THIS COMMON INHERITANCE

BRITAIN'S ENVIRONMENTAL STRATEGY

D1464680

*Presented to Parliament by the Secretaries of State for
Environment, Trade and Industry, Health, Education and Science,
Scotland, Transport, Energy and Northern Ireland,
the Minister of Agriculture, Fisheries and Food
and the Secretaries of State for Employment and Wales
by Command of Her Majesty
September 1990*

Cm 1200
LONDON: HMSO

£24.50 net

'Is there not the Earth itself, its forests and waters, above and below the surface?
These are the inheritance of the human race...
What rights, and under what conditions, a person shall be allowed to exercise
over any portion of this common inheritance cannot be left undecided.
No function of government is less optional than the regulation of these things,
or more completely involved in the idea of a civilised society.'

JOHN STUART MILL: 'PRINCIPLES OF POLITICAL ECONOMY'

CONTENTS

1

FIRST PRINCIPLES

INTRODUCTION

1.1 The Government's decision to produce Britain's first comprehensive White Paper on the Environment is timely.

1.2 There are moments in history when apparently disparate forces or issues come together and take shape. Almost half a century ago that was true of arguments about the welfare state. In the last decade, the case for market economics has emerged, coherent and formidable, as a blueprint for prosperity and a guarantee of freedom. Today it is the environment that captures headlines and excites public concern.

1.3 This White Paper looks at all levels of environmental concern and describes what the Government has done and proposes to do. It starts from general principles and objectives and it discusses the Government's approach to the environmental problems affecting Britain, Europe and the world. Many organisations and individuals have sent in papers or talked to Ministers and officials during the preparation of this White Paper. The Government is grateful for all the advice and comments received, and has drawn on it in preparing its proposals.

GROWTH AND THE QUALITY OF LIFE

1.4 From Western Europe to Eastern Asia, the more widespread implementation of market principles in economic management has enabled people and countries to flourish. As people have enjoyed the benefits of economic growth, they have become increasingly preoccupied with the quality of their daily lives. This can be seen in aspirations for healthier living, in the desire for cleaner air, water and streets, in popular enthusiasm for protecting the best of our urban and rural surroundings, and in the intense hope that we can pass on what we value most about our own heritage to our children.

The challenge is to integrate economic growth and environmental good sense

1.5 These are admirable goals. Economic growth is not an end in itself. It provides us with the means to live better and fuller lives. We should naturally avoid policies which secure growth in the short term at the expense of blighting our broader, longer term ambitions. But we should not be misled. Growth is a necessary though not a sufficient condition for achieving the higher quality of life that the world wants. In countries already rich beyond the dreams of a generation ago, growth is still needed to provide the resources to clean up the pollution of old industries and to produce the technology to accommodate tomorrow's industrial processes to cleaner surroundings. In countries still miserably poor, growth which will last is essential to overcoming the ruinous impact that poverty itself has on the environment. There is, therefore, no contradiction in arguing both for economic growth and for environmental good sense. The challenge is to integrate the two.

Coherent policies

1.6 If greater prosperity is making people more interested in the quality of their lives, it is proper to look at how public policy and administration attempt to reflect this. The Government needs to ensure that its policies fit together in every sector; that we are not undoing in one area what we are trying to do in another; and that policies are based on a harmonious set of principles rather than a clutter of expedients. This White Paper is the first comprehensive review of every aspect of Britain's environmental policy. The act of producing it has made us think hard about what we are trying to achieve. This cannot be the last word on the environment. But now that the Government has embarked on this comprehensive review, and published its conclusions, there can be no going back.

The pace of change

1.7 There is another reason for the upsurge of environmental concern: a reason which gives the debate drama and urgency.

1.8 Ever since the Age of Enlightenment, we have had an almost boundless faith in our own intelligence and in the benign consequences of our actions. Whatever the discoveries of science, whatever the advances of commerce and industry, whatever the rate at which we multiplied as a species, whatever the rate at which we destroyed other species, whatever the changes we made to our seas and landscape, we have believed that the world would stay much the same in all its fundamentals. We now know that this is no longer true. This perception could have consequences for national action and inter-national diplomacy as far-reaching as those which resulted from the splitting of the atom.

1.9 A main reason for this change of view is the pace and complexity of all the other changes in human history's recent stages. In a very short time, human activity has become so varied and complex that it is having effects not only at local and national level, but on the whole world itself. If our own species, Homo sapiens, had evolved only 25 years ago we would have discovered agriculture about 9 months ago, learnt to write a little over 4 months ago, and begun to use iron less than 3 months ago. Having taken more than 24 years to discover the circulation of the blood, it has taken us only 9 days to crack the genetic code itself. And although it took all but 25 years to expand the species to 2.5 billion for the first time, it has taken only one further day to get to 5 billion. Having discovered only the other day that our world is round, we are suddenly finding it

uncomfortably small and fragile.

1.10 Increasingly we understand that the ways we multiply, produce energy, use natural resources and produce waste threaten to change fundamentally the balance of our global environment. We may not be seeing the end of Nature. But Nature is certainly under threat.

International dimension

1.11 It is a threat that can only be overcome if all nations work together. The world's problems are the aggregate of local and regional pressures on the environment. One country's pollution can be every country's predicament. Our oceans and our atmosphere will only be saved by the aggregate of the world's actions. This will involve co-operation on a literally unparalleled scale.

1.12 Pooling knowledge and resources internationally allows faster progress towards scientific understanding of environmental problems and their solutions. To be successful in the diplomacy that lies ahead we need to be understanding in other ways. Lecturing one another on our respective virtues and failings is no basis for environmental statecraft. What is relatively easy in one country may be much more difficult in another. Developing countries will face particular problems, and they will require assistance from industrialised countries. For

We have a moral duty to hand on our planet in good order to future generations

instance they need access to the environmental know-how of the developed world on fair and affordable terms.

Environmental problems in our daily lives

1.13 But the environment does not raise a single issue. It lumps together a wide and diverse collection of problems. Inevitably, people notice most those that affect their daily lives. They dislike dirty streets and want them cleaned up. They object to what they regard as the onslaught of planners and developers on their towns and villages and fields, recoiling in particular from buildings that seem out of harmony with their familiar neighbourhood. They are worried about health risks and want reassurance that their environment is not becoming a health hazard. They ask for cleaner water in their rivers and taps, cleaner beaches and bathing waters when they go on holiday, and cleaner air to breathe. They want goods that can be produced and disposed of without harming the environment. They want more quiet and less hustle, and to be able to escape from their towns and cities to a countryside that can cater for their leisure without losing its beauty and its character. They want the benefits of prosperity to include the improvement of their surroundings and the safeguarding of the natural world. What can a Government best do to address these aims? There are no easy

and instant solutions; much has already been done but there is still more to do.

The foundation of policy: stewardship

1.14 The starting point for this Government is the ethical imperative of stewardship which must underlie all environmental policies. Mankind has always been capable of great good and great evil. That is certainly true of our role as custodians of our planet. The Government's approach begins with the recognition that it is mankind's duty to look after our world prudently and conscientiously. It was the Prime Minister who reminded us that we do not hold a freehold on our world, but only a full repairing lease. We have a moral duty to look after our planet and to hand it on in good order to future generations. That is what experts mean when they talk of "sustainable development": not sacrificing tomorrow's prospects for a largely illusory gain today. We must put a proper value on the natural world: it would be odd to cherish a Constable but not the landscape he depicted. The foundation stone of all the policies in this White Paper is our responsibility to future generations to preserve and enhance the environment of our country and our planet.

1.15 In order to fulfil this responsibility of stewardship, the Government has based the policies and proposals in this White Paper on a number of supporting principles. First, we must base our policies on fact not fantasy, and use the best evidence and analysis available. Second, given the environmental risks, we must act responsibly and be prepared to take precautionary action where it is justified. Third, we must inform public debate and public concern by ensuring publication of the facts. Fourth, we must work for progress just as hard in the international arena as we do at home. And fifth, we must take care to choose the best instruments to achieve our environmental goals.

Fact not fantasy: best evidence

1.16 Experience has taught us that actions and processes can damage the environment in ways no-one foresaw. Man-made chemicals like chlorofluorocarbons (CFCs) were once thought to be a benign scientific advance giving us aerosols, refrigeration and air-conditioning; no-one dreamed that the same chemicals would damage the ozone in the stratosphere. The addition of lead to petrol was seen as a great boon because we thought only in terms of improving vehicle performance; no-one then thought how the lead in exhaust fumes might damage health. International conferences are now organised to discuss the difficult and expensive ways of rectifying those mistakes and others like them. They are reminders of the care that we must take before stepping into the unknown. We must strengthen all our procedures for screening new products and processes to avoid causing unforeseen damage. And actions taken to protect one aspect of the environment can sometimes themselves cause other damage elsewhere. These are not arguments for taking no steps at all, but they point up the need, in environmental decisions as elsewhere, to look at all the facts and likely consequences of actions on the basis of the best scientific evidence available. Precipitate action on the basis of inadequate evidence is the wrong response.

1.17 The ways in which human activities affect the environment and our health are complex, with long chains of chemical, physical and biological effects. To identify, monitor and analyse them all in detail is an enormous task. There needs to be a major and growing scientific effort to understand them fully and to identify the most effective and appropriate ways of intervening to protect the environment. Much more research is needed, particularly on global issues such as the effects of human activities on the oceans and on the atmosphere. We must act on facts, and on the most accurate interpretation of them, using the best scientific and economic information.

Precautionary action

1.18 That does not mean we must sit back until we have 100% evidence about everything. Where the state of our planet is

at stake, the risks can be so high and the costs of corrective action so great, that prevention is better and cheaper than cure. We must analyse the possible benefits and costs both of action and of inaction. Where there are significant risks of damage to the environment, the Government will be prepared to take precautionary action to limit the use of potentially dangerous materials or the spread of potentially dangerous pollutants, even where scientific knowledge is not conclusive, if the balance of likely costs and benefits justifies it. This precautionary principle applies particularly where there are good grounds for judging either that action taken promptly at comparatively low cost may avoid more costly damage later, or that irreversible effects may follow if action is delayed.

1.19 This is similar to the responsible approach which the Government adopts on financial policy. Just as we believe that it is irresponsible for Governments to be extravagant with taxpayers' money, so we see even stronger arguments against wasting the world's, or this country's, natural resources and bequeathing a burden of environmental debts tomorrow. We must have development and growth in the world; but they must be sustainable. It is scarcely surprising that young people show so much sensitive interest in environmental matters. Much of the debate, after all, is about the state of the

We must base our policies on the best scientific and economic information

world which they will inherit. We must ensure that they are not disappointed by basing our actions on sound science and by taking precautionary action where justified.

Public information

1.20 The Government has made access to environmental information a key part of Britain's new comprehensive system of pollution control, and it warmly supported the European Community Directive on this subject. Chapter 17 describes new proposals for supplying regular, sound and authoritative statistical data on the environment, and for a system of environmental labelling of products. If people are given the facts, they are best placed to make their own consumer decisions and to exert pressure for change as consumers, investors, lobbyists and electors. We hope that this White Paper itself will help to raise the level of public debate and hence improve the quality of environmental decision-making by all concerned, not just the Government.

1.21 Facts and knowledge can be heavily contested ground in environmental policy-making. There is a temptation, to which some people occasionally fall prey, to exaggerate or distort evidence in order to excite public anxieties and drive policy

forward in particular directions. The best defence against these tactics in a free society is to make available the fullest and best information. The answers to environmental questions are not usually straightforward. How much are people prepared to pay for cleaner towns, for a greener countryside or for preserving historic buildings? How should we decide between building more homes or more bypasses and protecting our landscape? The best approach to such questions is to tell people the facts and what they mean, and to give them every opportunity to make their views known. That is the way to stimulate sensible public discussion and to earn public confidence in the approach to environmental policies.

International co-operation

1.22 Many of the world's environmental problems are global in scale. International action to deal with them is increasingly necessary. Action by one country alone to tackle global problems would be ineffective, and might simply damage its own economic position relative to others without doing anything significant to help the world's problems. Action to protect the stratospheric ozone layer is a good example. There is wide recognition that unilateral action is not enough, and that concerted international action is needed to phase out the chemicals that cause the damage. The Government was pleased to host and chair the successful international conference in London in June 1990 on the Montreal Protocol, which secured agreement on tackling the problem of ozone depletion. The process leading to that agreement provides a model for future diplomacy on biodiversity and climate change.

1.23 Britain will continue to play its full part in international discussions designed to develop the necessary concerted approach to global environmental problems. We are doing this through the United Nations and its subsidiary bodies, and through the Organisation for Economic Co-operation and Development (OECD), the European Community and other international organisations.

Where the state of our planet is at stake, precautionary action will sometimes be needed in advance of conclusive scientific evidence

The best instruments

1.24 Once it is clear which environmental problems need to be tackled and with what urgency, the next question is how best to tackle them. Safeguarding the environment can be very costly in the short term, whatever the longer term benefits. Control of pollution is estimated to cost 1-1.5% of Britain's gross national product - perhaps £7 billion in 1990. Action on the environment has to be proportionate to the costs involved and to the ability of those affected to pay them. So it is particularly important for Governments to adopt the most cost-effective instruments for controlling pollution and tackling environmental problems. And we need to ensure that we have a sensible order of priorities, acting first to tackle problems that could cause most damage to human life or health, and could do most damage to the environment now or in the future.

1.25 If Governments want to stop something happening, or make something happen in a different way, they have broadly two choices: they can by law lay down rules and regulations on standards to be met or equipment to be installed; or they can use the market to influence the behaviour of producers and their customers. Whichever course they choose, the objective is to make those who cause environmental damage face the costs of control in full, without subsidy. That is called the "polluter pays" principle which the Government, in common with many other Governments, adopts. If we impose higher standards centrally, this puts extra costs on producers and on their customers in turn; if we use price signals, for example by imposing charges or taxes on certain activities, extra costs again fall on the manufacturers, and then on their customers. This "polluter pays" principle is an important means of influencing potential polluters.

Regulation

1.26 In the past, governments in Britain and elsewhere have mostly used regulation to control pollution. "Fog everywhere", wrote Dickens about Victorian London. Eventually, the British Government used the

Those damaging the environment must face the full costs of pollution control

law to impose regulations to clean up London's air. And there are large numbers of laws and regulations to protect the quality of our water and air and to control disposal of wastes on land. This regulatory approach has served Britain and other countries well, and it will remain an important part of future environmental controls. For example, our new system of integrated pollution control will regulate industrial processes of all types to ensure the best outcome for the environment as a whole.

1.27 Regulation, however, does have limitations. It can be expensive to monitor and difficult to up-date quickly in response to scientific and technical advance. It cannot always pitch controls at the level which strikes the most cost-effective balance between environmental benefits and compliance costs. Compliance costs can fall widely - on business, on Government, and on consumers - and are easy to underestimate in advance. And so long as it remains the responsibility of the regulator, usually central Government, to lay down the ways in which pollution targets should be met, there will always be the danger that insufficiently flexible systems will be created and some better options overlooked. In short, regulation has always been required and is still required, but it has its shortcomings.

Market forces

1.28 For these reasons the Government, along with other Governments throughout the world, has begun to look for ways to control pollution which avoid some of these problems by working with the grain of the market. The ideas include various forms of pollution charges, as well as taxes and other economic instruments, all designed to encourage consumers and producers to behave in ways which benefit the environment. Annex A describes some of the options and gives examples of how they might be used.

1.29 These new approaches have been described loosely as the market-based approach to the environment, since they involve integrating economic and environmental concerns and applying market economics more broadly. In the Government's view, market mechanisms offer the prospect of a more efficient and flexible response to environmental issues, both old and new. There is nothing new about markets being influenced by environmental factors: houses in the quieter parts of towns have generally commanded the best prices; and, recently in particular, people across the world have been voting with their purses and wallets by preferring merchandise which seems environmentally-friendly, and manufacturers and suppliers have responded. Many Governments are now considering going a stage further by deliberate Government intervention to establish a new set of price signals.

1.30 We know what happens when price levels send the wrong environmental signals: the Amazon rain forests have been devastated at least in part because state subsidies there distorted economic choices and artificially favoured forest clearance instead of more sensible policies. The new Brazilian Government is trying to put that right. Just as the wrong price signals can cause disasters like that, so the right price signals should be able to cause very significant environmental improvements. There is evidence of that nearer to home. We have known for some time that lead in petrol produces harmful emissions, but motorists were slow to respond by switching to unleaded petrol. It was only when the Government intervened through a differential tax to give motorists a price incentive to switch to unleaded petrol that things started to move quickly.

1.31 The price mechanism will be the key, too, to the environmental consequences of the consumption of energy, which will much preoccupy people all over the world over the next 50 years. It is the price of energy more than any Government regulations or controls which will drive us to be more efficient about its use and more resourceful about the means of producing it. This is regardless of the political complexion of governments. It is impossible to be precise about the level of energy prices year by year, as the events of Summer 1990 have demonstrated. Increases in energy taxation or other measures directly raising the relative price of energy, outside transport, will not be necessary in the next few years. But we do not seek to duck the fact that energy prices will inevitably rise eventually, and we propose measures for promoting energy efficiency and reducing greenhouse gas emissions against that background.

1.32 The market can also help pay for improvements to the environment. Investment in cleaning up our rivers and beaches was held back for years by constraints on public expenditure under successive Governments. It took the privatisation of the water industry to allow the market to help. The new water companies will raise private funding for an extensive overhaul of the industry's capital equipment and for significant improvements to environmental standards. This will be reflected in the level of charges, and consumers will see for themselves the true market cost of the services that they consume and the quality they rightly demand. Private investment reflected in consumer charges is securing a public good. The forthcoming privatisation of the electricity supply industry will bring similar benefits.

Implications for people

1.33 We are all used to the idea that developments which change our surroundings bring gains to some and losses to others. A new industrial process can provide more jobs and more national wealth, but at the expense of the quality of our landscape or the air we breathe. A new housing estate on a green field can provide better living standards for those who move into it, but at the expense of those who delighted in this previously unspoilt countryside. Environmental gains and losses like this are familiar, and we have found ways of trying to reconcile them through public consultation and participation, the planning system and compensation schemes. Not everyone can be satisfied, but we have established systems to achieve a fair balance between different interests.

1.34 We are not, though, as used to balancing shorter term economic losses against longer term environmental gains. Closing down polluting industries can lose jobs but help preserve our inheritance. Changes in the pattern of energy use can cause problems and expense for some individuals, some industries and some countries, but are necessary if global warming is to be avoided. We may find ourselves apparently both gaining and losing in different parts of our lives; different groups in every country and different countries in every region will face similar adjustments. There can also be conflicts between environmental objectives: a tidal barrage produces emission-free electricity but floods important wildlife habitats.

1.35 The fact that almost every environmental issue faces us with an arduous agenda of choices in which some may initially have to shoulder greater burdens than others is another strong argument for basing decision-making on the best available evidence, and on the fullest possible public debate. If we avoid these difficult decisions, we will be putting our short-term convenience ahead of the lasting needs of future generations.

Changes to our surroundings bring gains to some and losses to others: we need full public debate

CONCLUSION

1.36 Attempting to bring together all the policies which affect the environment is not and cannot be an exact scientific process. There is no anatomical or mechanistic relationship between them all. We cannot calibrate with precision the effect of this or that policy switch or modification on all the other related parts of the whole. To try to reduce all these issues to a table of figures is neither helpful nor honest: these are three-dimensional problems in a fast-changing world. So we are not dealing with a science, but with an area where political judgement will properly have a central role, constrained by the impertinent but implacable realities of the world.

1.37 We are attempting to cope not only with immense and imprecise complication, but also with great diversity. We travel all the way from chalk-land to the heavens, from saving the wild orchids and sea cabbage on the cliffs above Dover to beginning the international environmental negotiations which will ensure that the atmosphere around our planet is no longer treated like a dustbin. In almost every area of work, there is already writing on the page; we do not begin with a blank sheet - we should be in deep trouble were it otherwise. So progress is not made from a standing start. We are already on the move but recognise that we have to go further and faster.

We all share
responsibility for
protecting and improving
our environment

A shared responsibility

1.38 This Chapter sets out the main principles which underly the Government's approach. Another principle is this. The responsibility for our environment is shared. It is not a duty for Government alone. It is an obligation on us all. We set out in this White Paper how everyone can help and what everyone can do – business, government (central and local), schools, voluntary bodies and individuals – so that caring for the environment becomes an instinctive characteristic of good citizenship as this century turns into the next.

1.39 This White Paper records what we are doing already and what we plan to do to make our air and water cleaner; to preserve the beauties of our countryside and historic buildings; to improve the quality of life in our towns and cities; to encourage more efficient use of energy; to promote more

research and public information as the foundations of good environmental policy; to develop a more open and constructive dialogue with industry, local government, and voluntary groups; to develop the institutions that monitor and regulate environmental quality; to explore new ways of using economic pressures to achieve environmental goals; to play our full part in the environmental diplomacy that will dominate the international agenda in future decades; and much else.

1.40 Important as all these subjects are, nothing will matter more than mobilising the energies and commitment of individual men, women and children. Everyone has a contribution to make. "Nobody", as Edmund Burke wrote, "made a greater mistake than he who did nothing because he could only do a little." We all have a part to play, however small, in conserving this common inheritance.

SUMMARY OF GOVERNMENT ACTION

S.1 Chapter 1 sets out the principles underlying the Government's approach to environmental policies. This is a summary of the action that the Government is taking, described in the following chapters, to put those principles into practice.

THE ENVIRONMENT IN BRITAIN

S.2 The Government's approach to improving the environment in Britain includes the following overall objectives:
• protecting the physical environment through the planning system and other controls and incentives (2.7);
• using resources prudently, including increasing energy efficiency and recycling, and reducing waste (2.9);
• controlling pollution through effective inspectorates and clear standards (2.11); and
• encouraging greater public involvement, and making information available (2.14).

EUROPE

S.3 To help combat the greenhouse effect, the Government will encourage the European Community to:
• introduce a scheme for labelling electrical appliances with information about their energy efficiency (3.15);
• set minimum efficiency standards for some categories of domestic and industrial appliances which vary widely in their use of energy (3.15);
• carry through its research and development on renewable energy sources (3.16); and
• amend or repeal anomalous regulations which hinder reductions in greenhouse gas emissions, such as the Gas Burn Directive and restrictions on 'cabotage' (3.17).

S.4 To improve Community pollution control, and encourage national self-sufficiency in waste disposal, the Government will:
• encourage the development of an integrated EC system of pollution control based on the model provided by the Environmental Protection Bill (3.19);
• call for improved standards of air quality monitoring (3.20);
• press for higher standards of hazardous waste incineration (3.20);
• urge tougher controls over vehicle emissions, including smoke and oxides of nitrogen from heavy diesel vehicles (3.20);
• press for consistent and compatible Community-wide arrangements for monitoring and reporting water quality standards (3.21); and
• argue for the retention of strong controls over the transboundary movement of all wastes after the completion of the internal market (3.23).

S.5 To help protect the Community's countryside, the Government will:
• argue for environmental considerations to play a greater role in the Common Agricultural Policy (3.22).

S.6 To improve consumer awareness and help ensure the proper implementation of community legislation, the Government will:
• press for the adoption of a European labelling scheme for environmentally friendly products (3.24); and
• press for stronger monitoring of Member States' compliance with EC obligations (3.25).

S.7 To help improve environmental standards in Eastern Europe the Government will:
• contribute to work on international bodies dealing with regional issues (3.26,31); and
• support appropriate international and Community action to help Central and Eastern Europe cope with environmental challenges (3.31–33).

BRITAIN AND THE WORLD ENVIRONMENT

S.8 To help developing countries play their part in combating global warming, the Government will:
• provide financial and technical support (4.17); and
• develop new energy efficiency aid initiatives (p.50).

S.9 To encourage the sustainable management of forests, the Government will:
• work to strengthen and reform the Tropical Forestry Action Plan, which co-ordinates aid for forestry in developing countries (4.20);
• continue to help the International Tropical Timber Organisation ensure that trade is carried out in a sustainable manner (4.21);
• provide bilateral aid to address the social and economic reasons for forest loss, and to promote agroforestry and the reforestation of degraded land (4.22); and
• fund research projects aimed at improving the productivity of forests in developing countries (p.51).

S.10 To support developing countries' efforts to restrain population growth, the Government will continue to:
• channel substantial aid for family planning activities (4.15);
• provide bilateral funding for projects aimed at alleviating poverty and promoting economic and social development (4.15); and
• directly fund projects to improve the health and education of women and to reduce infant mortality (4.15).

S.11 To help developing countries play their part in conserving the world's biological diversity and managing internationally important wildlife species, the Government will:
• support international efforts to agree a Convention for the conservation of biological diversity (4.26);
• continue to provide bilateral aid to support conservation projects (p.52);
• implement a five-point plan, including finance for major studies on the status of the world's biodiversity (p.52);
• continue to support anti-poaching projects

and the management of wildlife reserves (4.28); and
• continue to give strong support to the UN Convention on International Trade in Endangered Species of Wild Fauna and Flora (4.28).

S.12 To encourage the sustainable management of the world's oceans, the Government will:
• continue to contribute to improvements in scientific understanding of the oceans (4.30);
• help developing countries to practise sustainable methods of catching fish (4.32);
• continue to oppose indiscriminate fishing practices such as large-scale ocean drift net fishing (4.33);
• continue to oppose the resumption of commercial whaling until it is clear that stocks can be safeguarded at a healthy level, and urge the development and use of non-lethal research techniques for the study of whale populations and biology (4.34); and
• press the International Whaling Commission to agree similar measures for smaller cetaceans such as dolphins and porpoises (4.36).

S.13 To ensure proper protection of the world's polar regions, the Government will:
• continue to support the Antarctic Treaty System which provides strict measures for the conservation of wildlife (4.40);
• call for the introduction of a comprehensive environmental management plan for the Antarctic (4.40);
• continue to support the rigorous environmental safeguards in the Convention on the Regulation of Antarctic Mineral Resource Activities (4.41); and
• provide strong support for polar research through the British Antarctic Survey and the creation of an international Arctic Science Committee (4.43).

S.14 To reduce chlorofluorocarbons (CFCs) and other man-made chemicals which deplete the ozone layer, the Government will:
•continue to contribute to the scientific study of the problem and to the evaluation of alternative chemicals (4.45);
• continue to take a leading part in international action to eliminate ozone depleting substances (4.46);
• in line with the agreement at the 2nd London

Conference in 1990 on a revised Montreal Protocol, phase out CFC production and consumption in Britain by 2000 (p.56);
• press the European Commission to bring forward proposals for phasing out of CFCs in the Community by 1997 (p.56);
• contribute up to £9.4 million over three years towards the costs that developing countries will incur in complying with the revised Protocol (p.56); and
• provide bilateral assistance to India for its plans on phasing out CFCs (p.56).

S.15 To encourage the necessary global co-operation to manage the world's environmental resources, the Government will:
• help strengthen environmental institutions in developing countries through technical advice, training and environmental education (4.48);
• encourage business to take environmental considerations into account and make its expertise available to developing countries (4.52);
• ensure that international trade agreements respect the international environment and take account of the dangers associated with shipments of hazardous waste (4.53);
• continue to support the work in developing countries of a wide range of voluntary organisations (4.54);
• continue to support the environmental work of international bodies, especially the European Community, the United Nations Environmental Programme, the World Bank and the Organisation for Economic Co-operation and Development (4.55 on); and
• work to ensure the successful conclusion of the 1992 Conference on Environment and Development (4.63-66).

BRITAIN'S RESPONSE TO GLOBAL WARMING

S.16 To help reduce Britain's contribution to global warming, the Government will:
• continue to press for international action to reduce greenhouse gases through an international framework convention setting a broad strategy (5.16);
• promote measures which encourage people to use energy more efficiently, or are otherwise worthwhile in their own right, and consider

further measures in the longer term (5.24-5.25);
• set itself the demanding target, if other countries take similar action, of returning emissions of CO_2 to 1990 levels by 2005 (5.20); and
• take the following measures on energy, transport, forests and methane.

Energy

S.17 To improve the efficiency with which energy is generated and used, the Government has:
• required public electricity suppliers to promote efficiency in the use of electricity (C.7);
• introduced competition among electricity generators giving a strong incentive to generate electricity more efficiently (C.5); and
• introduced higher thermal insulation standards for new buildings in the Building Regulations (C.15).
In addition it will:
• develop the Energy Efficiency Office's (EEO) activities, including its Best Practice programme (5.30, C.8 on);
• promote wider use of combined heat and power to make use of waste heat from electricity generation (5.30, C.12);
• help to make buildings more energy efficient by for example: advice from EEO; encouraging energy-saving measures in local authority housing; and the new Home Energy Efficiency Scheme for low-income households (5.31,C.13 on);
• seek savings of 15% in the total energy bill for the Government Estate over a five year period (C.24-25);
• encourage everyone, at home and at work, to make energy efficiency improvements (5.27-30); and
• set up a new Ministerial Committee on energy efficiency to stimulate improvements in all sectors of the economy (5.32).

S.18 To encourage the use of energy from renewable sources, the Government will:
• work towards a figure of new renewable electricity generating capacity of 1000MW by 2000 - about a ten fold increase in current capacity, leaving aside the hydroelectric plants in Scotland (5.40):
• implement a comprehensive programme to

take forward renewable energy technologies which show promise of commercial viability in Britain, and review future policy in 1991 (5.40, C.47-55).

Transport

S.19 To make people more aware of the environmental impact of their transport decisions, the Government will:
• improve and extend its guidance on fuel economy and good driving practice (5.45);
• consider whether further changes should be made in the taxation of fuel and vehicles which might encourage people to seek greater fuel economy (5.51); and
• explore the scope for a code of practice on vehicle advertising (5.52).

S.20 To improve vehicle fuel consumption, the Government will:
• work with the EC on measures to improve the fuel consumption of motor vehicles (5.49);
• improve enforcement of speed limits (5.49);
• extend the MOT test and so improve the tuning of vehicle engines (5.49); and
• continue to help develop better vehicle technology (5.47).

S.21 To encourage transport choice, the Government will:
• continue to support the present high levels of investment by British Rail and London Transport (5.57-58);
• consider funding for cost-effective light rail proposals (5.59);
• promote effective measures to make the bus a more attractive means of travel (5.59);
• continue research to help to identify improvements and additions to transport networks which can increase choice and reduce congestion (5.61); and
• study ways of locating development to reduce travel distance and increase transport choice (5.65, 6.34).

Forests

S.22 The Government will:
• continue to encourage tree planting schemes, including community forests, and the planting of more broadleaved species: trees provide an effective means of absorbing and locking up

carbon dioxide (5.67).

Methane

S.23 To reduce emissions of methane gas, the Government proposes:
• action by local authorities over 5 years to improve some 1000 landfill sites and collect methane where possible (5.70); and
• to continue to restrict consents to vent methane from onshore and offshore oil and gas fields and terminals to the minimum necessary for safe and economic operations (5.71).

LAND USE AND PLANNING

S.24 To ensure that the planning system properly reflects environmental priorities, the Government will:
• review national planning policy guidance (6.33);
• develop planning policy guidance on planning to conserve energy (6.34);
• work to improve the operation of environmental impact assessment (6.38);
• align planning and pollution control mechanisms over special industrial activities (6.40),
• provide greater flexibility for planning agreements to offer environmental improvements alongside new developments (6.42);
• encourage the best location and design of new housing (6.44 on);
• review methods to achieve the best balance between economic and environmental costs and benefits in transport planning (6.52);
• improve the arrangements for considering the environmental impacts of new railways (6.55);
• review the operation of the law on aftercare conditions for mineral workings (6.57); and
• legislate to improve compensation payments where homes are affected by major new developments (6.59).

S.25 In development control, the Government will:
• seek to speed up decision taking, for the benefit of the environment and the economy, and ask the Audit Commission to examine local authorities' performance (6.12);
• consider extensions of planning control over

satellite dishes and the demolition of houses
(6.14);
• consult on whether to require prior
notification of new farm and forestry buildings
and to increase the size of holding to which
ordinary development controls apply (6.15-16);
• extend the tree preservation order system to
cover hedgerows of importance (6.17); and
• improve the enforcement of planning control
(6.18).

S.26 In development plans, the Government
will:
• make the preparation of district plans
mandatory and quicker (6.20-22);
• legislate for a streamlined system of county
structure plans, (6.26); and
• extend its regional guidance to assist these
new arrangements for development planning
(6.31).

S.27 To ensure that vacant, derelict and
contaminated land is brought into better use
quickly, the Government will:
• consider further steps to bring vacant land in
public ownership back into use (6.60);
• require district councils to prepare registers of
contaminated land and develop new standards
for cleaning it up (6.63); and
• discourage new dereliction and set new
priorities for the Derelict Land Grant
programme (6.64-69).

COUNTRYSIDE AND WILDLIFE

S.28 The Government is working towards the
integration of environmental considerations
with economic activity in the countryside. It
has taken a number of steps to build
environmental protection into the following
agricultural policies:
• Set-aside (7.17);
• Nitrate Sensitive Areas (7.15, 12.20);
• Extensification Schemes for Beef and Sheep
(7.14); and
• Farm and Conservation Grant Scheme (7.16).
It will:
• review the operation of the Countryside
Premium Scheme which offers farmers extra
conservation payments for Set-aside land (7.18);
• examine whether existing environmental
benefits afforded by Hill Livestock

Compensatory Allowances should be made
more specific and consult on these ideas (7.19);
• seek where possible and worthwhile to
develop the integration of agricultural and
environmental policies within the EC (7.20);
• continue to encourage organic farming and
consult on a grant scheme to assist conversion
to organic farming under the EC
Extensification Schemes (7.21);
• mount a campaign to advise farmers how to
safeguard and market their countryside assets; and
review the provision of conservation advice (7.22);
• continue to encourage environmentally
sensitive tree planting through existing grant
schemes (7.27-28);
• continue to encourage tree planting on better
quality agricultural land (7.28);
• make grants available from 1992 for woodland
management (7.29);
• support the development of new forestry initiatives, as in Central Scotland and Community
Forests, and consider proposals for a new
national forest in the English Midlands (7.30);
• continue to work through the Rural
Development Commission to promote
enterprise and economic activity in the
countryside (7.33);
• continue to encourage farmers to seek new
ways of improving their income benefit the
rural economy and rural communities (7.34);
• carry out a new study into how tourism can
contribute to the rural economy with least
damage to the environment (7.36);
• improve road design and environmental
practices (7.38); and
• examine the scope to recreate habitats affected
by road schemes, including the involvement of
landowners and farmers (7.38).

S.29 To encourage landscape conservation and
improvement, and provision of opportunities
for recreation the Government will:
• continue to support the work of the
Countryside Commission and discuss with it a
national countryside initiative to conserve key
landscape types and promote public access to
them (7.40-41);
• endorse the Countryside Commission's target
to bring all public footpaths and bridleways into
good order by the end of the century (7.43);
• continue to encourage voluntary activity and
business sponsorship in the countryside (7.44);
• continue to support the National Parks,

consider proposals for more and consider the Countryside Commission's recommendations from the National Parks review (7.48-52);
• encourage the Countryside Commission to follow up the review of Areas of Outstanding Natural Beauty (7.54);
• review the operation of Environmentally Sensitive Areas in 1991 (7.57);
• keep the special problems of the urban fringe under review (7.59); and
• work towards better arrangements for common land management and access (7.59).

S.30 To conserve the diversity of wildlife, the Government will:
• support the re-organised nature conservation agencies in all their nature conservation functions (7.63-65);
• issue new planning policy guidance on wildlife and planning (7.67);
• work towards designating more Marine Nature Reserves (7.68);
• consider whether to extend the Marine Consultation Area scheme concept to all British waters as well as Scotland (7.69); and
• follow through the British initiatives at the third North Sea Conference on protecting porpoises and dolphins and co-operate on site and species protection with other North Sea states (7.75).

TOWNS AND CITIES

S.31 To ensure that planning decisions respect the environment of towns and cities, the Government will:
• explore the part towns can play in improving the environment as a whole (8.4);
• encourage the best use of land in urban areas to keep pressure off other areas of environmental value and to improve local conditions (8.6); and
• issue new guidance asking local authorities to reflect in their decisions the need for good recreational land (8.8).

S.32 To civilise traffic in towns, the Government will:
• not generally provide or encourage others to provide new road capacity simply to facilitate

additional car commuting into already congested areas (8.11);
• help improve the quality of local traffic management through effective parking controls, the fuller understanding of traffic calming techniques, bus priorities, better signing, and more sophisticated traffic control systems (8.12);
• introduce 'Red Routes' in London at the earliest opportunity to help get traffic moving (8.14);
• continue to encourage the development of safe and convenient cycling networks, including a cycle network across London (8.16);
• encourage the use of quieter, cleaner lorries, operated more efficiently (8.17);
• provide bypasses where appropriate to relieve towns of through traffic and study traffic management measures to maximise their benefits (8.18); and
• continue to support public transport investment and examine the case for funding for light rail schemes (8.19).

S.33 To foster good design in new buildings, the Government will:
• support the use of design guidance and briefs (8.27-28);
• sponsor design awards, and schemes such as Art for Architecture which bring design into regeneration projects (8.31 on); and
• strive for a high quality of design in its own buildings (8.34).

S.34 To make specific improvements in the urban environment, the Government will:
• continue to target areas of greatest need for environmental improvement and ensure action programmes fully reflect environmental concerns (8.37 on); and
• support other specific steps to improve urban areas, including help for the expansion of the Groundwork Trust movement in England and Wales (8.45).

THE HERITAGE

S.35 To ensure the continued preservation and enjoyment of our heritage of historic buildings and landscape, the Government will:
• continue to ensure the properties it manages are kept in good condition and open to visitors; and fund a building programme for national museums and galleries (9.8 on);

• promote the educational value of sites, including new work by English Heritage (9.13);
• commission a register of battlefield sites to inform planning decisions which may affect them (9.13);
• work with the tourist boards to spread tourism between sites, and across the year (9.15);
• set up a Ministerially chaired forum of leading experts to discuss heritage policy (9.16);
• continue tax reliefs and grants to support the heritage (9.20, 9.22);
• place more emphasis within the grant system on buildings in towns and the industrial heritage; and make grants available to help Cathedrals (9.23 on);
• extend the work of the Royal Commissions in drawing together the country's database on archaeology and architectural history (9.30–31);
• complete resurveys of the whole country's heritage sites (9.32);
• continue to operate and strengthen where necessary current legislative protection, and give new guidance (9.34–35);
• transfer the responsibility for protecting historic wrecks to join that for archaeology on land (9.36); and
• improve the protection for ancient monuments (9.37).

BRITAIN'S APPROACH TO POLLUTION CONTROL

S.36 Following the enactment of the Environmental Protection Bill, in England and Wales the Government will:
• introduce a system of Integrated Pollution Control (IPC) (10.4);
• ensure that Her Majesty's Inspectorate of Pollution (HMIP) controls all major emissions to air, land and water from the most polluting industrial processes (10.9);
• prescribe the processes to be subject to control and publish criteria (10.9); and
• ensure that potential polluters curb the creation of wastes by applying the best available techniques not entailing excessive cost after obtaining prior authorisation from HMIP's Chief Inspector (10.10).

S.37 HMIP will:
• set higher environmental standards as the available technology improves and is available

without excessive cost (10.11);
• recover the bulk of the costs of IPC by charging for authorisations (10.12); and
• publish its guidance to inspectors on how to enforce IPC (10.13).

AIR

S.38 To improve controls over emissions to air outdoors, the Government will:
• base actions increasingly on air quality standards with the advice of a new expert advisory panel (11.8);
• develop 'critical loads' for different pollutants to target effective action on the areas of most need (11.10);
• extend and improve existing monitoring arrangements, and make information widely available – including in weather forecasts (11.11–13);
• ensure industry adopts new cleaner cost-effective technologies as they become available (11.15); and
• press for new European agreement to control ground-level ozone and incineration of toxic wastes (11.50, 11.59).

S.39 To reduce the levels of emissions from specific sources, the Government will:
• press the EC to finalise tighter emissions standards for cars and introduce emissions testing as part of the annual vehicle test (11.17);
• press the EC for tougher standards for emissions from diesel lorries and buses, increase road-side spot checks, and place emphasis on emissions standards in granting goods vehicle operator licensing (11.18);
• press the EC to improve the quality of fuels (11.20);
• pursue methods of reducing the amount of fuel which evaporates before it reaches the tank (11.20);
• extend controls under the Clean Air Acts to remove remaining pockets of dense smoke (11.22);
• ban straw and stubble burning by 1993 in England and Wales (11.24);
• ensure that power stations and other large combustion plants meet stringent EC requirements for reduced emissions of pollutants which cause acid rain (11.36);
• support international work and further action

on acid rain and ground level ozone (11.34-51); and
• extend new pollution controls to all incinerators and remove immunity from prosecution for NHS hospitals (11.59).

S.40 To reduce the risks from indoor air pollutants, the Government will:
• keep the building regulations under review and strengthen them where necessary (11.69);
• help develop specifications for safe building products in the EC (11.71);
• increase awareness of the dangers posed by a range of pollutants through guidance and publicity (11.72);
• issue new advice on avoiding passive smoking (11.77);
• continue to identify properties threatened by radon and methane penetration or damp, and help fund remedial action where the occupier cannot afford the works (11.82-91); and
• continue to pursue research into methods of reducing risk, and monitor the incidence of pollution (11.92);

WATER

S.41 In order to protect and improve the quality of drinking water, rivers and surrounding seas, the Government will:
• establish statutory water quality objectives, on the basis of advice from the National Rivers Authority (NRA) (12.6);
• bring drinking water and bathing water up to standard by the mid 1990's and improve river quality. To support this the private water companies will invest £28 billion including:
• £1.8 billion over the next five years to bring drinking water up to standard (12.7);
• £13.7 billion to improve sewerage works which includes £2.9 billion to bring all bathing waters up to EC standards by the mid-1990s through building long sea outfalls and treating the sewage discharged through them (12.12);
• introduce regulations setting minimum standards for the construction of silage, slurry and agricultural fuel oil stores and consider the scope for similar regulations for chemical and industrial fuel oil stores (12.16);
• ensure regular reports on water pollution and farm waste are published (12.16);
• continue to provide 50% grants towards

improving or providing facilities for storage, treatment and disposal of agricultural wastes and silage effluent (12.16);
• issue new advice on good agricultural practice to reduce pollution (12.16);
• keep under review the need for more controls over livestock waste (12.16);
• monitor the 10 pilot Nitrate Sensitive Areas (12.21) and 9 Advisory Areas and work towards an EC Directive on nitrate leaching (12.22);
• raise to £20,000 the maximum fines which magistrates courts can impose for water pollution offences (12.24);
• support the introduction by NRA of pollution control charges and consider greater use of economic mechanisms to discourage pollution (12.25); and
• keep under review the effectiveness of the water bodies' statutory responsibilities for conservation and recreation (12.27).

S.42 To protect and improve the quality of marine waters, the Government will :
• set targets for the reduction of the inputs of Red List substances by 50% between 1985 – 1995 (12.33);
• phase out the use of polychlorinated biphenyls (PCBs) by 1999 (12.34);
• halve atmospheric inputs of 17 harmful substances to sea by 1999 (12.34);
• aim to stop dumping at sea by ships of liquid industrial wastes and power station flyash by 1992, of stone waste from mining by 1997 and on beaches by 1995; stop dumping sewage sludge at sea by 1998; and stop incineration of British waste at sea by the end of 1990 (12.35);
• take further action to prevent pollution from ships and oil rigs (12.37, 12.39); and
• continue to work both in the EC and internationally to conserve marine fish stocks (12.40-42).

HAZARDOUS SUBSTANCES AND GENETICALLY MODIFIED ORGANISMS

S.43 To control the use of chemicals which carry risks to human health or the environment because of their widespread use, persistence in the environment or marked toxicity, the Government will:

• reduce human exposure to lead wherever practicable (13.8);
• support the EC proposal to ban cadmium use where it is not essential (13.9);
• reduce discharges into the North Sea of both lead and cadmium by 70% between 1985 and 1995 (13.9);
• reduce levels of dioxins in the environment (13.10);
• phase out and destroy all identifiable PCBs by the end of 1999 (13.11); and
• monitor the levels of these and other toxic substances in the environment to determine whether further controls are needed (13.12).

S.44 As part of a systematic approach to evaluating fully the potential environmental effects of the large number of industrial chemicals, the Government will:
• continue to subject new chemicals coming onto the market for the first time to rigorous scrutiny before they may be supplied for use, and share the information with EC partners (13.14);
• obtain information on chemicals already in use to assess their potential for harm (13.17);
• with EC partners, draw up a priority list of chemicals on which more information is needed (13.18); and
• participate actively in an Organisation for Economic Co-operation and Development review of chemicals produced in large volumes (13.19).

S.45 To control the use of pesticides, the Government will:
• continue to subject pesticides to a rigorous and independent approval system (13.22);
• limit their use to the minimum necessary (13.22);
• treble by 1993 the annual evaluation rate of older pesticides already in use before the statutory approval system was introduced (13.24);
• press in the EC for proposals to review all non-agricultural pesticides in use (13.25);
• enhance the monitoring of pesticide residues in food and wildlife (13.27);
• seek to reduce pesticide usage in water catchment areas where concentrations of pesticides in drinking water exceed the standards of the Drinking Water Regulations (13.29);

• implement recently revised international agreements on the export of pesticides and other hazardous chemicals to developing countries (13.31); and
• continue to sponsor training courses for people from developing countries on the assessment and safe use of hazardous chemicals (13.32).

S.46 In order to reduce the risks of major accidents during the manufacture, processing or storage of hazardous chemicals, the Government will:
• continue to oblige the relevant industrial installations to identify the risk of a major accident and demonstrate the safety of their operations (13.38);
• in the case of potentially more hazardous installations, continue to ensure the preparation of on-site and off-site emergency plans and restrictions on the design, location and construction of such installations (13.39); and
• extend controls to include consideration of environmental as well as human risks (13.40).

S.47 To ensure the safe use of genetically modified organisms (GMOs), the Government will:
• introduce regulations to implement controls of GMO research and controlled release into the environment (13.48-13.51);
• continue to fund extensive research into GMOs (13.50); and
• continue to work within international fora to encourage the preparation of international guidelines on the use of GMOs (13.52).

WASTE AND RECYCLING

S.48 To minimise the production of waste, the Government will:
• promote waste minimisation by industry through Integrated Pollution Control (14.4);
• widen its support for clean technologies through a joint Department of the Environment/Department of Trade and Industry grant programme (14.7); and
• establish a strict environmental regime for waste disposal: one effect of this will be higher disposal costs, which will provide a strong incentive to industry to reduce its waste (14.8).

S.49 To encourage recycling the Government will:
*   start two research projects to examine the scope for recycling building and mining wastes (14.16);
• aim to meet a target of recycling half of recyclable household waste by 2000 (14.23);
• introduce a system of recycling credits whereby savings in landfill costs will be passed on to those who remove materials for recycling (14.24);
• support pilot projects to test separate collection and sorting techniques (14.26);
• require local authorities to prepare and publish recycling plans and encourage recycling facilities at new shopping developments (14.29);
• discriminate positively as a consumer in favour of recycled products (14.38); and
• introduce an environmental labelling scheme, which will take account of the recycled content and recyclability of products, to enable consumers to make an informed choice (14.39).

S.50 The Government will introduce tougher new requirements for waste disposal. It will:
• impose a duty of care and aftercare on all those involved in waste disposal (14.45);
• separate regulators from operators by creating separate regulation authorities and disposal companies in England and Wales (14.45);
• introduce stricter licensing conditions for those involved in waste management (14.45);
• require local authorities to produce waste disposal plans and issue planning policy guidance to assist them in determining applications for new facilities (14.50);
• publish detailed regulations and guidance on waste disposal techniques (14.52);
• earmark funds to tackle problems at old landfill sites (14.59);
• call on all developed countries to become self-sufficient in waste disposal (14.61);
• call on the EC to ratify the Basel Convention, which aims to reduce transboundary movements of waste (14.62);
• take powers to control imports of waste where there is a risk of pollution or to conserve disposal capacity (14.64); and
•monitor the availability of waste disposal facilities across the country and compile information on trends in volumes, types and costs (14.69).

S.51 To combat litter, the Government will:
• place a new duty on local authorities and various landowners to keep public areas clear of litter (14.72);
• increase the maximum fine for leaving litter from £400 to £1,000 (14.72);
• introduce a Code of Practice on litter which will describe standards and recommend best practice (14.73);
• enable people to apply to magistrates for litter abatement orders against any authority which fails to keep its land clean (14.74); and
• continue to support the anti-litter work of voluntary bodies (14.76).

NUCLEAR POWER AND RADIOACTIVE WASTE

S.52 To ensure high safety standards, the Government will:
• commission further research into medical aspects of radiation (15.16);
• consider the implementation of any new recommendations on radiation dose limitation which the International Commission on Radiological Protection may publish (15.18);
• continue research into nuclear safety (15.21);
• maintain and enhance emergency arrangements and establish the second phase of the RIMNET overseas emergency monitoring system (15.24); and
• subject any proposal by UK Nirex Ltd for development of an underground waste disposal site to a full public inquiry (15.29).

S.53 In advance of a full scale review of nuclear policy in 1994 the Government and the nuclear industry will take several initiatives:
• the Government will keep under review whether the sea disposal option needs to be maintained (15.30);
• the Government will ensure that waste arising from post 1976 reprocessing contracts will be returned to overseas customers (15.35);
• UK Nirex Ltd. will speed up investigations into a potential underground waste disposal site (15.38);
• the Government will publish a strategy for nuclear research and development (15.38); and
• the nuclear generating companies will improve the economic efficiency of nuclear stations and complete Sizewell B (15.38).

NOISE

S.54 To reduce the extent of noise pollution at source, the Government will:
• press in the EC and elsewhere for reduced noise from vehicles and aircraft (16.9-13);
• introduce mandatory controls over burglar alarms and act to improve car alarms (16.15);
• examine ways of making roads quieter, through better surfaces, sound barriers and design (16.17-18);
• undertake research into nuisance caused by night flying (16.22);
• review current arrangements for mitigating noise nuisance at smaller airfields (16.23);
• issue new guidance on siting developments to avoid noise nuisance (16.26);
• examine action to limit the temporary use of land for helicopter landing and take-off (16.27);
• continue present arrangements of insulation or compensation for homes affected by noise nuisance caused by roads and aircraft, and develop equivalent arrangements for new rail lines (16.28-16.32); and
• improve the requirements for sound insulation in the Building Regulations, including new standards for flat conversions (16.34).

S.55 To make controls over noise more effective, the Government will:
• make it easier for local authorities to set up noise control zones (16.35);
• consider extending the scope of powers to control construction site noise to other similar activities (16.36);
• introduce a pilot 'quiet neighbourhood' scheme (16.39);
• strengthen the penalties for noise nuisance and the powers to control it (16.43);
• encourage local authorities to provide a consistent level of service on noise complaints (16.45); and
• continue to undertake research into reducing and recording noise (16.46).

RESEARCH, MONITORING AND AWARENESS

S.56 In order to base its policies on the best possible scientific, economic, and technological evidence, and building on the strengths in British research, the Government will:

• maintain Britain's contribution to international work on global climate change and to European environmental technology projects (17.7, 17.13);
• increase expenditure on environmental research in economic and social research programmes (17.9);
• target research priorities on the development of cleaner technologies and more efficient use of energy (17.14);
• improve our capacity to identify risks to health from the environment (17.18);
• increase environmental monitoring (17.20); and
• establish a network of scientific researchers and institutions to participate in the work of the European Environment Agency (17.24-25).

S.57 In order to increase awareness both generally and among consumers the Government will:
• produce at regular intervals a statistical report on the British environment (17.23);
• issue proposals on the arrangements to be made to ensure that environmental information on industrial emissions is widely available (17.27);
• press the EC to agree to a Europe-wide environmental labelling scheme, and establish a unilateral British scheme if necessary (17.31);
• decide whether food labels should be required to give details of production methods and crop treatments (17.32);
• encourage the energy labelling and environmental labelling of building products (17.32); and
• consider legislating to make clear that environmental claims for products or services must be capable of substantiation (17.33).

EDUCATION AND TRAINING

S.58 In order to improve the contribution of the education system to extending environmental awareness, the Government will:
• increase the profile of environmental education in the National Curriculum, both through subjects like science and geography and in developing it as a cross curricular theme (17.35-41);
• increase the specific grant for local authority in-service training, including work on

environmental education (17.43);
• ensure that pre-service teacher training courses cover the teaching of environmental matters (17.44);
• sponsor a comprehensive guide to environmental education and a database of relevant courses on offer at higher and further education establishments (17.47); and
• improve the provision of environmental further and higher education by:
- establishing an expert committee to identify the needs of the next decade (17.49);
- sponsoring a series of conferences to bring industry and course providers together (17.50); and
- producing a new leaflet designed to inform school children of job opportunities in environmental subjects, and what further and higher education is needed for each (17.50).

S.59 To ensure that education and training organisations increase their response to environmental needs the Government will:
• encourage Regional Technology Centres to focus on environmental issues (17.57);
• establish a new unit in the higher and further education sector to improve communications between businesses and those providing environmental education and training (17.57); and
• ensure that vocational standards are in place across the whole range of the environment (17.61).

GOVERNMENT INSTITUTIONS AND CONSULTATION

S.60 In order to integrate environmental concerns into decision taking within Government, the Government will:
• retain a Ministerial Committee to co-ordinate the approach to environmental issues (18.3);
• nominate a Minister in each Department with responsibility for its environmental policies (18.4);
• use annual Departmental reports to describe action following up the White Paper and other environmental initiatives (18.5);
• publish guidelines for environmental policy appraisal (18.6); and
• produce an environmental action guide for Government Departments containing guidance

on purchasing, building and land management (18.7).

S.61 In order to strengthen the role of the pollution inspectorates, the Government will
• make HMIP a candidate for becoming a 'next steps' agency (18.15);
• appoint an independent advisory committee for it (18.15); and
• consider other options for changing institutional arrangements in the medium term (18.16 on).

S.62 In order to improve the dialogue on environmental issues with those outside Government, and involve the voluntary sector more, the Government will
• set up improved arrangements for consulting local government (18.28), business (18.31) and voluntary organisations (18.34–35);
• establish a fund to finance specific environmental initiatives by voluntary organisations (18.36); and
• consider increasing the capacity of the Royal Commission on Environmental Pollution (18.38).

WALES

S.63 In order to protect and improve the special environmental qualities in Wales, the Government will:
• continue to take particular care when designing new road schemes (19.4);
• ensure that basic support for agriculture takes account of environmental factors (19.8);
• continue to protect the countryside through designated Environmentally Sensitive Areas, National Nature Reserves, Sites of Special Scientific Interest and Marine Nature Reserves (19.7, 19.9); and
• establish the Countryside Council for Wales by merging the Countryside Commission and the Nature Conservancy Council for Wales (19.11).

S.64 In order to improve further the urban environment, the Government will continue to:
• support a major land reclamation programme through the Welsh Development Agency's Land Grant (19.13);
• support urban renovation through its Urban

Programme (19.14);
• carry out housing improvements through Home Renovation Grants (19.15);
• restore unused and unsightly land and buildings through the Urban Investment Grant (19.16);
• regenerate the South Cardiff area, including the former docklands, through the Cardiff Bay Development Corporation (19.17); and
• improve conditions in the deprived urban communities of the South Wales Valleys through the Programme for the Valleys (19.18).

S.65 To promote the conservation, appreciation and enjoyment of the built heritage of Wales, the Government will:
• continue to protect scheduled monuments and listed buildings and consider increasing their numbers (19.20);
• provide major financial support for repairs (19.21); and
• establish Cadw: Welsh Historic Monuments as an executive agency (19.22).

S.66 To promote energy efficiency, the Government will:
• implement its strategy for the efficient use of energy in Wales (19.27).

S.67 To promote better understanding of the importance of caring for the environment, the Government will:
• give greater emphasis to environmental education, in schools and teacher training (19.29-32).

SCOTLAND

S.68 In order to conserve Scotland's wildlife and landscape more effectively, the Government :
• intends to set up a Scottish Natural Heritage agency combining the powers of the Nature Conservancy Council for Scotland and the Countryside Commission for Scotland to develop a new and more comprehensive approach and public understanding of the issues (20.5, 20.16-17).

S.69 In order to ensure that any proposed land use is compatible with the high quality of the Scottish environment the Government will :

• comprehensively review National Planning Guidelines and other planning advice (20.10);
• encourage Regional Councils to prepare indicative forestry strategies (20.11);
• have regard to Marine Consultation Areas in decisions affecting marine development (20.12);
• further improve control arrangements on the siting of marine fish farms (20.13);
• pursue measures suited to Scottish circumstances to integrate environmental protection into agricultural policies (20.18);
• give priority to major environmental improvement, for example through the Central Scotland Woodlands Initiative (20.19);
• work closely in support of the voluntary sector efforts to improve the environment (20.20);
• encourage environmentally sensitive tourism (20.21); and
• review the case for National Parks and other ways of managing Scotland's mountain areas (20.23).

S.70 In order to improve the urban environment and the quality of life in Scottish urban areas, the Government will :
• continue to encourage and support major urban renewal schemes (20.25);
• regenerate some of the worst peripheral housing estates through Government-led Partnership initiatives (20.26-27);
• ensure that the problems of other peripheral housing estates are tackled under the leadership of local authorities, Scottish Homes, the Scottish Development Agency and the private sector (20.29); and
• contribute to improvements in the quality of urban life through the Urban Programme (20.29).

S.71 In order to conserve and improve the Scottish built environment, the Government will :
• continue to make major resources available to protect ancient monuments and to assist in the repair of listed buildings (20.31-32);
• encourage higher standards in modern buildings (20.34); and
• issue new guidance on the location and design of rural housing (20.34).

S.72   In order to improve the physical environment and reduce pollution in Scotland,

the Government will:
• ensure that air emissions are more strictly controlled and that air quality continues to improve (20.35-36);
• support River Purification Boards and local authorities in controlling discharges and improving the quality of rivers, lochs and bathing waters (20.40);
• require all substantial sewage discharges to be treated at sewage treatment works (20.41);
• stop the dumping of sewage sludge at sea by the end of 1998 (20.41); and
• ensure that its Pollution Inspectorate and the River Purification Authorities will work closely together to develop a new integrated pollution control regime to protect the environment more effectively (20.45).

S.73 In order to improve understanding and public appreciation of environmental issues in Scotland the Government will :
• carry out research into key aspects of Scotland's environment (20.47-49);
• pursue its recent initiative on the identification of possible health risks from the environment (20.50); and
• give priority to environmental issues at all levels in the Scottish education system (20.51)

NORTHERN IRELAND

S.74 To preserve and enhance the Northern Ireland countryside, the Government will:
• adopt good conservation practices in the management of its own estate (21.6);
• provide advice, research and grant aid to farmers to reduce pollution from farms and to encourage environmentally sensitive farming (21.6);
• continue to protect habitats by completing the survey and declaration of Areas of Special Scientific Interest and National Nature Reserves (21.8); and
• complete its review of Areas of Outstanding Natural Beauty (21.10).

S.75 To prevent environmental pollution in Northern Ireland the Government will:
• continue to support the creation of smoke control areas so that levels of smoke and sulphur dioxide fall still further (21.16);
• aim to double the use of unleaded petrol (21.17);
• aim to manage rivers and estuaries so that water quality is 'good' or 'fair' (21.18);
• further improve the River Lagan as a key element in the regeneration of the Belfast river front and dock area (21.19);
• extend the monitoring of water quality to all main rivers and estuaries and to Strangford Lough (21.22); and
• improve sewage treatment and end the sea disposal of sewage sludge (21.22).

S.76 To protect the built heritage of Northern Ireland, the Government will:
• complete the listing of pre-1960 buildings of architectural or historic interest by 1994 (21.26); and
• complete its survey of all historic monuments by 1995 (21.27).

S.77 In order to encourage energy efficiency in Northern Ireland, the Government will:
• continue to provide financial assistance, practical advice and promotional seminars (21.30);
• take enabling powers to allow the replication of the Home Energy Efficiency Scheme (21.30);
• seek to reduce public sector energy usage by 15% by 1995 (21.31); and
• prepare a comprehensive strategy for the Province (21.32).

S.78 To increase awareness of the environment through education, the Government will:
• introduce two compulsory areas of study into the curriculum: 'Environment and Society' and 'Science and Technology' (21.34); and
• continue to promote the exploration of environmental issues in other educational themes (21.35).

THE ENVIRONMENT
IN BRITAIN

This is the first White Paper which comprehensively covers all aspects of Britain's environment

INTRODUCTION

2.1 This Chapter describes the Government's approach in Britain. It summarises some distinguishing features of Britain's environment and sets out the Government's main objectives for action, in line with the general principles set out in Chapter 1. Chapters 5 to 18 deal in more detail with different aspects of environmental policy in England or Britain generally. Chapters 19 to 21 cover particular aspects of policy in Scotland, Northern Ireland and Wales. Throughout the White Paper 'Britain' is used as shorthand for England, Scotland, Northern Ireland and Wales.

OUR COMMON INHERITANCE

2.2 The British environment has many strengths. We have a beautiful countryside. We have large expanses of upland moor and heath land, and the longest coastline in Europe. Our land is productive and is home for a large variety of wildlife. We have thriving towns and cities that provide homes, employment, commerce, culture and leisure activities. We have a rich heritage of buildings some of which date back for many centuries. We have an almost stable population, a mature economy and a fairly settled pattern of land use.

2.3 Nevertheless we face significant environmental challenges. Britain is a small country, but as we grow richer, we need more land to expand our businesses and to build more homes. We demand more cars and more roads to drive them on. At the same time we want increased protection of the natural environment and a better quality of life in our towns and cities. Congestion and noise are becoming bigger threats at the same time as they are becoming less acceptable.

2.4 Along with other developed countries we are major consumers of the world's natural resources, many of which are non-renewable. We need new efforts to make more efficient use of resources and to give preference to renewable resources, if we are to hand on a stable and sustainable way of life to future generations.

2.5 There is still too much pollution after

Britain has a rich cultural and architectural heritage

200 years of industrial development in Britain. We still have too many dirty rivers, too much derelict land and too much air pollution.

2.6 So the three critical issues for the British environment are:
• how to resolve the conflicts between pressures for development and mobility and the conservation of what is best in the environment of our countryside and towns;
• how to maintain economic growth without making excessive demands on natural resources; and
• how to combat the dangers of pollution without jeopardising economic growth.

Protecting the environment

2.7 We have well developed systems for planning and land use and for conserving special features of the environment. The systems are tried and tested, and familiar with the problem of reconciling development and conservation pressures. Chapters 6 to 9 describe these systems, and how the Government proposes to strengthen and use them to improve the environment. The Government's broad objectives are:
• to improve the quality of life in our towns and cities;
• to ensure that the planning system works to provide for homes and jobs, and to meet our desire for mobility, at the same time as conserving our heritage and protecting our environment;
• to integrate agricultural and environmental policy;

• to maintain the green belts around our towns and cities and to extend protected areas of natural beauty; and
• to maintain, and where necessary strengthen, measures to preserve our wildlife habitats and to provide access to the countryside without damaging it.

Prudent use of resources

2.8 The oldest and best way of controlling the pace at which we use up natural resources is to let the market work. If one resource is in short supply, its price goes up, and somebody develops alternatives. But some market signals are distorted or ineffective, and it is the Government's job to encourage more efficient use of resources, and the development of renewable resources that will continue to be available when other non-renewable sources run out.

2.9 The Government's objectives are:
• to increase the efficiency with which we use energy, at work and in our homes, and in our cars and use of public transport
• to reduce the amount of waste produced and increase the amount of material recycled;
• to ensure better use of resources in the Government estate and the rest of the public sector; and
• to see that we meet announced targets for reduced emissions of gases causing global warming, ozone depletion and acid rain.

2.10 Chapters 5, 11 and 14 describe the measures the Government proposes in support of these objectives.

Public participation is the key to improving our environment

Pollution control

2.11 In Britain we have well developed systems for controlling and regulating pollution. The Water Act 1989 and the Environmental Protection Bill of 1990 include measures to strengthen the powers and resources of the various inspectorates. The Government favours strong pollution inspectorates with clear remits to impose high quality standards. Chapters 10 to 16 explain how the legislation is to be implemented. The objectives are:
• to make our air cleaner and safer;
• to achieve further improvements in the quality of our water, and in the state of the North Sea and our other coastal waters;
• to establish the levels of emissions that our air and waters can safely tolerate, and set up control mechanisms based on that;
• to maintain, and strengthen where necessary, controls over pollution from industry, including farming, and over dangerous chemicals and other substances; and
• to provide the necessary incentives to industry to improve their environmental standards and develop clean technologies.

A comprehensive approach

2.12 A large number of Government policies affect the environment. The Department of Environment is itself responsible for some of these, including planning policy, urban policy, policy on countryside and wildlife and on the heritage, and policy on pollution control. But other critical policy areas come under other Departments, including transport, energy, agriculture, health, industry and education. In order to build up a comprehensive approach to environmental issues all the relevant Government Departments have been involved in the preparation of this White Paper. And all will continue to be involved in its implementation and follow-up.

Involving people

2.13 Parliaments can pass laws and Governments can produce White Papers. But the environment will only improve if we ourselves have the will to do what lies in our own hands. We should encourage wider participation in the many responsible voluntary bodies which tackle environmental issues at national and local level. There is more public participation in Britain on environmental issues than ever before and it is crucial to make the most of the expertise and experience of Britain's voluntary bodies in the environmental field. It is people as well as Governments that are essential participants in a successful environment policy.

2.14 That is as true in Britain as anywhere else. The recognition of it underlies all the Government's proposals. It underlies too the following particular objectives covered in Chapters 17, 18 and 22:
• to make more information available about the state of Britain's environment;
• to increase effort on research and monitoring;
• to place greater emphasis on the environment in our schools, colleges and training institutions;
• to encourage a greater sense of responsibility for the state of the environment among people, schools, firms and local authorities;
• to involve voluntary environmental bodies in the evolution of environmental policy and support their practical work; and
• to encourage individual people to do what they can to improve the environment themselves by giving them better information and financial incentives in some cases.

 3

EUROPE

Since 1973 the Community has agreed more than 280 measures to protect the environment

INTRODUCTION

3.1 A number of the environmental issues which cross national boundaries, while not of global importance, are important in regional terms. For Britain, this means that the issues concerned will have a European dimension; and the means of following them through will often - though not always - be the European Community (EC).

THE EC AND THE ENVIRONMENT

3.2 Britain's accession to the Treaty of Rome on New Year's Day 1973 was a critical moment in our history. Membership of the European Community has brought us great dividends in terms both of economic success and political co-operation. Conversely, Britain's contributions to developing the Community's work and institutions have helped it greatly.

3.3 In the environmental field too, the Community has brought added value to Britain, and we have brought added value to it. That is the best benchmark for measuring the success of environmental co-operation, just as it is in trade and economics. This Chapter describes what the Government is aiming to achieve through the Community's environmental policies, in the rest of Europe and as part of the wider world.

3.4 There are two reasons for the European Community to have a role in environmental policy. The first is that the Member States are neighbours. Pollution from one Member State often affects another, so joint action is required if it is to be tackled effectively. The second is trade. If industry and farmers are to compete fairly, then it will be helpful if the environmental rules governing how they produce things are aligned at a Community level, where that is practicable.

3.5 The Community has adopted environmental legislation since early in its history. And under the 1986 Single European Act (SEA), Member States agreed that the Community should include among its objectives environmental protection and improvement, protection of human health and prudent use of natural resources. The SEA lays down that these objectives should only be pursued at Community level to the extent that this is more effective than action at the level of individual Member States (the principle of "subsidiarity"). For example, it is quite right for the Community to set targets for each Member State for reducing pollution from power stations which crosses national boundaries. It is equally right that it should be for Member States to decide how to go about achieving those individual targets.

The EC and the world

3.6 The 'clout' that the Community carries in the wider world is greater than the sum of each Member's influence. This is no less true for the environment than for external trade and other areas of foreign policy. It is all the more valuable now that global co-operation on issues such as the ozone layer and climate change is taking on greater urgency. Where the EC can speak with one voice on issues like these, the Government will encourage it to do so.

Britain and the Community

3.7 In the Community, as in Britain and the wider world, the Government believes in treating the environment as a shared trust. We must act with prudence and concern, but be clear-sighted about the problems themselves and hard-headed about our choices for dealing with them and the costs and benefits they entail.

3.8 The Government therefore believes that the Community's programme for the environment must be vigorous and forward-looking, tackling issues in ways which are consistent with the responsibilities we owe to future generations and which encourage people to use Europe's natural resources in sustainable ways. The polluter must pay wherever possible. Action must be based on the best science available, but scientific uncertainty must not be an excuse for delay where there are clear threats of damage that could be serious or irreversible. As in Britain, we must weigh the costs of proposals for action carefully against the benefits and try to make sure that priority is given to measures that give the best and most urgent results most cost-effectively. It is the Government's aim to make sure that the standards that the Community sets do their job effectively, and that they do not put British people and firms at an unfair disadvantage; and to see that all EC policies – not just those on the environment itself – take environmental questions properly into account.

3.9 These principles are in harmony with the Treaty of Rome as modified by the Single European Act. The Treaty says that action to protect the environment should take particular account of scientific and technical evidence and the potential benefits and costs of taking action or of not taking action. It

Left: An EC Directive
protects wild birds
across Europe

Right: Each member
state ought to aim to
dispose of its own waste

also endorses the principles of preventative action, of priority for rectifying environmental damage at source and of ensuring that the polluter pays.

3.10 These common ground rules, which the SEA has now written into the EC Treaty itself, are just one aspect of the close understanding that Britain has increasingly enjoyed with its Community partners on environmental matters. On some issues, British thinking has come more closely into line with that of other Member States; sometimes it has been the other way round. For example, Britain used to be virtually alone in basing standards for the control of pollution on the effects that the pollution itself actually has on the environment, rather than relying solely on uniform emission control standards. Now this approach is widely accepted. Thanks to painstaking work,

Community decision making

Most environmental legislation of the European Communities is adopted by a unanimous vote in the Council, acting on a proposal from the European Commission under Article 130s of the Treaty of Rome. Proposals for such legislation are adopted following consultations with the European Parliament and the Economic and Social Committee.

led by British scientists, we have developed the critical loads approach as a basis for controlling air pollution. We are urging that this should become the basis for action within the EC in the future.

Achievements so far

3.11 Since 1973, the Community has agreed no less than 280 measures to protect the environment. Among the most important have been regulations and directives to
• combat acid rain by controlling pollution from power stations and other large combustion plants;
• improve the quality of air by setting stringent pollution standards for new small cars from the end of 1992, obliging Member States to make unleaded petrol widely available and requiring new cars to be able to run on it from 1990;
• move towards eliminating or reducing pollution of inland and territorial waters by curbing pollution from some dangerous substances and raising the quality of water for drinking and bathing;
• tighten controls on dangerous substances by introducing new arrangements for assessing new chemicals and requiring notification to be given before some kinds of hazardous waste are imported or exported;
• protect the environment from nuclear contamination by bringing in measures under the Euratom Treaty, including controls on the import of agricultural produce following a

nuclear accident and an agreement on rapid notification procedures;
• control the use and release of genetically modified organisms; and
• conserve wildlife by providing a system of protection for all species of wild birds found in Europe.

The future

3.12 The Commission of the European Communities will shortly be drawing up a new action plan on the environment – the fifth – with proposals for a new strategy to take over from the current plan, which expires in 1992. The heads of the Member States gave clear guidance to the Commission for the preparation of this plan by issuing the Dublin Declaration of the European Council on the Environment in June 1990, reflecting many of the themes that the Government is keen to develop at the Community level. The following paragraphs set the main priorities on the Government's agenda for Community action.

Better information about the environment

3.13 The Government supports the moves now being made in Europe to provide better information about the environment and better access to it. Information and access are essential so that everyone – Government and others alike – knows what is happening to the environment, and can bring effective pressure to bear to ensure that adequate standards are

set and maintained. The Community has recently agreed a directive about providing new rights of public access to environmental information, and in Britain this will be supplemented by the detailed provisions of the Environmental Protection Bill. Britain is also supporting the establishment of the new European Environment Agency which will assemble reliable data across Europe for policy makers and enable proper comparisons to be made of the state of the environment and of implementation in different countries.

Global warming

3.14 The Community will clearly have an important role in the measures necessary to reduce global warming, including action to increase energy efficiency. (The Government's policies on global warming are covered in full in Chapter 5 and Annex C.) The Community has expressed its concern over the continuing destruction of tropical forests and the effect that this is having on global warming and the world climate. Member States have undertaken to protect their own forests and to strengthen programmes of afforestation.

3.15 The Government is pressing the Commission to produce specific proposals on other matters that need to be taken forward at Community level, and is participating in Community studies on economic instruments that may be helpful to supplement the role of regulation. On energy efficiency, the Government will press for an effective Community scheme, if possible a voluntary one, to label electrical appliances with information about their energy efficiency. This would help consumers to choose appliances which are cheapest to run and best for the

The Government will press the Community to apply a system of integrated pollution contro

The Commission is
funding an extensive
research and
development programme
on renewable energy

environment, and encourage manufacturers to make them. The Government will also press for minimum energy efficiency standards to be set for a range of appliances – including central heating boilers, fridges, washing machines and industrial heaters – which vary widely in energy efficiency.

3.16 Using energy from renewable sources such as wind and water, including the tides, can help to combat global warming. The Government will take an active interest in the extensive programme of research and development that is already being funded by the European Commission. As arrangements for completing the single market in 1992 are carried forward, the Government will try to ensure that energy is fully priced everywhere, and that there is no impediment, beyond

The EC needs a better
system of monitoring and
reporting on river quality

normal safety requirements, to the use of energy sources, such as natural gas, nuclear or renewable energy, which produce less or no greenhouse gases.

3.17 There still remains some existing legislation within the EC which actually makes reducing greenhouse gas emissions more difficult. The Gas Burn Directive contains obsolete bureaucratic controls which make it harder than it need be to switch to gas from other, more polluting, fuels for generating electricity. Increased greenhouse gas emissions can also be caused by restrictions on 'cabotage' (the ability to pick up and deliver goods entirely within another Member State) which can cause lorries to run empty. The Government will work to get anomalous rules of this kind amended or repealed.

Pollution control

3.18 Great strides have been made since 1973 on pollution control, but there is more to be done. In some cases, Britain can lead the way.

3.19 The Government will argue in the Community for pollution control to be based on the same kind of integrated arrangements which it is proposing for England and Wales in the Environmental Protection Bill. This approach, which is discussed in Chapter 10, bases controls on an understanding of the effects of pollution on the environment as a whole, and not risking a false picture by looking at the effects on air, water or land in isolation. The Government will press for a new system of integrated controls at Community level, based on the arrangements that it has pioneered at home.

3.20 The Government also wants to see improved air quality monitoring arrangements throughout the Community. At present, monitoring in some countries is better than in others: it needs to be brought up to a consistent, high standard so that we can reliably track progress against the standards that we have now, and assess the need for new measures. The Government believes that higher standards are needed in some key areas, like the incineration of hazardous wastes and pollution from motor vehicles, especially smoke from lorries and other vehicles with heavy diesel engines.

3.21 For water, too, the Government believes that the EC needs a framework within which the whole Community can develop quality objectives. As in the case of air pollution, this will call for stronger arrangements to ensure consistency and compatibility of monitoring and reporting.

Countryside

3.22 As Chapter 7 shows, farming remains the main force shaping Britain's rural economy, and the appearance of our countryside and landscape. An important part of the Government's policies in the Community will be to make sure that environmental considerations play a greater role in the Common Agricultural Policy at all levels where that would be practical and cost-effective. Concern for the countryside must go hand in hand with concern for nature conservation: the Government is already working for progress on the draft habitats Directive, which it hopes will soon lead to agreement on a worthwhile measure which will produce real conservation benefits across Europe.

Waste disposal

3.23 As standards for waste disposal increase, so inevitably does the temptation to export

The Government supports checks that Member States are living up to their EC obligations

the problem, particularly of toxic and other difficult wastes, rather than deal with it within the country where it is produced. The Government has already taken a strong lead by calling for each country to aim to become self-sufficient in disposing of its waste, and the Community has now adopted this principle. As the next step, the Government has made it clear that the completion of the single market in 1992 must not result in waste being allowed to move freely across frontiers. It will argue strongly that controls over the transboundary movement of all wastes must remain.

Consumer awareness

3.24 As Chapter 1 says, the best foundation for public confidence in environmental matters in a free society is to make available the fullest and best information. The Government will press in the Community for further measures to increase public and consumer awareness of the issues. In particular, it will support proposals for a European labelling scheme for environmentally friendly products,

Environmental considerations should play a greater role in the Common Agricultural Policy

coupled with arrangements to ensure that the scheme is clear, effective and safe from abuse. It will also aim to ensure that Community legislation in other fields, for example the Construction Products Directive, sets standards for products which take environmental concerns into account, and allow Member States to require high environmental performance in their public purchasing.

Meeting Community obligations

3.25 The Government looks forward to Britain playing a leading part in the Community's future work on the environment. But, as part of the Community's next steps on the environment, the Government also wants to see the development of better means of checking that Member States are living up to their obligations under EC law. We have one of the best records in the Community of honouring the commitments that we agree to: this is one reason why Britain has been a tough negotiator, aiming to ensure that agreements are realistic. The Government wants to work with others to develop better ways of judging the records of Member States compatibly, and welcomes the steps recently taken in that direction by the Commission and the strong interest taken in this area by the European Parliament. A very important part of the job of the new European Environment Agency will be to identify and provide the information needed if these comparisons are to be made properly.

EUROPE OUTSIDE THE COMMUNITY

3.26 Europe does not, of course, mean the EC only. Co-operation in a wider European framework is also important. The World Bank has a major lending programme in both Eastern Europe and the Mediterranean. As well as projects specifically tailored to environmental problems (such as a recent loan to Poland), with Britain's support it is becoming increasingly sensitive to environmental concerns in all its operations. The UN's Economic Commission for Europe (ECE) is already helping to develop a European approach to air pollution control (as Chapter 11 describes) and can be expected to become an even more effective East/West forum in the future. It has a valuable history of co-operation between the EC, the European Free Trade Association (EFTA) and the countries of Eastern Europe. The Council of Europe does excellent work in several areas including nature conservation, and is responsible for the Bern Convention on the conservation of European wildlife and natural habitats. On matters such as harmonising technical standards of pollution control, liaison with the member countries of EFTA is of growing importance. Chapter 12 discusses work

Britain is helping Eastern Europe to tackle its environmental problems

done in the North Sea Conference to deal with the environment and pollution problems in the North Sea.

3.27 Another significant development, for which Britain pressed strongly, is the decision to offer participation in the European Environment Agency to non-Community countries. The Agency will be charged with collecting objective, reliable and comparable information to help to implement environmental policies effectively and to inform the public on the state of the European environment.

3.28 The European Region of the World Health Organisation, representing some 32 European states, has also been active in the field of environment and health. A conference at Frankfurt in December 1989 endorsed a Charter setting out the broad principles for protection of the environment and human health, and proposed a number of specific priority areas. These principles and priorities are fully in line with Britain's own policies on the environment and health, as set out in this White Paper.

Eastern Europe

3.29 A key theme of the recent momentous changes in Central and Eastern Europe has been the open recognition by reformers of the damage and pollution that their countries have suffered over the past 40 years. Improving the environment is one of the objectives the new governments have set for themselves. Effective programmes of economic reform will be of great importance in this.

3.30 Some of the problems are so serious that they will call for major industrial restructuring and changes in energy sources if the Eastern countries are to achieve real improvements. To take two examples, one Eastern country, despite the stagnation of its economy over decades, is the biggest producer of carbon dioxide per head in the world. And pollution problems with water in another Eastern state are so bad that it risks having virtually no serviceable supplies by the end of the century. Britain and the other Community governments can help the efforts of the reforming governments by providing skills and know-how, for example:

• scientific surveying and monitoring skills to identify and measure the main pollutants and establish where they come from and to determine the extent of harm to human health and other species in the worst-polluted areas;

• advice on ways of regulating pollution and developing strategies and plans for cleaning it up, and on ways of making cost-effective energy efficiency improvements;

• training and educating people in industry and the pollution control agencies on ways of avoiding and policing pollution; and

• planning investment so that the Eastern countries are able to use the finance available to tackle the worst problems first.

3.31 Britain is already helping in these areas. It has taken a full part in meetings organised during 1990 to allow the Environment Ministers of the Community, the Eastern European countries and the USSR to meet to discuss the problems and exchange views on how to deal with them. The Government is building on these initial meetings, both by continuing contacts directly with particular Eastern European countries, through use of the Government's Know-How Fund, and by taking part in the Community's assistance programme. Direct contacts include participation by British experts in international working groups advising the Russian Red Cross and Red Crescent and the Soviet Government on action needed to protect health after the Chernobyl disaster.

3.32 The European Bank for Reconstruction and Development, to be based in London, will invest in economically sound and environmentally sustainable development in Central and Eastern Europe: it will report annually on the environmental impact of its operations. By encouraging the development of a productive private sector, the Bank will help create the wealth needed to tackle the environmental legacy of central planning.

3.33 Resources to help to get the restoration of the Central and Eastern European economies under way are already coming from the West. As part of its wider aid effort for Eastern Europe, the EC, with support from Britain, has allocated a budget of 500 mecu (£350million) for aid projects to Poland, Hungary, Czechoslovakia, the GDR and Yugoslavia in 1990, including a number in the environmental field. Other priority areas are agriculture and training. So far, about 20% of the budget has been allocated for environmental projects.

CONCLUSION

3.34 Each of the Community initiatives discussed in this Chapter, whether past or future, needs action in Britain to carry it into effect. Later chapters turn their attention to that action, and how it is affected both by the Community initiatives that this Chapter has been discussing and by our national needs and aspirations.

4

BRITAIN AND THE
WORLD ENVIRONMENT

Britain helps developing
countries to take
account of the
environment in their
wider development plans

INTRODUCTION

4.1 Environmental problems arising in one country can often be dealt with by that country on its own. But some of the most important environmental problems affect more than one country, as Chapter 3 describes; and some affect the whole world. Problems on this scale need concerted action between countries if they are to be tackled successfully.

4.2 Environmental problems of this kind include:
• the threat of global warming arising from the over-production of greenhouse gases;
• the threat to the ozone layer in the upper atmosphere arising from the production of certain compounds containing chlorine;
• threats to the oceans from dumping wastes and from over-fishing;
• threats to the polar regions from unregulated development;
• loss of species and habitats, reducing the world's biological diversity;
• excessive use of non-renewable resources

through wasteful or inefficient exploitation.

4.3 All these problems arise fundamentally from development that has taken place with too little regard for resource management and environmental consequences. Since human activity has now become so much the dominant influence on the environment of the whole planet, we can no longer afford to ignore the environmental consequences of our actions. Global warming could raise sea levels and threaten crops and forests in all parts of the world. Damage to the ozone layer could let through more of the sun's radiation with a consequent damage to crops and increase in skin cancers and eye cataracts. Loss of non-renewable resources and of species of plants and animals could leave future generations without the resources they need to sustain reasonable development and standards of living. Drought, sea-level rise and the degradation of land could lead to social instability and create environmental refugees.

SUSTAINABLE DEVELOPMENT

4.4 The Government therefore supports the principle of sustainable development. This means living on the earth's income rather than eroding its capital. It means keeping the consumption of renewable natural resources within the limits of their replenishment. It means handing down to successive generations not only man–made wealth (such as buildings, roads and railways) but also natural wealth, such as clean and adequate water supplies, good arable land, a wealth of wildlife and ample forests.

4.5 To achieve sustainable development requires the full integration of environmental considerations into economic policy decisions. The Government is supporting research in the Organisation for Economic Co-operation and Development (OECD) on how best to record and value the stocks and flows of natural resources at the national level. Concern for the environment is not a luxury which only developed countries can afford. It is a necessity for all. For poor countries which depend heavily on their natural resources it is a matter of survival.

4.6 The Government is convinced that economic development and environmental protection need not be irrevocably opposing principles but can complement each other. Both are necessary: development to improve the standard of living in poor countries and to sustain prosperity in developed countries; environmental protection to ensure that the development is sustainable. Development provides the wealth to invest in cleaner methods of production, the means to husband

Britain's aid programme supports sustainable development

natural resources prudently and the freedom to adopt a longer term perspective of the value of environmental assets. The Government is making sustainable development an integral part of its domestic and international policies.

Developing countries

4.7 Chapter 2 and later chapters describe how the Government is integrating environmental considerations into all policy areas and promoting sustainable growth in Britain. This Chapter describes Britain's action to encourage sustainable development in its relations with developing countries, which face many immediate and additional challenges. These include devising effective policies for economic development, handling public expenditure issues, creating conditions which favour overseas investment and the private sector, minimising movements of capital abroad, encouraging exports and dealing with debt.

Environment and debt

Many developing countries suffering environmental deterioration also faced serious economic difficulties and heavy debt burdens in the 1980s. Britain supports international efforts to help these countries to pursue the economic reforms essential for lasting economic growth. Growth will in turn help provide the resources to tackle environmental problems.
A number of developing countries are now participating in 'debt for nature swaps'.

These arrangements usually involve a debtor country providing local currency for conservation, in return for an environmental organisation buying some of the debtor country's foreign debt from its creditors at a discount and cancelling it. The Houston Economic Summit in July 1990 agreed that debt for nature swaps can play a useful role in protecting the environment.

4.8 Developing countries of course vary widely in their particular circumstances, from the poorest and predominantly rural countries of parts of Africa to the newly industrialised countries of parts of South East Asia and Latin America. But for many the problems are acute. They need to alleviate poverty by raising living standards, producing clean water and more food, providing better health care, extending and improving education and providing proper shelter and sanitation. They also face the most acute local environmental problems. Their ecosystems are often more

fragile and more liable to flood, cyclone and drought. Rapidly growing populations are putting pressures on rural areas and towns. Villages are threatened by soil erosion and drought. Burgeoning cities are generating increasing pollution of air and water. Developing countries are short of appropriate technologies to combat these problems and of the institutional capacity to deal with them. And it is the world's poorest countries which may face the greatest hardship from the effects of global warming. There is an inextricable link of cause and effect between poverty and the environment. The need to reconcile the alleviation of poverty with environmental protection is one of the most critical problems facing the world.

4.9 The Government recognises our global interdependence and believes that helping developing countries to tackle local and global environmental problems is in all our interests. Britain's close historical relationship with many developing countries gives it a special insight, as does our active involvement in a number of international organisations which offer scope for better co-operation and understanding between the developed and developing worlds on environmental problems. The Commonwealth is particularly well placed to contribute to this aim.

4.10 The Government will work towards international agreements, conventions and protocols that help to sustain the global environment, and will develop strong domestic policies to contribute to international action. It will work with the Commonwealth and with international organisations to seek common solutions to common problems, while respecting the national sovereignty of other countries and their right to manage their own resources.

4.11 Assistance towards solving environmental problems in developing countries will be an increasingly important priority for the aid programme. The Government accepts that developing countries will need financial resources to help them respond to certain environmental problems, especially global ones. Assistance will include help for developing countries to

World population growth 1750 - 2100

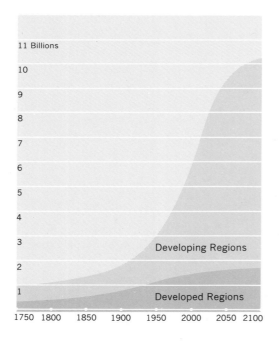

Rapid population growth is exacerbating environmental pressures. The Government supports developing countries' efforts to restrain it

build up their institutional capacity for managing their environmental resources.

4.12 Both the developed and developing worlds have contributed to our planet's environmental problem; for example, the developed world through the emissions of its industries, and the developing world through deforestation and its consequences. The important thing now is for all countries to recognise the mistakes of the past and the damage they have caused and to work together in the future to build a better framework which will enable us to manage the global environment for the benefit of all.

POPULATION GROWTH

4.13 The rate of population growth is exacerbating environmental pressures. The world's population doubled between 1950 and 1987. It now stands at over 5 billion and is expected to exceed 6 billion by the year 2000. 90 million people (over 1.5 times the population of Britain) are added to the global population each year: this is some 250,000 each day. 94% of these are born in developing countries.

4.14 As populations increase, so do demands for food, fuel, water and land. Farmers are forced into cultivating marginal land, which encourages soil degradation. The rising demand for wood, which is a major source of fuel in developing countries, and the need for agricultural land are important factors in deforestation. Since 1950 the world has lost nearly one-fifth of the top soil from its agricultural land and one-fifth of its tropical forests. Population pressures on the land lead to rural unemployment, large-scale migration from villages into towns, social disintegration and the rapid and unplanned growth of unhygienic slum dwellings. The effects of these pressures, particularly in urban areas,

Population growth

The Government has almost trebled its aid for the population sector, from £6.5 million in 1981 to £17.3 million in 1989. Most of this aid is channelled through the two multilateral population agencies – the United Nations Population Fund and the International Planned Parenthood Federation.

Bilaterally, the Government is supporting family planning activities in Africa and Asia. This support increasingly forms part of broader programmes to improve the health and welfare of mothers and children.

The Government also supports family planning programmes through British voluntary bodies.

will be enormous and widespread. The Government will therefore work internationally to improve the planning and management of urban growth, and to address the environmental problems that it can bring in developing countries.

Left: By 2000 almost half the world population will live in cities, compared with 14% in 1900. This causes social, environmental, and health problems

Right: The Government funds mother and child health projects as well as family planning programmes

4.15 The Government supports developing countries' own efforts to restrain population growth to levels which are consistent with their resources. There is now increasing evidence of a substantial demand by couples in many developing countries for family planning, particularly where basic health services are improving and women are becoming better educated. Britain's aid programme helps reduce population growth by alleviating poverty, promoting economic and social development and directly helping to meet demand for family planning. The aid programme also helps by funding projects to improve the health and education of women and to reduce infant and child mortality, which are crucial if smaller families are to be encouraged.

GLOBAL ENVIRONMENTAL RESOURCES

4.16 This section illustrates the Government's application of its principles through brief reference to key global environmental resources: a sustainable climate; tropical forests; biological diversity; wildlife; marine ecology; the oceans; the polar regions; and the ozone layer.

Climate

4.17 Very serious problems will arise if the speed and size of changes in the world's climate outstrip societies' ability to adapt. Chapter 5 gives a full account of the processes involved in climate change, and sets out the Government's programme of domestic action. Britain accepts its responsibility, alongside that of other countries, to curb its own emissions of gases such as carbon dioxide, methane and CFCs which contribute to global warming. Developing countries too will need to cooperate in a global strategy. If per head emissions of greenhouse gases grow too rapidly in developing countries, the effects will be devastating, regardless of the benefits of any steps which developed countries such as Britain may take. The Government recognises that developing countries will need financial and technical support if they are to participate fully in the international response to global warming. It is committed to playing its full part in co-operation with other developed countries to ensure that developing countries get the help they need.

Energy efficiency

The Government is developing new energy efficiency initiatives to help developing countries to contain their demands for fuels. This will minimise both their emissions of greenhouse gases and their fuel bills, and extend the lifetimes of non-renewable sources of energy. These initiatives include projects in:
- *India*: a £50 million grant programme to improve efficiency in both energy supply and energy use;
- *Bangladesh*: a major project in Dhaka to improve electricity distribution systems;
- *Pakistan*: a project, in conjunction with the World Bank, to improve the efficiency of all Pakistan's thermal power stations; and
- *Uganda:* a project, in conjunction with the World Bank, to rehabilitate and expand the Owen Falls hydroelectric project.

The Government has launched a major initiative to help developing countries manage their forests sustainably

Tropical forests

In 1989 the Prime Minister announced at the United Nations that the Government would aim to commit a further £100 million to tropical forestry activities over the next three years. At the end of 1988, the Government was financing about 80 forestry projects with a total value of £45 million. By mid-1990 it was supporting over 150 projects with a further 60 in preparation, at a total cost of £160 million. The Government's bilateral programmes include assistance to :
• *India*: £40 million for local costs for environmental, mainly forestry, projects.
• *Brazil*: a Memorandum of Understanding on technical co-operation on the environment. Eight forestry projects have been approved in principle, and a further seven are under consideration. The first of these - a £2.5

million research project into the effects of deforestation on climate involving the Institute of Hydrology - is to begin in September 1990.
• *Indonesia*: a £10 million package of institutional support for the forestry sector covering management assistance, training, research and conservation activities.
• *Ghana*: a £4 million forest management project concentrating on the management of individual forest reserves.

The Government is also financing 56 forestry projects run by voluntary organisations such as Oxfam and the World-Wide Fund for Nature (WWF). The Government funds about 40 forestry research projects, mostly managed by the Oxford Forestry Institute, to improve the productivity of forests in developing countries.

The Government supports international efforts to conserve forests

Tropical forests

4.18   The world's tropical forests are being destroyed at an alarming rate. An area about 1.5 times the size of England is cut down or burned each year.

4.19   Deforestation has both local and global effects. It destroys the livelihood of local people dependent on fuelwood and other products harvested from the forest; adversely affects watersheds and water resources; deprives the national economy of materials for export; and reduces the productivity of the soil, leaving the land impoverished or

even barren. Deforestation is also responsible for up to a quarter of man-made emissions of carbon dioxide, the principal greenhouse gas: burning forests puts large amounts of stored carbon back into the atmosphere.

4.20   Deforestation is a global problem requiring a concerted response. The Government supports the calls for international action made by the European Council in June 1990 and by the Houston Economic Summit in July 1990. The Government is working to strengthen and reform the Tropical Forestry Action Plan (TFAP) which should be the principal mechanism for

Deforestation contributes to global warming, loss of plant and animal species and reduced agricultural productivity

Map showing extent of tropical forest deforestation

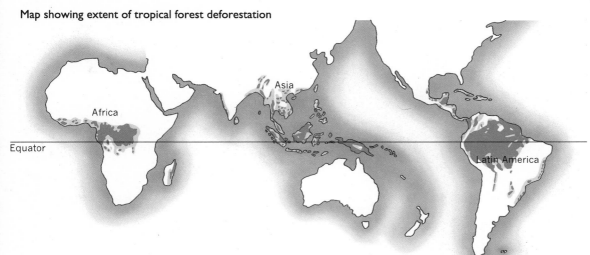

Previous Extent of Tropical Rainforests

Current Extent of Tropical Rainforests

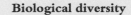

coordinating aid for the forestry sector in developing countries. In keeping with its domestic environmental policies, the Government wishes to see a more open and informed public dimension to the TFAP. The Plan needs to involve local people as well as the highest levels of Government in developing countries, and to place increased emphasis on conservation. It also needs to address policies, including those which encourage forest destruction.

4.21 The Government will also continue to play a constructive role in the International Tropical Timber Organisation, especially to promote measures to ensure that trade in tropical timber is carried out in a sustainable manner. It supports the proposal for an international agreement on the conservation of forests, perhaps as a Protocol to a Climate Change Convention.

4.22 The Government has launched a major new aid initiative to help developing countries maximise the economic and social benefits they enjoy from their forests in a sustainable way. The Forestry Initiative addresses the social and economic reasons for forest loss in order to help achieve sustainable forest management. The initiative also promotes agroforestry and the reforestation of degraded land.

Biological diversity

4.23 No one knows how many living species of organisms inhabit the earth. There may be up to 50 million, of which as many as a third could become extinct by about the year 2025. The tropical rain forests cover 7% of the world's land surface but may well contain over 90% of its living species. Species are disappearing rapidly as a result of over-hunting, over-collection and pollution, but most of all through destruction of their habitats, especially wetlands and tropical forests.

4.24 As species disappear, the world may be losing potentially valuable sources of food, medicine and industrial materials. All of our crop plants originated in the wild and many valuable drugs are based on natural plant

The Government's five-point plan will help conserve the world's genetic resources like this periwinkle

Biological diversity

The Government finances a variety of projects to help developing countries conserve biological diversity. These include help with the conservation of the Korup rainforest in Cameroon, assistance to the Government of India on the establishment of a Conservation Monitoring Centre and funding for a Manual on Centres of Plant Diversity.

The Government has prepared a five-point plan to give a further boost to the conservation of biological diversity in developing countries. It is:
• financing a major study on the status of the world's biodiversity;
• commissioning a strategic study on the biodiversity of tropical forests and outlines of projects for future funding;
• funding a similar study on 'wildlands' like the Savannah of Africa, the origin of many of our food crops;
• commissioning studies on the biodiversity of the marine environment; and
• funding research on the economic value of biological diversity.

products. For example, the most effective drug in the treatment of some childhood leukaemias comes from a tropical periwinkle. The world's existing stock of genetic resources may become increasingly valuable to future generations as climatic conditions change. Our descendants may need to grow different crop plants or to develop strains of livestock which are better adapted to the new conditions.

4.25 The Government is the second largest contributor to the International Board for Plant Genetic Resources, which promotes the collection and conservation of plant genetic resources. It also funds a number of collections in Britain, most notably the Seed Bank at Kew, which is of global standing and importance.

4.26 The Government is helping developing countries with their economic aspirations while ensuring that development projects are ecologically sustainable. It is committed to promoting the conservation of biological diversity in partnership with developing

The Government supports efforts to conserve wildlife in developing countries, especially endangered species

countries. The Government is supporting international efforts led by the United Nations Environment Programme (UNEP) to agree a global Convention for the conservation of biological diversity. This will impose conservation obligations on all countries which sign the Convention. The Government considers that all those who benefit from the conservation of biological diversity should contribute as far as they are able to its costs.

Wildlife management

4.27 Developing countries contain a wealth of wildlife and many of the world's endangered species. The decline in numbers of some species, especially the African elephant and the black rhino, has given rise to great concern. The estimated numbers of wild elephant in Africa, for example, have fallen from around 1,300,000 in the early 1970s to some 600,000 in 1989. Poaching and illegal trade, for instance in ivory and rhino horn, are particular threats.

4.28 British development aid supports wildlife conservation projects related to tourism throughout Africa to help developing countries manage internationally important species. It funds a number of projects aimed specifically at strengthening anti-poaching activities, like the Tanzanian project to protect the black rhino. Britain was one of the first countries to join the United Nations Convention on International Trade in Endangered Species of Wild Fauna and Flora (CITES), which exerts controls over international trade. The Government has been a leading supporter of CITES: in addition to its normal CITES subscription, it provides financial assistance to help developing country delegates attend meetings and play their full part in them; it also helps to maintain the ivory monitoring unit in the CITES secretariat. Britain was instrumental in persuading the European Community to agree a ban on ivory imports in June 1989: this ban preceded that declared by CITES and imposed stricter controls.

Sustainable management of the oceans

4.29 Man is a land-based animal, but in many parts of the world we have relied on the seas for our livelihood since prehistoric times. It is becoming clear that we need to improve our understanding of the seas and to treat them in a sustainable way.

4.30 Britain makes a major contribution to international efforts to improve man's scientific understanding of the oceans. This fundamental scientific understanding is essential if we are to appreciate the role of the oceans as a global resource and their influence on global warming, for example in absorbing carbon dioxide. The Government is also committed to policies designed to protect and preserve the marine environment, in particular through the prevention of pollution and the management of living resources.

4.31 Fish and other forms of marine life provide a major source of nutrition and employment in many countries. Maintaining the stocks of fish in the world's oceans and the ecosystems on which they depend requires responsible methods of catching them and preservation of the coastal marine

The Government supports sustainable fishing practices

practice and warmly supports the efforts of the Pacific nations most affected to conclude international agreements banning it.

4.34 The world's population of many species of whales has declined radically as a result of unsustainable levels of exploitation over the centuries. Britain has not been a whaling nation for many years and played a leading role in achieving the moratorium on commercial whaling declared by the International Whaling Commission in 1982, which is to be further reviewed in 1991. The Government will firmly oppose any resumption of such whaling except on the basis of scientific evidence that stocks of the species concerned are above naturally sustainable levels, and that the size of any catches proposed clearly poses no threat to species or to local populations. Further, the Government is clear that there has to be a revised management procedure which will avoid over-exploitation.

environment. Over-fishing and ocean pollution threaten not only stocks of fish but also the sea-birds and other animals, such as seals, which depend on them for their food. Biological diversity is under threat in the world's seas no less than in its forests, and they too need to be managed sustainably.

4.32 Dynamite fishing off coastal reefs is one example of an unsustainable practice. It yields short-term gains but impoverishes natural resources in the longer-term by damaging coral reefs, mangrove swamps and tidal lagoons, which are the habitat of many species of fish. The Government provides help to coastal communities in developing countries to promote sustainable fishing methods.

4.33 The Government is concerned at the use of large-scale ocean drift nets (some as much as 30 miles long) by a minority of Pacific nations. These cause gross and needless damage to marine life, including turtles and dolphins, as well as severely depleting the ocean's stock of fish. The Government condemns this destructive

4.35 Some nations have undertaken research studies of whales during the moratorium without fully demonstrating that these catches will help to provide scientific information essential to stock management. Britain will press for improvements to the procedure for overseeing whaling permits for scientific research and will urge the further development and use of study methods which do not involve taking whales.

4.36 The Government is also seeking agreement within the International Whaling Commission to implement similar measures for smaller cetaceans, such as porpoises and dolphins.

Britain supports the international ban on commercial whaling, and measures to conserve porpoises and dolphins

Polar regions

4.37 The Government wants to see proper protection of the polar regions. That will require more extensive scientific co-operation on an international scale. Britain's scientific expertise and long history of scientific study in these regions mean that it is well placed to play a leading role in that work.

4.38 Sustainable management of the Arctic and Antarctic is crucial to the world environment. The Antarctic ice-sheet plays a key role in setting world climate patterns and sea levels, and the polar regions are home to many unique wildlife species. The scale of the polar regions is vast. The Arctic Ocean is nearly five times the size of the Mediterranean Sea. The continent of Antarctica is more than double the size of Australia and considerably larger than Europe.

4.39 It is vital that man's activities in both the Arctic and Antarctic do not increase the risks to the world environment. Activities in most of the Arctic are controlled by the countries which have territory in the region. In the Antarctic, activity is controlled by consensus through the Antarctic Treaty System. The system ensures good relations between about forty states, despite territorial disputes, and promotes international scientific research and environmental co-operation.

4.40 The Antarctic Treaty System provides strict measures for the conservation of Antarctic wildlife. Equally strict measures are now needed for the protection of Antarctic habitat. The Government is therefore calling for the introduction of a comprehensive environmental management plan for the Antarctic to be negotiated within the Antarctic Treaty System. This would regulate all potentially damaging activities such as waste disposal, marine pollution and tourism. It would also provide for mandatory environmental impact assessment, environmental monitoring, a coherent system of area protection and strengthened compliance and enforcement.

4.41 The Government supports the rigorous environmental safeguards in the Convention

on the Regulation of Antarctic Mineral Resource Activities (CRAMRA) and associated conservation measures (such as the Convention on the Conservation of Antarctic Marine Living Resources) which together would regulate any exploitation of the natural resources of the Antarctic. The Government accepts that entry into force of CRAMRA will almost certainly have to await progress on a comprehensive environmental protection strategy for the Antarctic.

4.42 Many scientific questions about the global environment call for international scientific co-operation in the polar regions. For example understanding of the way in which global warming may affect the Antarctic ice-sheet, which has the potential to flood the world's low lying areas, is crucial to the world community. We still have much to learn. Research is needed on a scale beyond the capacity of any one Antarctic Treaty country.

4.43 The Government has substantially increased its funding for polar research by the British Antarctic Survey. It has given strong support to initiatives towards the creation of an international Arctic Science Committee, which it sees as an essential development. And, as the high priority of this work is recognised, it is encouraging universities to devote more of their resources to Arctic research.

Britain is calling for an international environmental management plan to protect the Antarctic

The ozone layer – the 1990 London Meeting

In June 1990 the Government hosted the Second Meeting of the Parties to the Montreal Protocol. The Parties agreed that CFCs should be phased out by 2000 with intermediate cuts of 50% by 1995, and 85% by 1997. Halons are to be phased out by 2000, except for essential uses, with a 50% cut by 1995. Two other substances were added to the Protocol for the first time – carbon tetrachloride and methyl chloroform. Carbon tetrachloride will go by 2000 with an interim cut of 85% in 1995. Methyl chloroform will be frozen at 1989 levels by 1993, cut by 30% by 1995, 70% by 2000, and phased out by 2005.

• Several countries including Britain wanted faster action, and the European Commission has been asked to make proposals for banning CFCs within the Community by 1997, subject to exemptions if necessary for essential uses such as medical aerosols. The Parties will review the Protocol in 1992 with a view to bringing forward the phase-out date.

• The Parties also reached agreement on a financial mechanism to help developing countries meet the costs of complying with the revised Protocol and to provide the necessary transfer of technology. Britain will contribute a minimum of £5.6 million towards the first three year programme. This will be increased to £9.4 million when other developing countries such as India and China, which are potentially major producers of ozone-depleting substances, join the Protocol. Britain's contribution will be separate from the aid budget for developing countries. Both the Indian and Chinese delegations to the Meeting agreed to recommend that their Governments join the Protocol. Meanwhile Britain is helping the Government of India with plans on phasing out CFCs and is assisting developing countries to play a full role in international discussion.

The ozone layer

4.44 The ozone layer acts as a shield against ultra-violet radiation from the sun. In 1984 the British Antarctic Survey detected significant ozone depletion over the Antarctic in spring and this was later confirmed by satellite measurements. The depletion is caused by certain very stable man-made chemicals such as halons, used in fire-fighting equipment, and chlorofluorocarbons (CFCs) which are used in aerosols, refrigeration, air conditioning, foam blowing and as solvents. As they reach the stratosphere they are broken down by strong sunlight, releasing chlorine which in turn destroys the ozone in the ozone layer. The resulting increased levels of ultraviolet radiation reaching the earth's surface may cause skin

Ozone depletion process

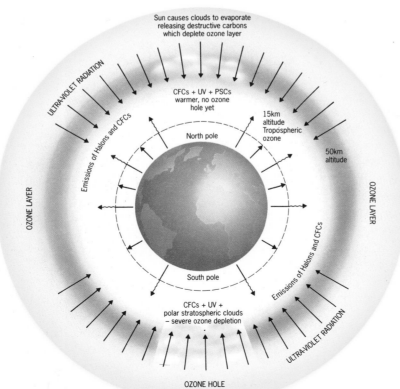

Research – ozone layer

British public and private sector research plays a major part in improving understanding of the state of the stratospheric ozone layer and how to protect it. Britain hosts the Cambridge Co-ordination Centre for monitoring of stratospheric ozone trends. Other work includes projects
• to monitor stratospheric ozone trends and assess their implications – Department of the Environment and Natural Environment Research Council (£0.75m in 1989/90)
• to investigate the chemical and photochemical reactions that occur in the atmosphere, using space-based and

laboratory-based instruments – Science and Engineering Research Council (£3.2m in 1990/91)
• to study the mechanisms by which ultraviolet light causes damage, such as skin cancer – Medical Research Council (£0.1m in 1989/90)

British companies have joined with other producers of chlorofluorocarbons worldwide to test possible alternatives in uses such as refrigeration, production of plastic foams and aerosol propellants.

cancer in humans, damage crops and kill plankton, fish larvae and other important links in the sea's food chain.

4.45 The Government has made a leading contribution to the scientific study of the problem, and in 1989, with support from other interested countries, it founded a centre in Cambridge to coordinate monitoring of the ozone layer. The Government is also supporting an evaluation of alternatives to CFC solvents and the establishment of a refrigeration training scheme to encourage the recovery and recycling of CFCs.

4.46 Britain has been in the forefront of action to protect the ozone layer. It played a leading part in concluding the 1985 Vienna Convention and the 1987 Montreal protocol which set the first international limits on consumption and production of CFCs and which has been ratified so far by 60 countries. In March 1989, the Government hosted a major conference in London on 'Saving the

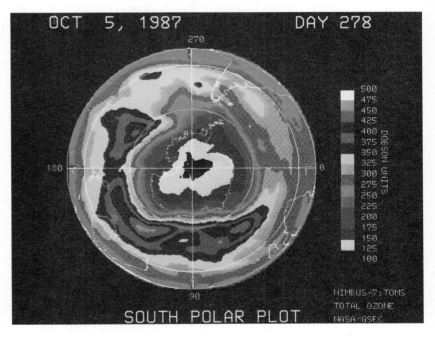

Ozone Layer' to raise world-wide political awareness of the problem. The conference was attended by 123 countries, and 20 undertook to join the Montreal Protocol.

Britain has taken a leading part in international measures to protect the ozone layer

PARTNERSHIP

4.47 The management of global environmental resources calls for global co-operation. The Government is committed to working in partnership with others - with developing countries, business, voluntary organisations and international bodies.

Developing countries

4.48 The Government is helping to strengthen environmental institutions in developing countries by encouraging environmental awareness and improving the professional environmental skills necessary to

The Government supports the British Council and other agencies which provide education and training in developing countries

promote sustainable development and a healthy environment. It is important that developing countries build up their capacity to identify environmental issues so that they can respond to them effectively and integrate environmental considerations into wider development planning.

4.49 The Government aims to achieve this objective by:
• providing technical advice on environmental policy and to environmental protection institutions;
• providing support for the transfer of environmentally benign technologies to help

The British Council

The aim of the British Council, in keeping with its Royal Charter, is to provide access to British thought, experience, achievement and expertise across the cultural spectrum, including the environment. Through its offices in 90 countries, the Council is proposing to strengthen its environmental activities in the following ways:
• promoting British environmental expertise and experience overseas, through consultancies and visits by British specialists and teachers;
• assisting with country-specific needs through institutional links and research collaboration between British and overseas institutions; and
• managing training activities, specialist courses, seminars and projects in Britain and overseas.

The Council pursues these activities through its programmes of exchange of people, information services and management of projects and programmes on behalf of the Government and other international sponsors.

economic and social development;
• offering training in a wide range of disciplines such as environmental science, soil conservation, wildlife management and water resource management;
• providing institutional links and research collaboration designed to develop local capability in specialist areas;
• financing environmental education projects

Natural Resources Institute

The Natural Resources Institute is the scientific arm of Britain's Overseas Development Administration. It is centrally involved in the sustainable management and use of renewable natural resources in developing countries – a key objective for governments and aid donors. Major aims are to:
• increase agricultural productivity and the incomes of farmers through the more effective management of resources and of land use. The work covers primarily land degradation issues, optimal forestry management, improved agronomy and cropping systems and the

contribution of livestock to integrated farming systems;
• develop pest management strategies which are adapted to local conditions. Environmental considerations are at the forefront of this work and emphasis is given to natural regulatory mechanisms; and
• reduce post-harvest losses and improve the quality of agricultural products. Post-harvest technology programmes reduce the pressure on the environment by increasing the productivity of the food and agriculture sector.

designed to encourage greater environmental awareness, for example among school-children, farmers and conservation officers; and

• involving local people in the planning of development projects affecting the area in which they live.

4.50 By strengthening the commitment and the ability of developing countries to manage their environmental resources in a sustainable manner, the Government's aid programme will promote primary environmental care. This concept involves everyone – from governments to local communities and individuals – shouldering responsibility for the management of their environmental resources and working together to prevent environmental degradation.

Business

4.51 Business is taking on an increasingly important role in promoting sustainable development in industrialised and developing countries. It holds the power both to pollute and to find solutions to environmental problems. For example, the same multi-national corporations which manufactured CFCs are leading the effort to develop environmentally benign alternatives.

4.52 The Government is encouraging industry to:
• continue to respond to the rising public concern over the environment;
• apply its substantial expertise and resources to help sustain environmental assets;
• develop environmentally more benign products, cleaner technologies and methods of conserving energy and raw materials;
• establish voluntary environmental controls;
• set high standards of health and safety in connection with exports to and operations in developing countries; and
• share its expertise with developing countries through the transfer of technical and managerial skills.

4.53 The Government is firmly of the view that the rules and regulations governing inter-national trade should be compatible with national and international policies to protect

The Government supports the work of voluntary bodies, in developing countries, as with this Walkabout Sawmill which enables mature logs to be removed without damaging the forest

and improve the environment. The General Agreement on Tariffs and Trade (GATT) allows nations to take trade measures to protect human, animal or plant life or health. Britain, with the European Community, is playing an active part in the GATT negotiations on the export of goods which are prohibited domestically. The Government will ensure that the negotiations:
• respect international environmental agreements; and in particular
• take full account of the dangers associated with shipments of hazardous waste.

Voluntary bodies

4.54 Many British voluntary bodies concerned with the environment and development have a high international reputation. The Government values their expertise and their special ability to help at the local community level. It meets them regularly to exchange ideas and encourages their participation in promoting sustainable development. On occasions where their contribution is relevant and appropriate the Government invites non-governmental experts to participate in British delegations to international environmental meetings, for example UNEP Governing Councils. Under the aid programme's Joint Funding Scheme, the Government supports the work in developing countries of a wide range of non-governmental agencies. Since 1985 this budget has quadrupled, and it is increasing by a further 25% in 1990/91 to £20 million.

OECD Development Assistance Committee (DAC)

The OECD Development Assistance Committee (DAC) is an informal liaison group for the development activities and policies of OECD members, who are the major aid donors. In 1989 the DAC set up a working group on the environment. Britain is contributing to work on:
• the role of aid agencies in tackling global environmental problems;
• environmental institution-building;
• biodiversity;
• links between population and the environment; and
• environmental economics.

International organisations

4.55 Britain plays an active part in the environmental work of many international bodies. About 40% of Britain's overseas aid is channelled through multilateral institutions, notably the European Community, the World Bank Group and the regional development banks in Africa, Asia, South America and the Caribbean, and United Nations agencies such as the World Meteorological Organisation, the United Nations Development Programme and the United Nations Children's Fund. The World Health Organisation too is giving increased emphasis to the environmental aspects of health protection. In all of these organisations, Britain plays a full part and uses its membership to press for the integration of environmental considerations into development programmes.

4.56 Four international organisations are particularly important because they offer scope for co-operation on a wide range of environmental matters.

4.57 The European Community has a number of agreements with other European countries and developing countries throughout the world. These include the Lomé Convention - an aid and trade agreement between the EC and African, Caribbean and Pacific countries; concessional financing arrangements with Asian and Latin American countries; and financial protocols with several Mediterranean countries. Lomé IV, which was concluded in December 1989, has an aid component worth over £17 billion and involved Britain in making its biggest ever single aid commitment (£1.3 billion). The protection of the environment has a prominent role in the new Convention, reflecting agreement that the effects on the environment must be taken into account *before* development projects are approved. Similar concerns are reflected increasingly in the Mediterranean and the Asia/Latin America programmes. At the Dublin summit in June 1990 the Prime Minister endorsed a call for greater emphasis on the preservation of the tropical rainforests, including those in Brazil.

4.58 The United Nations Environment Programme (UNEP) provides a forum in which the world's nations can consider and take action on common environmental problems. Major achievements include its Global Environmental Monitoring System; its Regional Seas Programme; the development of international agreements on the import and export of chemicals (the 1987 London Guidelines) and of toxic wastes (the 1989 Basel Convention described in Chapter 15); and the 1985 Vienna Convention and the 1987 Montreal Protocol on the Ozone Layer (see Chapter 5). It is now helping to develop

Britain supports the UNEP 'Basel Convention' which prohibits dumping of hazardous wastes in developing countries

strategies for dealing with global warming and the depletion of biological diversity. UNEP also has a key role because of its responsibility for stimulating environmental action in other United Nations bodies although it has not always had the resources or the necessary influence to force the pace on every issue.

4.59 The Government has been calling for an expanded role for UNEP in coordinating international environmental action. In 1989 it more than doubled Britain's financial contributions to strengthen UNEP's work and its voice in the United Nations system.

4.60 The World Bank has an important role in developing an internationally coordinated programme of action to help developing countries tackle global environmental problems. The Government welcomes the Bank's initiative for a Global Environmental Facility for assisting action by developing countries on climate change, biodiversity, ozone depletion and pollution of the world's seas. This should embrace other international institutions, including the multilateral development banks and the United Nations, as well as funding mechanisms for the proposed environmental protocols and conventions.

4.61 The Organisation for Economic Co-operation and Development (OECD) brings together the world's 24 most developed nations and is particularly important in helping to steer economic development in directions which do not cause excessive environmental damage. It has carried out pioneering work on environmental economics for example and on the control of chemicals. Its Development Assistance Committee (see opposite) is doing innovative work on the relationship between aid and the environment. Britain also looks to the OECD to provide a sound analysis of the possible economic and social effects of climate change. Britain will give strong support to OECD's Ministerial Conference in 1991 on Environment and Economic Policies.

4.62 Britain is also a State Member of the International Union for the Conservation of Nature and Natural Resources, which is the leading international organisation in the conservation field with a membership of some 63 states, 108 government agencies and over 400 non-governmental organisations. It plays a major role in developing strategies for the conservation of biological diversity and the sustainable use of the environment and it coordinates conservation action worldwide through national committees and a triennial General Assembly.

CONCLUSION: THE UN CONFERENCE ON ENVIRONMENT AND DEVELOPMENT

4.63 The 1972 Stockholm Conference on the Human Environment was the first opportunity for the international community to focus on the many and various environmental activities within the United Nations system. One result of that seminal Conference was the establishment of UNEP as an agent for stimulating and coordinating the environmental work of the UN. Twenty years later, with interest in the environment at an even higher and more urgent level, the UN Conference on Environment and Development will be held in Brazil in 1992. The Conference has the ambitious target of securing agreement on two global conventions – on climate change and biological diversity. It will also take forward action on many of the other international issues addressed in this chapter.

4.64 The Government sees the Conference as a crucial opportunity for the pursuit of sustainable development and it intends to stimulate the widest possible participation. The Government supports the innovative process developed at the Bergen Conference on Sustainable Development in May 1990 in which a range of non-governmental groups were partners with Government representatives. The Government is

Britain hosted a meeting in June 1990 which agreed tough new measures to phase out chemicals which destroy the ozone layer

help prepare Britain's national report for the Conference.

4.65 Britain was one of the first countries to contribute to a voluntary fund to enable developing countries to take part in preparations for the 1992 Conference. The Government's initial contribution is designed to bring in environmental experts from the least developed countries.

4.66 The Government looks to the Conference to set the international environmental agenda well beyond the end of the century and in doing so to decide how the United Nations itself should become more environmentally responsive. The Conference will conduct a rigorous examination of how the UN brings together environment and development matters. The Government expects recommendations to emerge on strengthening UNEP as an integral component of a more effective UN approach. The Conference should also provide firm guidance on streamlining international cooperation, on broader adherence to international environmental law, and on ways in which the industrialised world can cooperate better with the poorer countries of the world. Britain is determined to play a leading role in helping the 1992 Conference to a successful conclusion.

promoting the Bergen process as a model for the 1992 Conference and will continue to build on the partnership theme in its own domestic preparations. An important focus will be the UK Committee for UNEP whose members come from business, politics, the media, science, environmental groups and academic institutions as well as the Government. The Committee is being asked to play a major part in Britain's preparations by arranging a series of public meetings on the key issues. In addition the non-governmental community will be invited to

Research – Britain in the world environment

Britain's objectives for public sector research on the world environment are to improve understanding of natural processes; to improve long and short term monitoring systems; and to work closely with international bodies with related research programmes.

Some examples are projects
• to study the physics, chemistry and biology of the oceans as they relate to climate change and pollution – Natural Environment Research Council (£15.4m in 1989/90)
• to investigate whales, seals and dolphins and other cetaceans – mainly through work commissioned by the Fisheries Departments and the Department of the Environment and undertaken via the Natural Environment

Research Council (£0.4m in 1989/90)
• to use satellite data to study ecological and land use aspects of large-scale environmental problems including desertification, deforestation and global climate change – Natural Environment Research Council (£0.5m in 1989/90)
• to investigate how renewable natural resources can be used in agriculture, forestry, fisheries, livestock production and tackling health problems – Overseas Development Administration (£12.3m in 1989/90)
• to support British participation in the European Space Agency's Earth Resources Satellites programmes – Department of Trade and Industry through the British National Space Centre (£12m in 1989/90)

BRITAIN AND GLOBAL WARMING

5

INTRODUCTION

5.1 Global warming is one of the biggest environmental challenges now facing the world. It calls for action by all the world's nations, as no single nation can solve the problem on its own. This Chapter explains the processes that appear to be causing warming and changing the world's climate. It describes the steps that Britain, with others, has taken to clarify the scientific uncertainties and provide a sound basis for decisive international action, co-ordinated through the United Nations and its agencies. It also proposes measures to help to achieve the challenging target that the Government has announced that it is prepared to set for Britain, if other countries take similar action, of reversing the upward trend in emissions of carbon dioxide and stabilising them at 1990 levels by 2005 (Britain's emissions of carbon dioxide account for about 3% of the world total). If the Government's policies on all greenhouse gases (GHGs) are taken into account, and weighted according to the GHGs' potency, then achieving such a target should reduce the global warming potential of Britain's emissions by 2005 to a level some 20% lower than levels in 1990.

THE GREENHOUSE EFFECT

5.2 The energy which drives our weather and climate comes from the sun. The Earth receives energy, largely in the form that we see as visible light. About a third is reflected directly back into space. The rest is absorbed, heating the atmosphere, the oceans and the land. The warm Earth radiates infra-red energy back into space, but, on the way, some of it is absorbed by gases in the atmosphere. This is similar to the effect of glass in a greenhouse, which allows the sunlight in but keeps some of the radiated heat from escaping. Hence the gases in the atmosphere which absorb radiated heat are called the greenhouse gases, and the process is known as the greenhouse effect.

5.3 Greenhouse gases occur naturally in the atmosphere. The natural greenhouse effect keeps the temperature of the Earth some $30^{\circ}C$ warmer than it would be otherwise. Without it the Earth would be too cold to support life.

5.4 Water vapour is the most important natural greenhouse gas. Its concentration in the atmosphere depends on the Earth's temperature. The concentration of other natural greenhouse gases is determined by the balance between the processes which produce them ('sources') and those which absorb them ('sinks'). The main natural greenhouse gases are:
• carbon dioxide (CO_2), which is released when living things breathe, die and decay, and which is absorbed by plants and the animals that feed on them;
• methane (CH_4), which is produced when organic material decays in the absence of air, as in marshes and wetlands, and by digestion in the stomachs of cattle and sheep, and is destroyed by chemical reactions in the atmosphere;
• nitrous oxide (N_2O), which is given off by

How the greenhouse effect works

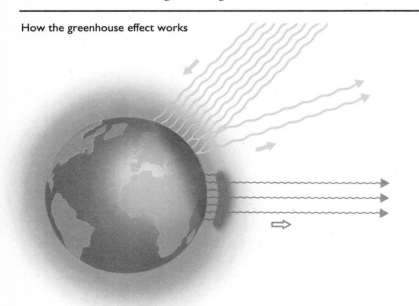

Energy received from the sun as visible sunlight heats the earth's surface' which emits energy. Some escapes to space but some is trapped by greenhouse gases and returns additional heat to the earth.

Contribution of different gases to greenhouse effect

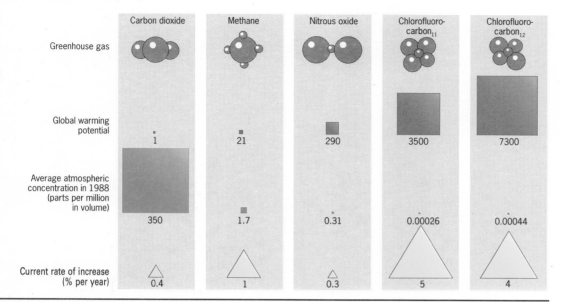

	Carbon dioxide	Methane	Nitrous oxide	Chlorofluoro-carbon₁₁	Chlorofluoro-carbon₁₂
Greenhouse gas					
Global warming potential	1	21	290	3500	7300
Average atmospheric concentration in 1988 (parts per million in volume)	350	1.7	0.31	0.00026	0.00044
Current rate of increase (% per year)	0.4	1	0.3	5	4

The Government will continue to press for action to reduce greenhouse gases through an international convention

vegetation and soils, and eventually breaks down chemically in the stratosphere;
• ozone (O_3), which is generated by the sun's rays in the stratosphere, and by chemical reactions in the lower atmosphere, and destroyed by other natural chemical reactions.

5.5 While the natural greenhouse effect is essential to life, a problem arises because human activity causes the release of additional greenhouse gases and these releases do not seem to be balanced by additional 'sinks'. The result is an increase in greenhouse gas concentrations, and in the greenhouse effect. *Carbon dioxide* comes in large quantities from fossil fuels – oil, coal and gas – burnt to provide the energy we need to run our homes, offices and factories, as fuel for transport and for other purposes and from burning forests. *Methane* comes from agriculture (mainly rice-growing, but also from the digestive processes of cattle and, to a lesser extent, sheep), coal mining, natural gas extraction and distribution and from waste disposed of on land. *Nitrous oxide* is thought to come mainly from farming and from burning fossil fuels and other materials. *Ozone* is produced in the lower atmosphere when nitrogen oxides, mainly from burning fuel, and organic compounds, some natural, some man-made, react in sunny weather.

5.6 All these gases have been increasing in

the lower atmosphere over the last 100 years. The trend has increased in recent decades as world population has grown and as less-developed countries have industrialised. In addition, a powerful family of GHGs is entirely man-made. These are the chlorofluorocarbons (CFCs), compounds containing chlorine, fluorine and carbon. They have been widely used in aerosols and refrigerators, for making insulating and structural foams, as solvents and for cleaning. Urgent action is already in hand to eliminate the CFCs because of the damage they do to

Greenhouse gases have been increasing in the atmosphere over the last 100 years

the Earth's protective layer of ozone in the upper atmosphere (see 4.44-4.46). But, weight for weight, their greenhouse effect ranges from several hundred to several thousand times that of CO_2, and eliminating them will help to combat global warming.

5.7 The additional heating due to GHGs has increased to a level at which it is now at least equivalent to natural factors such as volcanic activity and variations in the sun's output.

The effects

5.8 For over a century, some scientists have speculated that man-made emissions of CO_2 could cause climate warming. It is only over the last decade that the role of other gases has been fully recognised. Computer models are now available which aim to predict the response of the whole climate system to warming. Many elements of that response - for example higher levels of water vapour in a warmer atmosphere or shrinking ice-caps - may themselves increase the warming effect. But the effect of changes in clouds remains difficult to assess so far.

Britain has taken an active part in international efforts to study the problem of climate change and suggest responses

5.9 Our understanding of atmospheric chemistry has also greatly improved. There is now a consensus that many greenhouse gases, particularly carbon dioxide, nitrous oxide and CFCs, persist for a century or more after they are released into the atmosphere.

The scientific challenge

5.10 Even if preventative action is taken quickly, the concentration of man-made greenhouse gases already in the atmosphere will inevitably lead to some further warming in the future.

5.11 In 1988 the international community, with strong support from Britain, set up the Inter-Governmental Panel on Climate Change (IPCC), operating under the auspices of the United Nations Environment Programme and World Meteorological Organisation. Its task was to study the science of climate change, consider its possible impacts on the world and suggest response strategies that could be used to tackle the problem. The diagram on the left shows the organisation of the IPCC's work. Britain has chaired Working Group 1 on scientific assessment, which has involved more than 300 of the world's leading scientists, and took an active part in the other Working Groups and sub-groups.

5.12 The Second World Climate Conference will consider the IPCC's report in autumn 1990. As a result of its work, there can no longer be serious doubt that the global climate faces significant change because of the accumulation of man-made GHGs. But there is still uncertainty about detailed projections. More work remains to be done over at least the next 10-15 years to predict the global effects, and on ways to predict the local and regional consequences. But the IPCC Working Group I reached some important conclusions:

• emissions resulting from human activities are substantially increasing the atmospheric concentrations of greenhouse gases;
• these increases will enhance the greenhouse effect, causing an additional warming of the earth's surface;
• carbon dioxide is responsible for over half

IPCC working groups structure

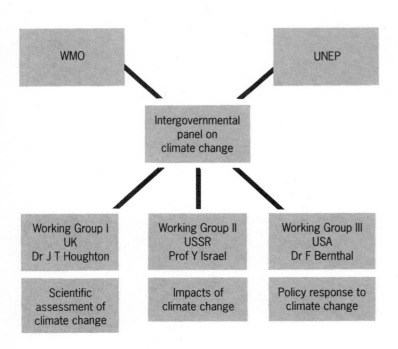

the man-made greenhouse effect in the past and is likely to remain so in the future;
• continued emissions of many of these gases at present rates would commit us to increased concentrations for centuries ahead; and
• the longer emissions continue to increase at present day rates, the greater reductions would have to be for concentrations to stabilise at a given level.

Using the best available models, Working Group I predicts that:
• if we continue as we are, global mean temperature would increase by 0.3°C per decade (within a range of 0.2° to 0.5° per decade); this is greater than the world has seen over the past 10,000 years. Global mean temperature over the next century would become higher than at any time over the last 150,000 years; sea-level would rise by 6cm per decade (within a range of 3-10cm per decade) over the next century, three to six times the rate seen over the last 100 years;
• rapid changes in climate will change the composition of natural living systems: some species will benefit, while others will be unable to migrate or adapt fast enough and may become extinct; and
• the effect of warming on biological and chemical processes seems likely to increase the atmospheric concentrations of natural greenhouse gases in a warmer world.

The consequences

5.13 These changes could have major effects on the world. Changes in sea level, mainly due to thermal expansion of the oceans and the melting of some land ice, would submerge low-lying coasts and turn some fresh water salt. Changes in climate and weather could happen faster than natural vegetation and crops could adapt to them, damaging agriculture and natural systems and making some land infertile. Some diseases could spread into countries in which they are not at present endemic. The human consequences of such changes, and their effects on international security, could be very severe. Even if drastic action in the future could avert the worst effects, their economic cost could be very great.

Action

5.14 The Government believes that this generation has a duty to act to meet the threat of global warming. The discipline involved must apply not only to the developed countries which currently produce most GHGs, but to the international community as a whole, including developing countries which are aiming to expand their economies significantly.

5.15 New approaches to pollution control may be needed that increase reliance on the operation of the market, in contrast to the more traditional approach of setting standards in laws and regulations (see Annex A). Britain will continue to play a leading part in work on these ideas in the Organisation for Economic Co-operation and Development and elsewhere. The developed world will also need to continue to provide the developing world, on fair and affordable terms, with technology and know-how which can help towards limiting emissions of GHGs.

5.16 Britain has proposed that the best way to act on global warming is through an international framework convention setting a broad strategy. Specific protocols could then be added, for example on forestry - since trees are a reservoir for carbon - and on controlling emissions. Britain believes that negotiations for a convention should begin as soon as possible after the Second World Climate Conference.

5.17 The Government believes that the work of the IPCC provides the sound scientific basis necessary for agreeing action internationally. But, helpful as it is, the IPCC's work has shown that a good deal of further work is needed to narrow the uncertainties. We have more work to do on observing the world's climate, improving our climate models and understanding climate processes. The view of IPCC is that this work will take some 15 years to complete. But in the meantime, the risks clearly justify action to begin to reduce greenhouse gases, so that the problem is contained while the longer-term analysis continues.

Pie chart showing sources of CO_2 emissions

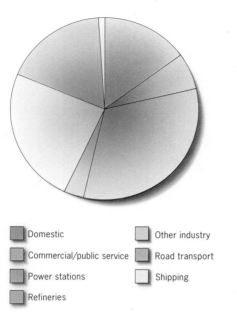

■ Domestic

■ Commercial/public service

■ Power stations

■ Refineries

■ Other industry

■ Road transport

□ Shipping

5.18 Britain is urging its partners in the European Community and in the rest of the industrialised world to begin now to develop their own strategies with specific measures for promoting energy efficiency and other steps that will limit or reduce greenhouse gas emissions. And as Chapter 4 describes, Britain is also taking vigorous action to help the developing world manage its economic growth in ways that will limit the growth of greenhouse gas emissions, by promoting energy efficiency, sustainable forestry and other measures.

Britain's strategy

5.19 The rest of this Chapter describes the strategy which Britain is developing to reduce its own greenhouse gas emissions. A major part of any strategy to contain GHG emissions must involve limiting emissions of carbon dioxide released from the consumption of fossil fuels (coal, oil and gas).

5.20 The Government has announced that Britain is prepared, if other countries take similar action, to set itself the demanding target of returning emissions of carbon dioxide, the dominant greenhouse gas, to 1990 levels by 2005. It is also pursuing measures to reduce emissions of methane

from various sources. Britain is committed to phasing out the production and consumption of CFCs, the most powerful greenhouse gases, by the end of the century and is pressing for even faster action within the European Community. Taking action on all greenhouse gases together, the global warming potential of Britain's emissions in 2005 should fall significantly, by approximately 20% compared with levels in 1990.

Controlling CO_2 emissions

5.21 Keeping CO_2 emissions to no more than 1990 levels by 2005 will mean important changes in the way we use energy in industry, to heat and light our homes, for transport and for other purposes. If nothing is done, energy consumption in Britain will grow substantially over the next 15 years. Projections prepared by the Government in 1989 and published in Energy Paper 58 in 1990 suggested that Britain's emissions of carbon dioxide into the atmosphere from all sources might be in the range 178-225 million tonnes of carbon (mtc) by 2005 if no action were taken – compared with emissions in 1989 of about 160 mtc.

5.22 These earlier projections assumed a level of new nuclear generating capacity by 2005 which is now unlikely to be reached. Adjusting for this would tend to increase projections of CO_2 emissions. On the other hand, it has become clearer that Government action already in hand will help keep emissions down.

5.23 For example, in the electricity industry the changes being brought about by the Electricity Act 1989 are likely to have a beneficial effect in reducing electricity CO_2 emissions. The Act will introduce competition among electricity generators, giving a strong incentive to generate energy more efficiently, and encourage electricity generation from non-fossil fuels. Indeed the two major non-nuclear electricity generating companies in England and Wales (PowerGen and National Power) believe that their intended installation of high efficiency gas-fired plant, and greater use of renewables, will hold their CO_2 emissions approximately constant for the foreseeable future, whereas the Government's earlier projections for the electricity supply industry assumed some growth. Similarly, in the transport sector the extension of the MOT test to emissions will improve tuning and so reduce projected vehicle emissions by a modest amount.

5.24 But more needs to be done, and difficult choices will need to be made. Meeting the target that the Government is prepared to set will call for adjustments in our everyday lives and the many ways in which we use energy. There are measures which the Government can and will take in the short and medium term which encourage people to use energy more efficiently or are worthwhile in their own right for other reasons. These are outlined below and described more fully in Annex C. The Government's approach to nuclear power, which can also contribute, is described in Chapter 15.

5.25 Even after all these measures are taken, it will clearly be necessary to take a number of further measures over a period of years to stabilise CO_2 emissions at 1990 levels by 2005. In the long term these will inevitably have to include increases in the relative prices of energy and fuel. This could be achieved by taxation or other means, such as tradeable permits. If achieved by taxation, the general level of taxation need not be significantly affected; higher taxation of energy and fuel could be offset by lower taxation elsewhere so that, in the medium term, there need be little net effect on the general price level. In deciding on measures to restrain CO_2 emissions, the Government will need to take into account the argument that market-based instruments will often be more efficient and less expensive than regulation in reducing emissions because they allow producers and consumers, rather than regulators, to decide how energy can best and most economically be used.

5.26 Long term measures affecting the relative price of energy can only sensibly be taken when competitor countries are prepared to take similar action. Unilateral action by Britain would do little to influence global warming. It would have a damaging impact on activity and employment in the energy-intensive sectors, relative to our competitors, to little purpose. In the immediate future the reduction of inflation is of overriding importance. Given this, and our best assessment of how long it will take to achieve an international consensus, tax or other measures directly raising the relative price of energy outside the transport sector will not be introduced in the next few years.

The Government will encourage everyone to make energy efficiency improvements at home and at work, and will give help in the form of advice from the Energy Efficiency Office and grants for households

ENERGY

5.27 This section describes the steps the Government will take to help to stabilise CO_2 emissions caused by the use of energy in buildings and in industry.

Energy efficiency

5.28 Energy efficiency improvements can help to combat acid rain (see Chapter 11) as well as global warming. They are also in the economic interests of energy consumers – from individuals in their own homes to large companies. Many of the Government's initiatives aim to inform consumers of these benefits and encourage them to take action.

5.29 The Government already actively

Left: The Government will encourage the use of combined heat and power in industry and commerce

Right: The Government will press the EC for a common energy labelling scheme for appliances, and minimum efficiency standards for some

promotes energy efficiency measures: there were improvements in the energy ratio (energy consumption per unit of gross domestic product (GDP)) every year during the 1980s, in spite of falling energy prices in real terms for most of that period. In 1989 Britain produced 25% more GDP than in 1979 without using any more energy. Since 1983 the Energy Efficiency Office (EEO) has spent some £130 million on programmes to stimulate better energy management. This has resulted in continuing savings estimated at over £500 million a year.

5.30 The Government is drawing on this experience to give a renewed boost to energy efficiency. The EEO's budget for 1990-91 has been increased, principally because of the new Home Energy Efficiency Scheme (details in Annex C), which draws together Government resources to improve further the energy efficiency of low-income households. The EEO will:

• continue to develop and promote energy efficiency technologies and management techniques in industry and buildings through its Best Practice Programme;

• develop further services to promote the implementation of energy efficiency measures; and

• continue to use its Best Practice programme to promote the use of the highly fuel-efficient technology of combined heat and power to achieve as much as possible of its identified potential of a further 2000 megawatts capacity by the year 2000.

5.31 The Government is taking action to make buildings, which account for nearly half of Britain's energy use, more energy-efficient

by means including :

• advice from the EEO for businesses and householders;

• monitoring the tougher Building Regulations for energy efficiency which came into force this year to see how they might be strengthened further;

• encouraging energy-efficiency measures in local authority and housing association properties coupled with advice and grants for households in both the public and private sectors; and

• a campaign to achieve further savings of 15% in the total energy bill for the Government Estate over a five-year period. The Government will also press for agreement in the European Community on a common energy labelling scheme for electrical appliances, and minimum efficiency standards for equipment such as central heating boilers, fridges, washing machines and industrial heating. Fuller details of all these measures are in section A of Annex C.

Ministerial committee

5.32 The Government will set up a new Ministerial Committee to maintain the momentum for improvement. Chaired by the Secretary of State for Energy, it will raise the profile of energy efficiency by working with Government Departments, Local Authorities, and organisations representing energy users in all sectors of the economy to stimulate improvements. The Committee will also monitor the Government's energy efficiency programmes and the new initiatives announced in this White Paper and assess the need for further action.

Local authorities

5.33 Local authorities are major property owners and energy users. A report in 1990 by the Audit Commission suggested that there was potential for energy savings in local authority buildings of as much as £100 million a year, and both central and local government are considering how these savings could be made. Annex C describes the contributions that schools and local authority housing are making to efficiency measures. Local authorities are also well placed to set a good example in energy efficiency, and many are adopting this aim as part of wider, formal policies for preserving and improving the local environment. More broadly, local authorities have an important role in promoting energy efficiency in their local communities and in assisting households with grants for energy-related improvements.

Voluntary organisations

5.34 Voluntary organisations can play an important part in informing people and motivating them to take action. The Government hopes that voluntary organisations will actively encourage the uptake of energy efficiency measures among the general public, including especially their own members. Voluntary organisations are already heavily involved in the EEO's Community Insulation Programme, and the Government hopes that they will play a similar part in the new Home Energy Efficiency Scheme described in Annex C.

Individual action

5.35 Energy efficiency improvements are the cheapest and quickest way of combating the threat of global warming. The success of the Government's initiatives will depend largely on decisions made by individuals – to insulate their homes, to invest in more efficient equipment at home and at work, to use more energy-efficient transport or to ask retailers for the most efficient electrical appliances. (See Chapter 22 for an action checklist).

RENEWABLE ENERGY

5.36 Another important contribution towards reducing carbon dioxide emissions can come from renewable energy. The Government has supported the development of a wide range of renewable technologies over the last decade. The Government's future programme, including its participation in the EC programme of research and development mentioned in paragraph 3.16, is designed to increase their contribution to energy supply through to the end of the century and beyond.

Advantages

5.37 Some renewable sources of energy, such as wind and tides, produce no emissions. The use of biofuels, including wood, recycles carbon dioxide and reduces the amounts of fossil fuels burnt. Increasing our use of renewables at the expense of fossil fuels helps to reduce our emissions of environmentally harmful gases such as CO_2, sulphur dioxide and oxides of nitrogen. There are other reasons for the use of renewables. First, fossil fuels are a finite resource. We in Britain are fortunate in having large reserves of coal, oil

Left: The Government is contributing to studies of a possible tidal barrage on the Mersey

Right: The Government will increase the contribution towards reducing carbon dioxide emissions that comes from renewable energy

and gas. But inevitably, as the larger and cheaper deposits are exhausted, prices will rise. By contrast, use of renewable energy sources does not diminish their future availability. Second, the use of renewables increases the diversity of our energy supply. The past twenty years have seen major fluctuations in energy markets. We need to insure ourselves against unforeseen developments by taking our energy from as many different sources as possible.

Further steps

5.38 The Government will continue to stimulate the development and use of renewable energy wherever it has the prospect of making an economic contribution to our energy supply. Some technologies, such as the use of methane from landfill sites, have immediate potential and are already commercially viable in some circumstances. Others will require more research and investigation before they can compete with existing energy supply systems. And some of them bring environmental effects of their own which need to be considered carefully. The Government proposes a comprehensive programme to take forward all the technologies relevant to Britain. This programme will involve action on a wide range of issues including research and development, demonstration and promotion.

5.39 The range of technologies, and the ways in which the Government is supporting them, are discussed in detail in section B of Annex C. The Department of Energy's strategy document published in 1988 included estimates for the possible contribution of renewable energy in the period up to 2025. This estimated that if all the current research and development were successful and the technologies could be commercially exploited, renewables might contribute up to the equivalent of nearly a quarter of current electricity supply by 2025.

5.40 Government policy is to encourage the development and application of all renewable energy sources, such as biofuels, wind and tide where they show promise of commercial viability in Britain. Through enhanced programmes on novel technologies, including research, development, demonstration and promotion, and through the non-fossil fuel obligation, the Government will work towards a figure of new renewable electricity generating capacity of 1000 megawatts in 2000. That would be about a tenfold increase over the current capacity (setting aside the long-standing use of more than 1000 megawatts of conventional hydro-electric plant in Scotland). The Government will review its programmes during 1991 and will assess the extent to which renewables could help further to restrain greenhouse gas emissions.

TRANSPORT

5.41 Transport contributes some 20% of our total carbon dioxide emissions, most of which comes from road transport. Transport is also a significant contributor to other gases which have a greenhouse effect: oxides of nitrogen and hydrocarbons, which also form ground-level ozone, and carbon monoxide (see Chapter 11 on Air).

5.42 As in the energy sector, reducing CO_2 emissions means using less fossil fuel. The best results will come if people choose the most efficient form of transport available and use it as economically as they can. The most efficient form of transport will vary widely

with the circumstances. In the long term, measures may also be possible to reduce the need or demand for transport.

Vehicles and road transport

5.43 The demand for personal travel, and in particular for private and business car travel, is greater than ever and seems certain to grow further: the diagram at opposite left shows how levels of car ownership in Britain in 1989 compared with those in other developed countries. People use their cars more than they did: the average in Britain is now 16,000 kilometres a year, compared

Cars and taxis per 1000 population

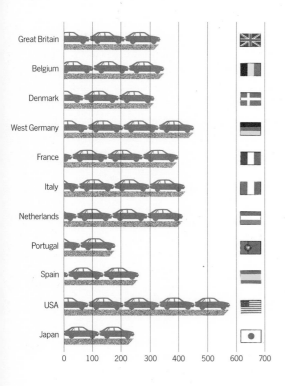

Wide car ownership is an important aspect of
freedom and choice

Contribution of transport to CO$_2$ levels

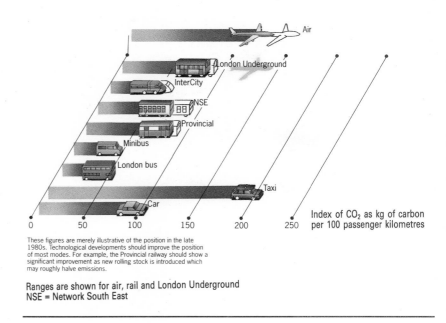

Index of CO$_2$ as kg of carbon
per 100 passenger kilometres

These figures are merely illustrative of the position in the late
1980s. Technological developments should improve the position
of most modes. For example, the Provincial railway should show a
significant improvement as new rolling stock is introduced which
may roughly halve emissions.

Ranges are shown for air, rail and London Underground
NSE = Network South East

---

with just 12,000 in 1960.

5.44 People understandably set great store by
the mobility and freedom that cars bring, and
the Government welcomes the continuing
widening of car ownership as an important
aspect of personal freedom and choice. The
speed and flexibility of motoring make it
indispensable for much business travel, which
in turn is vital for the economy.

5.45 Nevertheless, motorists can and must
contribute to controlling carbon dioxide
emissions. The Department of Transport will
improve the guidance that they already give
to motorists on ways of increasing fuel
economy. The motorist can contribute
directly by choosing a fuel-efficient car and
driving it in an economical way. Individual
action can achieve a surprising amount: for
example, the fuel consumption of 1300cc cars
now on sale varies by as much as 45%, and
careful driving can reduce consumption by 15%.

5.46 It is also obviously more fuel-efficient if
people share car journeys. On average, cars
carry less than two people. The Government
commends the efforts of organisations such as
the Automobile Association who are
operating or planning car sharing schemes.

5.47 The Government, industry and
independent researchers are looking into
ways of improving the efficiency of vehicles
themselves. Vehicle manufacturers have
already made huge progress in developing
more efficient engines and improved
materials and aerodynamics. In the longer
term, more radical solutions may be needed
including alternative fuels which require less
carbon in their production or emit less
carbon when burnt. The industry has a major
opportunity here for innovation.

5.48 Balanced and sensible regulation can
also play a part in ensuring that this potential
for more fuel-efficient vehicles is realised.

5.49 The European Commission is
considering proposals to improve the fuel
consumption of motor vehicles. The
Government intends to play a full part, in
consultation with the motor industry, in
making sure that this initiative is followed
through sensibly and effectively. In advance
of any agreement at European level, it

Travellers can and must
contribute efforts to
reduce CO$_2$ emissions

The Government will include an emissions test in the annual MOT and work in the EC to improve the fuel economy of vehicles

proposes to take immediate steps to:
• include an emissions check in the MOT test to ensure that vehicles are kept in tune:
• introduce measures to improve the enforcement of speed limits. Vehicles are at their most efficient when running in free traffic at moderate speeds. For the longer term, lower speed limits may be appropriate.

5.50 There are also other ways in which the Government can encourage people to take full account of the effects of their motoring decisions on the environment.

5.51 The Government has already introduced market-based measures which influence the environmental effects of motoring. It has taken action to reduce the tax advantages of company cars. The switch in the balance of taxation in recent years from Vehicle Excise Duty to petrol duties has meant that people who drive more miles or use less fuel-efficient cars pay a greater share of taxes than those who drive fewer miles or use more fuel efficient cars. Similarly, lower prices for unleaded petrol have resulted in a strong and growing market for this less polluting fuel. The Government will consider whether these measures need to be supplemented by any further changes in the taxation of fuel and vehicles which might encourage people to seek greater fuel economy in their motoring.

The Government will improve guidance to motorists on fuel economy and consider whether further changes in taxation are needed

5.52 The Government is exploring the possibility of a code of advertising practice which would encourage car manufacturers to lay less stress on power, speed and acceleration and more on efficiency, economy and safety. Few cars are designed to perform best in the conditions they are likely to meet in everyday traffic.

Freight

5.53 At present, 59% of freight tonne miles are by road. For those areas where rail or inland waterways can provide an alternative, grant is available towards the cost of freight handling facilities and rolling stock if there are worthwhile environmental benefits. Grant is paid where it would tip the balance on the choice between road and rail or waterborne freight. The Government is currently reviewing the grant rules to reflect wider environmental concerns.

5.54 Rail and water have strong market shares of freight transport in the bulk movement of goods between fixed points. Of all coal movements 40% are by rail, a further quarter by water. But rail and water cannot offer the flexibility of road for shorter, more varied journeys – the cost of transferring goods from one mode to another is prohibitive – and trying to use them for such journeys would lead to more CO_2 emissions than continuing to use road.

Roads

5.55 The Government is investing in an extensive trunk road programme, much of which is designed to improve our major inter-urban routes, which are already becoming congested.

5.56 The programme is intended to reduce congestion, benefit the economy and help the local environment through the bypasses provided to take traffic out of towns. Reducing congestion will help to reduce CO_2 emissions by increasing fuel economy and efficiency. Trying to control traffic volumes by restricting road building and allowing the growth of congestion would not only harm the economy, but could increase CO_2 emissions as fuel-efficiency declined.

Public transport

5.57 Public transport, where there is sufficient demand for it, will often be the most efficient transport choice. The Government is supporting the highest levels of investment by British Rail for over 25 years and record investment by London Transport. Compared with 1980, investment by BR was 30% higher in 1989/90. In London Transport's case, it was double.

5.58 In some areas, and particularly in London, rail is the most efficient means of moving commuters on journeys into major work centres: about 75% of commuting into central London is by rail, a significantly higher proportion than in other large Western European cities. This is a highly effective system; without it central London simply could not function. Between 1980 and 1989 rail commuting during the morning peak increased by 20%, representing a 9% increase in rail's market share. British Rail is investing heavily in its commuter lines to increase capacity. New, longer trains are already in operation on Liverpool Street services and Network South East (NSE) will benefit from new high capacity 'Networker' trains progressively from 1991. NSE has a good record on providing car parking spaces – a further 5,000 new spaces were provided in 1988, and 5,000 in 1989. In the last few years the London Underground has seen its services increase by 9% by better management of the existing network. Planned investment will substantially increase the capacity of the Central and Northern lines. And there is a massive programme to increase the capacity of Underground stations.

5.59 Outside London, buses will continue to be the main form of public transport. Buses are flexible and relatively cheap, but their market share has declined steadily over the years, although the Government's deregulation of the bus industry five years ago has revolutionised the position by increasing passenger choice and the responsiveness of bus services. This has increased in particular the numbers of minibuses, which are a very flexible and highly fuel-efficient form of transport. To be economically viable the demand for travel by bus and other transport needs to be commercially attractive - there must be a sufficient number of potential customers, for example, and demand needs to be spread widely enough over time to ensure that valuable vehicles and equipment are not left idle for too long. But where demand exists, local authorities can do much to foster bus use through measures such as bus lanes and traffic lights which give priority to buses. These can all help to make the bus a more rapid and comfortable form of travel. Chapter 8 explains how the Government is encouraging these efforts. It is also prepared to consider grant for light rail systems where they are the most cost-effective, and is at present funding such a scheme in Manchester. In considering light rail systems, the Government will look closely at the environmental benefits that other lines could bring.

Modern and cost-effective public transport can help to reduce CO_2 emissions

5.60 Public transport is not a panacea for controlling CO_2 emissions. Most forms of public transport at present tend to be more fuel efficient than the car, but that efficiency depends on their being well used. The diagram on page 73 right shows the CO_2 emissions of public transport, compared with those from cars, calculated at current average occupancy rates. Providing extra services would only make emissions worse if few passengers used them: trains are highly fuel-efficient when fully loaded, but in practice it is not possible to achieve high loadings all the time. Moreover 93% of passenger journeys are by road. Even if it were possible to double demand for rail travel by transferring passengers from the roads, that would only reduce road traffic by about 10%. On recent experience, that would be the equivalent of perhaps two or three years' growth in road traffic.

5.61 But there is an important place for public transport in Britain's strategy on CO_2. In combination with other measures, modern and cost-effective public transport can draw traffic at the margin from the roads and contribute to overall reductions in CO_2. The Government will continue research into why people make the transport choices that they do. This helps to identify improvements and additions to public transport networks which can increase choice and reduce road congestion. The major public transport operators already do extensive research into areas where they can expand their markets in this way - British Rail's reopening of local stations for commuters is one result of this work. The Government will continue to support efforts like these.

Air

5.62 The contribution of air transport to total CO_2 emissions is small at present. Air travel is set to expand, but the effect on CO_2 emissions will to some extent be offset as new, more fuel-efficient aircraft replace older ones. The Government has been pressing for international agreement to speed up this replacement process. There is also some interest in the possible global warming effects of water vapour emitted by aircraft in the upper atmosphere, and the Government is studying this.

Walking and cycling

5.63 Most journeys are very short. For these, walking and cycling provide carbon-free means of travel that are good for health. The Government has supported the development of a number of projects to demonstrate the value of safe and convenient cycle routes and is helping a number of London boroughs to develop a cycle network across the city.

Reducing the demand for travel

5.64 Leaving aside the costs of transport relative to other goods and services, many factors affect the underlying demand for transport, including:
• the growth of incomes and leisure;
• the way in which towns and cities are planned and laid out, and the physical distances between different types of building and land use; and
• the state of development of electronic and other means of communication between people at a distance.

5.65 In the short term it is not possible to make sudden changes in the layout of towns and cities. But in the longer term the interactions between planning and transport become increasingly important. If the inner areas of towns are allowed to degenerate and become unattractive places to live, so that people move further afield to suburbs and beyond, demands for transport are substantially increased. Conversely, the measures that the Government is taking to revive and regenerate inner city areas (see Chapter 8) should help to limit or reverse this trend and make public transport more attractive. The interactions between planning and transport are complex, and the Departments of Environment and Transport are proposing a joint study, described at paragraph 6.34, of the relationship between development and travel patterns and ways of locating development to reduce travel distances and to increase transport choice.

FORESTS AND CARBON DIOXIDE

5.66 The world's forests play a part in controlling carbon dioxide levels in the atmosphere. Photosynthesis, the process by which trees and other plants use the sun's energy to grow, traps carbon from CO_2 in the atmosphere. As forests grow, they lock up free carbon that would otherwise contribute to the greenhouse effect: unlike most other vegetation, trees store CO_2 for very long periods in the form of wood. Once forests are mature, they no longer have any net effect on the amounts of carbon in the air, but they continue to store the carbon absorbed during their growth. This carbon returns to the atmosphere slowly if the tree decays, and immediately if it is burnt; but it stays locked up indefinitely if the timber is put to long-lasting use. This is a good reason to avoid wasting or wantonly destroying the world's timber, and to manage forests as they mature by selective harvesting and regeneration. Using wood and wood wastes as a fuel, which the Government is encouraging, recycles carbon and thus reduces total emissions if it replaces the use of fossil fuel.

5.67 The part that forestry can play in keeping levels of CO_2 in the atmosphere down is one of the reasons for Britain's contribution to international efforts to conserve and regenerate the tropical rain forests (see Chapter 4). In Britain itself, the Government's initiatives to encourage tree-planting, including the creation of new community forests and special emphasis on planting more broadleaved species, will also help to keep CO_2 in the atmosphere down. The Government has already made grant-aid available to encourage tree planting: Chapter 7 gives further details of the Government's approach. Trees of all types, whether in gardens, hedgerows, woodlands or forests provide an effective way of absorbing CO_2 and storing it for very long periods.

As they grow, forests lock up free carbon which would otherwise contribute to the greenhouse effect

METHANE

5.68 Methane is an important greenhouse gas. The IPCC has calculated that, when effects over 100 years are taken into account, it is about 21 times more powerful than CO_2 as a greenhouse gas. It is responsible for about 7% of the man-made greenhouse effect, and in Britain it accounts for about 15% of our contribution to global warming.

5.69 The main sources of estimated methane emissions in Britain are: agriculture (34%), coal mining (30%), landfill waste (22%) and gas venting and leakage (14%).

5.70 Changes already under way in agriculture and energy recovery from landfill waste should reduce Britain's emissions of methane substantially in the next 30 years. In particular, the Government has encouraged the use of energy from landfill waste. Many applications to fill the renewable energy tranche of the Non-Fossil Fuel Obligation (see Annex C) would make use of this source of energy, reducing methane emissions and helping to reduce emissions from other forms of power generation. The Government is considering what more can be done to reduce emissions of methane from landfill sites by encouraging its use as an energy source. It is also supporting action by local authorities over the next five years at some

1,000 landfill sites requiring remedial work. Some sites will be suitable for methane recovery for heat and power.

5.71 The Government has a robust policy of minimising waste of gas. It has always been a major concern of the Department of Energy, in examining oil and gas field development plans, to ensure the maximum safe and

Methane emissions by source

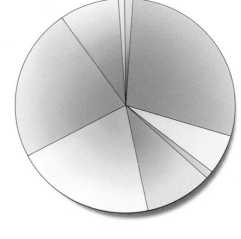

Domestic
Deep mined coal
Oil and gas venting
Road transport
Gas leakage

Landfill
Cattle
Sheep
Other animals

Britain's methane emissions should fall substantially over the next 30 years

economic recovery of gas. When a field or reception terminal comes on-stream, the operator needs the consent of the Secretary of State for Energy to vent (or flare) any gas. No consents are issued until he is satisfied that they are for the minimum amount necessary for safe and economic operation. Consents are for specified limited periods and can only be renewed against similar justifications.

5.72 Britain will encourage other countries to consider strategies which include measures to limit methane emissions as well as carbon dioxide. This will be particularly important for developing countries, where methane emissions come mainly from agriculture.

CHLOROFLUOROCARBONS (CFCS)

5.73 Britain is taking a leading part in international action to phase out the production and consumption of CFCs. Chapter 4 describes the steps the Government is taking. They will not only help to stop depletion of the ozone layer, but also make a significant contribution to the international response to global warming.

CONCLUSION

5.74 The threats facing the world's atmosphere, and in particular global warming, can be brought under control only through world-wide co-operation, which will require good faith, determination and ingenuity from us and from our partners in the developed and developing worlds. Controlling it could possibly be the first occasion on which the world adopts market-based solutions to a major international problem of pollution control. To achieve this, we shall need international statesmanship of an historic order.

5.75 In Britain, stabilising carbon dioxide emissions will require hard work, careful planning and substantial investment by the transport and energy industries and by vehicle manufacturers. No less importantly, it will require changes in our behaviour as individuals – making sure that our homes and workplaces are heated and lit as efficiently as possible, using the least polluting forms of transport available and using our cars economically and responsibly. The Government can help to set the right framework for improved economy, but achieving reductions will depend on individual action. The Government will monitor the results of the action proposed in this Chapter to ensure that we achieve the target reductions, and if possible improve on them.

Research – global climate change

Britain aims to play a full part in the world effort to assess the scale of future climate change, contributing in those areas where it has world class experience. The Government has established the Hadley Centre, a major international centre for assessing the potential impacts of climate change and studying abatement strategies – Department of the Environment (£6.0m in 1990/91). Other major international collaborations include projects
• to improve monitoring, understanding and prediction of the climate through better models of global atmospheric and oceanic circulation, and observations and studies of the underlying processes, including the World Ocean Circulation Experiment – Natural Environment Research Council (£8.9m in 1989/90) and Meteorological Office (£2.5m in 1990/91).
• to study the cycling of carbon and other elements in the ocean and related atmospheric exchanges through participation in the Joint Global Ocean Flux Study –Natural Environment Research Council (£4.7m in 1989/90).
• to support the development of novel satellite instrumentation for measuring the Earth's atmosphere from space – Science and Engineering Research Council (£2.5m in 1989/90)
• to investigate changes in the water and energy balance of land following deforestation through an Anglo-Brazilian Amazonian Climate Observational Study - Natural Environment Research Council (£0.3m in 1989/90)
• to estimate the CO_2 storage potential of trees and the effects of increased CO_2 on tree growth – Forestry Commission (£1.0m in 1989/90).

6

LAND USE

Land use policies must reconcile our demands for houses and jobs, with conservation and recreation

INTRODUCTION

6.1 Everyone wants to protect the best of urban and rural environments, so that we can pass on to our children what we value most about our own heritage. This and the following chapters look at our towns and countryside, our built and natural heritage. Land is the common thread. It is a finite resource, and we have to find enough for all our needs – homes, jobs, shops, food, transport, fuel, building materials and recreation – while protecting what we value most in our surroundings.

6.2 New buildings and other changes in land use are essential to help the economy grow and to provide people with jobs and homes. But, without some control, the myriad of proposed new developments would produce haphazard results which could damage the environment. The task of government is to set a framework of rules and incentives, so that patterns of land use reflect the interests of the community as a whole. That framework must encourage development in some places, through the designation of special areas, agencies and grants (such as enterprise zones, development corporations and city grant). And it must also protect the most sensitive environments. Thus, about a third of land in England lies within areas designated as Green Belts, National Parks and Areas of Outstanding Natural Beauty, where tight controls apply, as they also do in designated Conservation Areas.

6.3 In Britain, the framework for land use is largely provided by the long established town and country planning system. This aims to secure the most efficient and effective use of land in the public interest, and to ensure that service facilities such as roads, schools and sewers are built where they will be needed.

6.4 This Chapter explains how the Government and local authorities work through the planning system in England and Wales to reconcile the conservation of the environment with development needs, and to encourage the restoration of derelict and contaminated land. It is an overview – a full account of policies can be found in the planning guidance issued by the Government (see 6.32). The chapters which follow look in turn at rural and urban aspects of land use. Chapters 20 and 21 cover land use in Scotland and Northern Ireland.

Only about a tenth of land is built up

Percentage of land covered by agricultural and other uses

Forest and woodland [2]

Other agricultural [1]

Urban land & land not otherwise specified [3]

Agricultural: crops and fallow

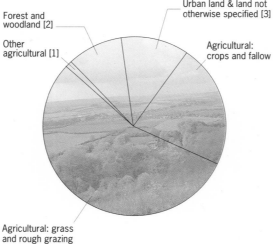

Agricultural: grass and rough grazing

[1] Farm buildings, roads, gardens etc
[2] Includes woodlands on agricultural holdings
[3] Includes roads, recreation areas, mineral works, semi-natural vegetation, etc

LAND USE AND THE PLANNING SYSTEM; THE GOVERNMENT'S OBJECTIVES

6.5 Conservation and development should not be seen as necessarily in conflict. For example, conservation enhances tourism, which provides 1½ million jobs in Britain (see also Chapter 7). Policies for land use must weigh and reconcile priorities in the public interest. Some priorities are primarily economic:

• growth in the national, regional and local economies;
• land and premises to provide people with jobs;
• housing to meet the needs of all sectors of society;
• a physically safe environment, in which planning helps to ensure for example that proper precautions are taken against the risks that flooding, subsidence or incidents at major chemical installations might pose;
• prime agricultural land for food production;
• safe and efficient transport systems;
• access to shops which provide choice and value; and
• the best use of mineral resources.

6.6 Other priorities have conservation as their common flavour:

• sustaining the character and diversity of the countryside, including its wildlife habitats;
• reserving use of high grade mineral resources for the most appropriate use, wherever practicable;
• defending green belts to check urban sprawl and provide a breathing space for city dwellers;
• maintaining the character, as well as the vitality, of town and city centres;
• revitalising older urban areas, so that they become more pleasant places to live and work in;
• safeguarding and improving the amenity of residential districts; and
• giving high priority to conserving the built heritage, to good design in new development and to encouraging the arts.

6.7 All these priorities are to do with enhancing the quality of life and public health. Taken together and expressed in published guidance, they amount to an overall policy for land use. They are the basis for all land use decisions, from planning permission for house extensions through to the designation in development plans of locations for new settlements or areas for industrial development.

How the planning system works

6.8 Planning decisions on proposals to build on land, or change its use, are usually made by local authorities in a process known as development control. Decisions should not be arbitrary, but must be considered against criteria adopted by the local authority, including the statutory development plan, and against central government's policy guidance on issues like green belt protection.

6.9 The system provides:
guidance, to help people plan the use of their land confidently and sensibly, and to help planning authorities to interpret the public interest wisely and consistently;
incentive, in that by designating land in their statutory plans for particular types of development, local authorities can stimulate such development; and
control, which ensures that developers cannot ultimately insist for private reasons on a change which would be against the wider public interest and that people affected by proposals for change can have their views and interests considered.

6.10 Over the past decade, the Government has reshaped planning into a slimmer, more flexible system, responsive to real strategic issues. Central government's regional and national guidance has been completely overhauled. Urban policies to encourage regeneration in inner cities mean that areas of urban decay are now seen increasingly as offering opportunities for new economic growth. This helps reduce development pressure in more sensitive areas by encouraging re-use of previously used urban land. The Government has also reviewed and updated the main instruments that control development, and has made proposals for simplifying the development plan system (see 6.19 on).

Green belts check urban sprawl and provide a breathing space for city dwellers

Comparison of approved green belts 1979 and 1989

Areas covered by approved green belts 1987

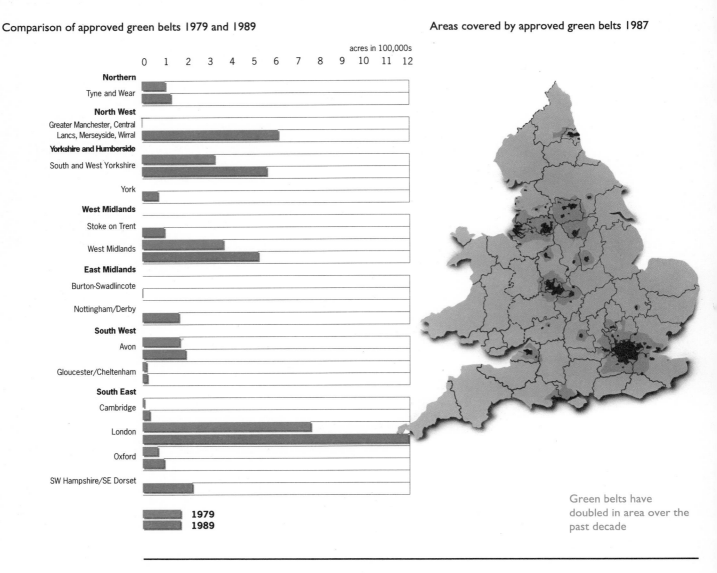

acres in 100,000s
0 1 2 3 4 5 6 7 8 9 10 11 12

Northern
Tyne and Wear

North West
Greater Manchester, Central Lancs, Merseyside, Wirral

Yorkshire and Humberside
South and West Yorkshire

York

West Midlands
Stoke on Trent

West Midlands

East Midlands
Burton-Swadlincote

Nottingham/Derby

South West
Avon

Gloucester/Cheltenham

South East
Cambridge

London

Oxford

SW Hampshire/SE Dorset

1979
1989

Green belts have doubled in area over the past decade

DEVELOPMENT CONTROL

6.11 Development control is the part of the planning process with which people are most familiar. Over 600,000 applications are made each year for development that requires planning permission. In considering these, the local authorities' task is to check whether the public interest (expressed in the development plan, in national guidance, or in relevant representations as a result of consultation) requires conditions to be attached to a permission, or consent to be refused. The option of an appeal is available if the applicant is aggrieved by a refusal, or by unacceptable conditions, or by the lack of a decision in the time allowed. The Secretary of State, or the planning inspector he appoints to decide the appeal, must consider the case on the same basis as the local authority.

6.12 Local authorities approve most applications. However, many local authority decisions, whether approvals or refusals, take much longer than the eight weeks allowed. The Government will discuss with the Audit Commission and the local authority National Development Control Forum how faster decisions can be achieved. There is no reason why faster decisions should threaten the environment: delay can itself create blight, or slow investment in cleaner industrial plant, or in new buildings with improved energy efficiency.

The boundaries of control

6.13 Central government sets the boundaries of development control. Many small changes to buildings do not require specific permission. Whether permission is required depends on the planning legislation. Some people think it should be drawn so that local authorities are entitled to prevent any change in the local environment. Others think that planning control is an unnecessary interference with individual rights. The Government's view is that the current balance is about right – councils can use planning controls to protect local character and amenities, while individuals have a reasonable degree of freedom to do what they wish with their property.

6.14   But the Government will continue to keep the degree of control under review. For example, it has recently sought views on whether to extend planning control to demolition of houses, and on controls over satellite TV dishes. The Government is also considering the need for more control over helicopter landing sites (see Chapter 16).

6.15   The Government will consult shortly on proposed changes to the controls over agricultural and forestry buildings. Modern agriculture sometimes needs buildings of a scale and design more akin to industry – buildings which may not blend into the landscape in the same way as more traditional barns and farmsteads. The consultation paper will propose that farmers should retain the right to erect most buildings other than dwellings without specific planning permission, but that local authorities should be able to exercise control over siting, design and external appearance; similar arrangements have applied in National Parks since 1986.

6.16   The consultation paper will also propose an extension of full development control over buildings on agricultural holdings of less than 5 hectares, many of which are not full-time agricultural businesses for which the exemption is intended (the current cut-off is 0.4 hectares). But special provision would be made for genuine holdings below that limit.

6.17   Tree preservation orders help protect important trees in urban areas, and woodlands of landscape value. Following a review, to be published shortly, the Government proposes:

The Government will give local authorities new powers to protect hedgerows

• to enable local authorities to protect hedgerows of key importance by making preservation orders, with appropriate payments to farmers to look after them properly; and
• to streamline the administration of tree preservation orders.
Full details will be included in a consultation paper later in 1990.

Enforcement of control

6.18   To take effective action to prevent environmental damage, local authorities must be able to respond quickly when planning rules are broken – for example, where a site is being developed without consent or in ways which breach a planning condition. Increasing concern about the effectiveness of enforcement powers led the Government to review the relevant provisions in the Planning Acts. It has now decided to introduce

(Left) The Government proposes to give local authorities more say in the siting, design and external appearance of farm buildings

ELKSTONE FARM DAIRY

legislation at the earliest opportunity to strengthen the powers by providing for:
• a new power to make it easier for planning authorities to seek a Court injunction to restrain an actual or threatened breach of planning control;
• better and quicker means of obtaining information about suspected breaches of control;
• 'stop notices' to halt unlawful development at once in especially serious cases; and
• much higher maximum fines for those convicted of enforcement offences.

DEVELOPMENT PLANS

6.19   Everyone has the right to know the basis on which planning applications are decided. Published development plans set out the main considerations. They comprise local plans (in which district councils set development control policies for a part or the whole of their area) and structure plans (in which county councils set out key, strategic policies as a framework for local planning by the district councils); or unitary plans (which combine the function of structure and local plans in London and metropolitan boroughs).

Local plans

6.20   The Government believes that local plans are necessary for effective development control and give the certainty that local communities and owners of land need. They also give an opportunity to look at the alternative forms that development could take, and the options for introducing local policies which respect the environment. As of the middle of 1989, 60 out of the 333 non-metropolitan district councils in England and Wales had local plans on deposit or adopted which fully covered their areas. Some 55 had no local plans at all, and many of the rest had local plans for only some of their areas.

6.21   The Government intends to legislate to make district-wide coverage of local plans mandatory. Local authorities are already aiming to cover 85% of England by 1993/94. Plans will be required to be consistent with national planning policies, with any regional planning guidance issued by the Secretary of State, and with relevant county policies.

6.22   Local authorities will consult widely as they draft their plans. The Government intends to legislate to streamline the process for adopting them, allowing:
• six weeks from publication for public objections or representations;
• a public local inquiry, where objectors can exercise their right to be heard by an independent inspector; and
• publication of any modifications to the draft plan, with six weeks for public objections to the modifications or to the adoption of the plan by the local planning authority.

6.23   The Secretary of State will have reserve powers to direct the local planning authority to consider modifying the draft plan; and to

Development plans help to guide the provision of services such as sewage treatment works and schools

call in the plan or parts of it for his own consideration. He will provide advice on good practice in plan preparation, based on research currently under way.

6.24   These procedures will help to ensure that the development plan system takes environmental considerations comprehensively and consistently into account. The new arrangements will complement the unitary development plan system already in place in London and the metropolitan areas. For the first time, all citizens in England and Wales will have an up-to-date, comprehensive, statutory local plan, adopted according to thorough procedures involving full public participation.

Planning by counties

6.25   Local plans must complement and be consistent with the structure plan prepared by the county council. This contains policies on planning issues which need to be considered county-wide. But approving and amending structure plans has tended to take a very long time – 28 months for an average county, in addition to the time taken in preparation.

6.26   The Government has therefore decided to introduce legislation to combine the most positive aspects of the existing system with proposals for improvements which it put forward in 1989. It proposes that county councils should continue to prepare structure plans but that they should be slimmer and concentrate on key, strategic issues – the scale and broad location of housing, industrial and commercial development, the rural economy, highways and other transport questions, mineral working, green belt and conservation issues, waste disposal, and land reclamation arrangements.

6.27   There will no longer be a requirement for the Secretary of State to approve all structure plans or amendments to them. Procedures will be similar to those for local plans (although there will still be a formal public examination of the proposals). The Secretary of State will have the power to call in plans or policies for his own decision and will still take a close interest in the

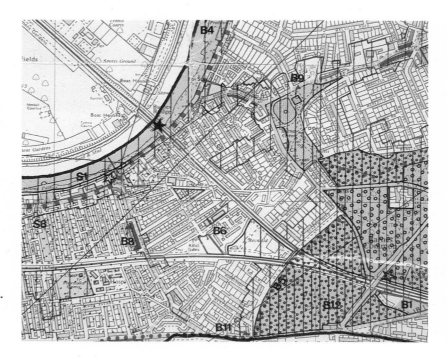

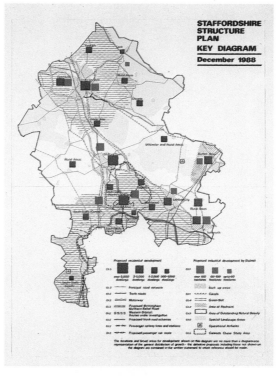

Local plans set out details; new county structure plans will concentrate on key strategic policies

consistency of the plan with national and regional guidance.

6.28   This change will make the development plan system simpler and more responsive, reducing costs for both the private sector and local authorities. Removing excessive detail from plans at the county level will leave a larger range of matters of local concern to be dealt with through local plans.

NATIONAL POLICY GUIDANCE

6.29 Development plans need to reflect regional and national priorities. The Government therefore sets out policies to be taken into account by local authorities preparing development plans, in the form of regional planning guidance and national planning guidance. National guidance is also taken into account in deciding individual planning applications.

Regional guidance

6.30 The Government's regional planning guidance sets broad strategic policies for land use and development where there are issues which, though not of national scope, apply across regions or parts of regions and need to be considered on a scale wider than a single county or district. Such policies are not the prescriptive economic planning of the type attempted in the past, but flexible guidance on ways of responding to economic forces to help local authorities plan for their areas.

6.31 The process starts with conferences or groups of local planning authorities getting together to produce proposals for guidance on issues affecting the region as a whole. Central and local government then confer before the Government publishes draft advice for public comment. It considers all the views expressed before formally issuing guidance for the region, in England in the form of a Regional Planning Guidance note, and in Wales as a strategic guidance paper. Regional guidance will form an important part of the new arrangements for county structure plans and local plans, described above.

National guidance

6.32 The Government prepares national guidance to be taken into account both in preparing development plans and in decisions on individual planning applications. The aim is to secure consistency of approach to decisions by setting out clearly the Government's policy priorities to be applied in each case. Since 1988, the Government has been issuing guidance in a new form – Planning Policy Guidance notes (PPGs) and Minerals Planning Guidance notes (MPGs). These are progressively replacing the guidance given in earlier planning circulars and are intended to provide clearer, more accessible and more systematic policy guidance.

Planning Policy and Minerals Planning Guidance Notes have provided clearer, more accessible and more systematic policy guidance since January 1988

Planning Policy Guidance Notes

PPG1   General Policy and Principles
PPG2   Green Belts
PPG3   Land for Housing
PPG4   Industrial and Commercial Development and Small Firms
PPG5   Simplified Planning Zones
PPG6   Major Retail Development
PPG7   Rural Enterprise and Development
PPG8   Telecommunications
PPG12   Local Plans
PPG13   Highway Consideration in Development Control
PPG14   Development on Unstable Land
PPG15   Regional Planning Guidance, Structure Plans, and the Content of Development Plans

Minerals Planning Guidance Notes

MPG1   General Considerations and the Development Plan System
MPG2   Applications, Permisssions and Conditions
MPG3   Opencast Coal Mining
MPG4   The Review of Mineral Working Sites
MPG5   Minerals Planning and the General Development Order
MPG6   Guidelines for Aggregates Provision in England and Wales
MPG7   The Reclamation of Mineral Workings

THE PLANNING SYSTEM AND THE ENVIRONMENT

Updating national planning guidance

6.33 The Government will continue its systematic review of existing planning guidance. The PPGs and MPGs already published will be revised and updated, and the series extended as necessary. The Government is also currently preparing PPGs on:
• archaeology and planning (see Chapter 9);
• sport and recreation (see Chapter 8);
• heritage (see Chapter 9);
• wildlife and planning (see Chapter 7);
• planning, pollution control and waste management (see below); and
• advertisement control;
and a new circular giving guidance on planning and noise. The Government will also issue further MPGs on topics such as cement, and oil and gas, and a booklet on the winning and working of minerals without excessive environmental disturbance.

6.34 The Government has already asked local authorities to have particular regard to the conservation of energy as an issue in development plans. This should contribute to reducing our emissions of greenhouse gases. In the longer term, the Government intends to issue planning guidance on the location of new development in relation to traffic generation as part of the need to tackle global warming. One aim would be to guide new development to locations which reduce the need for car journeys and the distances driven, or which permit the choice of more energy efficient public transport – without encouraging more or longer journeys – as an alternative to the private car. By the same token, the planning of transport routes should take account of the potential impact on settlement and development patterns. However, not enough is known about the relationship between choice of housing and employment location and transport mode to allow the Government to offer authoritative advice at this stage.

6.35 The joint Department of Transport and Department of the Environment studies

announced in paragraph 5.65 will therefore look at the relationship between land use and transport and the part different measures could play in reducing fuel use. These will in due course inform the proposed new guidance.

The Government will research the inter-relationship between development patterns and transport needs

Environmental assessment

6.36 Although the environmental effect of any proposed development has always been a major factor in development control, since 1988 some projects which may have significant environmental effects have been subject to specific 'environmental assessment' (also known as 'environmental impact assessment' or 'EIA') before development consent can be given.

6.37 EIA requires developers to assemble and publish the available information about the likely environmental effects of a proposal. Bodies with relevant environmental responsibilities, and the public, are invited to comment, and the information is taken into account by the decision-making authority. Requiring the environmental implications of a proposal to be set out in a clear and systematic way should:
• help developers to prepare planning applications in a way that strikes the right balance between the development proposed and all aspects of the environment; and

• enable the decision-making authority to handle the application efficiently and take environmental implications fully into account.

But EIAs impose costs both on developers who are required to assemble the information and on the authorities which must evaluate it. Any case for the extension of the application of EIA must therefore be considered carefully.

6.38 The EIA provisions implement an EC Directive. They are still quite new, and the Government has commissioned research on how they are operating. After further studies it will give guidance on how best to prepare and evaluate environmental statements.

Planning and pollution control

6.39 Planning control is primarily concerned with the type and location of new development and changes of use. Once broad land uses have been sanctioned by the planning process, it is the job of pollution control to limit the adverse effects that operations may have on the environment. But in practice there is common ground. In considering whether to grant planning permission for a particular development, a local authority must consider all the effects, including potential pollution; permission should not be granted if that might expose people to danger. And a change in an industrial process may well require planning permission as well as approval under environmental protection legislation.

The Government will enable developers to make binding commitments to provide local environmental improvements connected to development

6.40 The Government will shortly announce changes to simplify the special industrial classes of the Use Classes Order, which permits certain changes of industrial process to take place without planning permission. The aim is to bring planning control over changes of industrial process into line with integrated pollution control and air pollution control mechanisms. The Government will also consider the need for further guidance on the relationship between planning and pollution control in the light of new measures in the Environmental Protection Bill. Planning control over potentially hazardous developments is covered in Chapter 14.

Environmental considerations in planning agreements

6.41 The Government also proposes to issue revised guidance on 'planning agreements', which are sometimes concluded between local authorities and developers. They generally provide for the developer to supply, or pay towards, some kind of infrastructure – such as a road junction or extra sewage treatment capacity – in connection with a grant of planning permission. They supplement the conditions which authorities may attach to permissions, if necessary, to provide a wide degree of environmental protection. The Government's policy is that authorities must not try, unfairly, to use the applicant's need for planning permission to seek payments or other benefits which are not related directly to the proposed development.

6.42 The revised guidance will however make clear that agreements may include provisions to compensate for amenities or resources on the development site that would be lost or damaged as a result of the construction. The Government also intends to legislate to enable developers to enter binding commitments to undertake specified works connected with their development proposal. Together, these changes will make it easier for local authorities and developers to provide for the interests of nature conservation and of the environment more generally when preparing development proposals.

MAJOR DEVELOPMENTS AND THE ENVIRONMENT

6.43 The following sections address three particular major development types which can have significant environmental effects.

Housing

6.44 There will be a continuing and substantial demand for new housing in most parts of the country well into the next century. This demand flows from changes in life style and life expectancy rather than population growth or migration. Much of the demand is likely to be from small households of young or older people – one or two people rather than families with children. Adaptation and subdivision of existing houses can make a major contribution to meeting the need. Even so, substantial new housebuilding will be necessary.

6.45 It is one of the most important functions of land use planning to assess the need for new housing, and identify enough land in the right places to satisfy it. In future, the Government will prepare its own assessment of the requirement for each region, following consultation, and guidance will be given in the relevant Regional Planning Guidance note. It will then be for counties to indicate in their structure plans how much housing will be needed in each district.

6.46 District councils, in their local plans, must then identify suitable sites for those new homes. The Government believes it is right for local communities to decide themselves where new homes should be built, and will respect local plan policies reflecting the values which the local community places on its environment. But communities cannot expect to resist all development, and the Government will not hesitate to call in plans or to allow appeals if otherwise the overall requirement for the district would not be met.

6.47 Land in urban areas should be used to meet as much as possible of the demand for sites for new housing. This helps both to maintain the vitality of towns and cities, and to reduce the demand for new building in the countryside. New housebuilding should not mean the disappearance of the playing fields and green spaces which every town and city needs. In the suburbs too, there is a need to ensure that over-intensive infilling and redevelopment – sometimes called 'town cramming' – do not destroy the character of attractive residential areas. These are exactly the kind of issues which planning authorities must address in their local plans, taking account of local environmental concerns.

6.48 However well urban land is used, there will continue to be a need for building on 'green field' sites. It is important that new housing on such sites is carefully placed to preserve the open countryside and respects the quality of the landscape. Here again there are local choices to be made. One option is the creation of 'new villages' or larger settlements which could offer opportunities for high quality design and also relieve pressures on existing towns and villages. The Government believes that this is an option which should be considered by planning authorities and local communities in the preparation of their plans.

6.49 Attitudes to new housebuilding proposals are strongly influenced by the quality of their design. Chapter 8 shows what can be done to encourage designs which improve the quality of the environment, rather than detract from it.

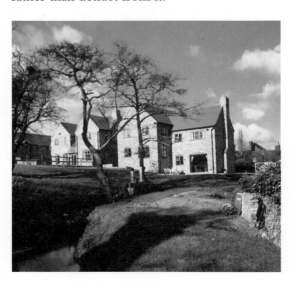

New housing on green field sites must respect the landscape

Transport

6.50 Efficient transport, and road transport in particular, is more vital than ever to everyday life in an age which depends on effective distribution of goods and rapid communications. But, both within and between towns and cities, proposals for new or expanded transport links can be a focus for environmental concern. Chapters 7 and 8 give details of proposals to improve urban transport and to improve the appearance of roads in the countryside. This Chapter explains how decisions on new road and rail routes will take account of environmental considerations.

6.51 The Government is committed to minimising the environmental impact of trunk roads. The public are consulted at an early stage on any significant proposal for a new road or improvements to an existing road, and the environmental advantages and disadvantages of the proposals under consideration are set out. The choice of a preferred route reflects local needs and concerns so far as possible. An environmental assessment is made of every scheme and all major schemes follow the procedure of the Department of Transport Manual of Environmental Appraisal. This meets the requirements of the EC Directive on Environmental Impact Assessment in full. Public inquiries are held for all major schemes to which there are objections, and the environmental assessment is one of the documents the inquiry will consider. The inquiry often results in changes to the original proposals and sometimes in their abandonment.

6.52 These procedures ensure that environmental concerns are taken into account at every stage of the road planning process. But the Government is examining ways to improve its assessment procedures. It has asked the Standing Advisory Committee on Trunk Road Assessment (SACTRA) to review its methods of environmental assessment, and in particular whether and how to put money values on environmental impact. The aim is not to replace the need for judgement, but to help achieve the best balance between economic and environmental costs and benefits. SACTRA hopes to complete its study at the end of 1990.

6.53 Other road schemes are planned and carried out by local authorities. Their procedures for environmental appraisal are similar to those of the Department of Transport, and most use the Department of Transport manual.

6.54 At present, construction of new railways is authorised by private Act of Parliament. Parliamentary procedures require promoters to consult affected local communities before depositing their Bills, and objections to schemes are considered by Select Committees. The Government has recently proposed that future railway and similar works should be authorised by an order-making procedure, subject in most cases to Ministerial rather than Parliamentary approval.

6.55 The new arrangements would require promoters to consult interested parties before applying for an order, and provide for public local inquiries into objections. The EC Directive on environmental impact assessment would apply to projects approved under the new procedures. The Government has also accepted that, where the private Bill procedure continues to be used for approval of works-type projects, the Standing Orders of Parliament should be amended to require EIA in appropriate cases. Legislation would be required to implement these changes.

Mineral workings

6.56 Minerals are an important national

resource. However, extracting them can be environmentally disruptive; they can only be worked where they are found, and strong conflicts of interest and controversy often arise. The environmental costs of transporting minerals must also be fully considered. Decisions about proposals to work minerals need to strike a careful balance between the interests of amenity and the need to exploit the resource. Operators must take account of best environmental practice and aim to be good neighbours. In the light of research already commissioned, the Government will continue to update the guidance it issues through MPGs on the environmental standards to be applied in the operation of mineral sites. The scope for recycling building materials (see Chapter 14) may also be relevant.

6.57 Environmental restoration and aftercare conditions have not always been applied to the high standards we expect today. Some old mineral workings and extant planning permissions date back many years. The 1981 Minerals Act provided for planning authorities to review all such sites and to update existing permissions; the Government now intends to review the operation of that Act and the compensation arrangements under it. It is also examining with British Coal the scope for improvement in areas such as soil disposal and coalfield dereliction, and will be reviewing British Coal's permitted development rights to see whether they should be brought into line with those of other mineral operators.

6.58 The Government and the minerals extraction industry have together sponsored a substantial programme of research into the reclamation of land used for minerals

Land used for minerals extraction can be put to good use once working has ceased

operations. It is essential that such land is reclaimed at the earliest opportunity, and is capable of an acceptable use once working has ceased. Work in hand includes an examination of best practice for restoring sites for agricultural and amenity uses, the landscaping of china clay waste tips and the shaping of large limestone quarry faces to blend with the surrounding natural land form.

Compensation

6.59 Major developments will continue to be necessary both for the country's economic well-being and in many cases to provide wider environmental benefits. But people whose homes are compulsorily purchased for such developments, or who live near them, may well be unhappy about them. The Government has reviewed the compensation arrangements which apply in such circumstances and has concluded that they are broadly fair in principle, but legislation will be introduced at an early opportunity to make significant detailed improvements to their coverage and operation.

RECYCLING LAND

6.60 Government policies are directed at making the best use of our finite supply of land. An important part of this is to bring previously-developed land back into constructive use. This is a major aim, for example, of the policies for inner cities (see Chapter 8). Analysis of land use changes has

shown that currently half the land developed for new housing was previously developed or vacant in urban areas. The Government has recently set in hand more research on the extent of vacant land through a national sample survey of the stock of vacant land in urban areas, to gain greater understanding of

Fourteen thousand
hectares of derelict land
have been reclaimed
since 1982

where further action may be needed. It is now considering what more could be done to bring into use vacant land currently in public sector ownership.

Derelict and contaminated sites

6.61 The 1988 Derelict Land Survey showed that, despite reclamation of 14,000 hectares since 1982, and an overall decrease in the total area of derelict land, large areas of land required action. A total of about 40,000

hectares was derelict, and about three quarters of it justified reclamation measures.

6.62 Contamination of land by chemicals and waste products is hard to define and measure exactly. But surveys suggest that over half of derelict land might be contaminated, and contamination is also found on other land. The nature of the contamination and the possible risks to health and groundwater supplies vary widely, and the Government needs better assessments of the scale of the problem.

6.63 Through the Environmental Protection Bill, therefore, the Government will introduce a new duty on district councils to compile registers of land that may be contaminated. Such registers will draw on historic land use data, to indicate areas where contamination may be found. By referring to the registers, developers will be able to decide where the risks demand more detailed surveys. The Government will also commission research to provide further guidance on quality objectives and standards, to be applied when contaminated sites are cleaned up.

Avoiding dereliction and contamination

6.64 It is important to try to prevent land becoming derelict or contaminated in the first place, and the Government is currently reviewing the existing law. On the basis of the polluter pays principle, those causing contamination and dereliction should pay for the costs of putting it right. Placing more responsibility on those who cause damage

Half the land for new
housing comes from
previously developed or
vacant urban sites

Previous uses of newly developed land

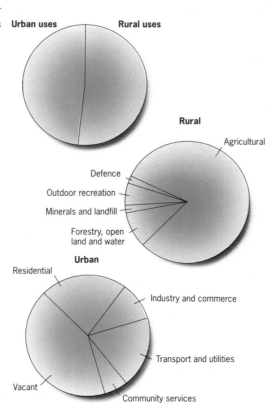

Urban uses   Rural uses

Rural

Agricultural

Defence

Outdoor recreation

Minerals and landfill

Forestry, open
land and water

Urban

Residential

Industry and commerce

Transport and utilities

Vacant

Community services

could reduce the amount of derelict land more quickly, and make it available for development or other uses to benefit the wider community.

6.65 Some existing measures can help to prevent damage, dereliction or contamination, and to reclaim derelict and contaminated sites. For example, the terms of planning permissions can discourage the degradation of sites, and permissions for minerals extraction may require operators (through restoration and aftercare conditions) to return sites to beneficial use after extraction or waste tipping ceases. The Environmental Protection Bill will help to prevent contamination of land, through:
• integrated pollution control for industrial processes (see Chapter 10); and
• new duties on operators of waste disposal sites to restore land to safe standards.

6.66 Further measures are needed to prevent dereliction. Options under consideration include:
• widening the types of development to which restoration and aftercare conditions may be attached, to development where industrial structures are specific to a particular use and are unlikely to have another use if the proposed use ends; and
• extending local authorities' existing powers to tackle dereliction on privately owned sites, by making the reclamation works eligible for grant assistance, but providing clear powers for any costs reasonably incurred to be recoverable from the owner, either immediately or when the owner sells the land (this would mean that authorities could reclaim derelict land without using their compulsory purchase powers and without incurring land acquisition expenditure). The Government will also consider the scope for market based instruments to discourage those who currently hold land derelict and vacant for a considerable length of time with-out taking steps to bring it back to beneficial use.

Derelict Land Grant

6.67 The Government believes that polluters should bear the cost of restoring land they

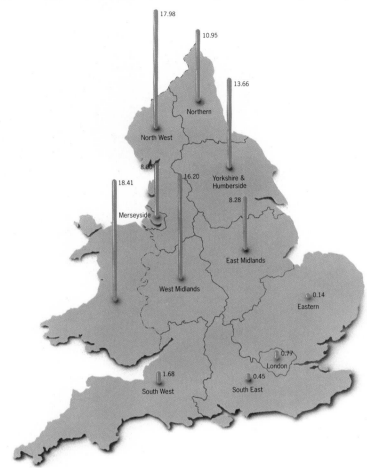

Expenditure on derelict land reclamation in England and Wales (£ million)

17.98

10.95

13.66

Northern

North West

8.00

18.41

16.20

Yorkshire & Humberside

8.28

Merseyside

East Midlands

0.14

Eastern

West Midlands

0.77

London

1.68

0.45

South West

South East

have damaged. But this is often not feasible where dereliction or contamination was caused many years ago, perhaps by firms that no longer exist. Experience from the United States has shown that there are great legal difficulties in trying to recover costs from original polluters. To restore derelict and contaminated land in these types of circumstance, the Government's Derelict Land Grant programme currently provides some £70 million a year in England. Where reclamation is for redevelopment, often to provide sites for housing or industry, this can stimulate private sector investment of up to 10 times the initial injection of grant.

6.68 The Government will shortly announce new priorities for this programme. These will:
• stress the importance of recycling derelict land;
• lay greater weight than previously on reclamation schemes that will improve the environment or deal with serious

The Government's Derelict Land Grant programme has restored many derelict and contaminated sites over the last decade. New priorities for the programme will target land which offers significant environmental benefits when restored, or where there is serious contamination

The Government is examining ways in which the cost of reclaiming contaminated and derelict land will in future fall on those causing the damage

contamination, especially those that can demonstrate new clean up methods; and
• encourage local authorities to develop a more strategic approach to reclamation involving both the private and voluntary sectors.

6.69 By stronger powers to discourage contamination and dereliction, by improving the amount of information available in the public domain, and by targeting resources in a way which gives greater priority to environmental concerns, the Government believes that major progress can be made in reducing the scale of the derelict land problem.

CONCLUSION

6.70 The amount of land is finite and in Britain almost all of it is used intensively. We need to look after it carefully. This Chapter explains how the Government intends to improve the town and country planning system and other rules that govern land and its use. It also explains some of the public sector initiatives to encourage re-use of derelict land, and the possibility of extending the polluter pays principle in relation to dereliction and contamination. Together these measures should do much to help ensure that environmental considerations are properly taken into account in land use policies. But the planning system cannot by

itself ensure that the environment is properly protected. The principle of stewardship requires everyone who owns, occupies or uses land – individuals, businesses, local authorities, government departments – to hold it in trust and to preserve it and enhance it where they can. Everyone needs to be involved in the task of ensuring that the best of our present environment is preserved for future generations, that the new development that is needed fits in harmoniously with what is here already, and that the ugly and derelict parts of our environment are restored and brought back into good use.

Research – land use

Research can help the Government to pursue its land use objectives in many ways. These include finding out more about the land itself, quantifying different uses and studying and monitoring their effects, and examining the implications of possible changes of policy.

Public sector research relevant to land use and planning includes projects
• to help with planning the extraction of minerals in environmentally acceptable ways and to investigate the problems that ground instability may cause for future development on minerals sites – Department of the Environment (£2.8m in 1989/90)
• to provide information for environmental impact assessment and wider planning purposes by increasing understanding of land resources and

monitoring and predicting change and interactions between land uses – Natural Environment Research Council (£2.0m in 1989/90)
• to improve the assessment of land availability for housing and of the operation of the Environmental Assessment Regulations – Department of the Environment (£0.6m in 1989/90)
• to assess the effectiveness of land use planning and in particular the role of new settlements and the influence of land supply on house prices – Department of the Environment (£0.2m in 1989/90).
• to study and develop the applications of Geographic Information Systems in research into land use and other environmental issues – Natural Environment Research Council and Economic and Social Research Council (joint programme of £0.4m in 1989/90)

7

COUNTRYSIDE
AND WILDLIFE

The Government aims to balance the need for food and other raw materials, the demand for jobs and homes, the opportunities for recreation and the need to safeguard wildlife and landscape

INTRODUCTION

7.1 Our countryside and coasts are a central part of our heritage. Most of us, wherever we live, visit them from time to time for pleasure. Our landscapes have been an inspiration for centuries to writers, painters and nature lovers. They help form our sense of national identity.

7.2 At the same time, the countryside is not a museum or a playground. It is a place where people live and work. Nature may have created the rocks, soils, plants and animals but man has moulded them to provide food, shelter, water and materials. What we see today is the result of centuries of this interaction between man and nature. The countryside is also an integral part of the world's living environment : it is a home for many wild species; its woodlands absorb carbon dioxide; and it is part of the natural cycle of water, carbon and nitrogen between air, land and sea.

7.3 No less than in other areas, the Government's policies for the countryside are based both on sound stewardship of the heritage and on creating the conditions for a healthy and growing economy. Most of the countryside is privately owned. Wherever possible, the Government works in partnership with its owners and managers to protect it through voluntary effort. Where necessary, however, the Government will continue to use the law to provide the necessary degree of protection.

7.4 The aims of the Government's policies for the countryside are
• to integrate environmental and economic activity in rural areas;
• to conserve and improve the landscape and encourage opportunities for recreation;
• to give extra protection to areas of special value;
• to conserve the diversity of Britain's wild-life, particularly by protecting habitats; and
• to provide scientific monitoring and research to support these aims.

INTEGRATING THE ENVIRONMENT AND THE ECONOMY

7.5 Agriculture and forestry take up 90% of the land and are the main influence on the appearance of the countryside. In the past they were also the foundation of the rural economy but the position has changed. Employment in agriculture continues to decline and light manufacturing, service industries and tourism are all growing in relative importance as a result of the Government's national economic policies and carefully targeted assistance.

7.6 The Government's aim is to ensure that the rural economy continues to prosper and to make its own contribution to the quality of the environment. Maintaining a healthy rural economy is one of the best ways of protecting and improving the countryside because so much depends on the availability of people and resources to invest in, and carry out, the work.

7.7 But the Government also recognises that some of the demands for countryside protection and improvement cannot be met through the market alone. Where this is so, it will continue to provide some financial support either indirectly through supporting economic activity, or directly through measures to encourage practical conservation.

7.8 The Government also accepts that some kinds of economic activity have the potential to harm the countryside. Chapter 6 explains how the planning system aims to make sure that the growing range of commercial activity does the least possible damage to the interests of conservation. The rest of this section, from 7.9 to 7.38, explains how the Government aims to ensure that environmental considerations are built directly into those policies that sustain economic activity in the countryside.

Agriculture

7.9 Agricultural policies since the war, including the Common Agricultural Policy (CAP) of the European Community, have aimed to provide the nation with a reliable source of food at a reasonable price and the farmer with a reasonable return. These policies have been successful in increasing output and food security. In recent years the Government has been leading attempts to reform the CAP by reducing its overall cost, by increasing the role of market forces and by curtailing support and protection.

7.10 The modernisation and intensification of farming since the war have also led to significant changes in the countryside. For

example, in some areas there have been major landscape changes and habitat losses as hedgerows have been removed, land drained and moorland reclaimed. Although the Government remains firmly committed to supporting efficient and productive farming, it recognises that if farmers are to protect the greater part of the countryside they need to be more sensitive to environmental needs.

7.11 Since 1986, Agriculture Ministers have had a legal duty to balance the interests of agriculture with rural and environmental interests, including the economic and social interests of rural areas, the conservation and enhancement of their natural beauty, wildlife and historic interest and public enjoyment of the countryside. The Government is working to integrate agricultural and environmental objectives across the whole range of its policies for the next decade. In some cases this requires concerted action in the European Community. Britain will continue to play a leading role in bringing pressure to bear to reform the CAP and to integrate environmental considerations into EC policy.

7.12 The Government is taking action at a number of levels. It is introducing environmental considerations into general policies for agriculture (paragraphs 7.13 – 7.20); it is encouraging the development of organic farming (7.21); it is underpinning this process by appropriate advice and research and development (7.76 – 7.79); and it has introduced some schemes specifically designed to encourage farmers to protect or improve the countryside while continuing to support farming (7.55 – 7.57).

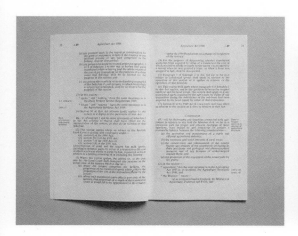

Left: Agriculture Departments are under a duty to balance agricultural needs with landscape, wildlife, recreation and the rural economy

Right: The Government aims to build environmental protection into agricultural policies

New agricultural schemes can require farmers to protect the environmental features of their land. The Government will seek to develop the integration of agricultural and environmental policies within the EC

HLCA arrangements have been criticised for encouraging overstocking with resulting damage to valuable habitats such as heather moorland. The Government will consult on changes to make environmental benefits more specific

Integrating environmental protection into agricultural policies

7.13 The Government has already taken action to build environmental protection directly into a number of agricultural policies.

7.14 Under the pilot Extensification Schemes for Beef and Sheep, farmers will receive payments in return for reducing output by at least 20%. Environmental protection is an integral part of the schemes. Apart from the benefit arising from less intensive use of land, the schemes will oblige participants to maintain and protect environmental features such as hedges and ponds and unimproved grassland, moorland and heath.

7.15 Nitrate Sensitive Areas have been designated to control nitrate leaching from soil (see Chapter 12).

7.16 In 1989, the Government introduced the Farm and Conservation Grant Scheme, which replaced earlier grant schemes aimed at supporting capital investment in the agriculture industry. It is mainly targeted at bringing about environmental improvements on farms. It strengthens the help given to farmers for improving the handling, storage and treatment of farm wastes (see Chapter 12), and adds new grants for the regeneration

of native woodlands and heather moors and for repairs to traditional agricultural buildings to existing grants for hedges, stone walls and shelter belts.

7.17 The Set-aside scheme offers farmers an incentive to reduce agricultural production. They receive payments for taking at least 20% of their arable land out of production for five years and putting it to fallow, woodland or non-agricultural use. Experience of the scheme has shown that some improvements were needed to the land management conditions. In future, new entrants to the scheme will be required to cut plant cover on fallow land twice a year instead of once; they will be required to maintain and protect a wider range of environmental features including stone walls, traditional buildings, moorland and heath; and some farmers will have the option to graze their set-aside land. Existing participants may also opt to observe these new rules.

7.18 Under the Countryside Premium Scheme, which is currently run by the Countryside Commission in seven counties in Eastern England, farmers receive additional payments for managing set-aside land for the benefit of wildlife, landscape and the local community. For example, payments are made for the creation of herb rich grassland for recreation and winter feeding areas for Brent Geese. The Government proposes to review the operation of this scheme at a suitable opportunity with a view to its being taken over by the relevant Government Departments.

7.19 The Government will continue to seek new ways of integrating environmental and agricultural policy further. For example, Hill Livestock Compensatory Allowance (HLCA) payments are made to farmers in the Less Favoured Areas to compensate for the practical and economic difficulty of farming in those areas. These payments, which, under EC rules, are made on the number of breeding cattle and sheep, help to prevent rural depopulation and countryside dereliction by providing essential income support for the farmers concerned. By supporting farming, HLCAs make a major contribution to the maintenance of landscapes in the hills and uplands which constitute about 50% of our countryside. But because the payments are linked to the number of animals, numbers have increased and in some areas this has led to grazing levels that have contributed to the loss of valuable habitats. Interested organisations have expressed particular concern about this overstocking and resulting damage to valuable and sensitive habitats, notably heather moorland, and damage to other environmental features such as hedges, ponds and stone walls. The Government has been successful in securing changes in the EC rules and is examining whether existing environmental benefits afforded by HLCAs should be made more specific. It will take account of the comments it has received and will consult fully before reaching conclusions.

7.20 The Government will seek, wherever possible and worthwhile, to develop the integration of agricultural and environmental policies within the European Community, including changes to Community arrangements so that those benefiting from EC support schemes will be required in return to protect and, where possible, enhance the environment on their holdings.

Organic farming

7.21 The Government supports the principle of organic farming – with its emphasis on using natural systems, avoiding pollution and using renewable resources. The Government has backed the United Kingdom Register of Organic Food Standards, which establishes standards for organic production. The Government also funds research, studies and surveys, and provides advice through the Ministry of Agriculture, Fisheries and Food's Agricultural Development and Advisory Service (ADAS) (see below). Farmers can make full use of existing grant schemes to help them convert to and invest in organic farming. The Government plans to consult on a grant scheme to assist those wishing to convert whole farms to organic production under the EC Extensification Schemes.

The Government provides conservation advice to farmers and will mount an intensive campaign in 1991

Advice

7.22 Farmers need advice to help them to adjust to changing circumstances. ADAS will be mounting an intensive campaign in 1991 to encourage greater conservation awareness among farmers and to demonstrate how they can make the most of opportunities for using and marketing the environmental assets of their farms. The object will be to encourage farmers to think more positively about habitats and wildlife and to give the public new opportunities for quiet recreation in the countryside. In addition to preparing a revised Code of Good Agricultural Practice for water protection, the Government will be publishing advice for all farmers on ways to protect the soil and air and to protect and improve the countryside.

7.23 The Ministry of Agriculture, Fisheries and Food will keep under review the capacity of ADAS to provide advice to farmers on environmental matters and the number of topics on which free advice is given. The Department of Environment will continue to support the provision of conservation advice.

7.24 Drawing on research results, and using the full range of advice and grant aid, the Government will continue to assist in the development of alternative farming methods and enterprises which are environmentally benign and sustainable. It will continue to encourage the development of means to rationalise and minimise chemical use, including alternatives to chemical pest control; and it will assist in the development of alternative energy sources on farms, for example using straw for fuel.

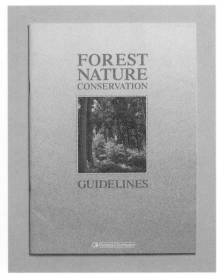

Left: The Government is encouraging environmentally sensitive tree planting and will introduce new grants for woodland management

Right: The Government advises on the best means of creating rich and diverse habitats in forests

Forestry

7.25 Forests, woodlands and trees, as Chapter 5 describes, provide one of the most effective ways by which carbon dioxide can be absorbed from the atmosphere and stored for long periods of time. They also provide timber which, if converted into durable products, can further prolong the storage process.

7.26 Forests and woodland occupy 10% of our land, roughly the same area as all of our towns. Post-war Governments have favoured an expansion of forestry chiefly to increase the supply of home-grown timber but this expansion has sometimes conflicted with protection of the environment. Since 1985 the Forestry Commission has had a legal duty to balance the interests of forestry and the environment and the Government has taken steps to build environmental objectives into its forestry policy.

7.27 For many years, the Government has encouraged planting of broadleaved trees through higher levels of grant aid and in 1985 it announced new policies, including a new and separate broadleaved woodland grant scheme. Since then the proportion of private broadleaved planting has increased from around 9% to 17% of total planting in 1987/88. The Forestry Commission introduced a new Woodland Grant Scheme in 1988, which sets higher environmental standards and gives particular encouragement

for planting native pinewoods and broadleaves by offering higher rates of grant. The Forestry Commission has since published detailed environmental guidelines to be followed by those planting under the scheme.

7.28 The Government is also encouraging planting on agriculturally improved land, first, by offering supplementary payments for better land under the Woodland Grant Scheme and second, through the introduction of the Farm Woodland Scheme. The latter scheme, which is experimental, aims to improve the landscape and benefit wildlife while reducing the cost of agricultural support, adding to farm incomes and employment and eventually increasing home-grown timber supplies.

7.29 In 1988 the Forestry Commission set up a review to consider the operation and effectiveness of its broadleaves policy. The single most important issue to emerge from the review was the need to encourage the multi-purpose management of woodland. The Government has recently announced that from April 1992, grants will also be available for the management of all types of woodlands, with a strong emphasis on maintaining and improving their environmental value. Higher grants will be payable over a longer period to encourage the management of woodlands of special environmental value including semi natural woodlands.

7.30 The Government aims to achieve 33,000 hectares a year of traditional planting plus 12,000 hectares a year under the Farm Woodland Scheme. The new Woodland Grant Scheme has been designed to ensure that planting positively enhances the visual and recreational potential of the countryside. The Government is also supporting a number of initiatives which, while contributing to the planting aim, will be directed specifically at improving the environment. For example, the Countryside Commission is working with the Forestry Commission to encourage the planting of Community Forests. These are new forests on the outskirts of major towns which provide opportunities for commercial forestry, for improving the landscape and wildlife of the urban fringe and for recreation. The Government has already approved three projects in Tyne and Wear, South Staffordshire and East London and will consider current proposals for further candidate areas from the Countryside Commission. The Government is also considering a proposal from the Countryside Commission for a new national forest in the English Midlands. The aim would be to harness substantial private sector and voluntary sector investment to create a forest of some 40,000 hectares over about 40 years. A similar project is being undertaken in Central Scotland. (See Chapter 20).

Rural development

7.31 One of the Government's main tasks in promoting rural development is to encourage a spirit of enterprise in all those who live and work in rural areas and to increase activity by the private and voluntary sectors. Another is to make the best possible use of limited public funds by encouraging others to contribute resources and by concentrating activities in the areas with the greatest economic and social needs. The Government takes action itself, where necessary, through legislation or by providing pump-priming finance.

Rural Development Commission (RDC)

7.32 The Government sponsors specialist agencies to put many of its policies for rural communities into practice. In England the

main agency for diversifying rural enterprise is the Rural Development Commission.

7.33 The Rural Development Commission's task is to create a climate in which businesses and communities can prosper in rural areas. In order to make the best use of its resources (about £38 million in 1990/91) the RDC concentrates its activities in the areas of greatest need, known as Rural Development Areas. Twenty seven Areas were defined in 1984 and cover 35% of England. All but eight now have unemployment rates below the national average. The RDC provides advice to Government, gives financial and technical support to rural enterprise and helps with the development of rural communities. Most importantly the RDC gets people and organisations in the private, voluntary and public sectors to work together to deal with rural problems. The Government will continue to work through the RDC to promote enterprise and economic diversity in a lively and prosperous countryside.

Community forests on the edge of towns, planted with Government aid, provide opportunities for forestry, landscape and wildlife improvement and recreation as on the above site before and after planting

The Government and the Rural Development Commission help to convert farm buildings to new uses

Farm Diversification Grant Scheme

7.34 Farmers are keen to use the assets of the farm and the skills and talents of the family and workforce in new ways that both improve their income and benefit the wider rural community. The Government's Farm Diversification Grant Scheme helps those who wish to diversify into appropriate and profitable businesses on their farm, such as farm trails, holidays and livery. This scheme is helping farmers to make an increasing contribution to the wider rural economy as well as producing food and caring for the countryside.

Tourism

7.35 Tourism can play an important part in the development and diversification of the rural economy. The past few years have seen many new developments in, for example, nature trails, farm museums, craft workshops and other activities designed to encourage tourism in rural areas. Tourist income is often essential to the maintenance of services and facilities. Many rural areas would have a greatly reduced range of shops and transport facilities were it not for the income generated by visitors. However, without sympathetic design and proper attention to visitor management, tourism can also damage the landscape and heritage on which it depends. The Government therefore welcomes measures like the English Tourist Board's rural development strategy, 'Visitors to the Countryside', and the recent agreement between the Countryside Commission and English and Wales Tourist Boards on 'green tourism' in the National Parks, which seeks to reconcile the growth of tourism with a full regard for the environment.

7.36 To help the industry overcome the problems that large numbers of visitors can bring to some of our most beautiful, but at the same time most environmentally sensitive areas, the Government has brought together a Task Force drawn from a range of organisations representing tourism and environmental interests. This Task Force is currently assembling information on best practice, in the light of which it will draw up guidance to the tourism industry on how to develop in harmony with the environment. This work is covering issues related to the effect of tourism on the heritage (Chapter 9) as well as tourism in the countryside. The guidance will be published in Spring 1991.

Roads and the countryside

7.37 The Government has a long-standing policy of keeping roads away from protected areas such as Areas of Outstanding Natural Beauty and Sites of Special Scientific Interest wherever possible. It also pays special attention to the effects of new roads on land owned by the National Trust. In National Parks, the Government is committed to ensuring that no new trunk road will be constructed and no existing road will be upgraded unless there is a compelling need which cannot be met by any reasonable alternative means.

7.38 The Government spends substantial sums minimising the environmental impact of new roads by contouring them and planting trees to help blend them into the landscape: it already plants 2 million trees each year and this number will grow substantially. The Department of Transport has recently appointed consultants to advise on improvements to its environmental practices and is planning to double staffing on landscaping and planting. The Government will also examine the scope for purchasing extra land on which habitats displaced by road schemes can be recreated and the scope for farmers or landowners to carry out environmental improvement work on its behalf.

The Government plants over 2 million trees a year to help new roads blend into the landscape

LANDSCAPE CONSERVATION, IMPROVEMENT AND RECREATION

7.39 As well as taking action itself to integrate environmental considerations with economic activity in the countryside, the Government also encourages others to take practical measures to protect and improve the landscape and to make provision for recreation. In England and Wales it does this mainly through the Countryside Commission. Local authorities and the voluntary sector also play an important part.

The Countryside Commission

7.40 The Countryside Commission works with and through public authorities, voluntary bodies and private individuals and organisations to protect and improve the landscape and provide new and improved opportunities for access and recreation. It is funded by the Government and advises it on all these matters. The Commission sees itself as a catalyst – seeking to get new initiatives off the ground by injecting new ideas, staff and finance at the right time and in the right place. The Government has recognised the importance of the Commission's role by doubling its funding in real terms in the last ten years.

7.41 The Government is discussing with the Countryside Commission the scope for including within its programme a new national countryside initiative in England. Such an initiative might offer landowners, managers and farmers incentive payments to manage or recreate landscapes particularly valued by the public while at the same time providing access to the public. This would complement agricultural policies for protecting Environmentally Sensitive Areas, which are described in the next section, and might focus on key landscape features which are under particular pressure from visitors in popular stretches of the countryside. For example, the scheme could encourage the conservation of herb rich grassland in chalk and limestone areas such as the North Downs; lowland heathland in areas such as Dorset and Suffolk; and the conservation of traditional landscapes adjoining rivers, lakes and other waterways; and their wider use for public access.

Recreation and access

7.42 More people than ever visit the countryside for pleasure and there is a growing demand for sport and recreation there. Some people take part in organised activities, or make use of facilities that have been specifically provided for recreation, but most go simply to walk, picnic and enjoy the fresh air and scenery.

The Government will discuss with the Countryside Commission new initiatives to protect key landscape features and extend public access

7.43 The 140,000 miles of the rights of way network provide the main means of public access to the countryside. The demands of the public are creating problems for the condition of the network in some areas, while elsewhere footpaths have become neglected and overgrown. The Countryside Commission has set itself the target of bringing the whole of the rights of way network into good order by the end of the century with the help of local authorities and landowners. The Government supports that objective.

Voluntary bodies

7.44 There is a vast range of bodies operating at local and national level that have a particular concern for protecting the countryside, especially wildlife, and making it accessible for public enjoyment. As membership of these organisations grows, so does their ability to finance projects of interest to them. The development of countryside policies and initiatives has been strongly influenced by their efforts over many years. The Government will continue to support their activities and to work in partnership with them.

7.45 The Government has provided a considerable amount of direct funding for voluntary bodies in rural areas. Through the Special Grants Programme it supports the central administrative costs of voluntary bodies that are mobilising conservation work within the community. For example, the Government has supported the British Trust for Conservation Volunteers (BTCV), with its workforce of 60,000 volunteers, since 1983. Agencies like the Countryside Commission work very closely with the voluntary sector and provide funds for specific projects.

Business sponsorship

7.46 The Government actively encourages industry to become involved in sponsoring environmental projects. The joint initiative the Government launched with the Worldwide Fund for Nature in 1983 has contributed more than £3 million to conservation projects in its first four years. The Government continues to support the expanding Groundwork movement (see Chapter 8) which harnesses the efforts of industry and the community at the local level.

Many footpaths and bridleways are unusable, but the Countryside Commission aims to have the whole network in good order by 2000

Above right: The footpath network provides one of the main ways for the public to enjoy the countryside

Below right: Voluntary groups play an increasing role in helping to maintain and restore our rural heritage

Reasons for unusable footpaths and bridleways in England and Wales

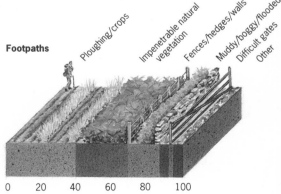

Footpaths

Ploughing/crops Impenetrable natural vegetation Fences/hedges/walls Muddy/boggy/flooded Difficult gates Other

0 20 40 60 80 100

Bridleways

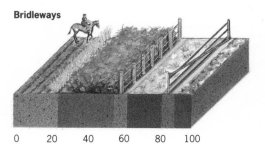

0 20 40 60 80 100

PROTECTING SPECIAL AREAS

7.47 Since the war successive Governments have established special arrangements for protecting parts of the countryside which are of particular environmental value.

National Parks (see map)

7.48 Our National Parks are the jewel in the countryside's crown and contain some of our most wild and beautiful landscapes. They were designated under the National Parks and Access to the Countryside Act 1949 with the twin purposes of protecting those landscapes and providing every opportunity for the public to enjoy them. The National Parks have for 40 years integrated the conservation and enjoyment of the natural beauty of the countryside with the interests of farming and forestry and the social and economic needs of rural areas. They are important in themselves and set standards for the countryside as a whole.

7.49 There are ten National Parks in England and Wales, covering some 13,500 square kilometres or 9% of the land area. In 1988 the Government created a statutory Broads Authority, which gives the Broads similar status to a National Park, though with some variations to take account of the special circumstances of the area. The Government attaches the greatest importance to the National Parks and provides 75% of their funds. It has increased its support in real terms by 20% over the past decade.

7.50 The Government will continue to give the protection of the Parks the highest priority. It will ensure that their special needs and priorities are reflected in policies affecting agriculture, forestry, transport, industry and minerals. Major industrial or commercial development will not normally be permitted in National Parks : only where there are proven national needs and a lack of alternative sites can any exception be justified. The Government has encouraged the Park authorities to prepare Park-wide development plans to ensure that their outstanding environmental quality is taken fully into account when proposals for new

The Government protects our most beautiful, wild or vunerable areas

■ Areas of Outstanding Natural Beauty
(England, Wales and N. Ireland)

□ National Parks
(England and Wales)

□ Environmentally Sensitive Areas

■ National Scenic Areas (Scotland)

The Government created the Broads Authority to give the Norfolk Broads similar status to a National Park

development are considered. The Government will bring forward legislation to make Park-wide plans a mandatory requirement.

7.51 It is important that the purposes, powers, administration and funding of the Parks are kept under review . The Countryside Commission for England and Wales has set up a panel to review the working of the National Parks which is due to report at the end of 1990. The Government looks forward to receiving the Commission's advice on the Panel's conclusions.

7.52 The Government will also consider any case for designating new National Parks in suitable areas where landscape conservation and recreation opportunities can be combined, either under the 1949 Act, or by creating further tailor made bodies like the Broads Authority.

Areas of Outstanding Natural Beauty (see map)

7.53 Areas of Outstanding Natural Beauty (AONBs) are areas where the landscape is of such beauty and quality as to be of national significance but which are not suitable for designation as National Parks because they do not have sufficient open country suitable for recreation. They are also designated under the 1949 Act. There are 38 AONBs covering some 20,000 square kilometres or over 13% of the total land area of England and Wales. In the past three years, the Countryside Commission has designated two new AONBs

In designated Environmentally Sensitive Areas, farmers are paid to maintain traditional farming practices which protect the landscape and wildlife

in the North Pennines and Howardian Hills and the Government is willing to support further designations if suitable areas are identified.

7.54 The Countryside Commission has recently published a review of AONBs and a new policy statement. The review has shown that a number of AONBs need further management effort to cope with increasing problems produced by greater pressures from visitors and development. The Government believes that AONBs are important national assets and will be asking the Countryside Commission to address these problems in co-operation with local authorities.

Environmentally Sensitive Areas (see map)

7.55 Environmentally Sensitive Areas (ESAs) are areas, designated by the Agriculture Departments, where the wildlife and landscape are of special importance and are particularly vulnerable to change arising from agricultural intensification. Some of them are in National Parks or AONBs and many contain important wildlife sites. The main difference between ESAs and other designated areas is that their special qualities are protected through incentive payments to farmers for the maintenance of traditional farming practices.

7.56 The Government has designated 19 areas in Britain, covering some 7,900 square kilometres or 3.5% of our agricultural land, and almost 4700 farmers have joined the scheme. They range in location from the mountains and moorlands of Breadalbane (in Perthshire) and the North Peak to the wetlands of Somerset and Suffolk. Each ESA is different and farmers are asked to do different things in each area : for example, restrictions on fertiliser and pesticide use may be combined with a requirement for hedges and ditches to be managed.

7.57 ESAs are demonstrably popular with farmers and conservationists. In 1991, with five years' experience of their operation, the Government will be assessing their value and deciding on the way forward.

Urban fringe

7.58 Agriculture in the urban fringe suffers from a range of problems including vandalism, trespass, litter and dumping; pressure for recreation; fragmentation of ownership and holdings which makes some land difficult to farm economically; and general neglect. The Government has helped to tackle this problem through the planning system, the Countryside Commission and Groundwork Trusts (see Chapter 8) and will keep the special problems of the urban fringe under review.

Common land

7.59 The 6,000 square kilometres of common land in England and Wales combine valuable wildlife habitats with extensive opportunities for quiet public enjoyment. The Government recognises the need for the status of this land to be safeguarded. It is working towards the provision of properly constituted and effective schemes of management to guarantee the conservation value and economic importance of common land, and improved arrangements for public access.

The coast

7.60 Britain's coasts, shores and cliffs are an important area for tourism and recreation and include some of our most outstanding landscapes. They also contain important and often rare species and habitats including many sites of international importance. The inter-tidal zone and shallow offshore waters are of similar importance for recreation and conservation and are important for fisheries and the extraction of oil, gravel and other minerals. The coast also offers important development opportunities, ranging from barrages, which could generate energy cleanly, to marinas and other leisure facilities.

7.61 The Government welcomes the initiatives which have been taken to conserve and plan coastal landscapes. The Countryside Commission's heritage coast designations now cover 1,455 kilometres in England and Wales and have provided a framework for managing recreation as well as protecting the landscape. The National Trust's Enterprise Neptune celebrates its twenty-fifth anniversary in 1990 and has contributed to the protection of some of our best coastal scenery.

PROTECTING AND ENHANCING WILDLIFE

7.62 The wildlife of Britain is an integral part of its countryside, towns and coasts and many of the measures outlined in this Chapter and elsewhere in the White Paper indirectly protect habitats and species. But in some cases special measures are needed to protect habitats or individual species directly, not least because of the mobility of wildlife and the fact that it does not recognise international frontiers. This section outlines the Government's current and proposed action on wildlife, including marine wildlife.

The Nature Conservancy Council

7.63 The Nature Conservancy Council (NCC) is the body which is mainly responsible for nature conservation. It is funded by the Government and is responsible for National Nature Reserves, for identifying and notifying Sites of Special Scientific Interest (SSSI), for advising the Government and others on matters affecting nature conservation, for disseminating knowledge about nature conservation and for supporting and commissioning research.

7.64 The NCC is being reorganised into three nationally based Councils. The creation of three national agencies will improve the effectiveness of the Government's nature conservation policies while also allowing them to focus more closely on the needs and circumstances of each country. The new Councils, like the old one, will found their activities on a strong science base. They will act together in a new Joint Committee to provide advice on British and international

NATURE CONSERVANCY COUNCIL

The Government has substantially increased funding to the NCC, the main body with responsibility for nature conservation in Britain

matters, to commission research on them, and to establish common standards for matters such as monitoring and data analysis. In this way, they will assist the Government in meeting its European and international commitments.

7.65 The Government greatly values the work of the NCC and has increased its resources by over 150% in real terms since 1981. It will continue to support the important work it does, in particular, protecting important sites and habitats to preserve rare or threatened species; underpinning the work of voluntary wildlife organisations such as the RSPB and RSNC by providing financial, scientific and technical support; expanding its advisory role on the long term management of sites and habitats; and educating the public about nature conservation.

Protecting habitats: Sites of Special Scientific Interest

7.66 The key to the protection of wildlife is the protection of the habitat on which it depends. The Wildlife and Countryside Act 1981 introduced the most comprehensive system of wildlife conservation ever seen in this country. It reinforced the NCC's statutory duty to identify the country's most important wildlife and geological areas as Sites of Special Scientific Interest (SSSIs) : the NCC has now designated over 5,300 in Great Britain covering about 16,270 square kilometres or 7% of the land. Most SSSIs are in private ownership. If the landowner or occupier wishes to carry out an operation that might damage the special interest of the Site, he must notify the NCC. The NCC may suggest an alternative approach, or persuade him not to go ahead and pay compensation under a management agreement. In 1987/88 the NCC spent £4.5 million on management agreements for SSSIs. SSSI designation has proved its worth: in 1980, before the Act, there were reports of damage to 6% of SSSIs. By 1986, this figure had fallen to 4%. Since then only 1% a year have suffered any significant damage. Some damage caused by ignorance or accident is virtually unavoidable. In other cases, even where nature conservation interests have been carefully considered, there will be times when these have to be overridden by more pressing legitimate interests, for example, the North Devon Link Road and the Dersingham By-pass, where the benefits of the roads outweighed the loss of small areas of SSSI. In other cases such as that at Lodmoor, Dorset, the conservation argument outweighed the economic benefits and permission was refused. Most damage has been more than compensated for by the continued expansion of the SSSI network.

7.67 The planning system is designed to balance environmental considerations against development which is necessary to sustain the local rural economy and to encourage diversification. The Department of Environment will be issuing further policy guidance to help local authorities take these particularly difficult decisions. The Government is also prepared to consider taking other action, for example, by confirming directions under Article 4 of the General Development Order to withdraw permitted development rights in particular areas, if there is evidence that the exercise of those rights (for example holding war games) conflicts unacceptably with policies to protect wildlife.

The NCC has designated more than 5,300 SSSIs to protect their wildlife and geological interest: landowners must consult them before carrying out potentially damaging operations

Government legislation protects most of our wild plants and animals. It is an offence to dig up wild plants

National Nature Reserves and Marine Nature Reserves

7.68 Britain's wildlife legislation also provides for the establishment of nature reserves, sites of such importance that they are managed primarily for nature conservation. Most are in private ownership and are managed under nature reserve agreements. Where the site is of national importance these agreements are with the NCC and there are now over 230 in Great Britain, covering over 1,650 square kilometres. Local authorities may make similar agreements on sites of local importance and over 167 have been established in Great Britain. The 1981 Act also established a new designation to protect important marine sites – Marine Nature Reserves (MNRs). The NCC have identified seven potential MNRs around the British coastline and the Government has designated two, Lundy in 1986 and Skomer in 1990. Consultation on two others is under way.

Coastal waters

7.69 The nature conservation interest of the marine environment extends beyond the Marine Nature Reserve programme and effective protection of this interest requires the voluntary co-operation of a wide range of sea users. The Government is currently examining how best this can be achieved and in particular is considering whether the Marine Consultation Area scheme introduced in Scotland and, based on a published directory of conservation interest prepared by the Nature Conservancy Council, should be extended throughout Britain. Such a scheme could also involve the preparation of Government guidelines addressed to sea users and would need to be closely monitored to assess its effectiveness. The Government will also examine existing legislation to see how this could help in the longer term to meet conservation objectives in the marine environment.

Protecting species

7.70 There are over 30,000 species of animals and birds and 5,000 species of plants in Britain. Many have adapted successfully to the changes that have taken place in their environment : the kestrel, for example, is often seen hunting for prey over the grass verges of motorways. Others have found it more difficult to survive. The Wildlife and Countryside Act gives protection to a large number of threatened species. The degree of protection varies according to the needs of each species and its rarity. For example, it is an offence under the Act to kill, injure, disturb, collect or sell the most endangered species, such as the otter. All wild plants and wild birds are protected under the Act and the list of species given special protection includes 93 plants, such as the military orchid, and 304 birds and animals, such as the slow-worm. Recently a further 22 species of British butterfly were added to the list. The Act has achieved a number of success stories : for example, the number of otters is increasing and in Scotland the white-tailed sea eagle is being successfully reintroduced to the wild. There is a review of the lists of protected species every five years: the next will take place in 1991.

7.71 The Act also includes a system of registration of the most endangered species of birds kept in captivity and this has been a major deterrent to taking from the wild and encouraged significant increases in captive breeding. The Department of Environment's Wildlife Inspectorate has played a key role in the implementation of the Register; and also in the controls over the trade in endangered species.

International obligations

7.72 The 1981 Act and SSSI designation not only form the basis of habitat protection in this country but also provide the main mechanisms through which we meet our international obligations. These include the designation of Special Protection Areas for Birds (SPAs) as required by the EC Birds Directive; and Wetlands of International Importance under the Ramsar Convention (The Convention on Wetlands of International Importance, especially as Waterfowl Habitat).

7.73 The Birds Directive seeks to provide Community-wide protection for all wild birds and their habitat, with special protection for some endangered and migratory species. The Government has designated 40 sites as SPAs and 44 wetland sites under the Ramsar Convention as part of a continuing programme to protect habitats for endangered species and has taken steps to protect all identified potential SPAs. Britain is also taking an active part in the development of the draft EC Habitats Directive to oblige Member States to establish a legal framework for the protection of all wild fauna and flora and their habitats.

The Government has designated over 40 wetland sites under the RAMSAR Convention

7.74 Britain was one of the first countries to become a party to CITES (The Convention on the International Trade in Endangered Species of Wild Fauna and Flora) which maintains controls to protect species from over exploitation through international trade. It is also party to the Bern Convention (on the Conservation of European Wildlife and Natural Habitats) which, under the auspices of the Council of Europe, seeks to conserve species of wildlife occurring in Europe. Finally, it is party to the Bonn Convention (on The Conservation of Migratory Species of Wild Animals), which is aimed at international measures to protect migratory species of all kinds throughout their migratory routes.

7.75 At the third North Sea Conference, all the North Sea states supported a British initiative to improve the protection of marine wildlife through a common and co-ordinated approach to developing species and habitat protection; and to develop appropriate conservation measures in the North Sea, especially for seals, sea and coastal birds. A specific initiative will provide greater protection for porpoises and dolphins: all the North Sea states signed a Memorandum of Understanding on Small Cetaceans in the North Sea which includes a commitment to protect these species and investigate potential threats to them and which should eventually lead to a full Cetacean Agreement.

SCIENTIFIC MONITORING AND RESEARCH

7.76 A full scientific understanding of the processes and changes which are taking place in the natural environment and the factors which affect them is the key to the development of policies for protecting and improving it. Government Departments, the conservation agencies, the research councils and others carry out a wide range of research into this field; the Table at the end of the Chapter gives some examples.

7.77 Much of this effort is devoted to monitoring the changes which are taking place in the natural environment and where possible evaluating potential causes. In some cases this is specifically targeted at evaluating the environmental effects of new policies. For example, the Agriculture Departments, in co-operation with the conservation agencies, are carrying out a detailed assessment of the effects of ESA designation. On a wider scale, the Department of Environment in partnership with the Natural Environment Research Council (NERC) is funding a major survey of the countryside in 1990 to assess the condition and rates of change of the main landscape features and habitats in Great Britain. In the marine environment, seabird populations are monitored at strategic sites and in appropriate cases dead birds are studied to indicate whether pollutant levels may be

significant. The NCC is developing detailed surveys of coastal conservation interest, including inshore areas, as part of the Marine Conservation Review, and paragraph 7.69 describes how this review might be built into new policies for marine protection areas.

7.78 At another level, research is devoted to the complex interaction between controlled ecosystems, such as agriculture and forestry, and the natural environment. A clear understanding of the effect of these regimes on wildlife, for example, will ensure that full account can be taken of their environmental impact as new policies and techniques are developed. Agriculture Departments have already increased the emphasis on environmental research in their research and development programmes and will keep this under review. The Ministry of Agriculture, Fisheries and Food spends some £42 million out of a total research budget of £120 million on environmental research, covering all aspects of its environmentally related research.

7.79 Finally, effort is also being devoted to evaluating and assessing the likely impact of future changes, particularly in climate. Scientists are evaluating the sensitivity of both controlled and natural ecosystems to predicted changes in climate to assess the likely effect, for example, on species distribution and food and timber production. Research projects commissioned by Government will lead to greater understanding of marine and coastal processes. In turn this will help towards the development of a strategy in response to predicted rises in sea level as a result of global warming.

CONCLUSION

7.80 This Chapter describes what the Government has done and intends to do to safeguard the beauty and character of our countryside and its wildlife while allowing economic activity to prosper there, so that future generations can enjoy the same or greater benefits than we do today. It seeks to achieve better integration of environmental and economic policies for the countryside; to encourage positive landscape conservation and recreation provision; to designate areas in need of special protection; and, where necessary, to control harmful activities by law. The Government bases all of its policies on a sound scientific knowledge of the rural heritage and constantly works to extend this.

7.81 Above all, however, countryside protection is a shared responsibility involving partnership between the Government, the owners and managers of the land, the special countryside agencies, local authorities, business, many voluntary bodies and the millions of people who visit and enjoy it. The Government will strengthen that partnership and common purpose.

Research – countryside and wildlife

The objectives of public sector research on the countryside and wildlife include monitoring changes in its wildlife, habitats, landscapes and economy and developing systems of production which are sensitive to the environment, while allowing economic growth and identifying ways to promote enterprise. The range of research is very wide, and includes projects
• to develop environmentally friendly agricultural practices and to protect and improve the rural environment, by
- reducing pesticide use through improvements in efficiency of pesticides and diagnostic techniques for pests and diseases and by developing and assessing safer uses of pesticides (£21.5m);
- improved understanding of nitrogen cycle and nitrate leaching; by developing improved, cost effective, methods of containing and disposing of farm waste (£7m);
- assessing various farming practices which encourage wildlife communities, alternative land use, soil contamination and erosion (£3.5m);
- conserving and augmenting plant diversity (£8m);
- and providing an improved understanding of effective, environmentally sensitive and economic means of flood protection and coastal defences (£2m)
(Ministry of Agriculture, Fisheries and Food – total £42 million 1991/92)
• to support regulatory activities on wildlife and nature conservation and policies for encouraging rural enterprises which reconcile agriculture, forestry, conservation and recreation activities – Department of the Environment (£1.2m in 1989/90)
• to support marine and coastal impact surveys, including the Marine Nature Conservation review, and coastal surveys and the international Seabirds at Sea Programme in conjunction with the oil industry – Nature Conservancy Council (£0.6m in 1989/90)
• to inform and support the development of national policies and regional practice by: monitoring social and environmental changes in the countryside; evaluating specific proposals or projects; developing and promoting new ideas; and spreading good practice – Countryside Commission for England and Wales (£1.0m in 1989/90).

8

TOWNS AND CITIES

INTRODUCTION

8.1 Most people in Britain live in towns and cities. So, if we are to have a good and healthy environment, it is vital that they are pleasant places in which to live and work, and that new developments and buildings improve the quality of life there.

8.2 Later chapters show how the Government proposes to improve the quality of air and reduce litter and noise, which will be of particular benefit in our towns and cities. This Chapter concentrates on the physical aspects of towns and the role good transport, new buildings and locally led effort can play in improving them.

8.3 The complexity of life in towns and cities means that many factors go to determine whether they enjoy a good environment. Chief among these are:
• the health of the local economy – a thriving local economy is the necessary base for a satisfactory environment;
• good planning and layout, with the different elements well related to one another, and adequate green space within and around the town;
• good transport, providing effective energy efficient mobility for the population, without damaging the environment; and
• good buildings, well designed and maintained.

Most can be achieved at the local level – through the efforts of individuals, of companies, and of local authorities. The Government's principal role is as a partner in these efforts, providing guidance on the best ways to plan for better towns and transport; and offering financial support where needed.

8.4 Towns are an efficient form of organising our lives and can be a very positive element in the environment as a whole. By concentrating development they help preserve the wider landscape, and can make travel distances shorter and sustain better public transport. And by concentrating demand for services, they offer economies of scale which can help measures such as recycling and combined heat and power systems to be cost effective. The Government hopes to build on these advantages, particularly in its work to reduce greenhouse gas emissions. This will be reflected in new planning guidance (see Chapter 6).

A good local environment makes the town more attractive as a place to work and invest

A STRONG LOCAL ECONOMY

8.5 For towns and cities no less than for nations, a good environment and a strong economy are dependent on each other. If a town has a strong economy, it is not likely that it will fall into dereliction and decay. And if the environment improves, its attraction as a place to live, work and invest will increase. Modern industry and commerce no longer create the dirt and noise of previous eras that gave rise to the phrase 'where there's muck there's brass'. Today we see that the worst urban environments are those with a weak local economy. Increasingly, firms place a premium on a good local environment and well designed accommodation when they come to make their investment and location decisions – poor buildings and surroundings are bad for business and recruitment. Strengthening the local economy is the major goal of the Government's action for the inner city areas which is described at 8.37 below.

Left: The Government is encouraging provision of open space in towns

Right: We need to ensure that our town centres retain their vitality, and contribute positively to the environment as a whole

GOOD PLANNING

Making the best use of urban land

8.6   The better the use we make of urban land, the less pressure there will be on the countryside and the greater the direct benefits in towns and cities. The Government has asked local authorities to look to the reuse of existing sites before allowing new land to be taken for development. The Green Belts round our larger cities help by preventing development from spreading into the surrounding green land and so encouraging developers to look to the urban areas (see Chapter 6). A recent study of land use in the South East showed that 58% of new housing is now being built on redeveloped or vacant urban land.

Greening urban areas

8.7   Providing attractive open space helps to breathe life into urban areas and gives opportunities for sport and recreation. But too often, urban green space is neglected or unsuitable for recreational use. The Government will encourage the creation and retention of suitable open space which is accessible to residents in urban areas, wherever this is practical.

8.8   Planning decisions must strike the right balance between the use of land for economic development and meeting local needs for green spaces. The Department of the Environment and the Welsh Office will soon issue a new planning policy guidance note on sport and recreation. This will ask local planning authorities to ensure that their planning policies address local needs for recreation and open space, protect valuable sites and identify suitable sites for additional provision, for example as part of redevelopment schemes. The guidance will also draw attention to the potential value of areas such as playing fields as recreational land for the wider community. The Government proposes to set up a register of sports sites to help monitor change in this area.

Ensuring the vitality of the town centre

8.9   Until a few years ago, people on shopping expeditions usually went into towns. Now many people go out of town, to the large supermarkets and shopping centres which have increasingly sprung up on the outskirts. This trend has its advantages: it has created new jobs, increased choice and given many people easier access to a wide range of goods. But there are disadvantages too: out-of-town shopping can be inaccessible to the least mobile people, including the old; it can lengthen car journeys; and it can sometimes threaten the town centre economy. The Government's guidance to planning authorities already emphasises the need to ensure that their planning decisions do not damage the vitality and viability of town centres as a whole. It will continue to stress this need.

In the larger cities, road congestion is caused mainly by local traffic. The Department of Transport is offering advice on traffic management policies, including priority for buses, and control of parking

TRANSPORT IN TOWNS

8.10   Good transport is vital to the well being of our towns. Good transport links can help overcome the problem of urban decay, avoid isolating certain groups in society, such as the elderly or disabled people, and stimulate employment and business. Transport should play a positive role in serving our towns and cities. To ensure this, the Government's aim is to civilise urban traffic – easing congestion, helping to improve the local environment and reducing air and noise pollution. Good traffic management and effective alternatives to the car can also help to reduce fuel consumption and emissions, including those of greenhouse gases.

8.11   In larger cities, road congestion is caused mainly by local traffic. The Government believes that what is needed is a balanced traffic management policy, taking pressure off unsuitable routes and allowing environmental improvements, together with improvements to traffic flow on the strategic road network and improved public transport with greater priority for buses. It believes that in most cases it does not make economic or environmental sense to increase capacity on roads leading into already congested areas simply to facilitate additional car commuting. Local highway authorities should consider the application of this policy in their own areas.

Better traffic management

8.12   Much can be achieved in the short term to improve transport in our towns by specific, often incremental, steps. These will generally be for local authorities to take, as they are responsible for the nation's local roads and have substantial powers to regulate traffic in consultation with local people and business. Examples of the steps that many local authorities have taken include the development of park and ride schemes coupled with city centre traffic management measures and pedestrianisation. The Department of Transport is preparing additional advice to help local authorities improve conditions further in towns and cities. This will include:
• better parking management and enforcement;
• ways of using bypasses and other road improvements, and increased public transport capacity, to take traffic out of residential areas and to put it on more suitable routes – including traffic calming measures to slow traffic on unsuitable routes and accommodating demand for cycling safely;
• the use of bus priority measures as part of traffic management schemes;
• more sophisticated traffic control systems to smooth the flow of traffic and reduce congestion; and
• improved traffic signing and driver infor-

mation systems to reduce wasted mileage.

8.13   Providing parking for more cars than the roads can easily cater for contributes to congestion. Similarly, parking that is too cheap encourages people to use cars rather than other forms of transport. The Government will pursue with local authorities the scope for more positive use of parking controls as a means of controlling traffic demand, while meeting the commercial and other demands of towns. It is also important that local authorities take into account the impact of new development on travel demands, especially in congested areas. For example, provision for car parking for employees should take account of the availability of other means of transport. Local authorities can ask developers to assist with road or public transport improvements where they are required to meet the demands of new development.

8.14   The Government has detailed proposals to improve traffic management in London. Proposed legislation would enable the Secretary of State to designate a priority route ('Red Route') network, including special measures to improve the movement of buses, reduce the impact of congestion and improve the local environment. The legislation would require local authorities to prepare local implementation plans for priority routes under their control and would introduce a new system of permitted on-street parking with increased powers to deal with breaches and powers to wheel-clamp and remove vehicles. It is for local authorities outside London to consider whether they wish to introduce priority routes in their areas.

8.15   With the co-operation of the London boroughs concerned, the Department of Transport is introducing a pilot 'Red Route' scheme to work out the practical details, such as how the benefits can be used to help buses and cyclists, and how to use traffic calming in surrounding areas.

8.16   The Department of Transport will continue to work to promote safe cycling. It is working with the local authorities to develop a cycle network across London. This follows successful work on schemes across the country – most recently the extensive system in Cambridge.

8.17   The Government wishes to make lorries quieter and cleaner. Its proposals are in Chapters 11 and 16. Local authorities can help by appropriate controls on lorry movements in urban areas for the benefit of the community as a whole. The Department of Transport's recent joint study with the Civic Trust and the County Surveyors Society ('Lorries in the Community') shows practical ways in which the impact of lorries can be reduced.

Taking traffic out of towns

8.18   The bypass programme has made a major contribution to improving urban conditions over many years. Bypasses redirect traffic to more suitable routes, and are particularly valuable in removing heavy lorries from towns. For example, the M25 has helped to take about 20% of heavy goods traffic off London's roads. 103 trunk road bypasses have been built in England since 1979 and over 170 are proposed in the current programme. The Department of Transport is considering pilot projects in conjunction with the local authorities concerned to link bypasses with traffic management measures in the towns bypassed. The aim is to find out how best to ensure that the environmental benefits a bypass brings to towns are lasting.

8.19   Chapter 5 discusses the role that public transport can play in helping to reduce vehicle emissions. Good public transport can also help reduce urban congestion and improve accessibility. The Government is currently supporting substantial investment in both British Rail and London Transport (£3.7 billion and £2.2 billion respectively over the three financial years from 1990/91). It has provided a grant for a light rail system in Manchester and similar systems are proposed for other cities. The bus priority measures mentioned above will help buses to provide faster and more reliable services.

8.20   In the long run some difficult choices

The Government supports the development of safe networks for cycling

Improved public transport has an important part to play in a balanced transport policy

may have to be made about traffic in our towns. It is simply not possible to cater for unrestricted growth of traffic in our city centres, nor would it be right to accept a situation in which traffic congestion found its own level, with inefficient use of road space and increased fuel consumption. Eventually it may be necessary to consider rationing use of road space by road pricing, but this approach is largely untried and there would be difficulties in ensuring an enforceable and fair system.

NEW BUILDINGS

Right: The best recent industrial development provides good working conditions, improves the landscape and sets high standards of architectural design.

Far right: Housing Associations have a good record of producing buildings which match tenants' needs and improve the street scene.

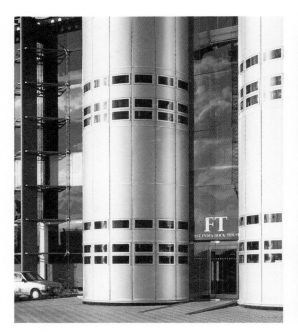

8.21 There has been much criticism over recent years of some of our newer buildings. This demonstrates not only the importance people place on good buildings as part of their environment, but also the potential impact, positive or negative, that new buildings can have. Good buildings result from the care and skill of those who commission and design them rather than regulation and control, but the Government wants to help good design to flourish.

Good design pays

8.22 Good design is the responsibility of everyone who commissions a building, however grand or small. Not only is a well designed building better for the wider environment, it also makes economic sense. It is a better building in or near which to live or work. Well designed commercial and industrial developments can help to increase job satisfaction, and increase the value of the property.

8.23 A well designed building should also be more efficient, especially in the use of energy, and other scarce resources. Careful use of materials, including low energy and recycled products, and design for energy efficiency can produce buildings which are more environmentally friendly. The Government wishes to encourage energy labelling schemes for buildings, and welcomes the independent schemes based on the assessment methods pioneered by the Building Research Establishment. A fuller account is given in Annex C of the part efficient buildings can play in reducing CO_2 emissions and so act against global warming.

8.24 But for most people, it is the appearrance of a building that will be of greatest importance. A good building can contribute to a sense of pride and of place. A really great building can become a positive symbol of its location and a major tourist attraction. At a time when people are increasingly concerned about new development, a design respon-

Far left: The public sector has a special responsibility to set high standards and to produce buildings which are attractive, economical and efficient.

Left: The work of the Property Services Agency has been recognised by national awards. The Government will continue to strive for good design in its own projects.

sive to local concerns can also contribute to making a new building acceptable.

8.25 The illustrations accompanying this section show the many ways in which good design can be expressed, through an imaginative and positive response to the needs of the building, its occupants and its location.

Design guidance

8.26 The planning system is not concerned with detailed design matters but many aspects of design are legitimate concerns of the planning system: location in relation to other properties; bulk; and overall relationship to the surroundings. In areas of great sensitivity other aspects can also be important, including the materials used. All of these factors contribute to good design and the appropriateness of the development for its site.

8.27 Local planning authorities need to be alive to the opinion of local and national bodies who offer advice on proposals for development and of course to the views of local people. It is often not enough simply to react to developers' ideas. Developers can appreciate a lead or guidance on development opportunities. Local planning authorities can have a positive effect on the quality of new development, for example through design briefs. These set out for potential developers the problems and opportunities of a site and the planning goals for it. A design brief can help an area to be developed with unity of purpose in a way that piecemeal development

proposals often cannot. It can be particularly valuable for sensitive development sites in historic centres, for example, Gloucester Green in Oxford or the Jorvik Development in York.

8.28 Even where large-scale redevelopment is not on the cards, it can be a good idea for a planning authority to issue design guidance for areas where special considerations apply - in a conservation area, for example, or an area with a high percentage of listed buildings. If it is pitched at the right level, such guidance can give developers a clear steer on the authority's outlook and its plans for the area without stifling creativity by taking too prescriptive an approach, and this should be good for the quality of the area as a whole.

Advice on design

8.29 The Royal Fine Art Commissions are established by Royal Warrant. Their main function is to advise on the aesthetic merits of major building and engineering works. The Commissions have a long history of influencing government departments, other public bodies and developers generally to seek the highest standards of architectural design and their advice has shaped and modified proposals for major developments. They also issue general guidance, including recent advice on urban design.

8.30 Many other national bodies (such as the Civic Trust) are very willing to assist with design issues, particularly where new developments are planned in sensitive areas.

Above: Housing design awards, which the Government helps to sponsor, encourage high standards of design

The Royal Fine Arts Commission offers valuable advice on design and, with the Sunday Times, gives awards. 1990 winners were:

Below right: New gallery, Imperial War Museum

Above right: the Imagination design group headquarters

Local public opinion and views of local societies will also be very valuable.

Encouragement to action

8.31 The Government sponsors award schemes to encourage high standards of design. Together with the existing privately sponsored schemes, these cover the full range of built design.

8.32 The Government sponsors Housing Design Awards Schemes in England and Wales jointly with the Royal Institute of British Architects and the National House Building Council. The aim is to encourage a high standard of good design and layout in public and private sector housing schemes. A new Project Award has recently been introduced to give recognition to housing developments still under construction. A common theme of recent award winning schemes is the care that has been taken to fit them into their surroundings.

8.33 The Government has sponsored the Art for Architecture scheme which involves artists and craftspeople in the design and develop-ment of buildings in ways which enrich urban regeneration projects. Through the Arts Council, it has also encouraged art as part of building projects. The voluntary 'Percent for Art' Scheme asks developers to set aside a proportion of project budgets for works of art.

8.34 The Government strives for good design

in its own projects. The Property Services Agency (PSA), which (under different names) has been central Government's Office of Works for several centuries, has won international and national recognition for its design capabilities. PSA has now become a separate entity – PSA Services – but it will continue to offer expert building and estate management services to government clients and business. Individual departments have taken over responsibility for the management of their estate and building programmes and will be committed to maintaining high stand– ards of design. Various departments have already issued advice on their approach to fostering good design combined with value for money.

8.35 The private sector has also long contributed to the encouragement of good design. Awards, presented by the Royal

Institute of British Architects, the Royal Town Planning Institute, the Civic Trust, The Times and the Financial Times, and industry, together with many local awards, recognise and publicise the best recent projects.

8.36 Design awards are valuable, but they cannot be enough on their own. A better understanding of building design, the problems it poses and the opportunities it presents, is essential. The recently established Art and Architecture Education Trust and Architectural Foundation provide platforms for the presentation of ideas, proposals for new buildings and public debate. These, and local exhibitions and meetings, offer the opportunity for everyone to share in the discussion of these issues.

PROGRAMMES AND FUNDING FOR URBAN IMPROVEMENT

8.37 Sometimes encouragement and planning controls are not enough and an area needs direct help in getting back on its feet. A number of local authority areas in England have been targeted for special action through the Government's "Action for Cities" initiative. This brings together a number of different Departmental programmes, and works with and through the private and voluntary sectors and local authorities. It aims:

• to encourage enterprise and new businesses, and create the conditions for existing businesses to grow stronger;
• to improve people's job prospects, their motivation and skills;
• to make areas attractive to residents and to business by, for example:
- tackling dereliction
- bringing buildings back into use
- preparing sites and encouraging development
- improving transport links and services
- improving the quality of housing
• to make inner city areas safe and attractive places to live and work by, for example:
- reducing crime
- improving education and health care
- developing better facilities for the arts, recreation and sport.

8.38 A range of training, enterprise and employment programmes exists to help create prosperous businesses and job opportunities, and to prepare people for them; initiatives to reduce crime and the fear of crime provide for safer cities in which to live and work; and the needs of ethnic minorities are addressed through specific grant to local authorities.

The availability, choice and quality of housing in urban areas is being enhanced, for example through Estate Action schemes, and run-down council estates are being revitalised. Central support and sponsorship

The Government will continue to target areas of need for special action

Map of urban initiatives

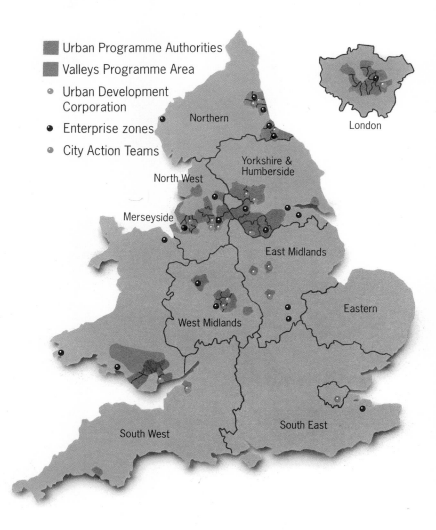

■ Urban Programme Authorities
■ Valleys Programme Area
● Urban Development Corporation
● Enterprise zones
● City Action Teams

Northern

London

Yorkshire & Humberside

North West

Merseyside

East Midlands

Eastern

West Midlands

South West

South East

are also given to provide good leisure facilities, including facilities for the arts, which not only provide direct employment and facilities for local people, but also attract tourism. Over 6 million people are expected to visit Glasgow in 1990 following its adoption as European City of Culture. The main aim of the programmes is to regenerate the local economy, and environmental improvement is a key element in the approach.

8.39 The Urban Programme and City Grant are good examples of parts of the programme designed to make a significant contribution to environmental improvement. This is in addition to the Government promoted National Garden Festivals in Liverpool, Stoke, Glasgow

The National Garden Festivals have reclaimed over 300 hectares of derelict land

and Gateshead (shown in the photographs) which have reclaimed over 300 hectares of derelict land in urban areas for profitable and attractive use, as well as drawing several million visitors.

8.40 Some 20% (or £45 million) of the resources of the Urban Programme, which is jointly funded by central and local government, is already spent directly on environmental improvements. Typical schemes include landscaping derelict and vacant land and improvements to commercial buildings, houses, walkways, parks and open spaces. Another feature of the Urban Programme is the emphasis that it places on harnessing the efforts of local people and community groups in improving their cities. In 1989/90 around £6 million of Urban Programme resources were spent on environmental schemes run by the voluntary sector. The Government has asked local authorities to give particular attention to the environmental effects of all projects put forward for funding in 1991/92.

8.41 Through encouraging redevelopment of derelict or neglected sites and buildings, City Grant makes a direct contribution to improving the urban environment. A typical project might involve refurbishing a building while retaining a listed facade, or clearing and redeveloping a major derelict area, giving opportunities to create whole new communities in developments containing both homes and jobs. The Government will shortly be issuing new guidance to developers who want to apply for City Grant, requiring them to submit fuller details of the environmental impact of their proposals, as well as their costs and economic benefits. This will make sure that the new schemes, many of which are for housing, provide a high quality of life for the people who live and work there.

Urban Development Corporations (UDCs)

8.42 The Government has created 11 Urban Development Corporations - independent bodies, generally with planning and funding powers, with the task of regenerating some of

The Government's urban
initiatives help improve
natural features of towns
like rivers and canals

the worst areas of dereliction in the country.

8.43 Landscaping, tree planting, and the
creation of public open space feature
prominently in the UDC programmes. The
aim is to enhance the quality of local people's
lives as well as encouraging more investment.
For example, Leeds UDC has planted
150,000 trees to date as part of landscape
improvements, and Teesside Development
Corporation is providing an international
nature reserve on local wetlands. So far,
UDCs have restored 1,300 hectares of
derelict land, with a further 360 hectares
targeted in 1990/91.

8.44 The Government is asking the UDCs
to pay particular attention to the contribution
that development can make to the local
environment, building on their success so far
in enhancing the natural environment in their
areas, for example by the refurbishment of
historic buildings and the positive use made
of waterscapes.

Further support for environmental improvement in towns

8.45 Urban initiatives in Wales, Scotland and
Northern Ireland are described in Chapters
19, 20 and 21. As well as programmes such as

Derelict Land Grant, described in Chapter 6,
which are of benefit to all areas, the
Government and its agencies also support a
range of specific local measures for urban
improvement. It is particularly eager to
support voluntary effort and is proposing an
initiative to promote this (see Chapter 18).
The Government is encouraged in this aim
by the success of the Groundwork Trusts.
There are currently over 20 of these Trusts in
England and Wales. They bring together
public agencies, private enterprise and
voluntary effort locally to achieve a wide
range of environmental improvements.
Central Government provides £2.3 million
to support Groundwork's administrative
expenses, as well as a range of project funding
– Urban Programme, Derelict Land Grant,
Countryside Commission grants – for the
Trusts. Trusts have shown that they can
mobilise effort and funds and deliver
significant environmental benefits at the local
level for relatively small public cost. The
Government is committed to further
expansion of the Groundwork network.

8.46 The Forestry and Countryside Commissions have jointly launched an important
initiative in developing urban or community
forests which improve the environment of
the urban fringe (see Chapter 7).

CONCLUSION

Government and local
people can work
together to improve
their local environment

8.47 This Chapter sets out how we can work towards making our towns and cities pleasant places in which to live and work which contribute fully to our wider environmental concerns. The Government wishes to see planning decisions which produce a better environment while helping other concerns – global warming, the countryside and the efficient use of resources. It wants the traffic in our towns to be civilised through a range of local measures. It will encourage good design in new buildings. And it will continue to support specific measures to help problem areas get back on their feet.

Research – towns and cities

Research on urban issues contributes to the understanding of the effects of urban land uses on the natural environment and supports Government policies to improve the urban environment and economy. Some examples are projects

• to understand the effects of traffic on the environment and communities, including people's perceptions, so that the environmental implications of new investment can be fully evaluated; to understand the causes of congestion on existing urban and interurban roads and how congestion and ways of relieving it affect communities and the environment; and to review practice for resolving conflicts over the use of road space in built-up areas, including assessment of the

performance of traffic calming techniques – Department of Transport (£1.25m in 1989/90)

• to minimise the effect of new transport investment on the environment and communities, for example by using noise barriers and quieter road surfaces; and to improve the efficiency of the existing network, for example by urban traffic control systems which cut congestion and pollution – Department of Transport (£1.1m in 1989/90)

• to inform policy and measures to regenerate inner cities, including assessment of the processes at work and developing best practice – Department of the Environment (£0.5m in 1989/90)

9

THE HERITAGE

Pride in our historic buildings encourages us to protect and improve the quality of the environment in which we live and work

INTRODUCTION

9.1 This Chapter sets out the Government's approach to preserving and enhancing our inheritance of historic buildings, sites and landscape.

9.2 Buildings, towns, monuments and other historic sites give us a sense of place. They remind us of our past, of how our forebears lived, and how our culture and society have developed. They tell us what earlier generations aspired to and achieved. They provide the context for new buildings, and for changes in our own way of life. They teach us lessons for the future.

9.3 The Government has direct responsibility for caring for many of the finest historic buildings and gardens in the land and strives to maintain them to the highest standard. They attract the admiration of millions of visitors from around the world. Yet by far the greatest part of our heritage is owned privately. Its preservation is due to the care shown by generations of individual owners.

9.4 Over the years the Government has built up a system of guidance, incentives and controls which protect and enhance our heritage. The Government believes this system has proved itself effective. Occasionally, of course, controversial

decisions arouse intense interest and comment. But the procedures allow full and public debate and make for an open and accountable process of decision making.

9.5 Perhaps more than in any other area of environmental policy, the secret of successful stewardship and care of our heritage is in the energy of private sector organisations and individual members of the public. Public interest in our heritage has never been greater. There are now over 1000 local amenity societies supported by the Civic Trust. Membership of the National Trust has grown from 0.9 to over 1.9 million over the last ten years and the Historic Houses Association now represents owners of 1300 historic houses and gardens. A number of local authorities have also joined together in the English Historic Towns Forum to develop understanding of the needs of such towns and share practical experience. Many authorities now have full time specialist conservation officers.

9.6 Government policy seeks to encourage these efforts. Where controls are necessary, it is careful not to stifle the natural desire of people to restore and improve the surroundings in which they live and work. The Government's policy for our heritage has

five main strands:
- looking after properties in Government care;
- promoting enjoyment and understanding of the heritage;
- encouraging private sector efforts, and making financial assistance available to help meet the extra costs of maintaining and restoring heritage property;
- identifying and recording the best of our heritage; and
- ensuring that the legislative system properly protects and preserves it.

9.7 This Chapter deals mainly with England, though many of the arrangements are similar in other parts of Britain. Chapters 19, 20 and 21 summarise what the Government is doing in Scotland, Wales and Northern Ireland. The Government relies on the expertise of a number of bodies in developing and implementing heritage policy. In England, the chief among these is English Heritage which was set up in 1984 to manage many of the monuments and buildings in public ownership, provide grants in support of heritage properties and advise the Secretary of State for the Environment on heritage matters.

PROPERTIES CARED FOR BY THE GOVERNMENT

9.8 The Department of the Environment maintains, on behalf of Her Majesty the Queen, the Palaces occupied by the Royal Family and the Royal Parks. Few buildings are more closely associated with the nation's heritage than Buckingham Palace and Windsor Castle. The great London parks like Regent's Park and St James's Park are attractive and restful places to relax in historic surroundings. The Government will continue to ensure that the use of the Royal Parks for events and leisure activities respects their historic fabric and traditional character.

Historic palaces and buildings

9.9 English Heritage manages some 400 castles, abbeys, historic houses and other sites and properties in England, which are open to the public. These include famous sites such as Stonehenge and Dover Castle, and less well known ones like Stott Park Bobbin Mill and Kirkham Priory. In 1989 they attracted about 5 million visitors. English Heritage spent about £11 million in caring for these properties in 1984/85. In 1990/91 it has allocated £34 million for this purpose. Through the Historic Royal Palaces Agency, the Government also manages five great historic buildings on behalf of Her Majesty the Queen: the Tower of London, Hampton Court Palace, the Banqueting House, Kensington Palace and Kew Palace.

Museums and galleries

9.10 The Government intends to bring the fine historic buildings which house our national museums and galleries into prime condition. It has allocated £180 million over the next three years to the building programmes of the national museums and galleries sponsored by the Office of Arts and Libraries. It also expects institutions to increase their own self-reliance by attracting private sponsorship and donations for major projects. A recent example is the substantial private sector support for renovation and repair work at the Sir John Soane Museum. Further substantial help will be available from the Museums and Galleries Improvement Fund, a joint initiative by the Wolfson Charities and the Government which will provide £12 million over the next three years.

The Government will continue to take great care of the Royal Parks and Palaces - like Kew Gardens

Government buildings

9.11 The Government owns many fine historic buildings which include offices, customs houses and military establishments. It has the opportunity to demonstrate by example, and Government Departments have direct responsibility for looking after their own historic buildings expertly and sensitively.

9.12 The Government constantly aims for the highest standards of conservation and will ensure that those responsible for its historic buildings are aware of the importance of the heritage they hold in trust. The Conservation Unit in the new Property Holdings organisation in the Department of the Environment offers expert advice to Government Departments both on individual projects and on conservation issues generally. Among many examples of recent restoration work of the highest quality was the refurbishment of offices in Richmond House for the Departments of Health and of Social Security and the restoration of the Victorian interior of the Foreign and Commonwealth Office building. PSA Services will continue to carry out much of this restoration and conservation work for the Government.

PROMOTING ENJOYMENT AND UNDERSTANDING OF THE HERITAGE

Our heritage can teach us about the past; our culture and institutions - they are lively places for learning

Education

9.13 English Heritage welcomed nearly 340,000 school visitors to their properties in 1989. They and the Historic Royal Palaces Agency have adapted their methods of presentation to present-day teaching objectives and techniques, providing more informative and colourful printed material and on-site education rooms. So far this has focused on the built heritage. The Government is now asking English Heritage and the Countryside Commission to develop their educational programmes, so as to make the public more aware of how the countryside, and historic landscapes, have evolved. It has invited English Heritage to prepare a register of landscapes and sites (such as battle fields) which have historic significance but where there are no longer any identifiable remains. Like the existing register of gardens of historic interest it will be informative, without direct legal effect. But through this register the Government, local planning authorities and others will be alerted to the significance of these sites when considering development plans and applications for planning permission.

9.14 The Government and its Commissions and agencies already publish a wide range of guides and educational material about our heritage. The Government has added a new pamphlet on the heritage to the Department of the Environment's successful 'Environment in Trust' series. It is designed as a readable guide to what public and private organisations are doing to preserve our heritage, and the enjoyment and interest our historic surroundings can provide.

Heritage and tourism

9.15 There has been concern recently that some of the most popular historic sites may be spoilt by over-visiting – by the wear and tear that results from the large numbers attracted to them at peak times, and by the facilities that have to be provided for them. The interest that overseas visitors and our own citizens are taking in the physical heritage is welcome, but it is also a management problem for the bodies in whose care the most popular sites happen to be. They are tackling the problem in a variety of ways – partly through visitor management, physical protection and admission charges, and partly by widening the range of heritage sites on offer to a public which is increasingly informed, discerning and ready to enjoy them. Together with the Regional Tourist Boards, and other public authorities, the heritage bodies also aim to spread visits to famous sites throughout the year. The effect of visitor numbers on some of the most popular sites is one of the main issues the Government's task force on tourism and the environment will consider (see Chapter 7).

A heritage forum

9.16 The Government is anxious to involve leading heritage experts more fully in the development of policies. It therefore proposes to set up a Ministerially chaired forum to discuss major heritage issues and opportunities. It will shortly announce the names of those invited to take part.

The Government has set up a task force to examine ways of making tourism kinder to the environment

ENCOURAGING PRIVATE SECTOR EFFORTS AND PROVIDING FINANCIAL ASSISTANCE

9.17 The main responsibility for maintaining our historic buildings and landscapes must rest with their owners. But heritage properties are expensive to maintain and financial help can sometimes be necessary to keep them properly.

Tax

9.18 Successive governments have recognised the importance of tax reliefs as a way of ensuring that we conserve and protect our national heritage for the benefit of the community as a whole.

9.19 The Government offers relief from capital taxes to encourage owners to keep and care for heritage property and to allow the public to visit. For example, in return for undertakings to preserve the property and allow access, exemptions from inheritance tax and reliefs from capital gains tax can be available for trust funds set up to provide for maintaining heritage property. The Government may also accept property in whole or part payment of a debt for capital transfer tax or inheritance tax. Many major works of art, which would otherwise have gone abroad, have remained in this country as a result. The growth in the value of acceptances to over £11.5 million in 1989/90 demonstrates the success of the scheme.

9.20 The Government will continue to offer such reliefs. It has improved the tax reliefs available for charitable covenants and introduced a new payroll giving scheme. From October 1990 it is making available a new tax relief on private and corporate charitable donations of between £600 and £5 million. This will be a major benefit to those many historic properties which are run by charitable trusts.

Grants

9.21 Central and local government also provide grants. In England the main source of public funding for the repair of historic buildings and monuments is English Heritage. They allocated £33 million for this in 1989/90 compared with an outlay of £11.9 million in 1979/80. Financial help is also available from the National Heritage Memorial Fund, set up in 1980. The Fund's aim is to prevent the loss to the nation of important works of art, historic documents and artefacts, land and buildings. It assists with negotiations and the raising of private funds to retain such items for the public to enjoy. As a last resort the Fund can offer grants and loans from the resources which Government provides – these now total £110 million since the fund's inception.

9.22 The Government will continue to provide such help and is examining proposals to fill a number of gaps in the present grant framework, as set out in the following sections.

Historic gardens

9.23 Britain has a great tradition of landscape gardens and other fine gardens. Grants are available for the most important architectural and structural features of these gardens, and English Heritage has introduced a scheme to make funds available to replace trees lost in the recent storms. County garden trusts continue to flourish and the Government welcomes the valuable work they do in protecting our gardens.

Historic buildings

9.24 The Government provides grants through English Heritage for the repair and restoration of nearly all kinds of buildings of architectural and historic interest. In future, English Heritage will give a high priority, within available resources, to buildings in historic town centres – houses, shops, market-halls and other buildings, many of which form part of conservation areas. These areas are readily accessible for large numbers of people to enjoy in their everyday life. They give character to surroundings and a sense of place, and show the continuity of the past with the present and the future.

Industrial heritage

9.25 The industrial revolution began in Britain, which pioneered and applied many of the technologies on which nineteenth and twentieth century development was based all over the world. Waterways, railways, shipbuilding, and modern merchant shipping were uniquely British in origin. Britain has contributed innumerable examples of advances in agriculture and medicine, and the techniques of civil engineering, aviation, defence, communications and computing.

Left: Britain has many fine historic gardens. English Heritage has funded tree planting following recent storm damage

Right: English Heritage supports the preservation and restoration of historic industrial buildings

This aspect of our national history – which we have shared with other western countries, themselves pioneers in many of these fields – is not as fully commemorated or as widely appreciated as it deserves to be. It is in the nature of economic development that successful methods of production are overtaken and the technology of each generation superseded and largely scrapped. Yet something of each major advance ought to be retained, as a record of achievement, as an inspiration for the future, and as a lesson in the nature of economic progress.

9.26 In recent years many private individuals and trusts have committed their efforts and enthusiasm to preserving some of the surviving remains of the industrial revolution, and to getting them back into working order. SAVE Britain's Heritage's recent book 'Bright Future' illustrates what has been achieved – and the opportunities that still remain for conserving industrial buildings. The Government believes that the enthusiasm and energy of private organisations and individuals can be harnessed to safeguard this part of our heritage. They will continue to have the support, in varying degrees and forms, from the National Museums, and from some local authorities. English Heritage has also made funds available for the preservation and restoration of mills, warehouses and industrial buildings, and structures of other kinds, and they will receive more attention in future.

Cathedrals

9.27 Historic churches and other historic places of worship which need help with repairs can receive grant from English Heritage. Cathedrals and other church buildings of comparable status have not in the past received such help because they have in general been well placed to raise all the necessary funds for repairs through public appeals. But sometimes there is a proven need which cannot be met by public appeal. The Government believes English Heritage grant should in principle be available in this event to cathedrals and comparable buildings of other denominations. This support cannot and should not replace individual giving,

which will remain the primary source of funding. The Government will discuss with English Heritage and the church authorities the way in which it can best offer support.

Redundant churches

9.28 In 1989 the Government commissioned a report from Mr Richard Wilding CB on the care of redundant churches. His report was published in May this year. The key proposed changes are:
• to give the Church Commissioners a more central role in steering the work of the Redundant Churches Fund (the body set up in 1969 to preserve Church of England churches of historical or architectural importance which are no longer needed for regular worship and are not suitable for alternative use). This would include the determination of policy, and the choice of priorities;
• to consider establishing a new funding scheme to assist the best redundant churches and chapels of other denominations, financed partly through Government and partly through private and charitable money.
The Government has welcomed the report and is consulting the Church authorities and other interested bodies on its proposals.

IDENTIFYING AND RECORDING THE HERITAGE

9.29 There is a very full system for recording our heritage, though some gaps remain. The Government is taking a number of steps to remove these.

The Royal Commission

9.30 Recording the historic monuments and structures of England in a national archive is the responsibility of the Royal Commission on the Historical Monuments of England. Many local authorities have also compiled lists for their local areas. These national and local records together comprise the country's database on archaeology and architectural history.

9.31 The Government has extended the Commission's responsibilities so that they now coordinate the efforts of County Councils and the Archaeological Trusts in preparing local Sites and Monuments Records; the aim is to compile records on a common basis. In England, the Government has provided extra funds to cover the costs of this growing programme of work, to aid the programme of recording, and to extend the National Monuments Record.

Listed buildings and scheduled monuments

9.32 The Secretary of State for the Environment has a duty to prepare statutory lists of buildings of special architectural or historic interest. The Government has just completed a systematic resurvey throughout England. The Government aims to make these records more widely accessible to the public and more usable. The Secretary of State may also schedule monuments which he considers to be of national importance, and English Heritage publishes lists of them in county volumes. Some 13,000 monuments have been scheduled in England. English Heritage is comprehensively assessing all known monuments to see whether more deserve to be scheduled.

World Heritage Convention

9.33 The World Heritage Convention was originally formulated by UNESCO and has two main purposes: to draw up a list of World Heritage sites which member states pledge to protect, and to operate the World Heritage Fund which gives practical support to conservation projects at threatened sites on the list. The Government gives its full support to the Convention. Thirteen sites in Britain have received recognition by the World Heritage Committee and more may be added in the future. Among existing sites are Hadrian's Wall and Durham Castle and Cathedral. The Convention also covers outstanding landscape sites such as St Kilda.

The legislative system

9.34 There is a mature and effective legislative system to protect our heritage which the Government will continue to operate and strengthen where necessary. It requires planning authorities to have regard

The Government has a programme to re-survey historic buildings. Many more buildings now enjoy the protection of listed building status

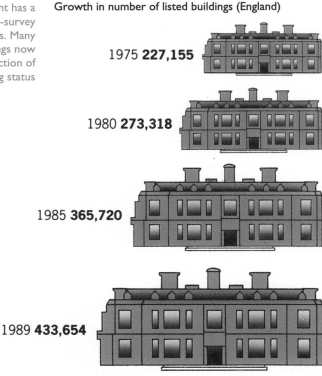

Growth in number of listed buildings (England)

1975 **227,155**

1980 **273,318**

1985 **365,720**

1989 **433,654**

to the setting of buildings of special architectural or historic interest – 'listed buildings' – when considering new development proposals which would affect them. The listed buildings themselves may not be demolished, altered or extended in a way which affects their character without the consent of the planning authority. Where a whole area is of special historic or architectural interest local authorities have powers to designate 'conservation areas'. Here consent is required before any building is demolished, and there are certain restrictions on the extent to which development can take place without specific planning permission. No works which are likely to affect or damage a scheduled monument may be carried out without consent from the Secretary of State for the Environment.

9.35 The Government wishes to ensure that local authorities, applicants and the general public have clear guidance on its policies for operating these controls. It is issuing a new Planning Policy Guidance note on archaeology and planning, aimed at reconciling the proper care of archaeological sites and development under the planning system. The Government will also shortly consult on new guidance on listed buildings and conservation areas. This will update existing guidance, and present it in a more accessible form.

Historic wrecks

9.36 The Government is responsible for identifying and protecting archaeological remains on the sea bed. It proposes that the Royal Commission on the Historical Monuments of England should begin work on a central record of historic wrecks. It intends the Commission to draw on the experience and expertise of the National Maritime Museum where appropriate. The Government also proposes to transfer from the Secretary of State for Transport to the Secretary of State for the Environment the designation of sites of historic wrecks in English waters and the licensing of diving and other activities around them. This will bring together control of archaeology on land with that under water. The Advisory Committee on Historic Wreck Sites and the Archaeological Diving Unit will offer advice on these new responsibilities. Similar transfers of responsibility will take place in Scotland, Wales and Northern Ireland.

Archaeology

9.37 The Government proposes to improve the legislation relating to archaeological

Below left: Britain has 13 World Heritage sites, including Hadrian's Wall

Below: The Government will consult on new planning guidance for listed buildings and conservation areas

The Government will
improve the legislation
on archaeological
monuments

monuments on land, including clarifying the
definition of damage to an ancient
monument and making it an offence to
remove objects from scheduled sites. It will
issue a consultation paper on these
amendments soon.

CONCLUSION

9.38 The Government has already done
much to improve the preservation of our
heritage, not least through creating the
National Heritage Memorial Fund and
English Heritage and by issuing
comprehensive guidance on listed buildings
and conservation area policy. More will now
be done to educate and involve the public in
our heritage. Grant programmes will reflect
new priorities, and the Government will give
assistance for repairs to cathedrals and similar
buildings. It will also strengthen the
legislation protecting scheduled monuments.
We have inherited many fine buildings and
landscapes from previous generations. These
measures build on the principles of good
stewardship already established and will
ensure our children can enjoy this inheritance
in the future.

BRITAIN'S APPROACH TO
POLLUTION CONTROL

Britain's new system of pollution control will regulate the most polluting processes

INTRODUCTION

10.1 Britain was the cradle of the industrial revolution, and industrial activity retains a central role in our economy. Industry has brought prosperity but also various forms of pollution. Despite the many advances which have been made, the quality of the air, land, rivers and coastal waters of our densely populated country is still under pressure from the very economic development which improves the quality of our lives in so many other ways. Subsequent chapters set out the Government's response to the threat of particular forms of pollution. This Chapter describes Britain's overall approach to pollution control and the principles which guide it.

Integrated pollution control recognises the interdependence of air, land and water. Pollution in one medium can affect the others

10.2 The Government applies the principles set out in the opening chapter. It takes a precautionary approach to the control of pollutants, relating the scale of effort to the degree of risks. It informs this approach with the best available scientific understanding and with sound economics. Its policy is to make available to the public full information about environmental issues and to involve the public in decision making. It recognises the international dimension of many environmental issues and works towards international solutions.

10.3 The Government's approach to pollution control is guided by a number of additional principles. It aims to:
- prevent pollution at source;
- minimise the risk of harm to human health and the environment;
- encourage and apply the most advanced technical solutions, while recognising the integrated nature of the environment and the need to achieve the best practicable option for the environment as a whole;
- apply a "critical loads" approach by assessing the levels of a pollutant which local environments can tolerate without significant damage, in order to focus protection on the most vulnerable environments; and
- ensure that the polluter pays for the necessary controls.

Integrated Pollution Control

10.4 The Government is uniting these principles in the system of Integrated Pollution Control (IPC). This will be applied to the most polluting industrial processes

Integrated pollution control

Her Majesty's
Inspectorate of Pollution
ensures that industrial
processes cause least
harm to the environment
as a whole

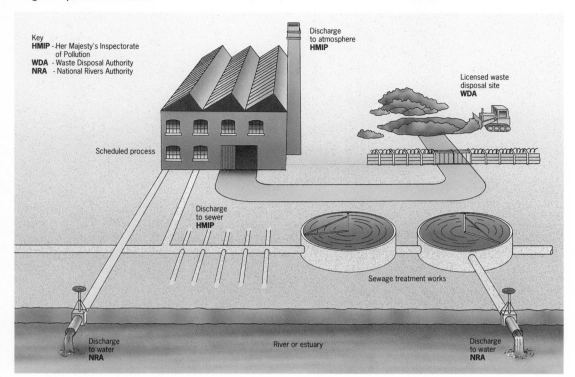

Key
HMIP - Her Majesty's Inspectorate
of Pollution
WDA - Waste Disposal Authority
NRA - National Rivers Authority

Discharge
to atmosphere
HMIP

Licensed waste
disposal site
WDA

Scheduled process

Discharge
to sewer
HMIP

Sewage treatment works

Discharge
to water
NRA

River or estuary

Discharge
to water
NRA

which have the potential to cause most harm to man and the environment.

10.5   Traditionally each sector of the environment – air, land and water – has had its own separate laws and systems of control. It has become increasingly clear in the 1980s that pollution in one medium can have implications in another. Burning fosssil fuels, for example, emits gases which can return to earth in acid rain, harming fresh-water life and reducing soil fertility. Heavy metals such as cadmium or lead, which are emitted into the air through combustion processes, can similarly return to the sea or land and find their way into our food chain.

10.6   Reducing disposal of waste to one medium may increase discharges of the same waste to another medium. As the Royal Commission on Environmental Pollution established, it is important to choose the method of waste disposal which causes the least overall damage to the environment. For example, flue gas desulphurisation involves a very substantial reduction in air pollution but some increased contamination of both land and water. On balance the overall impact on the environment of flue gas desulphurisation

is considered to be much less damaging than the air pollution which would take place without it.

10.7   Britain is going further than any other European country in introducing an integrated system of pollution control. The European Commission and several other countries have already shown interest in the strengths of IPC.

How IPC will work

10.8   In 1987 the Government took its first step towards realising the concept of IPC by forming Her Majesty's Inspectorate of Pollution (HMIP). This brought together three existing inspectorates, concerned with industrial air pollution, radioactive substances and hazardous wastes, and a newly created water pollution inspectorate. The creation of HMIP integrated pollution control institutions by forming a unified inspectorate capable of taking a cross-media approach.

10.9   Under IPC HMIP in England and Wales will control releases to air, water and land from the most polluting industrial processes. The Secretary of State for the Environment will prescribe the processes to be subject to IPC on the basis of published criteria. The regulation of pollutants from other sources will fall to the National Rivers Authority (NRA) (for water) and to local authorities (for air and land). Processes involving radioactive substances will continue to be controlled separately (see Chapters 11 and 15).

Advanced technical solutions

10.10 A significant feature of IPC is the application of advanced technical solutions. Potential polluters must curb the creation and discharge of wastes by applying the best available techniques which do not entail excessive cost (BATNEEC for short). This builds on the traditional British approach of Best Practicable Means in controlling air pollution and has won wide international acceptance.

10.11 Preventative action to limit environmental pollution is at the heart of IPC. Anyone wishing to operate a process which is subject to IPC will have to obtain prior authorisation from HMIP's Chief Inspector, who will set down specific

conditions which the operator must meet. The Chief Inspector will require the operator to use BATNEEC:
• to prevent or minimise the release of the most polluting substances;
• to render harmless all substances released; and
• to control releases in whichever way is best for the environment as a whole (the best practicable environmental option).
In addition, an authorisation will contain conditions which will require operators to comply with any relevant environmental quality objective and any relevant international requirement. Where there is a conflict between the requirements, the more stringent requirement will prevail. HMIP will set higher environmental standards as the available technology improves.

10.12 Potential polluters will have to pay for this control system. HMIP will recover the bulk of the costs of operating IPC by charging for authorisations.

Implementation of IPC

10.13 HMIP is now preparing some 200 guidance papers to inspectors on how to

Application of the most advanced technical solutions will minimise waste and curb pollution at source

Higher alcohols plant

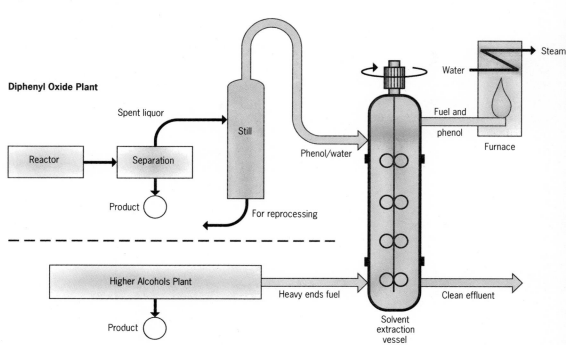

enforce the legislation controlling the most polluting industrial processes. These will cover about 5,000 industrial installations and will provide the most comprehensive pollution control guidance for those processes ever produced in this country. HMIP will publish the guidance papers so that industries can refer to them when applying for new authorisations.

Enforcement of standards

10.14 As an integral part of its pollution control strategy, the Government is committed to separating the powers of the producer and the regulator and to establishing strong environmental inspectorates. The Water Act 1989 created the National Rivers Authority, separate from the water companies, to enforce tough environmental standards (see Chapter 12). Chapter 18 descibes the Government's proposals for strengthening HMIP by making it an agency. The Environmental Protection Bill will reform waste disposal by local authorities according to the same principle of separation of powers, by creating new Waste Regulation Authorities, separate from waste disposal companies, responsible for licensing and enforcement (see Chapter 14).

Industrial processes subject to IPC will have to conform to high standards

The Environmental Protection Bill

10.15 The Environmental Protection Bill radically overhauls British pollution control systems. The promotion of IPC is the Bill's most important feature. It also introduces tighter environmental controls and stiffer penalties; it strengthens the power of HMIP and local authorities to control pollution; and it ensures for the first time that the public will have a systematic right of access to environmental information, including documents concerning authorisations made under IPC. Later chapters will cover other parts of the Bill in more detail.

The National Rivers Authority will control the discharge to water of less harmful pollutants. The effluent is treated before release

139

Environmental Protection Bill measures in the following Chapters

Chapter 11: Air Pollution
• new powers for local authorities to control air pollution from a range of less polluting processes.

Chapter 12: Marine Pollution
• new controls over the dumping of waste at sea.

Chapter 13: Hazardous Chemicals
• new powers to obtain information about hazardous chemicals and to control their use, storage and disposal;
• biotechnology – new controls over the release of Genetically Modified Organisms to the environment.

Chapter 14: Waste
• new powers to restrict trade in waste;
• stricter standards of control over waste disposal;
• a duty on local authorities to make plans for the recycling of waste;
• stricter penalties against litter louts;
• a duty on local authorities to keep public land free of litter.

Chapter 17: Knowledge
• access to information – a requirement that HMIP and local authorities keep copies of documents concerning authorisations under IPC and make these available to the public.

CONCLUSION

10.16 The Government is committed to preventing environmental pollution through the enforcement of rigorous environmental standards and the establishment of effective pollution inspectorates. Since the environment is a single, interconnected web, the new control systems aim to ensure that the most advanced technical solutions are applied in ways which achieve the best practicable option for the environment as a whole. The following chapters show how the Government applies these principles to control pollution of the air, water and land and from radiation and noise.

Research – Britain's approach to pollution control

Britain's approach to pollution control is based on a multi-media approach which seeks the best practicable environmental option in any particular case. Work on this aim is still at an early stage, but research will increasingly be directed towards ways of achieving it.

Public sector research relevant to Britain's approach to pollution control includes projects
• to support studies of the policy, planning and economic aspects of pollution control and environmental protection - Department of the Environment (£0.6m in 1989/90)
• to support the development of Integrated Pollution Control - Department of the Environment (£0.6m in 1989/90)
• to support a programme of environmental quality assessment using chemical and biological techniques with a view to identifying sources and types of inputs requiring control or reduction - Ministry of Agriculture, Fisheries and Food (£1.2m in 1989/90)

The Government is aiming for major improvements in Britain's air quality over the next decade

Air quality 1988

Air quality 2003

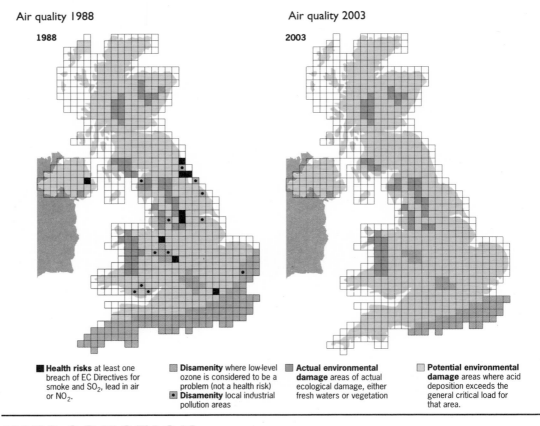

Health risks at least one breach of EC Directives for smoke and SO$_2$, lead in air or NO$_2$.

Disamenity where low-level ozone is considered to be a problem (not a health risk)

Disamenity local industrial pollution areas

Actual environmental damage areas of actual ecological damage, either fresh waters or vegetation

Potential environmental damage areas where acid deposition exceeds the general critical load for that area.

INTRODUCTION

11.1 This Chapter deals with the quality of the air we breathe, including the air in our homes and places of work. Nothing is so all pervading: good air quality is essential for human health and the health of the environment as a whole. Polluted air can seriously affect the quality of life, especially for those with asthma, bronchitis and similar breathing problems. It can damage historic buildings and kill sensitive plant life. In the long term it can even change our soil and water.

OUTDOOR AIR QUALITY

11.2 Little more than a generation ago, Britain's air was grossly polluted by smoke from domestic coal fires and from industry. The difference today is striking. The grime of the old urban smogs, and the health hazards that they brought, are things of the past. But if today's challenges are less glaring than those of the 1950s, they are still important. Smokeless zones and effective pollution control of industry have reduced local concentrations of pollutants, but the less obvious pollution from burning fossil fuels and from growing numbers of cars on our roads, still poses threats.

11.3 The Government's first priority is to ensure that statutory air quality standards set to protect public health are met throughout Britain. It is already very close to meeting this target, and will ensure that the remaining nine sites with elevated smoke, sulphur dioxide, nitrogen dioxide or lead concentrations are quickly brought within statutory standards.

11.4 It also intends to act against potential problems for the future. Levels of nitrogen dioxide - a contributor to acid rain - are increasing, especially in urban centres with growing vehicle emissions. The Government will tackle this in the European Community through new vehicle emissions standards. More vehicles and the wider use of certain organic chemicals in industrial processes and in every day life also threaten to increase levels of so-called 'photochemical smog'

Sources of emissions

Sulphur dioxide (SO₂)

Black smoke

Volatile organic compounds

Carbon Monoxide (CO)

Oxides of nitrogen (NOₓ) [1]

Domestic

Commercial/public service

Power stations

Refineries

Other industry

Road transport

Gas leakage

Forestry

Shipping

Railways

Processes/solvents

[1] expressed as Nitrogen dioxide equivalents

which first became notorious in Los Angeles. Pollutants which cause these problems can travel many hundreds of miles from their source, so the Government needs to act with its European partners to tackle them.

11.5 The Government also attaches great importance to combating the remaining local pollution problems. These arise largely from older technologies which currently fail to meet new standards. New powers will be available to the pollution inspectorates and local authorities under the Environmental Protection Bill to improve these plants.

11.6 Another important objective is to reduce acid emissions to a rate that is sustainable by the natural environment. Sensitive areas, such as North Wales, South West Scotland, or Southern Scandanavia, have been damaged over the last hundred years by acid rain often coming from sources many hundreds of miles distant. Once again the Government will need to act with its European partners to achieve effective controls.

11.7 The two maps at the head of this

Chapter show the present quality of Britain's air and the improvements for which we are aiming by the end of the century.

Standards

11.8 The Government intends action on air quality to be increasingly based on the definition of acceptable standards for the protection of health and the wider environment. There are at present three statutory air quality standards in Britain, which are also the subject of European Community Directives. These cover smoke and sulphur dioxide, lead in air, and nitrogen dioxide. The Government is strongly supporting the development of a further Directive setting guidelines for ground level ozone concentrations. The World Health Organisation (WHO) provides guidelines for a substantially larger number of pollutants. These are generally set at low levels, with substantial safety margins, intended to indicate to governments where new control strategies may be needed. The Government will establish an expert panel to advise on air quality standards in Britain.

11.9 For most air pollutants it is their concentrations in the atmosphere and the lengths of time for which concentrations are relatively high which is important. For other pollutants, notably those causing 'acid rain', what matters most is the total amount of the pollutant falling on a given area over a period. The level which a particular environment can tolerate without adverse effects is known as the 'critical load' of the pollutant.

11.10 The Government believes that development of an approach based on these 'critical loads' is central to further progress on the control of transboundary pollution of the kinds discussed in Chapter 3. Britain has taken a lead in developing this approach, and the Department of the Environment will have ready by the end of 1990 detailed maps showing the sensitivities of different parts of Britain to various pollutants. International inventories of emissions have also been taken and mathematical models have been developed to show how pollutants travel through the atmosphere. When all this information is brought together we shall be able to develop strategies for pollution control to protect particularly vulnerable environments and to give better value for our expenditure. Britain is collaborating closely with our partners in the UN Economic Commission for Europe (UNECE) on the critical loads approach: its feasibility should be established by the end of 1990 and by the end of 1991 a mathematical model should be ready using real data for both East and West Europe to provide a firm base for planning future pollution controls.

Monitoring

11.11 The first essential for implementing an air quality standard is a monitoring system. The Government has set up networks to monitor existing statutory standards and other pollution threats. These cost some £3 million to run. The information they provide is crucial in developing strategies to reduce pollution. There are networks of monitors to record levels for the three EC statutory standards (see 11.8). Other sites record levels of ground level ozone, acid rain, acid in water, and specific chemicals. The sites are carefully chosen to monitor areas where pollution is likely to be highest.

11.12 Key sites are already directly connected to the Department of the Environment, so that readings are immediately available. When there is a rise in levels, it makes the information public. The Government aims to expand the existing monitoring and modelling capability to plan for the future. We can already be confident that we have a good picture of the level of problem pollutants in Britain as a whole: the proposed expansion of the networks will give finer detail.

11.13 The Government will make information from its monitoring more widely available by including such information in weather bulletins. The Department of Health will provide guidance on whether those who might be affected by air pollution should be advised to take any special steps when levels are high.

The Government is helping to develop the critical loads approach illustrated below to target effective action on the areas of most need

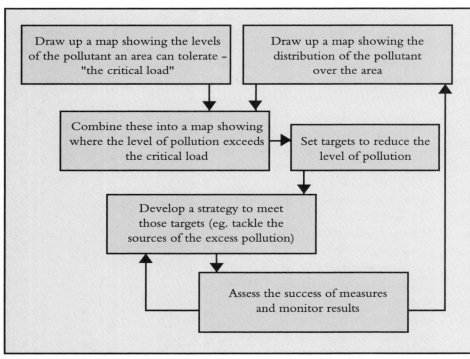

Draw up a map showing the levels of the pollutant an area can tolerate – "the critical load"

Draw up a map showing the distribution of the pollutant over the area

Combine these into a map showing where the level of pollution exceeds the critical load

Set targets to reduce the level of pollution

Develop a strategy to meet those targets (eg. tackle the sources of the excess pollution)

Assess the success of measures and monitor results

AIR POLLUTION CONTROL SYSTEMS

Pollution from industry

11.14 Britain's system for controlling air pollution from industry originated in the Alkali Acts of 1863 and 1874, which set up the Alkali Inspectorate. Its successors now form part of Her Majesty's Inspectorate of Pollution in England and Wales, Her Majesty's Industrial Pollution Inspectorate in Scotland and the Alkali and Radiochemical Inspectorate in Northern Ireland.

11.15 The previous Chapter describes the new approach to pollution control that the Government is proposing in the Environmental Protection Bill. As better air pollution control techniques become available without excessive cost, the new system will make their adoption compulsory, whether or not there is any specific evidence that harm is being caused. The Bill will pave the way for quicker application of new standards by obliging the Inspectorates to impose conditions which will ensure that air quality standards are met, international obligations are honoured, and the Government's plans implemented. The Bill will also improve the procedures for applying controls. It:
• gives improved enforcement powers to the Inspectorates, and new ones to local authorities;
• makes conditions in authorisations binding in law;
• gives the public an opportunity to comment before an authorisation is granted; and
• makes details of the controls imposed and of actual emissions from authorised plants available to the public locally.

11.16 As the new system takes effect, beginning in April next year, it will lead to a continuing long-term improvement in controls over air pollution from all major processes carried out on an industrial scale, and to a major strengthening of arrangements for informing and consulting the public about them.

Pollution from vehicles

11.17 Cars, lorries and other vehicles are an important and growing source of air pollution. Standards for new vehicles have to be agreed within the European Community before we can introduce them in Britain. As Chapter 3 mentions, Environment Ministers have recently agreed in principle that much tighter emission standards for cars should be in force by the end of 1992. A Directive covering small cars is now in place and the Government is pressing its European colleagues to agree on a Directive applying to larger cars as quickly as possible. We are also pressing for more progress in Europe on setting tighter standards for heavy diesel vehicles.

11.18 It is equally important to ensure that vehicles maintain acceptable standards not only when new but also throughout their lifetime. The Department of Transport will extend the MOT test to include a check on emissions to ensure that engines stay in tune. Heavy goods vehicles are checked visually for smoke from their exhausts in their annual tests and, between tests, they can be inspected at the roadside. The Government proposes more road side spot checks for heavy diesel vehicles. The Government will place considerable emphasis on the need to maintain good emission standards in licensing heavy goods vehicle operators and will be reminding them of this need. The public should let their local traffic area offices – which issue licences – know of unacceptably smoky heavy vehicles.

The Government is pressing in the EC for tighter standards and test procedures for emissions from heavy diesel vehicles

11.19 Cars tend to be most heavily used in their early years, so new standards have a rapid impact: roughly 10% of vehicles are new each year, and 44% of car miles are travelled by cars less than three years old. But new standards for heavy diesel vehicles, particularly buses, work through more slowly because these engines last much longer. It may be possible in some cases to improve the performance of old engines by fitting new technology, and the Government is examining the practicality of introducing tighter standards for such older vehicles.

11.20 The fuels used in vehicles affect the pollution produced. An integrated approach is necessary. The sulphur content of diesel fuel will have to be reduced to very low levels to enable heavy vehicles to meet future standards. The Government is pressing the European Commission for a commitment to this. Pollution from evaporating petrol will be much reduced by the proposed EC car standards, but the Government is committed to working with both vehicle and fuel industries to achieve further improvements.

Pollution from other sources

11.21 Pollution from domestic chimneys is controlled by the Clean Air Acts, under which local authorities create smoke control zones where only certain fuels may be burned. The Control of Pollution Act and Public Health legislation cover other sources of pollution. For example, they provide powers to control the sulphur content of liquid fuels for central heating and industry, and provisions to control air pollution from agriculture and nuisance pollution such as bonfires.

SMOKE

11.22 Britain led the world in smoke control. The Clean Air Acts of 1956 and 1968 have prevented many thousands of premature deaths from bronchial illness and changed our cities for the cleaner and better, as the figure opposite shows. Average visibility on a winter's day in London has increased from one-and-a-half to four miles. The Clean Air Act concept has been adopted by many other countries and has laid the basis for air quality standards now set on a European scale in an EC Directive. Except for the areas shown on the map at the head of this Chapter - mainly coal-mining areas where coal fires are traditional - Britain's air quality complies fully with agreed EC standards, and the Government will ensure

that these few remaining areas comply at the latest by the date allowed for compliance in the EC Directive (April 1993).

11.23 Local authorities can give grant to householders to help them pay for new boilers and fires in newly-declared smoke control zones. In certain existing smoke control areas, however, standards are in danger of erosion through illegal use of coal, often sold from local shops and garages. The Government is considering using powers in the Environmental Protection Bill to reduce this problem by banning sales of unauthorised fuels in smoke control areas.

11.24 Another source of smoke in some areas - straw and stubble burning - will be tackled by measures which the Government has already announced, leading to a ban by 1993 in England and Wales.

11.25 The remaining major source of smoke is diesel engines. The first standard for vehicle emissions was a limit on smoke. This was set in the early 1970s. Britain has sought over the years to persuade our European Community partners to tighten this old smoke standard. Of more recent concern are the smaller particles in diesel exhaust fumes ('particulates') that

Britain's air quality has improved substantially since the era of the London smogs

Average urban smoke concentrations

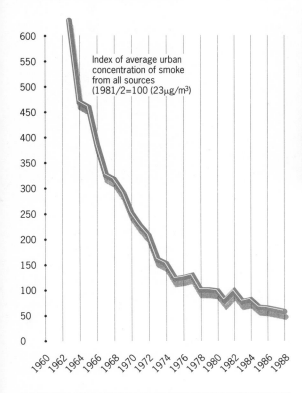

Index of average urban
concentration of smoke
from all sources
(1981/2=100 (23µg/m³)

11.26   The Government does not believe that the Commission's present proposals go far enough. They set new limits in two stages, which will affect new vehicles first from 1992/3, and then from 1996/7. The Government is content with the limits for Stage I, but not with Stage II. It has urged the Commisson to set standards and test procedures for this second stage as close as possible to the US 1994 standards, which are the strictest to be applied anywhere in the world at present.

have been identified as a possible contributor to cancer. There is a strict limit on these emissions from diesel engined cars. The European Commission has now made proposals to set stricter limits on emissions from heavy diesel vehicles, such as lorries, buses and coaches. For the first time the proposals include standards for the emission of particulates.

11.27   These controls will ensure that vehicles meet high standards when new. The Government will also introduce tougher testing and increased monitoring for emissions from diesels to minimise deterioration from these standards. As a first step, a thorough review is under way of the methods of testing emissions from heavy diesels.

ACID RAIN

11.28   Some air pollution crosses national boundaries, and calls for concerted action based on international agreement. This is true in particular of the group of pollutants which form acid rain.

11.29   The term is loosely used to describe both acidic gases in the atmosphere and, more precisely, rain, mist or snow containing acid compounds of sulphur and nitrogen. Two main gases contribute to the formation of acid rain: sulphur dioxide (SO_2), produced by burning fossil fuels which contain sulphur, such as coal and oil; and oxides of nitrogen (NOx), which are formed when anything is burnt. The formation of acids from these gases and the way in which they move

through the atmosphere are also affected by other pollutants, including ozone. The main sources of sulphur dioxide and oxides of nitrogen are power stations which burn fossil fuels, other large industrial combustion plant and motor vehicles.

11.30   Tall chimneys have largely solved the problem of intense local ground-level pollution around factories. Pollutants can however be carried long distances by winds, and lead to problems for neighbouring countries. For example, Scandinavian countries emit relatively low quantities of sulphur dioxide and NOx: most of their acid rain comes from neighbouring countries. Studies show that 17-27% of sulphur

deposited on Finland comes from the Soviet
Union; East Germany is responsible for 11–
17% of sulphur deposited on Denmark and
(due to prevailing winds) Britain is
responsible for 9–12% of sulphur deposition
in Norway. This shows why action on such
pollution needs to be agreed internationally,
through the EC, which sets standards in
Directives, and through the United Nations
Economic Commission for Europe
(UNECE) which covers the whole of Europe
and has an international Convention on long
range transboundary air pollution.

11.31 Acid rain can have a number of
adverse effects.
• By increasing the acidity of surface waters,
acid rain can kill fish and other freshwater
life. This effect, first noted in Scandanavia,
led to initial concern about acid rain. Similar

effects have also occurred in parts of Britain.
• For centuries, acids from air pollution have
contributed to the deterioration of buildings,
particularly in urban areas. Despite falling
concentrations of sulphur dioxide in these
areas, many buildings, some of historic
importance, are still deteriorating, in part
due to the continuing effects of past air
pollution.
• The effects of air pollution on trees in
Britain are still not fully understood. But acid
rain probably places additional stress on trees
which are close to their survival limit and
extreme levels of acidic air pollution from
Eastern Europe have undoubtedly damaged
and killed trees in some eastern areas of West
Germany.
• Acid rain can impoverish wildlife habitats.
Damage to one part of the food chain can
have effects higher up. For example, changes
in the numbers of insect larvae in streams can
affect the population of insect-eating birds.
This has already been seen to have an effect
on rare species such as the dipper.
• Nitrogen compounds such as NOx and
ammonia act as plant nutrients as well as
causing acidification. Excess nitrogen is
damaging the mosses which form peat in
some upland areas of Britain.

11.32 The effects of acid rain vary
enormously according to the type of soil on
which it falls. Alkaline soils based on
limestone can neutralise large amounts of
acid, whereas peat or granite soils have very
little ability to do so. The problem first came
to light in Scandanavia because its geology
makes it especially sensitive to the effects of
acid rain. Similar conditions and problems are
found in parts of upland Britain.

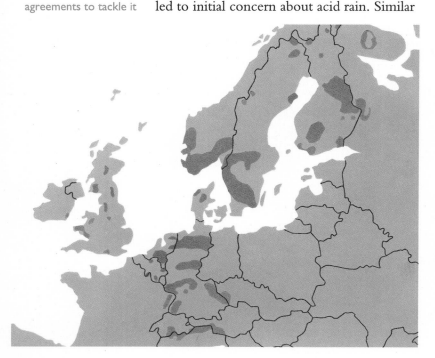

11.33 Acid rain is not a direct threat to human health in Britain, though acid gases in high concentration can be a hazard for people with bronchial and asthmatic conditions. By contrast the very high levels of air pollution in parts of Eastern Europe are known to have caused serious health problems.

Reducing sulphur dioxide

11.34 The Government has responded decisively to the threat of acid rain. Emissions of sulphur dioxide in Britain have declined significantly in recent years – by about 24% from 1980 levels and by almost 40% from 1970 levels. There are firm indications that this is already leading to an improvement in acidity levels in lochs in Southern Scotland. The Government has a substantial programme of action in hand to ensure that this trend continues.

11.35 Over 70% of Britain's emissions of sulphur dioxide come from power stations. The European Community is tackling the problem across the EC through the Large Combustion Plants Directive, which also includes other large boilers, accounting in all for 85% of our emissions. The Directive has stringent emission standards for new plants and sets a schedule for reductions from existing plants. Taking 1980 levels as the baseline, Britain has made legally binding commitments to cut emissions of sulphur dioxide from existing plants by 20% in 1993, 40% in 1998 and 60% in 2003.

11.36 The total investment of the electricity supply industry both on new, clean plant and new equipment for older plant over the next decade will be over £6 billion and will ensure that Britain meets its commitments under the Directive. Equipment to remove sulphur from flue gases is being fitted to some large power stations. This increases emissions of CO_2 slightly, and an alternative approach is to switch some power generation from coal to gas. This is happening increasingly as a result of investment prompted by privatisation. This will both reduce our emissions of sulphur dioxide (and NOx) and help to reduce carbon dioxide emissions, and so help reduce the greenhouse effect.

11.37 In 1984, the Government adopted the aim of reducing annual sulphur dioxide emissions from all existing sources by 30% on 1980 levels by the year 2000. We are on target to meet that objective and more. By 2003, total emissions should be 50% lower than in 1980. We can already see evidence that some sensitive environments in South West Scotland have begun to recover from the long term acidification they have suffered, though full recovery will take some time.

11.38 Britain and fellow EC Member States will review the Large Combustion Plants Directive in 1994. In doing so, the Government will assess the progress made in reducing sulphur dioxide emissions and measure this against the latest scientific understanding of the effects of acid rain, including the critical loads approach, and the need to reduce emissions of greenhouse gases.

11.39 Britain will also take a positive part in the revision of an existing UNECE Protocol on sulphur dioxide emissions. The new agreement should be based on the critical loads approach. The Government will be working hard with countries in both East and West Europe to agree on longer-term targets which will be both challenging and achievable.

Oxides of nitrogen

11.40 Parallel action is in hand on oxides of nitrogen (NOx) which come chiefly from large combustion plant and vehicles. In 1984 Britain set itself the ambitious policy aim of achieving a 30% reduction from 1980 levels by the end of the 1990s. Since then there has been substantial growth in road traffic which will make achieving this aim more difficult, but it remains an aim for which to strive.

Acid rain damages buildings as well as harming marine, plant and animal life

The emissions which cause acid rain come chiefly from power stations and road traffic

The Government's measures will greatly reduce the emissions which cause acid rain over the next decades

Emissions of sulphur dioxide (SO2) and nitrogen oxide (NOx) 1970 – 2000 (million tonnes)

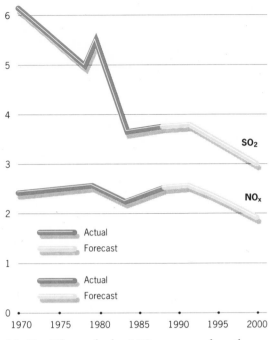

11.41   Through the NOx protocol to the UNECE convention, Britain is committed along with 25 countries across East and West Europe and North America, to freezing overall national emissions of NOx at 1987 levels by 1994. This applies to all sources of emissions. This protocol, which Britain signed in 1988, also commits us to developing further programmes for longer term reduction based on critical loads.

11.42   Within the European Community, the Large Combustion Plants Directive commits us to reducing NOx emissions from existing plant by 15% by 1993 and 30% by 1998. This will be achieved – in part by fitting low NOx burners to major coal fired power stations in Britain. The proposed tough new EC standards for passenger cars will require that from the end of 1992 emissions of NOx from each new car will be reduced by 75%. The standards will require all new petrol engined cars to be fitted with catalysts which will generally give greater than 75% reductions.

There will be a cost to the British motorist – perhaps £250–£500 a car – but there will be substantial environmental benefits as the number of cars fitted with catalysts grows, not least in urban areas where vehicles account for up to 85% of nitrogen dioxide emissions. Levels there should reduce by over a half by 2000. The Government will encourage fleets and individuals to buy cars equipped with catalysts in advance of the EC requirements, to reduce the current growth in emissions.

11.43   The amendments to the EC Directive on emissions from large diesel vehicles for which Britain is pressing, will reduce emissions of oxides of nitrogen as well as smoke. Diesel vehicles are now responsible for half of the emissions of oxides of nitrogen from road transport in Britain, and this proportion is set to rise rapidly once EC agreements on cars and light vans come into effect. The very features of diesel engines which make them so fuel efficient rule out using catalysts to remove NOx. Nevertheless, the Government is urging the Commission to adopt high standards for heavy diesels which will impel manufacturers to develop the necessary engineering solutions to achieve substantial reductions.

Ammonia

11.44   Ammonia is not an acid itself but can have similar effects in the soil. Ammonia emissions and deposition are not yet well understood although livestock farming is an important source. Atmospheric ammonia can contribute significantly to nitrogen inputs in some regions, providing up to two thirds of the deposited nitrogen. The Government is currently reviewing the effect of ammonia deposition on the environment through the Terrestrial Effects Review Group. The Government is also funding research which is looking at ways of curbing ammonia emissions from animal wastes and fertiliser use.

GROUND LEVEL OZONE

11.45   As the international community has developed measures to curb acid rain, concern in Europe has spread to a second air pollution problem which crosses national

boundaries: photochemical smog. This is a complex chemical mixture but its most important component is ground level ozone. (This is not to be confused with the beneficial layer of ozone in the upper atmosphere which absorbs some of the sun's harmful ultra-violet rays: see Chapter 4).

11.46 The action of sunlight on a mixture of NOx and volatile organic compounds (known as VOCs) leads to the formation of ground level ozone. Some VOCs come from natural sources, trees for example. But most are the result of human activity: chemical factories, cars and solvents in paints are all sources. The chemical reactions producing ozone are quite slow, so this pollutant builds up in polluted air over several days under suitable weather conditions. This air often comes from continental Europe and the problem is concentrated in southern England.

11.47 Ground level ozone has two kinds of harmful effects.
• High concentrations of ozone are harmful to human health and can exacerbate breathing disorders. Levels in Britain are generally substantially below this, though in hot summers several northern European cities – including London – can exceed the World Health Organisation guidelines for ozone levels. Peak levels in Britain rarely exceed 120 parts per billion (ppb), the standard aimed at in the USA. Readings over 300 ppb have occurred in Switzerland and Austria, and over 600 ppb in the USA. The highest value ever recorded in Britain is 250 ppb (in 1976).
• Ozone can be harmful to crops and trees. It is almost certainly responsible for some of the damage to forests in continental Europe, Scandinavia and North America.

Action on ozone

11.48 Because NOx plays a large part in the formation of both acid rain and ground level ozone, measures that Britain and her partners have taken to reduce acid rain also help to reduce ground level ozone.

11.49 The Government anticipates that peak ozone concentrations will still be above World Health Organisation guidelines through much of Europe if only NOx and car VOC emissions are tackled. To meet the guidelines, further action will be needed to control other sources of VOCs including the solvents used in paints, glues and varnishes, petrol evaporation and oil industry emissions. The Government is committed to developing this action quickly with our European partners, with the aim of reaching WHO guidelines by the end of the century.

11.50 Britain is taking a leading part in a Working Group of UNECE which is preparing a Protocol on VOCs. There is a wide recognition within UNECE of the urgent need to agree an action programme. The Government is urging that long-term action should be based on the critical loads approach, and although short-term action will have to be more pragmatically based, it should be designed to be as effective as possible. Different VOCs differ enormously in their potential to form ozone. Control measures should, in the Government's view, be targeted on the most damaging compounds. An indiscriminate percentage cut which reduced the least damaging emissions would deliver little environmental benefit.

11.51 Britain is supporting a European Commission initiative to complement the UNECE Protocol with an EC Directive. This will put an obligation on member states to monitor ozone levels and to set air quality guidelines.

In some countries ground-level ozone is a major health threat. Britain wants early action to reduce levels in Europe

LEAD

11.52 Lead is a toxic metal which can accumulate in the environment and in the body. In 1983, the Royal Commission on Environmental Pollution recommended a number of measures to reduce the amount of lead in the air. They did so on the grounds that the average blood-lead concentration of the British population was too high, even at about a quarter of the level at which signs of lead poisoning can occur. One of their recommendations was to reduce the amount of lead in petrol and to introduce unleaded petrol. Regulations reduced the permitted amount of lead in petrol by over 60% from the end of 1985.

Lead in air has fallen markedly thanks to less use of lead in petrol

Unleaded petrol - Market share

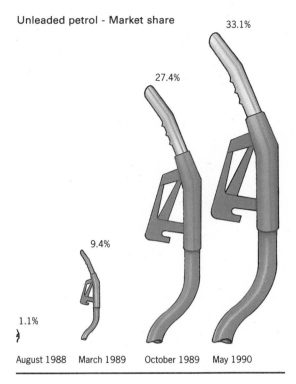

1.1%

August 1988 March 1989 October 1989 May 1990

9.4%

27.4%

33.1%

Ambient lead concentrations – average of UK network data

microgrammes per cubic metre

2.0 — EC Lead in Air Directive limit value

1.5

1.0

0.5

0

1985 1986 1987 1988

Britain has played a leading part in making unleaded petrol widely available within the EC

Availability of unleaded petrol in Europe (% of outlets)

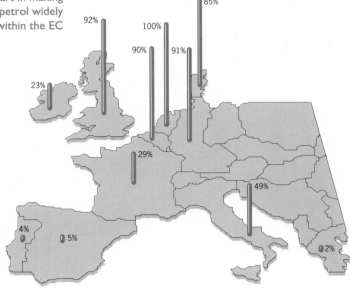

85%

92%

100%

90%

91%

23%

29%

49%

4%

5%

2%

shown how in the right circumstances environmental improvements can be achieved through the market, especially if tax incentives are combined with regulatory measures and greater information to the public.

11.54 The amount of airborne lead recorded at the Government's monitoring sites has now fallen by about 50% from levels in the early 1980s. An EC Directive on vehicle emissions includes a requirement that from 1 October 1990 all new cars must be capable of using unleaded petrol. Cars with catalysts must use unleaded petrol and, since new emission limits will shortly mean catalysts will have to be fitted to all new cars, use of unleaded fuel will be almost universal by 2000.

11.53 The Government took the lead in agreements within the EC on standards for unleaded petrol (agreed in 1985), and on making the fuel generally available throughout Member States' territories (by 1989). Unleaded petrol is now available throughout this country and the Government has encouraged its use with tax incentives. Sales of the new fuel have risen from nil at the beginning of 1987 to a market share of about 35% – and are still growing. This has

11.55 Certain industrial processes also release lead into the air. Extensive Government monitoring around all major sources has recorded levels of lead in excess of the limit set by the EC Directive on lead in air at only one site – a copper smelting plant in the West Midlands. Action has now been taken to bring the site into compliance with the limit within the time allowed in the Directive. By the end of the decade, as the use of unleaded petrol increases, the levels of lead in urban areas should fall by a further 40% – well inside international health standards.

CARBON MONOXIDE

11.56 Carbon monoxide (CO) is produced by incomplete combustion of fuel. It is poisonous and at moderate concentrations can cause drowsiness and impair mental and physical alertness. In Britain 85% of carbon monoxide emissions come from car exhausts. Concentrations have crept up over recent years, despite improvements in vehicle standards, as the levels of traffic and traffic congestion have grown. The introduction of new EC standards from the end of 1992 will require emissions from individual vehicles to be reduced by 75%. Catalyst fitted cars are likely to better this figure. This will be reinforced through tougher MOT testing. By the end of the decade, urban concentrations of CO should fall by over a half, taking peak levels below the WHO Guidelines.

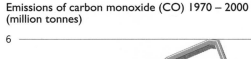

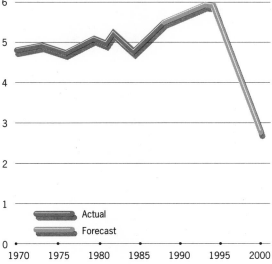

Emissions of carbon monoxide (CO) 1970 – 2000 (million tonnes)

OTHER POLLUTANTS

11.57 Many other pollutants which presented problems for our air in the past – notably heavy metals other than lead, such as cadmium and mercury – have declined as industry has modernised.

11.58 Recently attention has focused on newer pollutants such as polychlorinated bi-phenyls (PCBs) and dioxins (see Chapter 13).

11.59 The only satisfactory way to destroy PCBs and dioxins is through high temperature incineration. Incineration is also often the best method of disposing of much less dangerous wastes, taking all environmental effects into account. Yet poorly controlled incinerators can themselves emit traces of dioxins and other pollutants such as heavy metals and acids. Britain is commited to implementing EC Directives applying strict combustion controls and emission limits for incinerators: municipal waste incineration is already the subject of two EC Directives and the Government is pressing for early finalisation of a similar Directive on toxic and dangerous waste incineration – a field in which Britain has expertise and high standards. From next Spring all incinerators will be brought into the new pollution control system and the Government will remove Crown immunity from prosecution from National Health Service hospitals. By the end of the 1990s all municipal, hospital and toxic waste incinerators will meet extremely strict emission standards.

RESEARCH

11.60 The Government is firmly committed to a comprehensive research programme into all aspects of air pollution to provide the sound scientific basis needed for effective pollution control. The Government will sponsor over £6.8 million of research into local and transboundary air pollution in 1990/91 through the Department of the Environment's air pollution research programme, as well as fundamental research under Research Council funding. A selection of current projects is shown at the end of this Chapter.

11.61 The Government has several groups of independent scientific experts which monitor developments in air pollution research and recommend areas for changes in the Government's research programme. They cover such issues as ground level ozone and the effects of acid rain on buildings, vegetation and fresh waters.

11.62 The air pollution research programme makes a strong contribution to international work programmes. The UNECE has established the European Monitoring and Evaluation Programme as a primary basis for its work, and also a range of International Co-operative Programmes directed at particular effects of pollution. Britain supports all these programmes and is the lead country for the work on effects of pollution on crops. British researchers also contribute to European Community collaborative programmes.

INDOOR AIR QUALITY

Introduction

11.63 On average people spend 90% of their time indoors. 75% of that time is spent at home. Because buildings are closed environments, the threat posed by pollutants, if they are allowed to build up in sufficient quantities, can be significant. Radon, tobacco smoke and carbon monoxide can kill.

11.64 The Government's first priority is to find out the potential dangers, monitor levels of pollution in buildings and assess if there are any risks to people's health. It then controls the design of buildings and products to reduce those risks. Many pollutants are introduced into buildings by people themselves, by smoking, DIY and hobbies, so the Government also makes information available so that people can make choices about the way they live and the effects that this might have on their health.

11.65 Our understanding of indoor air pollution is constantly changing: the Government will take strong action to counter new risks from indoor air pollution.

Sources of indoor air pollution

11.66 The principal sources of indoor air pollution are :
• materials used in a building or in its construction;
• people's activities and household products;
• appliances and fires burning fossil fuels;
• emissions from the ground;
• damp conditions causing growth of mould and mites.

Reducing the risk

11.67 The Government has taken and will continue to take steps to minimise the dangers posed by indoor pollution, based on thorough research and a programme of specific measures. These include:
• improving standards in new buildings, principally by means of controls and guidance under the Building Regulations;
• improving conditions in existing housing, through targeted improvement programmes;
• controlling products which can give rise to pollution; and
• educating people on the risks and how to reduce them.

POLLUTION FROM THE BUILDING

11.68 Building materials and house contents can give rise to pollutants, albeit often at low levels. For example the colourless gas, formaldehyde, which can irritate the nose and eyes, may be given off from glues used in wood products (eg chipboard), and from some cavity wall insulation, floor coverings and fabrics. There are two main means of controlling pollution from the building - controls over the design and construction, and controls over the products used.

11.69 Building design can help to prevent pollutants from entering a building and make sure pollutants which do enter the building are dispersed quickly. The Building Regulations set out these requirements. The Government has recently amended the Building Regulations to introduce enhanced standards of ventilation for new dwellings.

Ventilation of a typical house

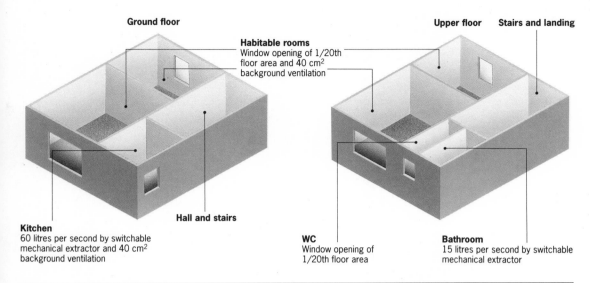

Ground floor

Upper floor **Stairs and landing**

Habitable rooms
Window opening of 1/20th floor area and 40 cm² background ventilation

Hall and stairs

Kitchen
60 litres per second by switchable mechanical extractor and 40 cm² background ventilation

WC
Window opening of 1/20th floor area

Bathroom
15 litres per second by switchable mechanical extractor

These requirements are intended to reduce accumulation of pollutants indoors and also to control levels of water vapour to reduce dampness. The Government keeps the regulations under review and strengthens them where necessary, for example to keep up to date with knowledge of such pollutants as radon (see below).

11.70 The Building Regulations 1985 require building work to be carried out with proper materials. This means that they must be fit for their purpose in terms of health and safety. Ways in which this can be demonstrated include conformity with an appropriate British Standard and the certification of a product by the British Board of Agrement (which approves new products and confirms certification from other countries). There are also specific requirements about the way in which certain wall insulation materials are manufactured and installed, which are intended to avoid the risk of formaldehyde fumes, for example, entering the building.

11.71 The EC Construction Products Directive provides for the development of European technical specifications for construction products. Products must enable the building to be constructed in such a way that it will not be a threat to the hygiene or health of the occupants. Risks that are

specifically referred to include:
• giving off toxic gas;
• the presence of dangerous particles or gases in the air;
• faulty elimination of smoke; and
• the presence of damp.
The Government and industry are making a substantial contribution to the development of these technical specifications. The Government bans substances and products found to present a health risk.

11.72 For older properties, where new building regulations can have no effect, the Department of the Environment issues advice leaflets on indoor air pollution issues. These currently cover radon, asbestos, mould and damp. It also provides more detailed advice to local authorities which environmental health officers can use to provide further information and advice to householders. The Department of the Environment will shortly produce a general leaflet for householders on indoor pollution, outlining the main risks and how to avoid them.

Sick building syndrome

11.73 Sometimes there can be a higher incidence of sickness for no readily identifiable reason amongst people who work in certain buildings - 'sick building syndrome'. There is no specific link between

The Government offers advice on the main sources of indoor pollution

Legionella bacteria can endanger life: the Government is working to improve controls further

any particular indoor air pollutant and sick building syndrome - the causes are varied. Investigation is difficult because the reported symptoms are usually mild and are indistinguishable from symptoms which might be caused by factors other than the building's internal environment. The Building Research Establishment is undertaking a programme of research into causes and remedies.

11.74 The Health and Safety Executive (HSE), which together with local authorities has responsibility for ensuring the safety of workplaces, has published guidance on sick building syndrome, and suggested various measures to reduce it. Symptoms may, for example, be reduced by increasing the fresh air circulation in the building. The work has been widely used by HSE inspectors and employment medical advisers called to advise on individual cases. HSE also publishes guidance on ventilation of the workplace which provides information on standards for fresh air.

Legionnaires' disease

11.75 A specific health hazard which can be transmitted through the air, not necessarily just indoors, is Legionnaires' disease. People catch this disease by inhaling airborne water droplets contaminated by Legionella bacteria. There are around 200-250 cases each year in Britain, many following infection abroad, but other outbreaks of the disease have been associated with hot water services, and particularly external tanks on buildings.

11.76 The Health and Safety Executive has published guidance on Legionnaires' disease and the Health and Safety Commission has recently gone out to consultation on proposals to strengthen existing legislation and guidance applying to the control of the disease. They are currently considering the results of this consultation. The Government has also set up a Working Group to review existing provisions for control and to advise on longer term action.

PEOPLE'S ACTIVITIES

Smoking

11.77 Smoking is a major source of many indoor pollutants. Tobacco smoke indoors can increase the likelihood of respiratory illness in children and the risk of contracting lung cancer among non-smokers. Several hundred lung cancer deaths a year may be attributable to such 'passive' smoking. Thanks to increased awareness of the problem, smoking is now restricted in many public places. The Government will shortly publish new guidance on best practice in segregating smokers and non-smokers to encourage this trend further.

11.78 Smoking also increases the danger posed by other pollutants - the risk from radon (below) is estimated to be ten times greater for someone who smokes 15 cigarettes a day than for a non-smoker.

Use of household and DIY products

11.79 Many products such as oven cleaners, paint stripper and glues contain hazardous

chemicals. Although they are safe if used as the manufacturer instructs, they can present problems if used in confined unventilated spaces. Manufacturers are required to indicate on the packaging what types of problems can arise and how to avoid them.

Care of appliances and fires

11.80 Inadequate air supply or ventilation for appliances such as gas or solid fuel fires can result in lethal concentrations of carbon monoxide. This causes as many as a hundred deaths a year. Lower levels of carbon monoxide, for example from poorly ventilated gas cookers or open fires, can lead to lethargy and lack of concentration.

11.81 If appliances are properly installed and subsequently maintained and serviced, they should not cause carbon monoxide poisoning. There are requirements in the Building Regulations 1985 to ensure that heat-producing appliances are capable of being operated without the products of combustion becoming a hazard to health.

The Gas Safety (Installation and Use) Regulations 1984 provide for the proper installation of flues where appropriate and the correct provision of ventilation. They also require that such work should be undertaken by a competent fitter.

Left: Smoking can increase the dangers posed by other pollutants

Right: Government regulations require fires to be properly installed

GROUND EMISSIONS

Radon

11.82 Radon is a naturally occurring radioactive gas produced from the radioactive decay of uranium, found in small quantities everywhere, but especially in areas of granite rock. Radon disperses quickly in the open, but can accumulate inside buildings. These accumulations can cause damage to the lungs and increase the risk of lung cancer. Recent estimates suggest that as many as one in twenty lung cancer cases in Britain might be caused by exposure to radon in the home.

11.83 The Government recommended action to reduce radon in houses in 1987, and set an action level above which precautionary measures were recommended. In view of the latest research on radiation dangers, the Government announced in January 1990 that the action level should be halved, to an annual average concentration of 200 becquerels per cubic metre. The National Radiological Protection Board (NRPB), which advises Government on radiation protection standards in Britain, calculates that radon and thoron (a form of radon) contribute 51% of the average annual radiation dose to the British population. Britain's action level is lower than those proposed elsewhere in the European Community and it is ahead in its programme of research and surveys.

11.84 The Government is pursuing urgently research into the methods of reducing radon entry into existing houses, or of removing it once it has entered. This can be done in three main ways. In most cases for best results a combination of two or more techniques may

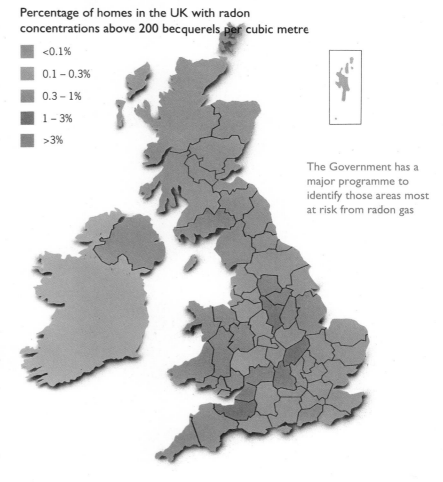

Percentage of homes in the UK with radon concentrations above 200 becquerels per cubic metre

- <0.1%
- 0.1 – 0.3%
- 0.3 – 1%
- 1 – 3%
- >3%

The Government has a major programme to identify those areas most at risk from radon gas

How radon enters houses

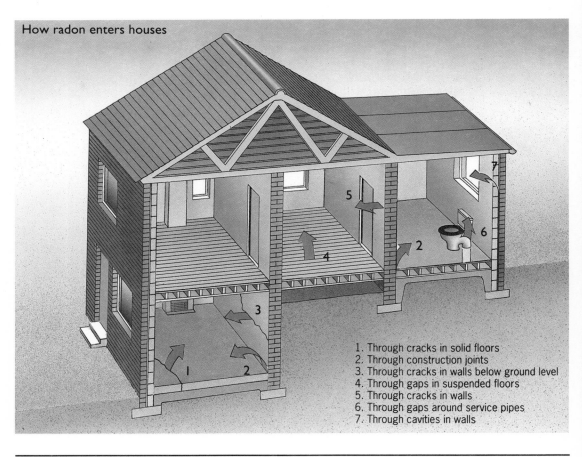

1. Through cracks in solid floors
2. Through construction joints
3. Through cracks in walls below ground level
4. Through gaps in suspended floors
5. Through cracks in walls
6. Through gaps around service pipes
7. Through cavities in walls

be needed. Firstly, the way a house is ventilated can be altered, to avoid, as far as possible, drawing air and radon through the floor. Next, the floor can be sealed to prevent radon getting through it. Finally, the air can be drawn from under the floor. For solid floors a sump, pipework and fan may be used: for suspended timber floors, natural or mechanical ventilation may be relied on to disperse the radon into the open air. The choice of method depends on the characteristics of the house, including the heating method, type of floor construction and layout. Grants can be available to those on lower incomes to cover the cost of any works.

11.85 The Government has launched a campaign to give wide publicity to the problem of radon, focusing on areas where concentrations are highest. It has published two free leaflets: Radon in Houses (January 1987), a short general leaflet of which more than 50,000 copies have been distributed, and The Householders' Guide to Radon (August 1988), a more detailed description of the

problem, written particularly for the householder who has had radon measurements made, giving practical advice on how to reduce radon concentrations. More than 30,000 copies have been distributed. A second edition was published in July 1990 offering fuller advice and reflecting the new lower action level.

11.86 The Government has issued interim guidance under the Building Regulations on protection against radon in new dwellings. This has applied to Cornwall and parts of Devon – the worst affected areas – since 1 July 1988. This guidance is now under review. Subject to advice from NRPB, it is likely that the area covered by the guidance will be extended.

11.87 Occupational exposure to radon is regulated by the requirements of the Ionising Radiations Regulations 1985, practical guidance on which was published by the Health and Safety Executive in 1988. Steps have been taken to identify workplaces where exposure to radon needs to be reduced. In these cases, occupiers have been required to introduce remedial measures similar to those described for houses, to reduce exposure to the extent required under the Regulations.

Methane

11.88 Another threat can come from methane emitted from old rubbish tips and mine workings. If sufficient gas accumulates in a building, this can lead to a risk of explosion. Such problems are localised and the Government is helping to identify and alleviate them wherever they arise. To tackle the problem £33 million has been made available in 1990/91.

11.89 The Government has advised planning authorities to avoid development on potentially hazardous sites, and is reviewing the Building Regulations as they deal with protection against contaminants in the ground. The revisions will include new detailed guidance about avoiding risks from methane and landfill gas. The Government has also given guidance to tip operators on measures to avoid risks. These include the potential for tapping methane for power generation which also helps reduce greenhouse gas emissions.

DAMP

11.90 Moulds and mites which can cause allergic illness can flourish in damp buildings. It has been estimated that three and a half million homes are affected and that a significant number of the allergic illnesses suffered by 15% of the population may be related. The Government acts to reduce the risks through a concerted programme of home improvements and by setting ventilation standards in the Building Regulations.

11.91 The Local Government and Housing Act 1989 reaffirms the statutory duty on local authorities to take action where any dwelling is found to be unfit for habitation. This specifically includes the health risks from condensation, damp and mould. Mandatory grants, based on a test of an applicant's resources, are available to improve conditions in badly affected housing up to a revised standard of fitness for human habitation. Discretionary grants are available for works above this standard. The Department of the Environment has also published guidance on steps to remove the risks of damp in all housing.

3½ million homes may be affected by damp. Grants are available to those who most need help with improvement work

RESEARCH

11.92 Over £2 million is being spent in 1990/91 by the Department of the Environment on research and monitoring of indoor pollution problems. A major part of the regular programme of research and monitoring is directed to targeted monitoring of levels of indoor pollutants to assess risks to people's health and the need for action. The Building Research Establishment has a programme of research into the key areas of concern – for example, ventilation, radon and methane penetration and emissions from products used in buildings. The Government can also draw on work and experience overseas through a series of international fora.

CONCLUSION

11.93 Britain is playing a major role in international steps to improve outdoor air quality. Our scientific understanding has given us a lead in many areas and has allowed us to help shape much of the present international legislation. The Government will continue to press for measures based on sound scientific understanding of air pollution and the risks it presents, and will target available funds and measures where they will have the greatest impact. The new emphasis on quality standards and the Government's leading role in the development of critical loads is central to this approach. These should enable us to set the specific limits necessary to address the problems experienced by our environment and so best help to sustain and improve our environment for future generations. The Government will also continue its effective work to control indoor air pollution and to increase understanding of its dangers.

Research – air

Research into air quality aims to establish the effects of possible pollutants on man and the natural environment. Examples of relevant public sector research are projects
• to monitor air quality to establish where the pollution comes from, how it can be controlled, reduced or treated, how it is transported through the air and how it changes chemically – Department of the Environment (£4.4m in 1989/90)
• to assess and quantify the effects of air pollution on the natural and man-made environment and to derive 'critical loads' – Department of the Environment (£1.9m in 1989/90)
• to support a consortium of engine manufacturers in developing techniques to improve the design of vehicle engines and reduce emissions from them – Department of Trade and Industry (£0.6m in 1989/90)
• to provide accurate information on the contribution of vehicles to noise and pollution and assess and predict how this might change in response to legislative changes, as the basis for developing appropriate standards – Department of Transport (£0.9m in 1989/90)
• to improve prediction of local and regional dispersion of air pollutants, including radionuclides, and to extend knowledge of the atmospheric chemistry of air pollutants – Meteorological Office (£0.4m in 1989/90)
• to improve understanding of the chemistry of the stratosphere and the troposphere in relation to air pollution problems near the ground; and to participate in the European Experiment on Transport and Transformation over Europe (EUROTRAC) providing basic information on the transport of pollutants such as acidic substances and photo-oxidants like ozone – Natural Environment Research Council (£0.2m in 1989/90) and Science and Engineering Research Council (£0.4m in 1991/92)
• to study the effects of nitrogen and sulphur-based acidic pollutants on sensitive organisms and ecosystems – Natural Environment Research Council (£1.0m in 1989/90)
• to study the effects of atmospheric pollutants on natural vegetation, soils and surface waters, including a joint programme with Powergen and National Power – Natural Environment Research Council (£1.2m in 1989/90)
• to develop new methods to quantify likely radon emissions in different areas – National Radiological Protection Board and the Natural Environment Research Council (£0.25m in 1989/90)
• to investigate the release into the air of asbestos, man-made mineral fibres and chemicals from construction products and other materials used in homes – Building Research Establishment and others (£0.25 million in 1989/90)
• to monitor the levels of indoor pollutants in homes, particularly for families with babies – Building Research Establishment (£0.5 million in 1989/90)
• to evaluate construction measures to reduce radon entry into houses – Building Research Establishment (£0.2 million in 1990/1991)

12

WATER

INTRODUCTION

Above: Water has many uses - the Government supports rigorous pollution control and good resource management

12.1 Water occurs in, on and around the earth and has been there since the beginning of time. It circulates constantly between the land, the oceans and the air, is a vital part of all living plants and animals and its presence in the air and oceans has a profound effect on the world's climate. It is above all essential to human life. We use it:

• at home, in industry and in agriculture,
• for waste disposal,
• as a means of transport,
• for commercial fishing and for informal recreation and organised sports.

12.2 Chapter 2 spells out the Government's objectives for the protection of Britain's waters and the North Sea, based on stewardship, sustainability and the other principles laid down in Chapter 1. The Government is committed to achieving further improvements in the quality of Britain's drinking water, rivers and surrounding seas and this Chapter describes how the Government intends to achieve these objectives. It concentrates on arrangements in England and Wales. Where they are different elsewhere in Britain, they are described in Chapters 19, 20 and 21 on Wales, Scotland and Northern Ireland.

INLAND AND COASTAL WATER

The Government has set up the NRA as an independant watchdog to control water pollution and coordinate the management of water resources

12.3 The Government aims to protect Britain's water resources – lakes and reservoirs, canals, rivers and streams, underground water sources and coastal waters – in four main ways :

• by establishing the right organisations to supply water to the public, to manage the water resource and to monitor and control its quality;
• by setting standards for water quality;
• by making regulations to prevent pollution and by advising on how to avoid it; and
• by setting guidelines for recreation and wildlife conservation.

The right organisations

12.4 In 1989 the Government made far-reaching changes to the structure and organisation of the water industry in England and Wales. It created new private sector companies to provide services to customers and set up a new regulatory body, the National Rivers Authority (NRA). Under the old arrangements the same authorities had been responsible for abstracting and supplying water, using it for discharges and protecting it from pollution. The new arrangements ended this potential conflict of interest by giving responsibility for preventing pollution and controlling abstraction to the NRA. Privatisation of the water industry ensured that the investment needed to improve water quality was properly identified and gave the industry access to the private sector funds needed to carry out the increased investment programmes.

12.5 The NRA has wide-ranging responsibilities for managing water resources and must balance the interests of all who use them. It has responsibilities for controlling pollution in inland, estuarial and coastal waters. The Water Act 1989 requires it to control pollution by issuing discharge consents; to monitor water quality and the achievement of national water quality standards and take enforcement action where necessary; and to manage water resources and protect their long term future by controlling abstraction rates. The NRA also has responsibilities for flood defence and land drainage, salmon and freshwater fisheries, navigation in some areas and nature conservation and recreation in inland waters and associated land. By bringing together all these functions under one single body, the Government has created one of the strongest environmental protection agencies in Europe.

Quality standards

12.6 Through the Water Act, the Government has established a stronger legal basis for preventing and controlling pollution. Before the Act, individual water authorities set water quality objectives on an informal basis and they varied from area to area. In future, the Government will set water quality objectives by law on a consistent basis and they will cover all types of water courses. These quality objectives will be set after public consultation and will provide a clear

framework for ensuring that different waters are of a high enough standard for all their uses, whether, for example, as a source for drinking water or for fisheries. The NRA will advise the Government on these objectives. In preparation for this, the NRA will identify water where current quality

River and canal water classification sceme

Class		Current Potential Use
1A	Good	Water of high quality suitable for potable supply abstractions; game or other high class fisheries; high amenity value.
1B		Water of less high quality than class 1A but usable for substantially the same purposes.
2	Fair	Waters suitable for potable supply after advanced treatment; supporting reasonably good coarse fisheries; moderate amenity value.
3	Poor	Waters which are polluted to an extent that fish are absent or only sporadically present; may be used for low grade industrial abstraction purposes; considerable potential for further use if cleaned up.
4	Bad	Waters which are grossly polluted and are likely to cause nuisance.

New statutory water quality objectives will build on this quality classification scheme

Britain' s water quality since 1958; data since 1985 confirm a steadily improving trend

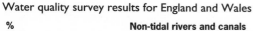

Water quality survey results for England and Wales

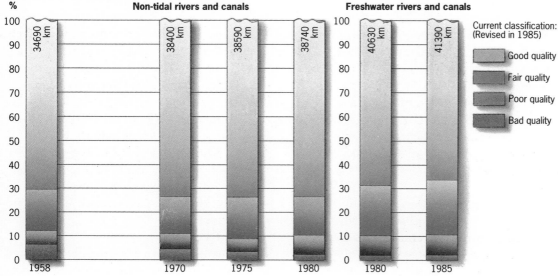

95% of our rivers are of good or fair quality, compared with 75% for the EC as a whole

The water industry is investing £2.9 billion to bring all our bathing waters up to EC standards by the mid-1990s

needs to be maintained or improved and set the timescale for improvements. It is carrying out a survey of river and estuary quality during 1990 and will carry out further surveys as necessary. The NRA is also reviewing its own monitoring practices to ensure that they provide a comprehensive and coherent picture of water quality throughout the country.

12.7 It is vital to protect the quality of drinking water which has to meet stringent standards to safeguard health and to ensure acceptable standards of taste, odour and appearance. The Government established the Drinking Water Inspectorate on 1 January 1990 to ensure that these standards are met. Many of the standards are based on the EC Drinking Water Directive but the Government has in some cases set more stringent national requirements, for example, on the standard for lead. The quality of all public supplies of water is high enough for drinking. But some supplies fall short of some standards and water companies in England and Wales will be spending £1.8 billion before the end of 1995 to put this right. This programme covers the removal of excess nitrate and pesticides and action to reduce the tendency of some supplies to pick up lead from customers' pipes.

12.8 The Government has done a great deal to maintain and improve the quality of our rivers which, (together with reservoirs), supply about two thirds of drinking water

and are also used for waste disposal, sport and recreation. A study conducted by the Water Research Centre in 1987 showed that, whereas in Britain 95% of river length was of good or fair quality, for the EC as a whole only 75% was of comparable quality. No other Member State bettered our position. But we must do more and the Government's policy is to eliminate the remaining class 4 rivers and improve those in class 3 to class 2 as soon as practicable. Rivers have to be used for waste disposal from industry (including the water industry) and domestic users; farm waste disposed of on land also contributes to river pollution. The 1985 River Quality Survey identified effluent from sewage works and agriculture as the main causes of pollution in rivers. The next section, on preventing pollution, describes the measures the Government is taking to deal with this.

12.9 Clean and unpolluted bathing waters are very important not only for health reasons but also for the pleasure which beaches give. The standards which the EC sets in the Bathing Water Directive apply mainly to pollution from sewage. The quality of our bathing waters is steadily improving. In 1986, only 51% complied with the Directive but by 1989 this figure had increased to 76%. The next section describes the Government's measures to bring the remainder up to standard.

Diagram of bathing water statistics

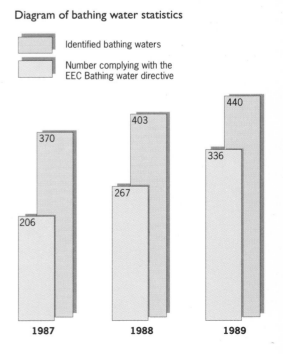

Identified bathing waters

Number complying with the EEC Bathing water directive

Left: Effluent from sewage treatment works is a major cause of river pollution

Right: The water industry is investing £1 billion to bring poorly performing sewage treatment works up to standard

Preventing pollution: introduction

12.10   Once water pollution has occurred it can be difficult and expensive to put right. This is why the Government's long term approach concentrates on prevention rather than cure. This section describes the measures which the Government is taking to deal with the pollution of our inland and coastal waters.

Sewage

12.11 · In England and Wales 96% of properties are connected to the sewerage system, the highest proportion in Europe, and 83% of all sewage is treated at inland treatment works. The ten water companies in England and Wales are responsible for the operation of about 6,500 sewage treatment works, most of which discharge effluent to rivers. In 1986, 23% of sewage treatment works were failing to meet their discharge consent conditions. By 1988, this figure had fallen to 17%. Failure to comply was often because plant was inadequate to deal with the increased load now placed on it.

12.12   Since 1989, some major steps have been taken:
• the water industry is committed to the largest ever investment programme of £28 billion (at 1989 prices) between 1990 and 2000. It will spend £13.7 billion on sewerage works, pipe networks and sea and estuarial outfalls. This will include £1 billion to enable poorly performing sewage works to comply with their discharge consents by March 1992 wherever possible. The privatisation of the water industry has given it access to the large sums of capital needed for this investment; and,
• as a priority, the NRA is reviewing the terms of the discharge consents for all known storm overflows (which can cause serious pollution).
The NRA will monitor river quality as these improvements take place and will advise the Government if it judges that further action is necessary.

12.13   Britain disposes of 17% of its sewage by discharging it to sea, mainly from coastal towns. In 1989, 24% of our bathing waters did not comply with the EC Directive and the Government announced a £1.4 billion investment programme to put this right. This programme includes the installation of long sea outfalls and improvements to sewage treatment works and storm sewage overflows. In addition, in March 1990, the Government announced a further £1.5 billion investment in sewage treatment works so that in future sewage will be treated before discharge to the sea.

12.14   These programmes will lead to a substantial long term improvement in the quality of our bathing waters and marine environment. The vast majority of bathing waters will comply with the EC Directive by the mid 1990's. In the short term, the Government has asked the NRA to take action to improve the position by ensuring that maximum use is made of screening raw sewage to remove solids and that disinfectants are used where they will not harm the aquatic environment. In addition, the Government has asked all local authorities to put up public notices describing the quality of the bathing water in their area. The measures described above will effectively bring pollution from human sewage under control by 2000.

Farm waste

12.15 Pollution from farm waste remains a major problem. Undiluted farm slurry is up to one hundred times more polluting than raw sewage. When it is broken down in water, so much oxygen is consumed that fish and other wildlife can suffocate. Silage effluent is even more polluting. Between 1980/81 and 1988, reported farm pollution incidents rose from 2,367 to 4,141, in line with increases in reported pollution incidents from other sources; and in 1988 half of all serious water pollution incidents reported were caused by pollution from farms. Although the level of reported farm pollution incidents fell by 30% in 1989 and serious incidents by 45%, probably due to the exceptionally dry weather, surveys carried out by the NRA in several regions indicate that the scale of agricultural pollution is more widespread than the number of reported incidents suggests.

12.16 The Government has recently introduced a number of measures to combat farm pollution of rivers and streams and has plans for more:
• in February 1989, the Government introduced the Farm and Conservation Grant Scheme, which provides 50% grants for providing, replacing or improving facilities for the storage, treatment and disposal of agricultural wastes and silage effluent;
• the Ministry of Agriculture, Fisheries and Food (MAFF) has published the 1989 Survey of Water Pollution and Farm Waste. This is its first joint report with the NRA (rather than the Water Authorities) and provides a factual picture of farm pollution incidents in England and Wales. There will be similar reports in future years;
• MAFF is preparing a revised free advisory package of Codes of Good Agricultural Practice for farmers which will include one relating to water. The Agricultural Development and Advisory Service (ADAS) also provide free initial advice on pollution control; and
• the Government will publish new regulations setting minimum standards for the construction of silage, slurry and agricultural fuel oil stores. These should greatly reduce the number of pollution incidents from structural failures. The regulations will also enable the NRA to require farmers to improve their existing installations, where it considers there is a significant risk of pollution.

Farm waste also causes river pollution. The Government provides advice on pollution control and pays grant for new and improved farm waste facilities

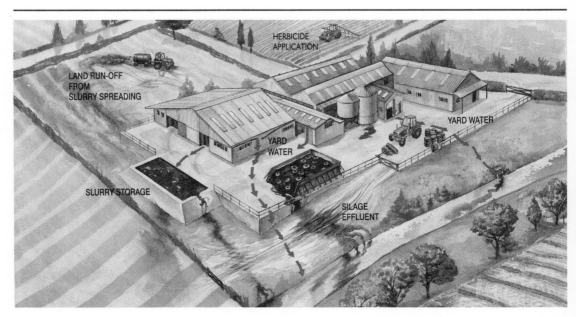

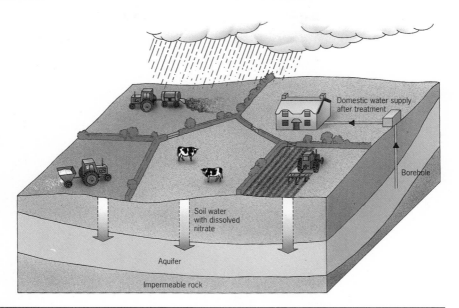

Nitrate, mainly from farmland, is carried through the soil and rocks in rainwater. The Government is taking action to reduce nitrate leaching

The Government remains determined to tackle the farm waste problem. It will monitor the effectiveness of the recently introduced measures, taking into account the NRA's own review of the impact of farm waste. It will continue to support research into the causes of and remedies for agricultural pollution and to investigate the best methods for preventing it, including advice, regulation, grant aid and charges. In particular, it will keep under review the need for more controls over livestock waste.

Chemicals

12.17 Britain has taken the lead within the EC in identifying the substances entering its rivers and estuaries which are potentially harmful both to them and to the sea into which they flow. It is taking action to reduce the pollution from these dangerous substances, known as the 'Red List', described in paragraphs 12.31 - 12.34. Most chemicals enter water as a by-product from industry and specific discharge consents are required. As with other types of discharge, consents can and will be reviewed and improvements sought, in order to meet water quality objectives. Pesticides, however, can reach water from diffuse sources as a result of general use and to tackle this problem the Government regulates their use and seeks to encourage good agricultural practice. Chapter 13 describes these measures.

12.18   The Government is considering the need for regulations to set minimum standards for chemical stores and industrial fuel oil installations, which are potential sources of pollution.

Nitrate

12.19 The EC Drinking Water Directive sets a limit for nitrate in water in order to avoid danger to human health. In some areas levels of nitrate in water are close to or above this limit. Agriculture is the main source of nitrate in water. It comes mainly from organic nitrogen in the soil and to a lesser extent from unused fertilisers. The release of organic nitrogen into soil water and hence into rivers and underground water sources is a natural process but some farming activities, such as ploughing grassland, can add to it and it also varies with crop types and climatic conditions. The speed with which nitrate reaches underground water sources varies but it can take a long time, so today's levels may reflect several decades of past activity. Controlling nitrate leaching is therefore a complex problem and will not be quickly or simply resolved.

12.20   The Government's aim is to reduce the amount of nitrate leaching from agricultural land and it has taken the power under the Water Act to designate Nitrate Sensitive Areas (NSAs) in which certain agricultural operations, such as cropping and fertiliser use, can be regulated. The Government designated ten pilot Nitrate

Pilot Nitrate Scheme

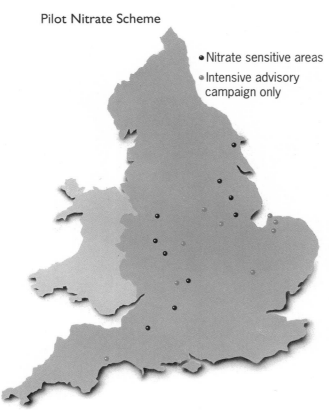

• Nitrate sensitive areas
• Intensive advisory campaign only

The Government is offering farmers payments to reduce fertiliser use and cereal cropping in ten new Nitrate Sensitive Areas

Sensitive Areas in England in 1990 (see map) covering some 15,000 hectares. In these areas farmers will get free advice on ways to reduce the risk of nitrate leaching into water. They can also qualify for annual payments to help them make substantial voluntary changes to their farming operations – such as switching from arable to low intensity grassland cultivation. In a further nine areas which are not designated NSAs, farmers will get similar free advice on reducing nitrate leaching.

12.21 Pilot NSAs and the intensive advisory campaign will provide a valuable insight into ways of controlling nitrate leaching. The Government will monitor the effectiveness of these measures very closely. It will keep under review the need for more action to reduce nitrate levels in water sources over the long term.

12.22 The EC has proposed a draft Directive for concerted action across the Community to control nitrate pollution. The Government welcomes its general approach and is playing a full part in the negotiations to ensure that the final Directive is compatible with Britain's environmental and agricultural interests.

Enforcement and charges

12.23 The Government has given the NRA wide powers to enable it to be a tough and effective regulator. By granting and reviewing discharge consents, the NRA sets standards for discharges to water which will ensure that water quality objectives are met. It is also responsible for ensuring that dischargers meet the conditions imposed on them. At the Government's request, the NRA has recently published a consultation document suggesting changes in the way in which it sets consents for all types of discharges and assesses compliance with them.

12.24 The NRA has already demonstrated its commitment to effective regulation and enforcement of water quality standards by prosecuting more offenders than ever before, by issuing many more formal warnings and by taking more cases to the Crown Courts – which can impose unlimited fines on polluters or up to two years in jail.   In addition, the Government is to increase to £20,000 the maximum fines which magistrates' courts can impose for water pollution offences.

12.25 The NRA is introducing a scheme for charging dischargers for the cost of investigating and administering their applications for discharge consents and of monitoring compliance with them. This should enable the NRA to recover most of the cost of running the system and monitoring discharges and it should be an incentive for dischargers to reduce pollution by making them more aware of the costs of their activities. In the longer term, the Government will consider using other fiscal mechanisms, such as pollution load charging, to discourage pollution. As soon as the NRA has finalised arrangements for its cost recovery scheme, the Government will commission studies in consultation with the NRA and HMIP into the scope for developing charging systems which take full account of the cost of pollution. They would provide a greater incentive to reduce pollution.

The NRA, water companies and internal drainage boards have a statutory duty to protect and enhance landscape, wildlife and historic features and to provide opportunities for recreation on their land and water

Conservation and recreation

12.26 Our inland waters and the land which the water companies own provide valuable habitats for wildlife and tremendous opportunities for recreation and tourism. Over 40,000 hectares, or about a third of the land and water owned by the water companies, are in National Parks or Areas of Outstanding Natural Beauty (see Chapter 7). The Government has imposed a duty on the NRA, the water and sewerage undertakers and the internal drainage boards, where they can, to :
• conserve and enhance natural beauty and to conserve flora, fauna and geological features of special interest;

• protect and conserve buildings, sites and other objects of archaeological, architectural or historic interest and public access to them; and
• ensure that water and land are made available for recreation.

12.27 The Government issued a Code of Practice in July 1989 about these duties. It also set up a Standing Committee of representatives of conservation and recreation bodies to monitor and review the application and effectiveness of the Code. The Government will review the adequacy of the Code in the light of their advice, or in response to changing circumstances.

THE SEAS

12.28 Britain's seas are affected by many natural factors including tides, currents, and weather; by the impact of human activities on land and at sea including coastal development, shipping and offshore oil and gas exploitation; and by pollution arising from those activities directly, via rivers and through deposition from the atmosphere. The marine environment is very complex and safeguarding it requires international co-operation and action. The Government, either on its own account or within international organisations, seeks to protect the seas by :
• controlling inputs of pollutants from rivers, estuaries and direct discharge from the coasts;
• controlling or stopping waste disposal activities at sea;

• controlling inputs of pollutants from ships and oil rigs; and
• conserving fish stocks.
Chapter 7 describes some specific measures to protect marine wildlife in the seas around Britain.

12.29 The Government is working closely with other countries that border the North Sea and Irish Sea to ensure that their quality is protected and improved where necessary. The quality of the Irish Sea is generally good, as is that of the North Sea, although there are localized problems, for example, in the German Bight, which is polluted because of the combined effect of slow circulation, shallow water and large inputs of pollutants.

Pollution from rivers, estuaries and coasts

12.30 The most important factor influencing the quality of the marine environment is the nature of wastes reaching the sea from land-based domestic and industrial sources, via rivers and direct discharge from coasts. The impact of dangerous substances can be particularly damaging.

Dangerous substances

12.31 In 1987, the Government hosted the second North Sea Conference, which agreed that inputs of dangerous substances to the North Sea via rivers and estuaries should be reduced by around 50% between 1985 and 1995. The Government has strongly endorsed the need to reduce, on a precautionary basis, inputs of the most dangerous substances.

12.32 Dangerous substances are substances which are persistent, toxic and liable to accumulate in living tissues. Britain took an early lead in producing a scientifically – based list of dangerous substances – the 'Red List'. It includes heavy metals such as mercury and cadmium, certain pesticides, chlorinated industrial chemicals and solvents. It is the list of 'prescribed substances' which HMIP will use in applying integrated pollution control (IPC) for discharges to water.

12.33 Plans to make the agreed reductions have been drawn up and progress has been made. For example, mercury inputs were reduced by 26% between 1985 and 1988 and cadmium inputs were reduced by 18%. Further reductions will be achieved through the application of IPC; by applying environmental quality standards to substances which did not have them before; by reviewing all discharge consents; and by introducing new controls on the production and use of harmful substances where necessary. Details of progress made and the steps the Government is taking were published in March 1990 in 'United Kingdom North Sea Action Plan 1985 – 1995.'

12.34 The Third North Sea Conference in 1990 agreed on further measures to improve our seas and the Government is committed to implementing them. It will take steps to ensure that the use of all identifiable polychlorinated biphenyls (PCBs) is phased out by the end of 1999 at the latest and that they are destroyed in an environmentally safe way. The Government will work together with industry to survey and identify equipment where PCBs remain in use, to publicise the need to withdraw them and to ensure their safe disposal within the agreed timescale. New regulations will ban any continued use of PCBs after 1999. In addition, the Government will halve by 1999 the amounts of 17 potentially harmful substances such as mercury and cadmium which reach the sea from the atmosphere. In co-operation with other North Sea states, it is carrying out studies, which will be completed by 1991, into the sources of these pollutants, how they reach the sea and how to monitor them. The Government has taken an early lead by publishing, in July 1990, in its 'Implementation Guidance Note', details of the steps it will take to implement the agreements reached at the third North Sea Conference.

The Government aims to reduce the inputs of these substances to the North Sea by 50% by 1995

Red List Substances

Mercury and its compounds
Cadmium and its compounds
Gamma-hexachlorocyclohexane
DDT
Pentachlorophenol and its compounds
Hexachlorobenzine
Hexachlorobutadiene
Aldrin
Dieldrin
Endrin
Polychlorinated Biphenyls
Dichlorvos
1, 2-Dichloroethane
Trichlorobenzene
Atrazine
Simazine
Tributyltin compounds
Triphenyltin compounds
Trifluralin
Fenitrothion
Azinphos-menthyl
Malathion
Endosulfan

Further substances may be added to the list from time to time where there are sound scientific reasons for doing so.

Waste disposal at sea

12.35 The Government is taking the following steps to limit or stop altogether the dumping from ships of waste at sea. In common with other North Sea states, it has decided that land-based alternatives will be found for the disposal of industrial wastes and sewage sludge. Sea dumping of liquid industrial wastes and flyash from power stations is due to stop by the end of 1992 and the dumping of sewage sludge will stop by the end of 1998. In addition, the Government has announced its intention to withdraw the licences for dumping stone waste from coal mining on beaches by mid 1995 and at sea by the end of 1997, unless disposal on land proves to be impracticable for the collieries concerned. The Government also plans to end the incineration of waste at sea by the end of 1990, a year ahead of the North Sea Conference schedule.

Pollution from ships

12.36 Shipping is a world wide business. Many of the ships using British waters have no connection with Britain and, for pollution control to be effective, it has to be co-ordinated internationally. Britain has taken a leading role through the International Maritime Organisation in establishing international regulations which set minimum standards for the construction, equipment and operation of ships in order to control pollution from oil, noxious substances and garbage. The Department of Transport's surveyors ensure that British ships comply with these standards and inspect foreign registered ships entering British ports.

12.37 Britain and other North Sea states have agreed to improve the control and enforcement of pollution prevention regulations over ships using the North Sea by:
• more inspection of ships;
• closer co-operation with other countries in exchanging information on suspected illegal discharges;
• implementing strict sewage controls on ferries sailing between North Sea ports after consultation with the industry;

Sea dumping of liquid and industrial wastes and flyash from power stations is to stop by 1992

• seeking higher world wide standards for oil and chemical discharges to sea; and
• increasing by 60% the Government's regular airborne surveillance patrols, which detect and deter illegal operational oil discharges from ships and British coasts.

12.38 Bulk transport of oil by sea is the most efficient way of distributing the large amounts of it needed by many countries. The risk of accidents involving oil spillage cannot be totally eliminated. Fast and effective means of dealing with oil spills will therefore always be needed and, in 1979, the Government set up the Marine Pollution Control Unit (MPCU) to deal with pollution incidents which could affect British seas and coasts. The MPCU has nine aircraft available at very short notice and has stocks of dispersant at 20 strategically placed sites around the coastline and special equipment for recovering oil both at sea and on beaches. In recent months, the MPCU has successfully responded to two significant spillages off the coasts of Britain - in September 1989 when about 800 tonnes of oil was spilt off the Humber Estuary, and in May 1990 when over 1,000 tonnes of oil was spilt off the South Devon coast.

Pollution from oil rigs

12.39 There are about 150 oil and gas production platforms in the North Sea producing about 100 million tonnes of oil and about 40 billion cubic metres of gas each year. The industry directly employs around 50,000 people in Britain and produces enormous benefits for the British economy. But it also uses a range of materials which may cause pollution - either as a by-product of extraction (oil-contaminated drilling muds) or as a result of accidental spillages. Britain has been active in helping to establish international standards and controls. These include :
• elimination of discharge of oil-contaminated drill cuttings from single exploration and appraisal wells by 1994 and from all wells as soon as possible thereafter; and
• international co-operation to produce a reporting and controlling scheme for the use and discharge of chemicals offshore; and in reviewing safety, risk assessments to the marine environment and platform disposal.

Conserving fish stocks

12.40 The waters of the North-East Atlantic support the most productive fisheries in the world and have done so for centuries. Around the North Sea and the coast of the British Isles, fishing and related industries play an important part in the life of many communities. Total fish catches in the North Sea rose from an annual average of 1.75 million tonnes in the late 1940s to a peak of 3.2 million tonnes at the beginning of the

1970s and have now stabilised at around 2.4 million tonnes. Catches of crustaceans (crabs and lobsters) show a similar pattern and production of other shellfish has increased in the same period. In the Irish Sea, catches of most species have increased steadily in recent years.

12.41 Most changes in fish stocks since the early 1900s can be explained in terms of fishing intensity and natural factors. A few species, such as skate, have declined significantly and sturgeon has almost disappeared from British waters. Others, such as salmon and sea trout, which spend part of their life cycle in freshwater, were affected by local pollution but have recently returned along with other species such as smelt, to rivers like the Thames and Tyne, where water quality has improved substantially.

12.42 Many important fish stocks such as haddock, cod and mackerel have suffered from intense fishing but all the major fisheries are now regulated by international agreements in order to manage and conserve the stocks. Populations of bottom-dwelling species such as flatfish have survived well : for example, catches of plaice doubled between 1957 and 1984. Other fish catches, such as cod in both the Irish and North Seas, have risen to a peak and then declined to earlier levels. Mid-water species, such as mackerel and herring, are particularly vulnerable to intensive fishing techniques but fisheries for both are being effectively controlled by the more comprehensive conservation measures that have been introduced by the Common Fisheries Policy of the EC.

SCIENTIFIC MONITORING AND RESEARCH

12.43 Government Departments and the NRA carry out extensive scientific assessment and monitoring in support of policies to protect the water environment and aquatic life. Their findings assist in the control of water quality and commercial fishing, add to the level of scientific knowledge and enhance our ability to join other countries in solving international problems. They also undertake and support research into drinking water quality and health; water resource and river quality management; the quality of estuarine, coastal and offshore waters; the disposal of sewage sludge to land; the causes and reduction of nitrate leaching from agricultural land; the safe and cost-effective management of farm waste; the assessment of dangerous substances and their effect on aquatic life; the occurence of blue-green algae in inland waters; health aspects of bathing waters; flood protection; and fish stocks and fish diseases. Because marine research needs international co-ordination if resources are to be effectively directed and used, Britain pressed for the establishment of the North Sea Task Force at the Second North Sea Conference. It will co-ordinate research and prepare a new assessment or health check on the North Sea by 1993. It has already identified 'critical gaps in

The Government supports a wide - ranging research programme into fresh and marine water resources: MAFF research vessels monitor many aspects of the marine environment - including fish stocks

knowledge' requiring further work and much British marine environment research, supported by studies on the inputs of pollution from inland waters and including the Government's £11.5 million a year marine environment programme, will be directed towards filling those gaps. The tables overleaf show examples of some of the research being carried out.

CONCLUSION

12.44 By establishing the NRA and creating ten new water companies in England and Wales, the Government has set in place the right framework to protect and improve the state of our drinking water, rivers and coastal waters. The water companies are now undertaking a massive investment programme to improve water quality and to make our bathing waters cleaner. The NRA will police existing regulations strictly and advise the Government if it thinks they need to be strengthened. It will enforce discharge consents and where necessary require improvements to be made by dischargers. The Government will set clear water quality objectives. It will also take action to improve

the quality of the North Sea and continue to work for international agreements with other North Sea states. Water quality will be comprehensively monitored and assessed and the Government will take further steps to improve the water environment where necessary for the benefit of its users.

12.45 Industry, farmers and individuals all have a responsibility to make sure that we use all our water resources responsibly and cleanly and to look constantly for ways of reducing pollution that could damage them. The Government will continue to work with the water industry, the NRA and with consumers of all kinds to meet this challenge.

Research – water (inland)

Water research in the public sector is designed to improve knowledge of the natural and man-made changes which affect the availability of water, its quality, and its interactions with the air, soil and ecosystems; and to support policy decisions at home and in Europe. This research is complemented by The National Rivers Authority programme for the management and regulation of the water environment.

Examples of public sector research relevant to inland water are projects
• to support policy development on quality standards for surface waters, dealing with concern over drinking water quality and health, sewage disposal, reservoir safety and examining the likely impact of climate change – Department of the Environment (£4.2m in 1989/90)
• to support work on control of river quality including the effects of upland land use, agriculture and fish farming, problems in urban catchments, estuaries, coastal waters, groundwaters, lakes and reservoirs – National Rivers Authority (£3.5m in 1989/90)
• to investigate the fate of agrochemicals in soil, especially nitrates and their levels in soil run-off water and aquifers – Agricultural and Food Research Council and the Natural Environment Research Council (£0.5m in 1989/90)
• to investigate the effects on freshwater resources of forestry, the development of urban areas, acidification, pollution and changing land use – Natural Environment Research Council (£3.7m in 1989/90)
• to investigate the ecosystems of lowland rivers with high pollutant loads – Natural Environment Research Council (£0.8m in 1989/90)
• to study the toxic effects of mercury, organochlorines, rodent poisons, and TBT (TriButyl Tin) in estuaries and coastal waters – Ministry of Agriculture, Fisheries and Food (£2.4m in 1989/90)

Research – water (marine)

Public sector research relevant to the impact of human activities on the life of the sea includes projects
• to establish the scientific basis on which to develop policies for the future management of the sea and estuaries to contribute to the work of the Oslo and Paris Commissions – fisheries Departments and Department of the Environment (£3.5m in 1989/90)
• to support a comprehensive study of the southern North Sea to produce a three-dimensional model of water quality, from which the fate of pollutants and the health of the Sea can be deduced – Natural Environment Research Council (£4.4m in 1989/90)
• to contribute to case studies of marine pollution in the North Sea and Mediterranean through the European Science Foundation programme in Environmental Science and Society – Economic and Social Research Council (£0.06m in 1990/91)
• to understand the behaviour of marine oil and chemical spills in order to assess potential risks of different materials; to develop adequate monitoring and clean up techniques; to develop the use of remote sensing in tracking oil slicks, and study the vulnerability of seabirds to oil at sea – Department of Transport (£0.8m in 1989/90)
• to research and monitor fish stocks in UK waters, to contribute to the work of the International Council for the Exploration of the Seas, which provides scientific advice on conservation and management of fish resources – fisheries Departments (£15.0m in 1989/90)

13

HAZARDOUS SUBSTANCES AND GENETICALLY MODIFIED ORGANISMS

INTRODUCTION

13.1 Many substances, whether man-made or natural, can cause harm to man or the environment. Some of these reach the environment in waste streams, and other chapters in this section describe how emission limits and environmental quality standards can reduce the amounts released. But others cannot be controlled in this way because they are released, not in industrial waste streams, but through the use or disposal of products which contain them. In many cases these substances pose little or no threat if the product containing them is used and disposed of properly. The right way to deal with them is usually through controls over their supply, use and disposal.

13.2 These substances include many of the most useful chemicals in modern society. Chlorine, for example, is used to disinfect drinking water, and pesticides enable farmers to grow more food. New drugs capable of curing diseases which were sometimes fatal a few decades ago are sometimes hazardous in use or disposal. Chemicals are also used in the manufacture of many everyday goods, for example televisions, radios and the microchips for computers and tele-communications equipment, plastics, paints and synthetic fibres for clothes. New technical advances have also produced genetically modified organisms, which have benefits especially for medicine and agriculture: these might give rise to biological, as distinct from chemical, risks that need to be controlled.

13.3 Our knowledge of the fate of chemicals in the environment is continually increasing through research and exchange of experience with other countries. The Government's aim is to achieve a systematic and forward-looking approach to hazardous substances which prevents problems from arising in the first place and so reduces the need to respond reactively. The greatest challenge lies with the large number of chemicals produced in bulk which are already on world markets and whose environmental effects are not well known. Britain proposes to play a major role in international efforts to review these substances.

13.4 There is large-scale international trade in chemicals, and a unified regime for the classification, packaging, labelling, transport and use of hazardous materials is essential if goods are to move freely and valuable new products are to become available quickly. Britain is participating in the development of this regime for new and existing industrial chemicals, pesticides and other chemicals in the European Community and in international organisations such as the Organisation for Economic Co-operation and Development (OECD), World Health Organisation (WHO), United Nations Environment Programme (UNEP) and the International Maritime Organisation (IMO).

Action by the Government

13.5 The Government takes action to prevent harm to people and the environment from hazardous substances. The form of the action depends on:
• the nature of the hazard: the manufacture and use of some chemicals carries the risk of fire or explosion; some are poisonous; some can cause serious illness if we are exposed to them over a long period of time; some can harm the environment; and
• the level of risk: the Government grades its controls according to the seriousness of the risk; for example, it has banned certain extremely dangerous substances, while at the other end of the spectrum it requires household disinfectant or paint to carry labels drawing attention to any special hazards.

13.6 This Chapter describes the precautionary strategy that the Government has developed to respond to:
• the threat to human health and the environment from certain hazardous chemicals;
• the dangers to the environment from the use of pesticides;
• the risk of major accidents involving dangerous substances; and
• rapidly emerging new techniques of genetic modification.

INDUSTRIAL CHEMICALS

13.7 Some persistent toxic chemicals were widely used before the extent of their presence in the environment was recognised. It is now known that some of these chemicals can carry risks for human health or the environment because of widespread use, persistence in the environment or marked toxicity. The Government is responding by controlling their use across all environmental media on an individual basis. The following paragraphs describe four examples of Government action.

Lead

13.8 Studies have suggested that even low levels of exposure to lead may reduce intelligence and affect behaviour in children. Although the scientific results are not conclusive and the possible effects are small, the Government is committed as part of its precautionary approach to reducing human exposure to lead wherever it is practicable. The Government has acted to reduce the lead content of petrol, industrial emissions, paint, cosmetics, ceramic glazes, food and drinking water. An extensive monitoring programme shows steadily declining amounts of lead in people's blood.

Cadmium

13.9 Cadmium is a useful industrial chemical, but if it is released into the environment it can be absorbed through the food chain and accumulate in the body. At high levels it could cause kidney or bone damage. There is no evidence of this occurring in Britain, but the Government strongly supports a European Commission proposal to ban the use of cadmium where it is not essential and where safe substitutes are available. The Government has also undertaken to reduce discharges into the North Sea of both cadmium and lead by 70% between 1985 and 1995.

Dioxins

13.10 There are 210 closely related chemicals known as dioxins. They are produced in trace quantities as by-products of some chemical and combustion processes.

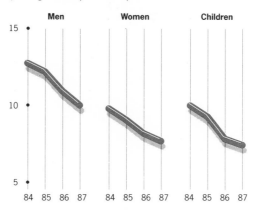

Distributions of blood lead concentrations for people exposed to heavy traffic: 1984-87 (microgrammes per 100 ml)

Men   Women   Children

Government action has helped to reduce concentrations of blood lead among people in Britain; these fell fastest in people exposed to heavy traffic after 1985 when the lead concentration of petrol was reduced

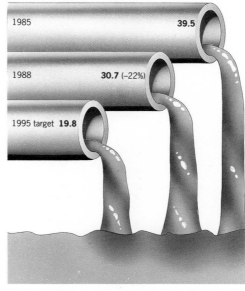

Cadmium discharged into the North Sea (tonnes per year)

1985   39.5
1988   30.7 (–22%)
1995 target 19.8

Britain will help improve the quality of the North Sea by reducing its discharges of lead and cadmium and phasing out PCBs

Some dioxins are toxic at low levels: the levels found in the environment are generally well below the threshold for any adverse effects but it would be prudent to reduce levels still further. Food is the principal route of exposure and dioxins can build up in body fat. Food only becomes contaminated as a result of environmental contamination. The Government is taking action to control sources of dioxins in order to reduce levels in food. For example, it has introduced strict controls on the production of chemicals which might be contaminated with dioxins; it is further tightening its controls on emissions from incinerators; and it intends to ban straw and stubble burning in England and Wales through the Environmental Protection Bill.

PCBs

13.11 Polychlorinated Biphenyls (PCBs) are oily substances that were used mainly in transformers and other electrical equipment. Studies showed that they are persistent if released into the environment and accumulate in the food chain. Even their disposal by incineration would produce harmful dioxins if this were not carried out at very high temperatures. Britain banned the use of PCBs in new equipment in 1986 and, along with other North Sea states, has agreed to phase out and destroy all identifiable PCBs already in use by the end of 1999 at the latest.

Research and monitoring

13.12 The Government is committed to monitoring the levels of these and other toxic substances in the environment to determine how much people in Britain are exposed to them and whether further controls are needed. As Chapter 17 describes, it will ensure that monitoring focuses on the most significant potential hazards and that new or changing risks from pollutants are identified as early as possible. It obtains advice on the possible effects on health of chemicals in the environment from independent expert committees.

13.13 The Government is responding to claims that pollution by chemicals from industrial plant causes ill health in nearby communities. It has set up an independent Small Area Health Statistics Unit to investigate such claims and will take action if the Unit finds any evidence to link clusters of ill health with industrial pollution.

New chemicals

13.14 Where a new chemical is placed on the market in the EC for the first time, the manufacturer or importer must provide detailed information on its properties. In Britain, the Health and Safety Executive (HSE) and Department of the Environment then evaluate its potential to harm man or the environment and share this information with other members of the Community. If a chemical is found to be potentially hazardous, appropriate action is taken to control it.

Chemicals in use

13.15 The Government will continue to respond to the problems posed by particularly hazardous individual chemicals. But it is also developing a more systematic precautionary approach to evaluate the environmental effects of the very large numbers of industrial chemicals in use.

13.16 Some 110,000 different chemicals were marketed in the European Community before 1981. About 5,000 of these are produced in quantities over 10 tonnes a year, and about 1,500 in quantities over 1,000 tonnes a year. There is little information about the environmental effects of many industrial chemicals which are produced in large volumes. Britain is taking steps both domestically and internationally to evaluate and if necessary control them.

13.17 The Environmental Protection Bill will give the Government powers to obtain information on chemicals so that it can assess the harm they could do to man and the environment. The Bill also strengthens the Government's powers to control the use, supply, storage or import of chemicals. These powers are an important element in the integrated approach to pollution control described in Chapter 10. A new statutory committee, provided for in the Bill, will advise the Government on the selection of chemicals for assessment and control.

13.18 The European Commission will soon propose Community legislation requiring all chemicals already on the market in large quantities to be thoroughly evaluated and if necessary tested. The Commission and the members of the Community will draw up a priority list of chemicals on which more information is needed. The manufacturers or importers of priority chemicals will be required to supply the information needed to evaluate any risk to human health and the environment and to carry out any necessary testing.

13.19 Britain is participating actively in a review by the Organisation for Economic Co-operation and Development (OECD), of chemicals produced in large volumes.

Reviewing a single substance takes a great deal of specialist scientific manpower, and it makes sense for developed countries to share the effort and avoid duplication. The OECD has identified a first priority list of some 150 chemicals which are produced in large quantities and about whose environmental effects little is known. Britain has undertaken to study its full share of these . This will be a co-operative effort with the chemical industry.

PESTICIDES

13.20 Pesticides are an essential part of modern agriculture and help farmers to grow better and cheaper food by controlling organisms which harm crops, including insects, slugs, moulds and weeds. They also have important non-agricultural uses, for example in controlling rats and mice or protecting houses against dry rot or woodworm. But because they have to be poisonous to some organisms, they are also potentially dangerous to man and the environment, and their use must be carefully controlled.

13.21 The Government introduced legislation in the Food and Environment Protection Act 1985 to put the control of pesticides onto a statutory basis. The Control of Pesticides Regulations 1986 established statutory controls in Britain over the sale, storage, use and advertisement of pesticides, including weedkillers, insecticides, fungicides and wood preservatives. The Government is advised on granting approvals for the use of pesticides by an independent committee of scientific experts - the Advisory Committee on Pesticides - which includes experts on the environmental effects of chemicals.

Principles

13.22 The Government has agreed on five principles to govern the assessment of risks and benefits when pesticides are approved:
• the amounts of pesticides used should be limited to the minimum necessary for the effective control of pests compatible with the protection of human health and the environment;
• in making decisions on the use of pesticides, the Government will take into account efficacy, human health and environmental factors;
• the Government will review all approvals at

Certain pesticides caused a sharp decline in the population of sparrowhawks and other birds of prey. As a result of the Government's tight controls, numbers are now on the increase

regular intervals and will withdraw them if significant new information about harmful effects on man or the environment comes to light;
• subject to essential commercial confidentiality, the information supporting decisions on the use of pesticides should be available for public scrutiny; and
• procedures for approving the use of pesticides must be fully independent of particular sectoral interests.

Assessment

13.23 Companies applying for approval to market a new pesticide are required to provide a comprehensive dossier of information on its physical and chemical properties, its efficacy, its safety for humans and animals and its effects on plants and animals. This information is carefully reviewed by Government scientists and by the Advisory Committee on Pesticides.

13.24 The Government has decided to review information on all the older pesticides approved before the statutory scheme was introduced. It is committed to trebling the annual evaluation rate of pesticides by 1993

The Government subjects all pesticides in Britain to vigorous controls and monitors pesticides residues in food and wildlife

and making substantial increases in the number of scientific staff carrying out this work. The costs of approving new pesticides and reviewing older ones are met by fees and a levy paid by pesticide manufacturers.

13.25 Britain's work will form part of a coordinated ten year European Community programme for the review of older agricultural pesticides. On non-agricultural pesticides, Britain has taken the lead in pressing the Commission to put forward similar proposals.

13.26 Possible effects on the environment are one of the main factors considered in the pesticides approval and review process, and environmental data forms a large part of the dossier submitted by manufacturers. The environmental data requirements for approval are at present being reviewed and updated, and the scientific methods used to evaluate the data are continually being improved.

Monitoring

13.27 The Government also monitors pesticide residues in food, animal feed, wildlife and human milk and tissues. It intends to strengthen this programme where possible using the results of the tests carried out by manufacturers, retailers and local authorities, which will greatly enlarge the data available to underpin the approval process. Ways of reducing the harmful environmental effects of pesticides and preventing damage to wildlife and beneficial species are investigated by Government

laboratories. Research into the effects of pesticides on the environment is also supported through the Natural Environment Research Council.

13.28 When new evidence of harmful effects on the environment becomes available, the approvals for the pesticide concerned are reviewed and can be modified to reduce the risk or completely withdrawn. Approvals for a number of pesticides have been withdrawn in recent years and it is possible that more will be withdrawn as the older pesticides are reviewed. If this happens there may be problems with disposing of existing stocks. If it is not safe to allow existing stocks to be used up, the Government will expect manufacturers and distributors to help to collect and dispose of them safely.

Pesticides in drinking water

13.29 Pesticides have been detected in 10% of drinking water sources at very low concentrations. Although in the view of the Department of Health these concentrations do not endanger health, they nevertheless exceed the standard of the Drinking Water Regulations. Water companies and the National Rivers Authority (NRA) are seeking to reduce pesticide usage within the affected water catchment areas and have installed or are investigating treatment processes for removing pesticides from water. If pesticides were to be detected in water supplies in excess of values which medical advisers consider safe for health, the water company would be expected to carry out intensive investigations and if necessary provide an alternative supply.

13.30 All water companies have devised monitoring strategies to meet their individual circumstances. The strategies will be checked by the Drinking Water Inspectorate, which will collect monitoring information to augment that collected by the NRA. Meanwhile, the use of three pesticides – Atrazine, Simazine and Isoproturon, which are those most commonly detected in drinking water – is being reviewed by the Advisory Committee on Pesticides. The Government is sponsoring a survey of the non-agricultural uses of pesticides which may enter water in order to reach a better understanding of the potential for water contamination.

Export of hazardous chemicals

13.31 There is concern internationally about the export of hazardous chemicals, especially pesticides, to developing countries which may not have the necessary expertise or training facilities to ensure that they are used safely. Britain played a major role in the development of the UNEP London Guidelines for Exchange of Information on Chemicals in International Trade and has also contributed to the Food and Agriculture Organisation (FAO) Code of Conduct on the Distribution and Use of Pesticides. A voluntary export notification scheme based on these agreements has been in operation since 1986, and an EC Regulation on export and import of dangerous substances is also now in force. The UNEP and FAO agreements have recently been updated to include a procedure for obtaining the prior informed consent of the importing country, and Britain will fully implement these revised agreements.

13.32 Britain makes a major contribution to the United Nations International Programme on Chemical Safety (IPCS) and the International Register of Potentially Toxic Chemicals, which provide developing countries with the necessary information to make decisions about the import of chemicals. The Government sponsors IPCS training courses for people from developing countries on the assessment and safe use of chemicals. It also makes an important contribution to advisory and training programmes on the use of chemicals in developing countries through aid programmes and sponsors research into integrated pest management and the safer use of pesticides.

MAJOR ACCIDENTS

13.33 This Chapter describes controls over the ways in which hazardous substances are used. But there remains a residual risk that hazardous substances could be unintentionally released to the environment as a result of an accident during manufacture, processing or storage. Three chemical accidents in particular have led to the tightening of safeguards in Britain and the European Community.

Flixborough

13.34 In 1974, 28 workers were killed at a petrochemical plant in Flixborough on Humberside after a massive explosion. In response to this tragedy, the Health and Safety Commission appointed an Advisory Committee on Major Hazards. The Committee produced three far-reaching reports over the next nine years. These have become the blueprint for controlling the manufacture of dangerous chemicals in Britain and throughout much of the developed world.

Seveso

13.35 In 1976 a reaction at a chemicals plant at Seveso in northern Italy got out of control. It released a cloud of poisonous chemicals which killed animals and plants and made people in the town ill. This accident triggered European Community action. In 1982 the Community agreed the 'Seveso' Directive. This lays down strict controls to prevent major chemical accidents and to limit the consequences for people and the environment of any which do occur.

Accidents at industrial plants can have serious consequences, as happened at this pesticides factory on the Rhine

The Government has put in place stringent precautions against major chemical accidents and is looking at ways of improving them

Basel

13.36 In 1986, a warehouse containing almost a thousand tonnes of agro-chemicals caught fire at a chemicals factory near Basel in Switzerland. The accident caused 30 tonnes of poisonous chemicals to enter the River Rhine and led to ecological damage along much of the river.

13.37 The fire near Basel focused concern on the environmental impact of chemical accidents. The European Community moved swiftly to update the Seveso Directive. It extended the scope to cover more storage of dangerous substances, thus increasing the number of installations subject to controls, and made more information about them available to the public.

Controls in Britain

13.38 In Britain those in charge of certain industrial installations must identify the risk of a major accident and demonstrate the safety of their operations. Stricter rules apply to the potentially more hazardous installations. These include a duty to:
• submit a written safety report to the Health and Safety Executive;
• prepare an on-site emergency plan; and
• provide certain information to people who live or work near the premises.

13.39 The local authorities must prepare an off-site emergency plan. They also have powers to limit new developments near major hazard installations to ensure that as few people as possible are exposed to risk. In addition there are rigorous restrictions on the location, design and construction of such installations. Safeguards such as these would have saved many lives in Bhopal, where at least 3,000 people died after an accident at a pesticides factory.

13.40 The Government intends to extend these controls to include consideration of environmental as well as human risks and is now studying further ways of preventing environmental disasters. A discussion paper, published in May 1990, recommends ways in which major hazard installations should take account of environmental risks in their safety report.

13.41 A major producer of chemicals, Britain has played an influential part in developing rigorous international controls. The Government remains committed to making available its expertise in support of the growing international interest in this area.

GENETICALLY MODIFIED ORGANISMS (GMOs)

13.42 People have practised biotechnology for thousands of years. For example we have used micro-organisms to make cheese and beer. And we have used traditional breeding methods to develop new varieties of crops with improved disease resistance, yield and quality. This breeding process has usually taken a long time, and we could only cross-breed characteristics between strains of the same species, such as two strains of wheat, or between closely related species, such as wheat and oats.

13.43 Using improved techniques, called genetic modification, scientists can now develop new strains more rapidly and transfer a much wider range of characteristics. They can also transfer genes between non-related species.

Uses of GMOs

13.44 Some of the first applications of genetic modification have been in medicine. For example, bacteria transformed to produce pharmaceutical products such as human insulin (used by diabetics) or growth hormone, can be used to produce them relatively cheaply and in a very pure form. Most of the insulin used by diabetics in Britain is now made in this way. We could also apply genetically modified organisms to help achieve environmental objectives, for example by using them to clean up oil spills, to control pests by biological means or to reduce the need for crop fertilizers.

13.45 The first planned releases of GMOs into the environment in Britain took place in 1986 and since then there has been a steady growth in such releases for research and development purposes. In 1989 there were six releases in Britain and 56 in the United States. Most of these were of plants. For example, bacterial genes have modified oil seed rape and tomatoes to strengthen their resistance to pests. There may well be a rapid growth in releases in the near future, both in Britain and in other developed countries.

Risks

13.46 The use of some GMOs may carry risks for the environment, for example:
• a new organism may be excessively competitive - like the rabbit in Australia or the grey squirrel in Britain;
• there may be unexpected side-effects;

Controls over GMOs

The Environmental Protection Bill will:
• require everyone intending to acquire, market or work with a GMO - whether a university researcher or a large company - to carry out an assessment of the environmental risks, and (depending on the circumstances) to notify the Secretary of State or to obtain his consent;
• impose a duty on all those involved with GMOs to use the best available techniques not entailing excessive cost (BATNEEC) to prevent environmental damage;
• give the Secretary of State powers to appoint inspectors to enforce these controls.

• characteristics may 'leak' from the original organism to others - the means by which some bacteria have acquired resistance to antibiotics.

13.47 These potential hazards are biological, as distinct from the chemical hazards described earlier. But in its response, the Government applies the same principles: it seeks to reduce the risk of harm to people and the environment through precautionary controls supported by rigorous research to improve our understanding.

The Environmental Protection Bill

13.48 The Government introduced specific controls to protect human health and safety from operations involving GMOs in 1978 and revised them in 1989. It is now taking urgent steps to protect the environment through measures in the Environmental Protection Bill. This establishes rigorous controls which will be flexible enough to stand the test of time and which will enable the Government to respond immediately to the development of new techniques.

13.49 When the Bill becomes law, the Government will follow it up with detailed regulations to implement the controls. These will interlock with those under the Health and Safety at Work etc Act 1974, which protect human safety. The Government has set up an Advisory Committee on Releases to the Environment to advise on the safety of specific proposals for release, on guidance for people working with GMOs and on key areas of research.

13.50 The Government recognises the need to improve the basis of scientific assessments of the risks which may arise from the release of GMOs into the environment. Research to meet this need is being funded by several government departments and agencies: expenditure in 1990/91 is expected to be nearly £5 million. This is in addition to

Treatment with human growth hormone, produced by genetic modification, enabled the older girl (on the left) to grow to the same height as her younger sister

Genetic modification of the baculovirus may control insect pests, as in this experiment which was Britain's first controlled GMO release

Genetically modified organisms may be used to destroy chemical pollutants

the considerable sums being spent by industry in order to ensure the safety of the products which they develop.

International action

13.51 The Government played an influential part in securing agreement on two EC Directives to control the contained use of genetically modified micro-organisms, for example in laboratories and industrial fermentation plant, and the release of all GMOs into the environment. The possible environmental effects of GMOs may not stop at national boundaries, and the Government supported the establishment of controls for the whole of the Community.

13.52 Genetic modification of organisms offers great promise for the economies of the whole world. It offers possibilities for new products less dependent on finite resources and holds out new prospects of combating disease and other pests which limit world agricultural production. Britain believes that public confidence in the safeguards must therefore be protected as the technology diffuses worldwide. It will be taking an active part in work in the OECD and the UN towards international guidelines on the exchange of information and expertise to bring about effective risk assessment and the management of activities involving GMOs worldwide.

CONCLUSION

13.53 The Government is taking action to protect people and the environment from the potential hazards posed by chemicals and new techniques of genetic modification. It is adopting a precautionary approach where necessary and setting in place a system of comprehensive controls. It is extending the research programme to find out more about potentially hazardous substances and their effects and stepping up environmental monitoring to check on the amounts of chemicals in the environment. In the emerging field of genetic modification, proposals for regulations to be made under the Environmental Protection Bill when enacted and the Health and Safety at Work etc. Act 1974 will be issued for consultation as soon as possible. The Government is working closely with international partners to share knowledge and coordinate action.

Research: hazardous substances and genetically modified organisms

For hazardous substances and genetically modified organisms, research aims to assess the risks and open new approaches to risk management. Public sector research relevant to dangerous substances includes projects
• to support policies to protect health and the environment and to provide scientific advice on limiting human exposure to toxic substances and environmental damage by toxic substances – Department of the Environment and the Medical Research Council (£2.4m in 1989/90)
• to provide information on rates of accidental release and dispersion into the atmosphere of hazardous gases or vapours from breached containers; and to investigate the factors causing gas or vapour explosions, the ignition and propagation of fires, and problems associated with explosives and reactive chemicals – Health and Safety Executive (£1.9m in 1989/90)

• to develop risk assessment techniques for the environmental release of genetically modified organisms – Departments of the Environment and of Trade and Industry, and the Agricultural and Food Research Council (£0.75m in 1989/90)
• to support the replacement of pesticides by the use of naturally occurring diseases of pests ('Viral Insecticides') – Natural Environment Research Council (£1.2m in 1989/90)
• to increase the efficiency of pesticide application and seek alternative non-chemical methods of controlling pests – Agricultural and Food Research Council (£4.3m in 1989/90)
• to help to produce crop plants and animals less dependent on agrochemicals and drugs – Agricultural and Food Research Council (£13.4m in 1989/90)

14

WASTE AND RECYCLING

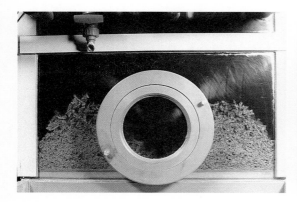

The Government's priorities are to reduce waste at source or reuse what is left, and dispose of the rest in the most environmentally responsible way

INTRODUCTION

14.1 Waste is inseparable from almost all areas of human activity. Britain, like other modern industrial economies, produces large amounts of it in many different forms. Chapter 12 describes the system of controls over waste discharges into the water environment from industry, sewage works and agricultural sources of pollution such as animal manure and silage. This Chapter focuses on waste for disposal on land. Industry generates about 100 million tonnes of such waste each year. Households are responsible for some 20 million tonnes – about a tonne of waste for each household. While we have not reached the levels of some countries, which produce twice our levels of rubbish, the quantity of some types of waste has grown rapidly in recent decades.

Modern waste contains a higher proportion of non-degradable products, such as plastics, and of chemicals: these can contaminate the environment if not properly controlled.

14.2 The Government's strategic approach to waste management aims to ensure that valuable raw materials are used efficiently and not discarded unnecessarily: and that unavoidable waste is disposed of safely and efficiently. To this end the Government will:
• encourage the minimisation of waste;
• promote the recycling of as much waste as possible – including the recovery of materials and energy;
• tighten controls over waste disposal standards; and
• take tough action to curb litter.

WASTE MINIMISATION

14.3 The Government's first priority is to reduce waste at source to a minimum. It intends to achieve this by imposing tough standards on industry through Integrated Pollution Control (IPC) and by promoting clean technologies.

Integrated Pollution Control

14.4 The Environmental Protection Bill promotes the minimisation of waste through the innovative system of Integrated Pollution Control. As Chapter 10 describes in more detail, IPC targets those industrial processes

which are potentially the most polluting. It requires them to prevent the release of pollutants. Where this is not possible, they must minimise releases and render harmless the substances involved.

14.5 IPC will deter industry from producing unnecessary waste. It will:
• control waste at source (industry must apply in advance to Her Majesty's Inspectorate of Pollution (HMIP) for an authorisation to operate);
• examine the potential impact of waste discharges on all three media (air, water and

land): this will enable HMIP to assess the best practicable option for the environment as a whole and to minimise the effect of waste on the environment;
• require industry to curb pollution by making use of the Best Available Techniques Not Entailing Excessive Cost (BATNEEC); HMIP may impose still higher standards where these are necessary; and
• lead to higher standards (HMIP will continually tighten up authorisations to reflect advances in technology).

Clean technologies

14.6 IPC's in-built dynamic towards higher standards relies on the development of new, cleaner technologies, and the Government encourages such technical innovation. The Department of the Environment launched the Environmental Protection Technology Scheme in 1988 to promote the prevention and abatement of pollution. In partnership with industry, the scheme is funding research projects into new methods of tackling pollution in Priority Areas where environmental standards need improving. Examples include ways of reducing emissions from waste incinerators and reducing the quantity of toxic substances discharged in industrial waste water. Through its Innovation and Environmental Programmes the Department of Trade and Industry is encouraging business to take voluntary cost-effective action to reduce waste.

14.7 The Government has now decided to strengthen its support for collaborative research in environmental technology. The Departments of Environment and Trade and Industry will merge their existing support by forming a joint Environmental Technology Innovation Scheme. This unified scheme will promote innovation and competitiveness in the environmental technology industry and pave the way for higher environmental standards in defined Priority Areas. As well as assisting research in Priority Areas, it will help innovatory projects in a wider range of subject areas including waste minimisation, recycling and new methods for treating and disposing of waste.

Waste disposal costs

14.8 The Government's policy is to harness market forces more effectively to encourage waste minimisation. The Environmental Protection Bill establishes a strict environmental regime for the disposal of waste, whether it is burned (incineration) or put in the ground (landfill). One effect of this will be to make waste disposal much more expensive. Increasing disposal costs will in turn provide a strong incentive for industry to cut down the volume of waste it produces and to make more use of cleaner technologies.

RECYCLING

14.9 Another Government priority is to encourage the re-use or recycling of materials which would otherwise be thrown away and the recovery of energy from waste which cannot be recycled.

14.10 Given the right conditions, recycling can make good environmental and economic sense. It will:
• conserve natural resources;
• save energy in production and transport;
• reduce the risk of pollution as well as saving costs in pollution control;

The Government is encouraging local authorities to provide recycling facilities and industry to set itself recycling targets

• reduce the demand for landfill space, especially near built-up areas where it is scarce; and
• produce goods more cheaply.

14.11 Recycling an aluminium can, for example, uses about 5% of the energy needed to make one from scratch, avoids extracting the metal and cuts down on pollution.

Constraints

14.12 The economics of recycling are far from simple. Not all forms of recycling are worthwhile. In some cases the amount of energy needed to collect, transport and process materials for recycling is greater than that needed to make a new product. It makes no sense to use up greater quantities of one material (for example oil, which emits carbon dioxide when it is burned) in order to re-use waste from another. The cost-effectiveness of recycling often involves a fine balance between the availability of waste materials, the costs of sorting and treating them, the market for recycled products and the price of raw materials.

14.13 A successful recycling scheme must combine:
• effective collection and sorting of the materials;
• the technology to convert them into a useful product; and
• a market demand for the product.

14.14 The costs and benefits of recycling vary from one material to another. There is currently limited (though growing) demand for recycled newspaper, although it is easy to collect; but not enough metal cans are collected to meet the demand. Some recent schemes in Europe and North America have run into problems because one part or other of the recycling chain has failed. The Government's recycling policy is therefore based on encouraging both the supply of recycled materials and the demand for them and on setting the right legislative framework.

Industry

14.15 British industry already recycles large amounts of waste. Our reclamation industry is well established: in 1986 it recovered some 27 million tonnes of re-usable materials, valued at over £2 billion; these included exports of about £700 million. British firms export recycling technology to a number of developing countries and to Eastern Europe. Britain is particularly successful at recovering waste metal from industrial processes: it re-uses some 82% of ferrous metal, 74% of copper and 66% of lead. Following the introduction of bottle banks, recycling of glass rose from 25,000 tonnes in 1977 to 310,000 tonnes in 1989. Many firms are carrying out reviews to improve their recycling performance. The rising costs of waste disposal will act as a powerful incentive to industry to step up recycling efforts still further.

Proportion of waste material used in industrial products in 1988

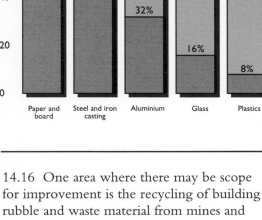

This de-inking factory will repulp 200,000 tons a year of newspaper and magazines by 1991

14.16 One area where there may be scope for improvement is the recycling of building rubble and waste material from mines and quarries. Two Government research projects are to examine the scope for making greater use of such materials, for example in building foundations, or in road construction. One project will study the availability of suitable materials and the economics of using them; the second project will explore the potential for broadening the specifications for building materials so as to encourage the use of waste.

14.17 The Government is encouraging industry to reduce unnecessary packaging of consumer goods. Industry has already improved its performance in this respect, but much more needs to be achieved. The Government will therefore discuss with industry and retailers proposals for:
• targets for packaging reduction;
• measures to reduce packaging through, for example, environmental auditing; and
• arrangements enabling consumers to discard or return packaging at the point of sale.
The Government will also encourage improvements in packaging design which will minimise waste and promote recycling or re-use. While the Government intends to proceed by voluntary means, it will if necessary consider the introduction of regulatory measures, such as deposit schemes, and will review measures applied in other countries.

14.18 The Government is discussing with newspaper publishers and newsprint producers the possibility of increasing the proportion of recycled paper used in newspapers and magazines.

14.19 The Government is monitoring local schemes to pilot the collection and recycling of used agricultural plastic sacks. In the light of these schemes, it will discuss their wider application with the plastics industry and farmers. More generally, it will work with the plastics industry and others to encourage the greater recovery and recycling of household plastic waste.

14.20 Industry is continually finding new uses for waste products. It can re-use glass in reflective coatings, for example, and waste paper for insulation. Many more opportunities remain to be exploited. The Government is giving support to research and development (£9.8 million in 1990/91). Industrial recycling has enjoyed much success and can look forward to a bright future.

Household waste

14.21 Britain's performance in recycling the waste we produce from our houses and offices is much weaker. We recover little more than 1 million tonnes a year from some 20 million tonnes of household waste.

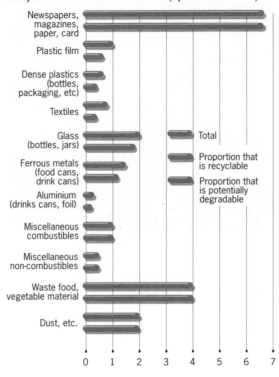

Analysis of UK Household waste (by million tonnes)

Newspapers, magazines, paper, card

Plastic film

Dense plastics (bottles, packaging, etc)

Textiles

Glass (bottles, jars)

Ferrous metals (food cans, drink cans)

Aluminium (drinks cans, foil)

Miscellaneous combustibles

Miscellaneous non-combustibles

Waste food, vegetable material

Dust, etc.

0 1 2 3 4 5 6 7

Total

Proportion that is recyclable

Proportion that is potentially degradable

14.22 Readily recyclable material – such as glass, cans, plastic bottles or paper – accounts for about 40% by weight of the average family dustbin. Vegetable peelings and other potential compost, which could help to offset the country's diminishing supplies of peat moss, are a further 10%. In all, about 50% of this waste is potentially recyclable: yet we achieve only 5%.

Target

14.23 The Government is setting the challenging target of recycling half our recyclable household waste by the end of the century. That is around 25% of all household waste.

Costs

14.24 Recycling, as well as waste-reducing technologies, will become a more attractive option for industry as a result of the Government's stricter environmental controls over waste disposals. But because householders, unlike industry, do not pay directly for the disposal of their waste, the Government is creating a comparable incentive for waste collection authorities to promote the recycling of household waste. The Environmental Protection Bill will introduce a system of 'recycling credits'. Recycling helps to reduce the volume of waste for disposal. The Bill will place a duty on waste disposal authorities to pass the savings in landfill costs that result from recycling to waste collection authorities. This will do much to make recycling more profitable. The Government has commissioned research into how such savings will be assessed and will consult fully on the findings before issuing formal advice to local authorities.

14.25 The Bill will also provide for landfill savings resulting from recycling to be payable to others who promote recycling, such as voluntary organisations. Again, the Government will consult widely on how this might be implemented.

Pilot projects

14.26 The Government is supporting a wide range of experimental projects in co-operation with industry, local authorities and voluntary organisations, to test collection and sorting techniques. 'Recycling City', is one such project. Sheffield and Cardiff are the first Recycling Cities; Dundee will follow in 1991 and other cities will be chosen. The schemes include a trial kerbside collection programme, in which householders are given special blue bins for their recyclable waste. The projects have also increased recycling 'banks' around the city where people can put paper, glass, cans, plastic bottles and batteries for recycling. The Government is encouraging kerbside collection schemes in other areas, and there are plans to start more projects. It will assess the results of these projects and others in the pipeline.

14.27 The results of such experiments will help to shape future strategy. The Government also intends to examine further ways of creating incentives for recycling, for example deposit schemes on bottles.

Recycling banks

14.28 The glass, newspaper and board industries already use large quantities of recycled material. Others are keen to obtain more material, for example steel and aluminium. The markets for other kinds of paper and some plastics are also developing. It is important that the collection of these materials keeps pace with demand.

14.29 The Government will therefore encourage the provision of recycling banks. It will:
• require local authorities, under the Environmental Protection Bill, to draw up recycling plans and publish them;
• issue guidance to local authorities on recycling, including the provision of new can and bottle banks (for example, where to site them and who should operate them);
• encourage industry to set itself recycling targets: for example, industry has already set a target of 10,000 bottle banks by 1995 (more than double present numbers); and 1,000 can banks by 1994 (more than five times present numbers);
• encourage large supermarkets to provide collection facilities wherever practicable;
• require local authorities to take recycling facilities into account when considering planning applications for large new shopping developments;
• encourage local authorities to invest in recycling centres and new equipment, such as magnetic separators for cans, in partnership with private firms;
• encourage industry to expand its capacity to process the extra material collected; and
• ensure careful review and evaluation of new and existing schemes.

Problem materials

14.30 Certain kinds of waste may create

The Government is requiring local authorities to draw up recycling plans including details of recycling centres and other facilities

serious environmental problems. Examples include small batteries, the chlorofluorocarbons (CFCs) in fridges, old tyres and used oil from cars. A number of local authorities and industries have schemes for collecting batteries; draining CFCs from fridges and returning them for recycling; and collecting waste oil for energy recovery. However, commercial recycling may not be sufficient to deal with these products. There may therefore be a case for placing an additional charge on them to help meet the extra costs of their collection and recycling or safe disposal. The Government's preferred option is for industry itself to come up with workable schemes and is actively discussing a range of proposals; but it will consider statutory measures if necessary.

14.31 The Government, in consultation with manufacturers and distributors, is considering the options for dealing with waste tyres, which are particularly difficult to get rid of safely. Buried tyres have a tendency to rise to the surface; shredding them, to make them easier to bury, has proved difficult because of their metal lining; and uncontrolled burning of them can give off poisonous fumes. One option is that an extra levy on each tyre sold would go into a central fund to pay for research into safe incineration or new methods of shredding.

14.32 Britain is also working with its European Community partners to improve the treatment of such problem wastes. A proposed directive on batteries, in the final stages of negotiation, will require their separate collection and disposal. It will also ban the marketing of batteries containing undesirable proportions of heavy metals.

Technology

14.33 Industry is increasingly aware of the need to design goods so that they can be recycled. The technology for recycling waste material is also advancing rapidly in many areas, as the commercial and environmental benefits become more clearly established. For certain materials, however, such as plastics, cloth and vegetable matter (which can be turned into compost), advances in technology need stimulating. The Environmental Technology Innovation Scheme will stimulate better technologies for recycling these and other materials.

14.34 The Government is encouraging energy recovery from waste materials which cannot be recycled. Some kinds of waste can either be incinerated directly or processed into refined fuels. The heat recovery can be used in industrial processes to heat buildings or to generate electricity. This can help to curb greenhouse gas emissions by reducing the consumption of other fossil fuels. Over 30 energy recovery plants from landfill gas are already in operation and a further 30 are being planned or built. As Annex C on renewable sources of energy describes, the Government is stimulating the further development and use of this technology.

Further steps

14.35 Successful recycling is not only a matter of economics and technology. All of us can help to recycle more waste.

14.36 Voluntary organisations have an important part to play. Some, notably Friends of the Earth, are active in trial projects. Others such as Wastewatch provide information on the availability of recycling facilities. The Government, with support from Wastewatch, is to produce a video on recycling for showing in schools and elsewhere.

14.37 Individuals can exercise consumer

power by buying more recycled or recyclable products. We can urge our local supermarkets and our local authorites to provide more recycling facilities, where needed. We can re-use products more, for example plastic carrier bags. We can compost waste vegetable matter for use in our gardens. And we can show greater discipline in segregating our waste, either for kerbside collection or for recycling banks.

14.38 The Government intends to use its influence as a major consumer. In future it will discriminate positively in favour of recycled products. It will, for example, use recycled paper wherever this is available, of adequate quality and represents value for money. The Government's guide to the environmental implications of purchasing and building management (see Chapter 18) will show ways in which the Government can use its purchasing power to encourage the market for cost-effective recycled materials. The best environmental practice guide for local authorities will set out ways of encouraging recycling in local government.

14.39 The Government will introduce an environmental labelling scheme to help consumers make an informed choice about the products they buy. (Chapter 17 describes this in more detail.) By taking environmental considerations into account, consumers will encourage manufacturers to produce goods and packaging which are environmentally more friendly. The Government is pressing for the adoption of a common scheme across the European Community including assessment of the recycled content and recyclability of products.

14.40 The Government will consider how to carry forward the work of the expert Advisory Group on Recycling, which included representatives from industry, local authorities and voluntary organisations as well as Government. It attaches importance to maintaining a pool of expertise on recycling issues in view of the likelihood of advances in technology and the need to develop recycling initiatives in co-operation with our European Community partners.

The major European glass manufacturers launched this logo for recycled glass jars and bottles in June 1990

WASTE DISPOSAL

14.41 The Government is introducing tough new licensing requirements for disposal of the waste which cannot be eliminated at source or recycled. It is also working with local authorities and the waste disposal industry to plan adequate disposal facilities across the country.

Disposal facilities

14.42 About 90% of our waste is disposed of in the ground - in some 4,000 controlled landfill sites. Britain's geology enables this to be done safely in many areas. There is no shortage of suitable sites in most parts of the country, though there are obvious shortages in some metropolitan areas. Britain has some 35 municipal incinerators which burn most of the remaining household waste. Four specialised high temperature incinerators deal with some of our most toxic waste. In the past, landfill disposal has been much the cheaper option for most waste: incineration has sometimes cost up to three times as much. The provisions of the Environmental Protection Bill for stronger licensing powers for Waste Regulation Authorities, described in the following paragraphs, will raise standards of landfill substantially and thus increase the costs of landfill relative to other forms of treatment and disposal.

The Environmental Protection Bill

14.43 Through the 1974 Control of Pollution Act Britain developed one of the world's first licensing systems for waste disposal control and subsequent EC legislation reflected this system. Under the 1974 Act, waste regulation and disposal authorities in England are the shire counties and a mixture of statutory and voluntary arrangements in metropolitan areas; in Wales they are the District councils, and in Scotland the District and Islands Councils.

14.44 In recent years the limitations of the Act have become apparent. In particular, it gave too few powers to enforcement bodies; and it focused controls at the point of disposal, with inadequate attention to earlier

Incineration reduces the amount of waste to be put in landfill sites. The Government is encouraging the generation of electricity from burning waste

stages of the waste chain or to the maintenance of old disposal sites.

14.45 The Environmental Protection Bill comprehensively overhauls this system:
• for the first time it imposes a duty of care on all those involved in the waste disposal chain to ensure that waste is disposed of safely (breach of the duty will be a criminal offence);
• local authorities in England and Wales may no longer act as both regulators and operators of waste disposal (as Waste Regulation Authorities free from operational responsibilities, they will have full responsibility for licensing and enforcement, while new arms-length waste disposal companies will compete with the private sector for contracts);
• applicants for waste management licenses will have to demonstrate that they have the financial and technical competence to do the job (holders of licences who manage sites incompetently or breach their license conditions may lose their rights to operate disposal sites, while remaining legally and financially accountable for any pollution they may have caused);
• the Bill imposes a new duty of aftercare (licence holders will continue to be responsible for sites once tipping activities have ceased until they are able to demonstrate that there are no continuing risks of

environmental harm and they will be responsible for restoring and cleaning up the site;
• Waste Regulation Authorities (WRAs) will be able to charge for waste management licences and recover costs associated with monitoring and inspection; and
• authorities will have a new duty to monitor and inspect old landfill sites, to undertake remedial work where necessary and to charge site owners for the costs.

14.46 These measures represent a radical advance, and forthcoming EC directives are likely to incorporate a number of them. The Government will publish detailed regulations and guidance to implement them and will keep the system under review.

Role of the private sector

14.47 The private sector, which generates most of Britain's waste, has already made great progress in minimising waste from its production processes and in recycling. The Environmental Protection Bill's new duty of care will encourage an environmentally conscious approach to waste disposal. Every producer will now have to take as much care of what happens to its waste as it does to consignments of it products.

14.48 Britain's private sector waste disposal industry, which manages almost all our industrial waste, will face three critical challenges. It will need to:
• provide the necessary investment to meet the rising standards of waste disposal;
• keep pace with the rapid developments in disposal technologies, including techniques for recovering energy from waste; and
• give comprehensive training to its workforce so that it can improve its technical competence in line with rising standards.
The Government is encouraged by the creation of the Waste Management Industry Training and Advisory Board by the waste management industry and the Institute of Waste Management. With the help of Government financial support, the Board will develop a programme of training in waste management. It will also create specific

qualifications for holding a waste management licence to meet the requirement of the Environmental Protection Bill that licence holders should be technically competent.

Role of local authorities

14.49 The Bill places major responsibilities on local authorities for planning, regulating and arranging the disposal of household and commercial waste in their areas.

Planning

14.50 Local authorities are responsible both for preparing waste disposal plans and for considering planning applications for new waste disposal facilities. These waste disposal plans must forecast future waste from all sources and estimate the type and quantity of facilities that will be needed to deal with it. They must be sufficiently accurate to enable the provision of an adequate range of disposal facilities. Local authorities should take into account the needs identified in their disposal plans when determining applications for new facilities. The Government will issue planning policy guidance notes to assist local authorities.

Regulation

14.51 Waste Regulation Authorities will regulate waste disposal. The Bill considerably strengthens their powers to give and take away licences and to take enforcement action.

14.52 The Department of the Environment will give guidance to the WRAs in the form of Waste Management Papers. These provide technical guidance on landfill techniques and the disposal of particular types of waste. The Department will strengthen this guidance by prescribing standards on disposal techniques and giving statutory guidance on licensing.

14.53 Her Majesty's Inspectorate of Pollution (HMIP) will check that the WRAs use their new legal powers to the full. It will closely monitor their performance and will advise the Secretary of State if it is unsatisfactory and there is any need for him to intervene.

14.54 At present there are about 100 licensing authorities in England and Wales. The standards of waste regulation vary considerably and the Government is pleased that local authorities in England have agreed to the creation of regional groupings of WRAs to bring about more consistent standards of planning, licensing and enforcement. The Government endorses this voluntary approach but will take powers in the Bill to introduce statutory arrangements if necessary. In Wales, the Welsh Office is discussing with the Council of Welsh Districts the steps that are needed to improve and strengthen the existing regional group arrangements.

Disposal

14.55 Local authorities will arrange for the disposal of waste collected in their area. The Bill requires them, in awarding contracts, to take into account not only costs but also the environmental effects of the proposed handling arrangements, including the benefits to be gained from recycling and energy recovery. Local authorities will thus promote environmentally conscious waste management and encourage new disposal and recycling technologies. As major waste producers they will be bound by the duty of care.

Costs

14.56 In future WRAs will be able to charge site operators (rather than local charge payers) for the costs of licensing and inspection. This important extension to the polluter pays principle will ensure that local authorities have adequate resources to carry out their responsibilities effectively.

14.57 The Environmental Protection Bill, through the new licensing conditions, will substantially increase the costs of waste disposal by all means, and particularly by landfill, over the next five years. Requirements for higher engineering standards for landfill will probably cause a

shift towards incineration, especially for hazardous waste. Any temptation to dispose of waste illegally, for example by flytipping, will be countered by the new duty of care on all who handle waste; and this will be backed by sanctions under criminal law.

Old landfill sites

14.58 Britain, like other industrialised countries, has to cope with the legacy of past waste disposal practices when authorities were less aware of the potential hazards. Some old landfill sites which contain poisonous wastes may leak and contaminate soil or water supplies in the surrounding area. Some are emitting methane gas, which carries the risk of explosion.

14.59 Local authorities and industry are starting a programme of remedial work at up to 1000 such old sites. The Government has earmarked £33 million for 1990/91 to help them tackle these problems. WRAs will be

The Government is introducing tough new standards for waste disposal. Sites must be restored and regularly inspected

Britain is self-sufficient in disposing of its waste, and is pressing for all developed countries to make similar arrangements

monitoring especially carefully those sites where past standards were inadequate.

International self-sufficiency

14.60 Partly because of poor standards at some old incinerators and landfill sites, there is public resistance in most developed countries to proposals for new waste facilities. No one wants a disposal site or an incinerator in his neighbourhood, and local environmental groups are active in opposing planning applications.

14.61 In recent years, this attitude has had serious international consequences. During the 1980s, some industries tried to evade tighter licensing or planning controls by exporting waste, particularly toxic waste. Some of this movement has been acceptable – because not all countries have had the specialist disposal facilities needed for certain types of waste; but some has been of dubious nature – in effect finding cheap disposal routes (for example in developing countries) with scant regard to environmental consequences. In some well publicised cases ships with cargoes of toxic waste have sailed the high seas in search of a country willing to accept their load. Britain has taken the lead in the EC and the OECD in calling for all developed countries to become self-sufficient in disposing of their own waste, and the European Community has now incorporated this principle into its legislation. The principle of self-sufficiency provides an incentive for countries to make proper arrangements for the disposal of their own waste and to encourage waste minimisation and recycling.

14.62 Britain supports the Basel Convention, drawn up by the United Nations Environmental Programme (UNEP), which introduces global controls on waste movements. Britain and other signatories of the Convention have agreed to minimise their production of waste and to provide adequate disposal facilities in order to reduce transboundary movements of waste. The Government is helping to finance the Convention's Interim Secretariat, which is developing further controls and compiling information for developing countries on waste management. It is also pressing the European Commission to bring forward a proposal enabling the Community and member states to ratify the Convention.

14.63 The completion of the internal market in 1992 will remove barriers to trade within the European Community. The Government believes that waste should not be regarded as a tradeable commodity like any other. It will seek to maintain effective controls on the transboundary movement of all wastes.

14.64 In the absence of binding international agreements, the Environmental Protection Bill gives the Secretary of State additional powers to control imports and exports of wastes. The Government will be able to ban the import of waste where there is a risk of pollution or in order to conserve disposal capacity. In particular the Government believes that waste should not be imported to Britain for direct landfill.

National self-sufficiency

14.65 At a national level Britain is self-sufficient in waste disposal facilities, and the Government intends that it should remain so. It recognises that weaker environmental standards in the past may have led to some pollution from incinerators and landfill sites, though these instances have been relatively few, and the pollution has not been on the scale experienced in some other countries. The Government acknowledges the genuine public concern at proposals for new waste facilities. But the waste generated by a modern industrial economy has to be disposed of somewhere. Opposition to all disposal facilities is not a responsible policy for any person or group to adopt.

14.66 The Government is taking vigorous action to ensure the very highest standards of human safety and environmental protection are maintained. Major new disposal facilities are also subject to a prior assessment of their environmental impact (see Chapter 6).

14.67 The Government intends that so far as practicable there should be adequate facilities within each region for dealing with all waste which arises there. It will work with local authorities in their regional groups and with the waste disposal industry to develop this principle of self-sufficiency. Local authorities also have an important part to play in raising public awareness of the need for waste disposal facilities.

14.68 The Government recognises the need for flexibility in applying this principle. Certain special types of waste may need to be handled at the nearest suitable facility. The Government may also have to play a part in planning decisions in determining the location of special waste disposal facilities.

14.69 The Government will monitor the availability of waste disposal facilities across the country. It will compile information on trends in the volumes and types of waste generated and on the unit costs of disposal in order to assess the effectiveness of the changes it is introducing.

LITTER

14.70 Waste disposal is not only a matter for industry and local authorities. Businesses and individuals have a role to play in disposing of their own waste properly.

14.71 Although there are no reliable statistics, there is growing concern that litter has increased in recent decades. Smokers are responsible for around a third of litter by dropping cigarette butts, packets and matches. The explosion of fast-food packaging and plastic carrier bags in recent years has caused a change in the nature of litter, but all litter is caused by individuals throwing waste onto the ground instead of into a bin.

14.72 The Environmental Protection Bill launches a two-pronged attack. It places a new duty on the Crown, local authorities, schools and certain private landowners, to keep their public areas clear of litter. The Government intends to put the same duty on transport operators, such as British Rail and London Regional Transport. Local authorities will be able to require shops and businesses to keep the pavement in front of their premises clear. The Bill also raises the maximum fine for leaving litter from £400 to £1000 and it empowers local authorities to operate fixed penalty schemes.

14.73 A code of practice will describe standards of cleanliness which those under the duty to keep land clear of litter should achieve and will recommend the 'best practice' methods for achieving them. The Government estimates that this new duty will add some £50 million to spending on street cleaning by local authorities in England: it has taken this into account in the local government finance settlement for 1991/92.

The Government is placing a new duty on local authorities and other landowners to keep public areas clear of litter

It is up to all of us to keep
our neighbourhoods
clean and litter-free

14.74 The Bill gives an important role to individuals. We all pay for our streets to be cleaned through the Community Charge. The Bill will give effective means of redress if standards slip. It will give individuals the power to apply to the magistrates' court for a litter abatement order against any authority which fails to keep its land clean. This enables individuals to act as litter watchdogs.

14.75 Individuals above all can reduce litter by not dropping it. We should:
• recycle our waste where possible, by taking bottles, cans, and other materials to recycling banks;

• re-use packaging as often as possible, for example, carrier bags, plastic bottles or cardboard boxes;
• dispose of our own waste by putting it in bins for collection and proper disposal; and
• keep the area in front of our own homes clean.

14.76 Voluntary organisations can help convince people to behave in ways which are environmentally and socially friendly. The Department of the Environment gives the Tidy Britain Group substantial grants to help them continue their campaigning and educational work on litter.

CONCLUSION

14.77 The Government's waste management strategy reflects the principles which guide its overall approach to environmental protection. It aims to make economic development more sustainable by encouraging less use of valuable natural resources, less use of land for disposing of our waste and less atmospheric pollution. And it aims to prevent pollution by minimising waste at source, by recycling as much waste material as possible, and by ensuring stricter controls over material which does need to be disposed of. The Government is using both strict regulation and market forces to achieve its goals and will rigorously monitor the success of these measures. It is working in close co-operation with other countries to extend the application of these principles internationally. It is encouraging industry, business, voluntary organisations and individuals to play their part in curbing waste.

Research: waste

Waste research is directed towards improving our understanding of how substances degrade, and how particular chemicals behave once disposed of. It aims at new techniques for waste minimisation and recycling, including the scope for new techniques for energy recovery. Public sector research includes projects:
• to conduct studies aimed at setting National Standards and assessing best available techniques for managing wastes – Department of the Environment and HMIP (£3.0m)
• to develop risk assessment procedures in waste management for operational and regulatory purposes – DOE, HMIP and NRA (£0.5m)
• to encourage best practice in areas such as design, production processes, and clean technology – Department of Trade and Industry (£1.0m in 1990-91 new programme)
• to minimise the effects from waste deposits on, for example, groundwater – Natural Environment Research Council (£0.2m in 1989/90 including work commissioned by the Department of the Environment)
• to investigate new clean technologies to prevent or reduce pollution in the agricultural, food and manufacturing industries – Science and Engineering Research Council and Agricultural Food Research Council (£0.4m in 1989/90)
• to investigate the possible uses of refuse derived fuel – Department of Energy, Department of the Environment (£0.2m in 1989/90)
• to investigate the possible uses of refuse derived humus, including use as compost and alternative to peat – Department of the Environment, Department of Trade and Industry (£0.3m in 1989/90)
• to introduce a system of recycling credits to encourage recycling rather than landfill Department of the Environment (£0.1m in 1990/91 new programme)
• to encourage greater recycling and new applications for waste construction aggregates and other building materials – Department of the Environment (£0.2m in 1989/90)

15

NUCLEAR POWER AND RADIOACTIVE WASTE

Britain's 18 nuclear power stations contribute nearly 20% of our electricity while emitting practically no carbon dioxide and sulphur dioxide

Proportions of electricity generated by nuclear power

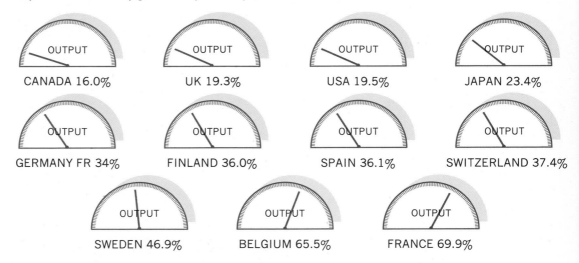

CANADA 16.0% UK 19.3% USA 19.5% JAPAN 23.4%

GERMANY FR 34% FINLAND 36.0% SPAIN 36.1% SWITZERLAND 37.4%

SWEDEN 46.9% BELGIUM 65.5% FRANCE 69.9%

INTRODUCTION

15.1 Nuclear power accounted for 16% of the world's electricity generation in 1989, when there were 426 nuclear power plants in operation. Over 30% of the electricity in the European Community is generated by nuclear power: in France and Belgium the proportion is almost 70%. Britain currently has 18 nuclear power stations which contribute as much as half of Scotland's electricity and some 20% of the electricity for the whole of Britain.

15.2 Nuclear power makes an important contribution to Britain's economy too, but it faces a challenging future. This Chapter describes the advantages of nuclear power; the Government's precautionary approach to pollution control, which aims to minimise the risk of human exposure to radiation; and the action the Government and the nuclear industry are taking to maintain high safety standards, improve methods of waste disposal, carry out research into health risks and other safety concerns and improve the industry's economic performance.

NUCLEAR ENERGY IN BRITAIN

15.3 Calder Hall in Cumbria, which opened in 1956, was the first industrial-scale power station in the world to demonstrate the commercial potential of generating electricity through nuclear fission. This is now a proven technology.

15.4 Two types of gas-cooled reactor produce most of Britain's nuclear electricity: we have nine operating Magnox stations and seven newer Advanced Gas-Cooled Reactor (AGR) stations. The most widely used design outside Britain is the Pressurised Water Reactor (PWR). The first British PWR is now being built at Sizewell B in Suffolk and will serve to replace some of the retiring Magnox capacity when it comes on stream in 1994/95.

15.5 The Government is privatising the electricity industry under the Electricity Act 1989, but the nuclear power stations will remain in the public sector. In England and Wales they will be managed by Nuclear Electric Plc and in Scotland by Scottish Nuclear Ltd.

Advantages

15.6 The Government recognises two main advantages to continued nuclear power generation. First, the use of nuclear power increases the diversity of our energy supply and thus helps to maintain security of supply. The past 20 years have seen major fluctuations in the price and availability of fossil fuels such as gas, oil and coal. It is important to insure ourselves against future unforeseen developments by deriving our energy from a range of different sources. Secondly, nuclear power can play a part in curbing acid rain and in combating global warming. Nuclear stations emit practically no sulphur dioxide (SO_2) or nitrogen oxides (NOx) (the principal ingredients of acid rain) and practically no carbon dioxide (CO_2)(the principal greenhouse gas). If the electricity currently provided by nuclear power stations were to be generated by gas, Britain would emit about 7 million tonnes more carbon, increasing total emissions by about 4.5% each year. If the same amount of electricity were generated by coal, our emissions would increase by around 15.5 million tonnes each year, increasing total emissions by nearly 10%.

15.7   In addition nuclear power has long-term potential. As currently used, proven reserves of uranium, which nuclear power uses as a fuel, are about equivalent in terms of power generation to those of oil. But reprocessing of uranium after use can allow around 95% to be recycled into more fuel. Technical developments in reactor design (including fast reactors) would also lead to more efficient use of fuel.

15.8   For these reasons the Government wishes to maintain the nuclear option, but only if nuclear power becomes more economic and the industry demonstrates that it can maintain high standards of safety and environmental protection.

Health and safety

15.9   All forms of energy entail risks if not properly controlled. Nuclear power is not unique in this respect. Both the coal and the off-shore oil and gas industries have experienced major disasters, such as those at Aberfan and Piper Alpha. The British nuclear industry has an excellent safety record. Nevertheless, nuclear power arouses special public concern.

15.10   The specific risks from nuclear power stations arise from the potential for exposure to additional sources of radiation through:

• the risk of an accident at a nuclear installation releasing radioactivity either within the site or, as at Chernobyl, into the environment;
• occupational risks to nuclear workers in the normal course of their work; and
• the risks to man and the environment of handling and disposing of radioactive waste material.

Radiation doses

15.11   Radiation is a natural phenomenon. About 87% of the radiation to which we are exposed each year comes from natural sources such as rocks, soil, cosmic rays, food and drink. Most of the remainder comes from medical uses, such as diagnostic x–rays.

15.12 Our exposure to radiation in the environment can vary according to where we live or what we do. For example, people living in parts of South-West England are exposed to more radiation than the average for Britain because of the radon gas released from the ground. Aircraft crew receive higher than average radiation doses from cosmic rays. Coal miners and medical staff, such as radiologists and radiographers, also encounter radiation in their work.

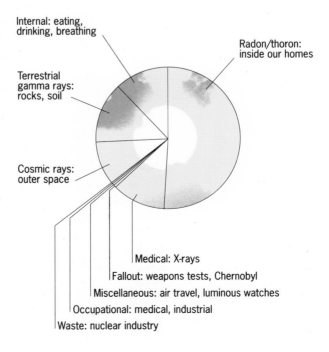

Sources of radiation exposure of the UK population

Internal: eating, drinking, breathing

Radon/thoron: inside our homes

Terrestrial gamma rays: rocks, soil

Cosmic rays: outer space

Medical: X-rays

Fallout: weapons tests, Chernobyl

Miscellaneous: air travel, luminous watches

Occupational: medical, industrial

Waste: nuclear industry

15.13 Only 0.1% of the annual radiation dose to which the British population is exposed comes from routine discharges from the nuclear industry. This compares with some 51% from the naturally occurring gases radon and thoron (a form of radon).

15.14 Radiation can be used in a number of beneficial ways – in medicine, industry and agriculture – but it can also damage body cells and cause cancer. For this reason all activities involving radiation are subject to strict controls. The National Radiological Protection Board (NRPB) gives independent and authoritative advice on the subject and keeps in close touch with international organisations such as the International Commission on Radiological Protection (ICRP).

15.15 The Government's policy, which is in line with internationally accepted principles, is to reduce exposure to radiation from industrial sources to levels as low as are reasonably achievable; and to ensure that in any case people should not be exposed, either as workers or as members of the public, to higher levels of risk than from other activities regarded as acceptable.

15.16 It recognises that present knowledge of the human effects of radiation risks is incomplete. In particular, the increased rates of childhood leukaemia around some nuclear sites, as established by the independent expert advisory Committee on Medical Aspects of Radiation in the Environment, are a matter of concern. A recent report has documented a statistical association between the raised incidence of childhood leukaemia in the

vicinity of Sellafield and employment of fathers at the plant. The causal link has yet to be identified. The Government is funding more research in this area; it will shortly commission further studies and act as necessary on their findings.

15.17 The current maximum levels of radiation dose for nuclear workers and members of the public were recommended by the International Commission on Radiological Protection in 1977 and endorsed by the National Radiological Protection Board. However, scientific data on the risks from radiation are continually reassessed. ICRP has recently reviewed the available evidence and is expected to recommend lower limits shortly. In the meantime, the NRPB has issued interim guidance that worker doses should not, on average, exceed one third of the previous limits.

15.18 The Government will consider such revised recommendations carefully, taking into account advice from the NRPB and the expected revision of the EC Directive on radiation safety standards. British exposure levels are within current ICRP limits, and radiation dose rates to the general public and to the vast majority of workers in the industry are already lower than the levels recommended by the NRPB in their interim guidance.

Operational safety

15.19 Because the consequences of a nuclear accident can be so great, the nuclear industry gives safety extremely high priority – from the initial designing of a plant through construction, commissioning, and operation to decommissioning. All these stages are subject to rigorous licensing procedures administered by the Health and Safety Executive's Nuclear Installations Inspectorate. The Inspectorate can require an operator to make changes in the interests of safety or if necessary to shut down a nuclear installation immediately. It regularly inspects nuclear installations to ensure safety standards are maintained.

15.20 An important principle governing

nuclear safety is that known as ALARP (As Low as Reasonably Practicable). This requires operators to reduce risks to the lowest level practicable and to maintain a constant search for safety improvements.

15.21 The nuclear industry and the Government will continue to fund research into nuclear safety to improve standards and reduce risks. The Government recovers costs through a levy on the industry.

Emergency arrangements

15.22 Although accidents at nuclear installations are very unlikely, the Government requires operators to prepare detailed plans to cover emergency procedures for the site and the surrounding area. The operators draw up these plans in consultation with Government, local authorities, the police and other bodies and they exercise and improve them regularly.

15.23 In the event of a nuclear incident overseas, Britain will receive initial notification under the International Atomic Energy Agency's Early Notification Convention. To enable Britain to determine what action is necessary the Prime Minister announced in 1987 the framework of a new National Response Plan for handling any future overseas nuclear incidents like Chernobyl. Under this Plan, the Department of the Environment has set up a national radiation monitoring network, RIMNET. An interim system, which monitors gamma radiation doses at 46 Meteorological Office sites throughout Britain, has been in full operation since early 1989. It will immediately detect any abnormal increase in

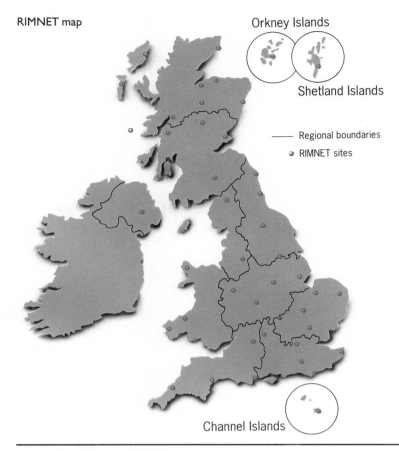

RIMNET map

Orkney Islands

Shetland Islands

—— Regional boundaries
⊙ RIMNET sites

Channel Islands

radiation levels and raise a central alert. The Government publishes summaries of RIMNET monitoring data at six-monthly intervals.

15.24 The second phase of the RIMNET system, which the Government aims to have in place by the end of 1991, will double the number of monitoring sites. This will help the Government to determine the scale of any hazard and the actions it may need to take in response. RIMNET is also equipped to relay immediate information to the responsible authorities and to the public.

Special monitoring sites would provide early warning of any nuclear incident overseas; the number of these sites will be doubled

RADIOACTIVE WASTE MANAGEMENT

15.25 Radioactive materials from any source, whether medical, industrial or from nuclear power, can remain radioactive for hundreds or thousands of years. The Government has therefore set strict safety standards for their use, storage and disposal. The Government and site operators carry out an extensive monitoring programme to ensure that these

standards are met. Major discharges are sampled, recorded and analysed.

15.26 The Government is responsible for radioactive waste management strategy in Britain. It aims to ensure that the creation of radioactive waste is minimised and that it is managed and disposed of safely.

The Government has set strict safety standards for the use, storage and disposal of radioactive waste

Organisations which produce radioactive waste are responsible for its safe and effective management and for meeting the full cost of such actions. The Government receives independent expert advice on these issues from the Radioactive Waste Management Advisory Commitee.

15.27 Radioactive waste is identified according to its level of radioactivity and longevity. Low-level waste includes only slightly contaminated material such as gloves, overalls or laboratory equipment. More active material, such as reactor components or sludge from waste treatment plants, is classified as intermediate-level waste. High-level or heat generating waste includes the very highly active products from the reprocessing of spent nuclear fuel.

15.28 Low-level waste, which constitutes about 94% by volume of all radioactive waste, is mainly disposed of at a 300-acre controlled landfill site at Drigg in Cumbria. The waste is not only from the nuclear industry: it comes from all users of radioactive substances, such as hospitals, research establishments and industry. It is packed into containers and placed in concrete-lined trenches which are subsequently sealed. Intermediate-level (about 6%) and high-level waste (about 0.3%) is currently stored at nuclear establishments.

UK Nirex Ltd is speeding up its search for a repository for the disposal of low and intermediate level radioactive waste

15.29 As part of its strategy for the disposal of intermediate-level waste, the Goverment gave UK Nirex Ltd the task of developing a deep underground repository to isolate the waste from the environment for the many thousands of years which will be necessary. In 1987 the Government agreed that the repository should also be used for low-level waste. Nirex is now carrying out detailed geological studies at Dounreay and Sellafield to identify a suitable site. These investigations are subject to normal planning procedures, and the Government will make any proposal for development subject to a full public inquiry as well as to compliance with strict safety standards.

15.30 Until 1982, Britain disposed of some low and intermediate-level waste in drums at selected sites in the deep ocean. In 1988 the

Government decided that this waste should be stored for future disposal in the Nirex repository. The Government has not ruled out sea disposal for large items such as boilers from decommissioned power stations but will keep under review whether this disposal option needs to be maintained.

15.31 High-level waste will be stored for at least 50 years at Sellafield and Dounreay to allow it to cool. It is currently kept in liquid form in cooled stainless steel tanks. British Nuclear Fuels (BNFL) will complete a new vitrification plant in 1990 at Sellafield. This will convert waste into glass blocks and reduce its overall volume by two-thirds.

15.32 Low-level liquid waste from nuclear establishments arises mainly from water used in cooling processes. After treatment to reduce its radioactive content it is discharged to the environment. All releases to the environment require an authorisation from the Government. Radioactive discharges are minimised in accordance with international recommendations and Government authorisations. BNFL is investing over £500 million in new treatment plants at Sellafield. These have reduced levels of radioactivity in discharges to the Irish Sea to less than 3% of what they were in 1979.

An artists impression of a cavern repository in hard rock for low and intermediate-level waste

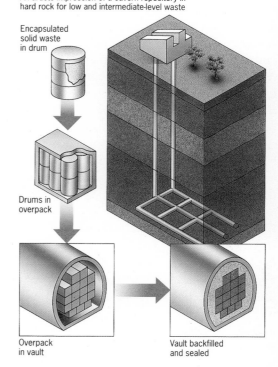

Encapsulated solid waste in drum

Drums in overpack

Overpack in vault

Vault backfilled and sealed

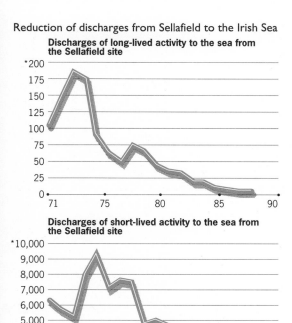

Reduction of discharges from Sellafield to the Irish Sea

Discharges of long-lived activity to the sea from the Sellafield site

Discharges of short-lived activity to the sea from the Sellafield site

*Terabequerels per year

15.33 The Government is confident that present disposal and storage arrangements are safe. But it recognises the need to provide methods of permanent disposal eventually for intermediate and high-level waste.

Reprocessing

15.34 Reprocessing separates recyclable material from waste. After several years in a reactor, the uranium fuel becomes less efficient and needs to be replaced. Reprocessing allows over 95% of the uranium and plutonium in the spent fuel to be re-used. It also puts the remaining waste into a better form for storage and eventual disposal.

15.35 A proportion of the spent fuel which is reprocessed at Sellafield comes from abroad. Since 1976 reprocessing contracts with overseas customers have allowed for the return of waste. The Government has made it clear that waste will be returned. No radioactive waste will be imported into Britain.

ECONOMICS

15.36 At current levels of fossil fuel prices, nuclear power is more expensive than electricity generated from new coal, oil or gas-fired stations. The Non-Fossil Fuel Obligation set under the Electricity Act 1989 (see Chapter 5) provides market protection for nuclear power and renewable sources of energy to ensure diversity and security of supply. It requires the Public Electricity Suppliers in England and Wales to contract for specified amounts of electricity from non-fossil sources (mainly nuclear) up to 1998. A levy on electricity sales allows electricity generated from nuclear power to be bought at a premium price, with the cost being passed on to the consumer. This levy will gradually decline.

15.37 In the longer term, nuclear power will have to improve its competitiveness. It will only attract investment if it is economic in comparison with other fuels. There will also need to be greater transparency in nuclear costs to reduce current uncertainties and allow an informed comparison to be made. One reason for the high cost of nuclear power is that it bears the environmental costs of its fuel cycle, in particular the safe disposal of its waste. The relative economics of nuclear power (and also of renewable energy) could improve if the environmental costs of fossil fuels are taken into account on a comparable basis: more work is needed to explore this.

GOVERNMENT ACTION AND POLICY REVIEW

15.38 The Government will carry out a full-scale review of the prospects for nuclear power in 1994 when the Sizewell B project will be nearing completion. The Government and the nuclear industry will take several initiatives in advance of 1994:
• to reflect the ICRP's revised recommendations, the Government will support amendment to the EC Directive on radiation protection and amend its own legislation;

Spent nuclear fuel is reprocessed allowing the uranium and plutonium to be re-used

• UK Nirex Ltd. will speed up its investigations into a potential underground waste disposal site so that a well-founded proposal can come to a public inquiry as soon as possible;
• the Government will ensure that waste arising from post-1976 reprocessing contracts is returned to overseas customers;
• the Government will keep under review whether the sea disposal option needs to be maintained;
• Nuclear Electric and Scottish Nuclear will take steps to improve the economic efficiency of their nuclear stations (Nuclear Electric will seek to extend the life span of older Magnox reactors if it is economic and safe to do so and will complete the new Pressurised Water

Reactor at Sizewell B to maintain this technology as an option for the future);
• there will be greater transparency in costs, provided in part through the publication by Nuclear Electric and Scottish Nuclear of annual reports and accounts;
• the Government intends to establish a group of those involved in the nuclear industry to consider what civil nuclear research and development should be undertaken outside Government to maintain the nuclear option (it intends to review its own civil nuclear R&D objectives in the light of that); and
• the Government, in consultation with the nuclear industry, will publish a strategy for nuclear R&D examining in part the scope for collaboration with other countries.

CONCLUSION

15.39 The Government will continue to take all reasonable precautionary action to ensure that human exposure to radiation from the nuclear industry is kept to the lowest practicable levels. It will ensure that comprehensive emergency plans are prepared and will complete its new network for monitoring any overseas nuclear incident. It will continue to monitor closely the safety performance of nuclear power stations to check that the highest standards are being maintained. It will also continue to monitor the storage and disposal of radioactive materials and will seek to improve waste disposal arrangements. The Government's full-scale review of the nuclear industry will enable it to assess the advantages and constraints of nuclear power and determine its potential for the 21st century.

Research – nuclear

Research on nuclear power and radioactive substances is directed towards improved methods for the management and treatment of radioactive waste and demonstrating the safety of its disposal and towards developing further our understanding of radioactivity in the environment.
Public sector research relevant to nuclear power and radioactive waste includes projects
• to improve understanding of pathways for human exposure to radiation – Department of Health, the National Radiological Protection Board, and Department of Energy (£6.2m in 1989/90)
• to study how radionuclides arising from natural sources or industrial discharges travel in the atmosphere and are taken up in the environment – Natural Environment Research Council (£0.4m in 1989/90)

• to improve understanding and support management of radioactive waste disposal – Department of the Environment (£8.3m in 1989/90)
• to monitor and protect the marine environment from radioactive contamination – Ministry of Agriculture, Fisheries and Food (£1.0m in 1989/90)
• to study the behaviour and effects of radioactivity in atmospheric, marine and land based ecosystems – Natural Environment Research Council (£0.5m in 1989/90)
• to help with the design, construction and safe operation of plants for storage, treatment and disposal of radioactive wastes – Department of Energy (£4.8m in 1989/90) in co-operation with the nuclear industry – total programme costs about £20m a year

16

NOISE

INTRODUCTION

16.1 Noise is a pollutant which in excess can damage health. It can irritate and annoy, interrupt sleep, increase stress and disrupt concentration at work. Prolonged exposure to loud noise can also do irreparable damage to hearing. Some noise is inevitable, but much can be done to minimise nuisance and reduce dangers to health through tougher standards, better controls, greater understanding of the risks and, perhaps above all, through greater consideration for our neighbours.

16.2 The Government's first priority must be to minimise the health risks posed by noise. These come chiefly, though not exclusively, from constant noise at work from heavy machinery, which is governed by strict health and safety regulations. Where noise cannot be reduced to safe levels at source, workers must wear ear protectors. This legislation has recently been strengthened by the Noise at Work Regulations 1989.

16.3 It is less easy to set priorities on the levels of noise which can cause nuisance but do not damage health. The Government aims to ensure that new technology is adopted as it becomes available to reduce noise at source and sponsors research to encourage such breakthroughs. And it takes account of public opinion and acts on areas of greatest concern.

In response to increasing complaints about neighbourhood noise, the Government commissioned an independently chaired review. Its report will be published shortly

Noise complaints

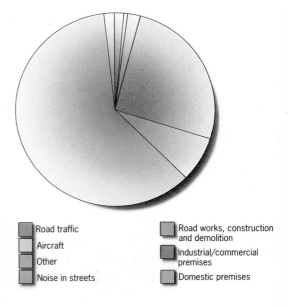

- Road traffic
- Aircraft
- Other
- Noise in streets
- Road works, construction and demolition
- Industrial/commercial premises
- Domestic premises

16.4 The figure above sets out the main causes of complaints about noise. The commonest source of complaint – bothering about one in seven people – is noise from neighbours. The number of complaints about this source of noise has increased by six times over the last ten years. Last year the Government commissioned an independent review by a working group of representatives of local government and voluntary bodies to examine it.

16.5 The report of the working group will be published shortly. Some of its recommendations which the Government intends to pursue are reflected in this Chapter. The Government will make these proposed changes, some requiring new legislation, at the earliest opportunity.

16.6 Noise is controlled in three ways: setting limits on the emission of noise at source; keeping noise and people apart, and ensuring that adequate controls exist over noise nuisance. The Government aims to ensure that standards are up to date and consistent, and that controls are effective.

MEASURING NOISE

16.7 Noise is measured in decibels (dB), a logarithmic scale. An increase of ten decibels will seem around twice as loud, while a change of less than 3dB is hard for the human ear to detect, although the sound energy will in fact have doubled. The usual form of measurement is dB(A) - the 'A' refers to the filter used in sound meters to mimic human hearing.

16.8 Measuring noise levels is not the same as measuring the nuisance they can cause. Different people are disturbed by different types of noise and comparison of occasional loud noise with constant moderate noise is difficult. For this reason limits for different noise sources may differ, but the Government's aim is to produce comparable standards so far as is possible. To achieve this the standards measure sound levels over different periods and with different weightings. For example, road noise is measured with L_{10} (18 hours) - the average of noise levels exceeded for 10% of each hour between 6am and midnight. This is well suited to a regular sound. A more

Noise levels and dB(A) equivalents

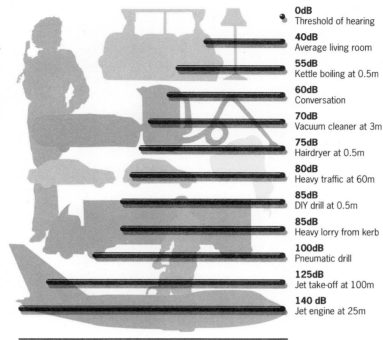

0dB	Threshold of hearing
40dB	Average living room
55dB	Kettle boiling at 0.5m
60dB	Conversation
70dB	Vacuum cleaner at 3m
75dB	Hairdryer at 0.5m
80dB	Heavy traffic at 60m
85dB	DIY drill at 0.5m
85dB	Heavy lorry from kerb
100dB	Pneumatic drill
125dB	Jet take-off at 100m
140 dB	Jet engine at 25m

intermittent sound may be measured in L eq - which averages peak sounds to an equivalent continuous noise level.

REDUCING NOISE AT SOURCE

Transport

16.9 National and international regulations for noise emissions exist for private cars, commercial vehicles, motorcycles and civil aircraft. No such regulations apply at present to railway locomotives and rolling stock but the European Community is examining railway standards as part of moves towards the single market, and is considering the inclusion of noise.

16.10 The Government has taken a leading role in international work on noise. Its aim has been to ensure the widespread adoption of the most effective new technology, which it also helps to develop through its research programmes. The results are significant. For example, the new generation of jet aircraft is much quieter than earlier ones, and replacement of older jets by the latest models will continue to bring benefits.

16.11 Older aircraft which fail to meet current noise requirements are now banned from Britain. From November, the Government will join other European countries in banning its national airlines from acquiring aircraft which fail to meet the latest tight requirements. The Government's introduction of controls on noise from microlight aircraft has led to a substantial reduction in the number of complaints and seems likely to form the basis of forthcoming international regulations. The Government is also pressing for world-wide agreement to phase out all aircraft which do not meet the latest noise requirements.

16.12 The Government is constantly seeking ways of

The Government has successfully pressed for quieter jet aircraft

Thanks to work carried out by the Transport and Road Research Laboratory on lorry noise, the Government has been able to demonstrate to the EC that lorries can be made significantly quieter

reducing the noise emitted by all transport sources. Tighter standards for vehicles have reduced noise levels by up to 10dB(A) over the last ten years. It should be technically possible to reduce noise levels set for cars by a further 2dB(A) and the work of the Government's Transport and Road Research Laboratory has demonstrated that lorry noise could fall by up to 5dB(A). The Government is pressing for such reductions to be introduced across the Community. The Government also took a leading role in new tighter EC standards for motorcycles and will follow this with new regulations to control the quality of silencers on the market.

16.13 It is important to make sure that vehicles continue to meet noise standards throughout their life time. It is already an offence to alter a silencer to make it louder, or to use a vehicle in a way which creates excessive noise. The Government is now examining the practicalities of introducing metered noise testing as part of the annual test and when inspecting vehicles at the road side.

Products

16.14 British and European standards for noise apply to a wide variety of products. Some products such as lawnmowers are specifically covered by EC Directive, others under Directives on product standards.

16.15 Generally standards are effective but the Government believes that burglar alarms and car alarms should perform better. Car alarms are permitted to sound for five-minutes but often continue for longer. They

are also prone to go off accidentally. The Government is examining how they can be improved. Burglar alarms are currently governed by a Code of Practice – which limits the alarm to 20 minutes duration – but this is widely ignored and the Government proposes to introduce mandatory controls.

16.16 The Government will also include noise levels of products when awarding environmental labels (see Chapter 17), so that people are able to choose quieter equipment.

Roads and airports

16.17 The Government has achieved much by requiring vehicles and civil aircraft to emit less noise, but the design and control of roads and airports can reduce it further.

16.18 The Department of Transport takes care to select lines and levels for its roads that minimise the impact of noise on local people. In addition, earth mounds and noise barriers are provided to deflect noise away from people, often, incidentally improving the appearance of the road. For the future, experiments in producing quieter road surfaces by the use of new or improved materials offer considerable potential for noise reduction, at source, in selected areas.

16.19 The Department of Transport is developing ideas for better environmental performance of roads, including ways to make them quieter. The Department is also beginning a trial to assess the cost-effectiveness of improved noise barriers.

16.20 Chapter 8 sets out proposals to civilise further the use of heavy lorries. This includes guidance on arranging lorry movements in towns to reduce disturbance to local residents.

16.21 At major airports, measures are taken to minimise the effects of noise on people living near by. 'Noise preferential routes' are designed so that aircraft taking off fly over as few people as possible. Noise limits, checked by noise monitors, are enforced at some airports. Manchester Airport has recently

The Government ensures that roads and airports are designed in ways which reduce noise disturbance

installed a system to monitor automatically the paths taken by aircraft (track monitoring). Gatwick, Heathrow, and Stansted are planning to install modern integrated noise and track monitoring by the end of 1992. Night restrictions are enforced at these airports. All these measures add to the benefits from making the aircraft themselves quieter. Some airports increase charges levied on aircraft landing when they exceed certain noise levels. The Government supports this use of market signals to penalise noisy aircraft.

16.22 The Government recently announced that it would commission research into aircraft noise at night to inform the 1992 review of the major London airports' night flying restrictions. Manchester airport has also been invited to participate.

16.23 Many smaller airfields are used primarily for leisure flying which can cause noise problems for those living nearby. This was studied in a research report into business and general aviation published by the Department of Transport in 1988. One finding was that those running small airfields should maintain close contact with local people about their operations, and discuss ways of reducing noise nuisance. As circumstances vary between airfields, the Government believes it is better for problems to be discussed and resolved locally if at all possible. It has power to require such consultation and has done so wherever asked. So far this covers 47 airports. If disputes cannot be resolved locally then it also has the power to require the Civil Aviation Authority to take account of environmental considerations in its licensing of the airport. The Government is ready to use such powers where necessary, and is reviewing current arrangements to ensure that they afford sufficient protection for local people.

16.24 The Ministry of Defence takes great care to minimise the impact of its airfields and its wider flight patterns and is conducting research on the problems of noise from military aircraft. It will re-examine the operational needs for low flying in the light of the review of defence requirements.

REDUCING EXPOSURE TO NOISE

Planning

16.25 Given that some noise is inevitable whatever measures are taken, an effective way of avoiding noise nuisance is to keep sources of noise away from people, and vice versa. It is important that planners of factories, roads and airports, and of houses, schools, and hospitals should consider potential noise problems carefully. A Government circular to local authorities already offers guidance on tolerance standards and on how to avoid conflicts of interest between noise-makers and the noise-sensitive.

16.26 The Government is preparing new guidance for consultation. It will set new noise standards and cover a wider range of

The Government will introduce noise standards for new railway lines

noise sources. There will be new recommended noise levels for different types of noise on which local authorities should act to reduce noise nuisance or to prevent it worsening.

16.27 The Government will also be examining whether there is a need for action to limit the temporary use of land for helicopter take-off and landing – an aspect of helicopter operations perceived as a growing source of complaint.

Insulation

16.28 Where noise and people cannot be kept apart and other methods of reducing noise such as physical barriers prove inadequate, sound insulation, usually in the form of double glazing, can help.

16.29 The Department of Transport provides secondary glazing to houses exposed to 68 dB(A) L_{10} (18 hours) – see 16.8 – by the development of a new trunk road. The Government has now extended these provisions to major trunk road widening and upgrading. No equivalent exists at present for rail. The Government intends to produce comparable standards for new rail lines shortly and is also considering extending the current provision for houses to schools and hospitals.

16.30 There is a statutory requirement for the principal London airports to provide sound insulation to surrounding homes within a specified boundary – equivalent to the provision for roads. Elsewhere insulation is discretionary but all the major airports (which are owned largely by local authorities) run similar insulation schemes.

Right: The Government proposes to strengthen the sound insulation requirements for new buildings and conversions

16.31 The Ministry of Defence offers grants for the insulation of homes subject to noise levels of 70dB(A) averaged over a continuous 12-hour period. It is currently carrying out noise surveys at some 40 military airfields and 25 insulation schemes have been introduced

to date. In addition to insulation grants, MOD will offer to buy homes subject to average noise levels over 83dB(A) at above market value.

Compensation

16.32 The Land Compensation Act 1973 provides for compensation to be paid to reflect depreciation in property value where this can be shown to have resulted directly from the nuisance caused by specified physical factors, including noise, arising from the use of new or altered public works. The provision puts owner occupiers in a similar position in respect of nuisance from public works to that in respect of nuisance from private works where they can pursue an action at common law.

Building Regulations

16.33 The Building Regulations require walls and floors between houses and flats to have sound insulation to a prescribed standard. This limits noise between houses and flats to acceptable levels given normal day to day noise.

16.34 In England and Wales, the present sound insulation requirements apply only to new construction. In June 1990, the Government consulted on proposals to extend these requirements to conversions to flats – a common problem area. Technical guidance on ways of meeting the requirement will be given and the provisions relating to new construction work will be improved and updated. Final decisions on these proposals will be taken by Summer 1991.

CONTROLLING NOISE

Noise control zones

16.35 The Control of Pollution Act 1974 gives local authorities powers to set up Noise Abatement Zones. These provide for local authorities to control noise levels in mixed residential and industrial or commercial areas. The Government aims to simplify the procedures to encourage authorities to use them more, principally by replacing the existing cumbersome noise measurement procedures by simpler ones set out in a Code of Practice.

16.36 Under the Control of Pollution Act 1974 local authorities have powers to control noise from construction sites, limiting nuisance in a situation where some noise is inevitable. The Government is considering whether it would be feasible to extend these powers to other inevitably noisy activities.

16.37 These schemes are aimed primarily at reducing the effects of industrial noise on people's homes. But the chief cause of concern is neighbourhood noise.

16.38 The Government is not persuaded that it would be right to make noise nuisance an immediate criminal offence, or to give the police further powers to control noise. Noise nuisance is often complex and subjective, making it very difficult to establish the clear cut levels required for legal action. While noise can be very annoying, criminalisation is a very heavy stick to take to it. The current powers, particularly the stiffer penalties proposed, and the recent strengthening of the separate penalties for illegal parties (to protect against the Acid House craze) already provide tough controls.

16.39 Where there are local problems, the Government believes a co-operative approach is needed. So it is sponsoring a pilot 'quiet neighbourhood' scheme. The key to success will be to encourage the residents of an area to co-operate in drawing up a code of conduct and agreeing on reasonable behaviour, perhaps with time restrictions on noisy activities. Such schemes might be developed to provide a mediation service for resolving disputes.

Tackling nuisance

16.40 There will always be those who are not prepared to be considerate to their neighbours and the wider community. Government and local authorities have legal power to deal with such noise-makers.

16.41 Noise from fixed premises is governed by the law of nuisance. The Control of Pollution Act imposes a duty on local authorities to inspect their areas from time to time to detect noise nuisance against which action may be taken. Local authorites have powers to serve noise abatement notices and prosecute if necessary. If this does not resolve the problem, they can take further court proceedings. The current maximum penalty for non-compliance with an abatement notice is £2,000.

16.42 The Act also allows individuals to apply direct to a court for the issue of an abatement notice. The notice is enforced direct by the court and the same penalties apply.

16.43 The Environmental Protection Bill includes two important changes in noise control:
• an increase in the maximum fine for noise nuisance from commercial and industrial sources to £20,000; and
• a power for local authorities to take action against noise makers in some circumstances without the need for prior action in the courts.

16.44 Recent evidence has suggested that the existing controls are not consistently effective, and that they are not uniformly applied. In particular, the response to noise

Local people can do most to reduce noise nuisance. The Government is developing a 'quiet neighbourhood' scheme to help

Right: The Government
is giving local authorities
new powers to control
noise

complaints varies from local authority to local authority: only a minority provide an out-of-hours service.

16.45 The Bill will make local authorities' existing responsibilities for noise control more explicit. At the same time, the Department of the Environment and the Welsh Office will issue new guidance to local authorities in England and Wales restating their duties under the Act and how they should tackle noise problems in their area, setting out what constitutes noise nuisance and suggesting measuring methods.

Research

16.46 The Government's Building Research Establishment has a team dedicated to noise research. They are working to develop a consistent approach to assessing neighbourhood noise to aid the work of local authorities and the courts. It is also developing improved methods of sound insulation. The Department of Transport continues to support research into the practicalities of reducing noise levels from aircraft and vehicles and the Government

supports research into the problem of low frequency noise, to which some people are particularly sensitive. The box at the end of the chapter gives some details.

Public awareness

16.47 We all need reminding from time to time of the need to take care over the amount of noise we create. The Government supports a range of voluntary organisations who campaign on noise and makes funds available to publicity campaigns. It will consider in the light of the report of the working group on noise whether more should be done to increase awareness.

CONCLUSION

16.48 The recent noise review and the continuing research in this field demonstrates the Government's commitment to reduce noise problems. The Government will continue to press for cost effective measures to reduce noise at source, based closely on its research work. In the light of the recommendations of the review it will also

seek further to reduce noise from products and strengthen controls. But Government action can only do so much. Action by individuals is needed to cure many of the current problems through greater awareness of the potential risks to health and more consideration for neighbours.

Research – noise

Noise research aims to improve our understanding of how noise is generated, its effects on people and the environment and practical ways in which its impact can be reduced. The Department of the Environment's Building Research Establishment has particular expertise.

Public sector research relevant to noise includes projects
• to increase understanding of 'neighbourhood' aspects of noise control and planning legislation, including studies of trends in the noise climate and

how and why particular types of noise create a nuisance - Department of the Environment (£0.5m in 1989/90)
• to support engineering research on reducing noise pollution and improving the built environment - Science and Engineering Research Council (£0.2m in 1989/90)
• to develop quieter road surface materials and more effective noise barriers - Department of Transport (£0.1m in 1989/90)
• to identify better ways of measuring vehicle noise and its nuisance to humans - Department of Transport (£0.1m in 1989/90)

KNOWLEDGE, EDUCATION AND TRAINING

We need research monitoring and training on which to base our policies for protecting the environment and controlling pollution

INTRODUCTION

17.1 In deciding on measures to protect the environment and control pollution, everyone concerned needs a sound understanding of the underlying science, of the natural processes at work, of the effects of man on the environment and of the environment on human health and well-being. Decisions should be based on sound information and sound analysis of the risks, costs and benefits.

17.2 The Government can help people to act in a balanced way by:
• promoting good scientific research and environmental monitoring;
• ensuring wide and clear dissemination of the results of research and other environmental data;
• encouraging individuals and the media to act on the basis of sound information; and
• giving proper attention to the environment at all levels in the education system.

17.3 The Government also needs to ensure that further and higher education and training courses are available to produce the specialists needed to fill key jobs in environmental protection – such as local authority environmental health officers and Her Majesty's Inspectors of Pollution (HMIP) – and to provide the environmental element in training for other employment.

RESEARCH

The Government's approach to research

17.4 Policy on the environment needs to be based on the best possible scientific, technological and economic advice and on a thorough assessment of the risks, costs and benefits of all options. A great deal is being spent on environmental research in both the public and private sectors. The private sector effort concentrates on market-directed research (for example on environmentally safer products and cleaner production). The public sector concentrates on basic and strategic research, such as climatic modelling, investigations of environmental processes and standard setting, where the outputs underpin public policy and the market cannot be expected to pay. Research in both sectors draws on a wide range of scientific and engineering disciplines where training is provided through Government support.

Public sector research

17.5 Most public sector work aims to discover how the environment works, how it changes over time both naturally and through human intervention, and how adverse effects can be tackled. The Government's research on environmental issues costs about £200 million a year. A significant element of this research effort is directed to issues of global concern, particularly climate change, where expenditure has recently trebled to £50 million a year.

17.6 Britain has considerable strengths in environmental research. But the global nature

Classification of government funded environmental research

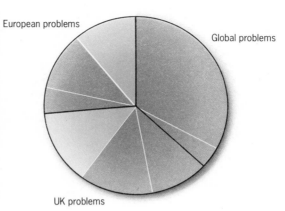

European problems

Global problems

UK problems

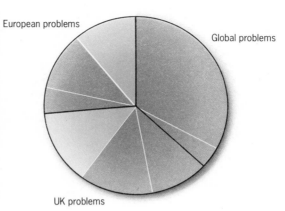

Processes   Impacts   Remedial

Processes physical, biological and chemical processes that determine the system being studied
Impacts impacts of changes in those processes on the environment
Remedial remedial measures to combat undesirable changes, including the development of alternative cleaner technologies

Left: Government research on global and regional issues concentrates on Britain's areas of strength, for example Antarctica

Right: The Government spends about £200 million a year on research on the environment

of many environmental issues, and the scale of the work required, demand international collaboration. Britain does not have or need an in-depth research capability in every aspect of the environment. On global and regional issues, Government policy is to concentrate on research areas where Britain has particular strengths and experience to contribute to the international effort, for example on polar research in Antarctica and on the World Ocean Circulation Experiment. On other issues, we need only a capability to take the work of others into account in Britain.

17.7 Britain encourages and works with the leading international scientific bodies such as the International Council for Scientific Unions, the World Health Organisation, the World Meteorological Organisation (WMO), the United Nations Environment Programme (UNEP) and the North Sea Scientific Task Force. The British contribution to international work on global climate change is an example of the Government's commitment. We are one of 80 nations contributing to the work of the Intergovernmental Panel on Climate Change, sponsored jointly by the UNEP and the WMO, and have chaired one of its three working groups, on Scientific Assessment: the other groups are chaired by the USA and USSR. The Government has also established a centre for climate change prediction at the Meteorological Office. The first objective of the new centre will be to develop an improved global circulation model in good

time for the negotiation of protocols to a climate change convention in 1992.

Economic and social research

17.8 Economic and social research provides another important input to policy on the environment. The aims are to understand the significance of environmental damage better and to assess the costs and benefits of environmental protection measures. The research programme includes analysis to show which policy instruments, including market-based instruments, are likely to be most cost-

The Government will continue to contribute to intenational research. Britain has established a centre for climate change prediction at the Meteorological Office

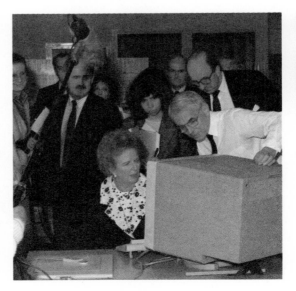

effective in achieving environmental ends, especially international ones.

17.9 There is a growing interest among academic social scientists for work on environmental issues. Both the Government and the Economic and Social Research Council (ESRC) are substantially increasing funding for research into the social and economic aspects of global climate change. As part of this, ESRC plans to establish the Global Environmental Research Centre.

Non-government organisations and environmental research

17.10 Non-government organisations such as Friends of the Earth are developing research programmes to help to respond to the public demand for accurate and authoritative information. Such groups' programmes include work on sustainable agriculture, the uses of CFCs, water quality, recycling and energy issues from nuclear waste disposal to the implications of the greenhouse effect on Britain's energy policy.

17.11 ODA's Joint Funding Scheme assists non-governmental organisations in their work on the environment. Under this scheme the Worldwide Fund for Nature, for example, receives over £1 million a year, mainly for forestry and environmental education projects, which it matches from its own resources. Many smaller organisations are also involved in practical projects concerned with environmental protection and development. Various independent research bodies have also increased their interest in environmental economics. The Government is supporting the UK Centre for Economic and Environmental Development, an independent body which promotes economic analysis of environmental issues.

Role of privately funded research

17.12 Commercial forces are the most effective spur for technological progress. Research and development funded by industry range from developing new pollution control methods - so-called 'end-of-pipe' techniques - to more radical ways of reducing pollution such as replacing a process with one which uses less raw materials or energy, or emits fewer pollutants.

17.13 Industry can supply skills, equipment and finance to correct environmental problems. The Government's new Environmental Technology Innovation Scheme (see Chapter 14) aims to stimulate industry to advance technology, and thus to develop competition and achieve higher environmental standards cost-effectively. In addition, the Government will offer support for companies and consortia wishing to demonstrate examples of environmental best practice to the wider market. Both these new schemes will focus on clean technologies, waste minimisation and recycling. Together with existing schemes such as LINK (a programme to help industry to exploit developments in science and to make scientists more aware of industry's needs) and EUREKA EUROENVIRON (a programme for collaborative international industry-led research and development), they will help industry to capitalise on the capabilities in British higher education, research and applied technology institutions, as well as building on industry's own ideas.

Future directions for research

17.14 The Government intends to target public sector research towards developing cleaner technologies and more efficient use of energy. This will mean more work on technologies where the scientific basis is well developed, but where costs are not yet competitive with existing technologies (such as hydrogen-fuelled vehicles, power generation from wind and nuclear fusion, and innovative refrigeration methods). It will also mean more effort on developing the basic science needed for longer-term possibilities (such as new applications of biotechnology, improved handling of radioactive waste, desulphurisation of coal and new and highly selective catalysts for the production of key chemicals).

17.15 In these areas the Government will help to take new technologies up to the demonstration stage, but will not impose its

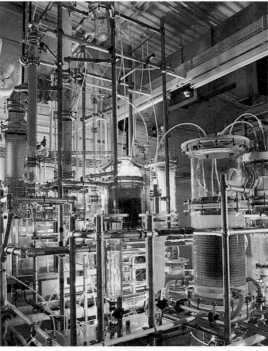

The Government will target public research on energy efficiency and clean technology: promising initiatives include work on alternatives to CFCs and improved handling of radioactive waste

own solutions. It will involve industry wherever possible, and highlight the problems so as to challenge scientists everywhere to develop their own ideas on the frontiers of

knowledge. One aim, for example, should be to achieve for waste minimisation what has already been achieved through energy audits in many industrial plants.

MONITORING

17.16 In addition to basic research, monitoring is crucial. Environmental monitoring is extensive in Britain; the government and the academic and industrial sectors all contribute, and more and more data are becoming available. The Government will continue to co-ordinate environmental monitoring, with emphasis on the consistent and cost effective capture, processing, storage and transmission of data.

17.17 General monitoring systems can assess trends in exposure to a wide range of known pollutants. But they cannot ensure that there are no unacceptable exposures to more localised forms of pollution, for example near industrial installations. Nor can they collect precise enough information to test allegations that particular pollutants are responsible for specific incidences of ill health, such as leukaemia clusters, in some parts of the country. The Government therefore set up the Small Area Health Statistics Unit, as an independent unit in the London School of

Hygiene and Tropical Medicine, to investigate such issues.

17.18 It is important to ensure that monitoring systems can be used to tackle the main current potential hazards, and that new or changing risks from pollutants are identified as early as possible. The Government therefore proposes:
• to improve the arrangements for collecting data on human exposure to toxic chemicals;
• to review ways of identifying potential new environmental hazards as early as possible; and
• to review arrangements for providing expert advice on the microbiological contamination of air, soil and water.

17.19 There is a need for a clear and unequivocal means to demonstrate the validity of measurement data. In a White Paper "Measuring Up to Competition" the Government suggested a national system to underpin all measurements within the United

The Government will keep monitoring systems under review and develop improved ones where justified

Kingdom. It recognised the importance of quality assurance and the need for initiatives to ensure the validity of analytical measurements. To follow up that White Paper, Government laboratories will collaborate with others and foster improvement in measurements.

17.20 The Government will keep monitoring systems under review and develop improved ones where justified. For example, Chapter 11 sets out substantial increases which are proposed in air quality monitoring, including a greatly increased number of sampling points and an increase in the range of pollutants covered. Developing technology will increase the effectiveness and efficiency of monitoring, especially in remote or hostile environments such as the North Sea.

ENVIRONMENTAL STATISTICS

17.21 Government departments, research organisations and other bodies, including industrial concerns and non-government organisations, collect, analyse and publish a great deal of information on the state of our environment and how it is changing.

17.22 The Government supports the regular provision of sound and authoritative statistical data on the environment to underpin properly informed debate and objective decision taking. An immense range of statistical material is already published, including the Government's annual Digest of Environmental Protection and Water Statistics. The Government believes that environmental statistics need to be brought together in a more coherent and comprehensive form to provide the necessary benchmark against which progress can be assessed.

17.23 It accordingly proposes to publish at regular intervals statistical reports covering a range of data on environmental topics. Annex B lists the statistical series which the Government proposes to include in this publication, together with explanatory charts and commentary. The Department of the

Environment will consult widely on the material to be included. The timing of publication will depend on the results of that consultation, but the Government hopes that the first such report will be published within 2 years. The database might be made available as an extension to current nationally available databases such as Campus 2000. Schools and colleges could draw on the information in support of environmental education.

17.24 Earlier this year the EC adopted a Regulation to establish a European Environment Agency. Its task will be to provide data and analysis to the Commission and member countries drawing on a network of national and international centres of excellence. It will ensure that the data underpinning environmental policy at the European level are comparable and reliable. The Agency will be open to non-EC countries, and this should help to create a wider European database.

17.25 In playing its part in the new Agency arrangements, Britain will establish a network that can be brought into play as needed, involving many scientific research and other institutions. The Government expects the initiative to result in a substantial improvement in the availability, comparability and reliability of data on the European environment.

The Government has played a leading role in moves to make environmental information publicly available in Britain and Europe

PUBLIC USE OF DATA

17.26 The Government believes that the public should have a right of access to information held by pollution control authorities. HMIP, local authorities, the National Rivers Authority, the Health and Safety Executive and some Government departments keep public registers of environmental and other information. These registers make information available in a form which is easy to use and have been widely welcomed.

17.27 The Government has played a leading part in moves to make environmental information publicly available through out the EC. In 1986 it proposed a Resolution calling for access to environmental information to be made available throughout the Community, and an EC Directive on this was agreed earlier this year. The Directive requires most environmental information held by public authorities to be made available to the public and comes into force at the end of 1992. The Government will propose arrangements, including registers, by which environmental information can be made available in Britain. It believes that the role of the public in monitoring environmental information and demanding improvements where necessary will be one of the most effective stimuli to improving the environment throughout Europe.

17.28 As more environmental information becomes available, the challenge is to the public and interest groups to make use of it in a balanced and constructive way. Interest groups can use this information to seek to influence those responsible for processes that pollute; where their claims are based on sound data, they will be more difficult to refute. For its part, the business sector will need to be equally objective, for example, in producing environmental statements in its annual reports to shareholders. It is for companies themselves to decide whether to produce such statements, but the Government believes that it is desirable and will often be in their interests to draw up and publish statements of their environmental policies and of their plans to deal with adverse effects.

The Government is working for an official eco-labelling scheme, EC-wide if possible. It intends to legislate to require products' environmental claims to be well-founded

how to judge one item against another.

Labelling products

17.29 Many people want to buy environmentally friendly products. If they are told the facts, they can exercise choice and can significantly influence the market place. Products which are environmentally unfriendly will lose their market. For some time Britain has had a system of negative labelling to warn people about hazardous products. Eco-labelling is the other side of the coin - a system of positive labelling to help people to identify goods which do least harm to the environment. If enough consumers want them, the market will provide cleaner products, even if they may cost slightly more. Consumers proved this when they shunned aerosols containing ozone-damaging chlorofluorocarbons.

17.30 The response of manufacturers and retailers has varied. Some have introduced more environmentally friendly alternatives to existing products or have laid down higher environmental standards for their suppliers to follow; others have simply given their marketing more environmental emphasis. More and more are introducing their own green labels and claims. It is not always simple for consumers to evaluate competing claims, some of which have failed to stand up to close inspection. There is a danger of people becoming confused and disenchanted, anxious to buy the right thing but unsure

17.31 The Government is therefore establishing an official eco-labelling scheme to provide authoritative advice to consumers and encourage the production of more environmentally friendly products. A flexible voluntary scheme, working with market forces and preferably operating throughout the EC, with a single label and consistent standards, would best meet these objectives. The scheme will need to be clear and its standards demanding. The environmental effects of each product throughout its whole life, from production to disposal, will need to be taken into account. The Government is pressing the European Community for early agreement so that a scheme can be introduced by the end of 1991. If consensus within an acceptable time proves impossible, the Government will take its own steps to introduce a British labelling scheme.

17.32 There are already detailed requirements for the labelling and advertising of foodstuffs. The Government has recently set in hand a study of food labelling, which is examining whether labels should be required to give details of production methods and crop treatments. Building product labelling has to be considered separately because of the limitations of the EC Construction Products Directive. Annex C describes the Government's proposals for more energy-efficient products, appliances and building materials, and the Government will consider how best to achieve an eco-labelling scheme for building products.

Controlling environmental claims

17.33 An eco-labelling scheme helps consumers to judge products, but does not prevent false or misleading environmental claims. The Government intends, when Parliamentary time is available, to legislate to tighten the provisions of the Trade Descriptions Act 1968 as regards environmental claims. The main aim is to put beyond any doubt that the Act covers environmental claims, and to require those making claims to produce evidence to substantiate those claims if challenged.

EDUCATION AND TRAINING

17.34 Public debate and decisions, including consumer choices, require sound knowledge and awareness of environmental issues. The education system must play an important part in promoting environmental awareness, understanding and competence. Environmental education in schools feeds back more widely, as children bring their knowledge home. Education beyond school can make the managers and leaders, scientists and engineers of tomorrow aware of the environmental perspective. Higher and further education and training must deliver the specialists we need to operate pollution control systems in both the public and the private sector. Adult education, business schools, agricultural colleges and voluntary bodies must all play their part too.

Schools: the National Curriculum

17.35 The environment already features widely in teaching in primary schools and in geography, science, history and other subjects in secondary schools. Good environmental education is not just about topical 'green' issues; the aim is to provide children with knowledge, skills and understanding relating to nature, scientific processes and the world's resources.

17.36 The National Curriculum being

introduced by the Government will provide a sure basis for developing and improving environmental education. Environmental education has been identified as an important theme, running through the curriculum, and featuring in the core and other foundation subjects of the National Curriculum.

17.37 National Curriculum science requires pupils:
• to know that human activities produce a wide range of waste products, some of which can be recycled, and some but not others decay naturally over time;
• to be able to describe the sources and implications of pollution and possible ways of preventing it;
• to understand the processes that affect water purity; and
• to understand the basic scientific principles associated with major changes in the biosphere, such as the greenhouse effect and ozone depletion, the extent to which these result from human activities, and the timescales on which they can be dealt with. National Curriculum technology requires children to take account of the environmental impact of what they design and make and of technological innovations.

17.38 National Curriculum geography, to be introduced from Autumn 1991, will be

Environmental education figures widely in primary schools and through geography, science and many other subjects in secondary schools

particularly significant. The current proposals are of wide relevance to environmental education and include an attainment target on environmental geography. They envisage that pupils should be able, among other things, to:
• discuss how people's attitudes can affect the exploitation of natural resources;
• discuss whether certain types of environment need special protection;
• explain why rivers, lakes, seas and oceans are vulnerable to pollution, and consider how some water pollution problems have been tackled;
• distinguish between renewable and non-renewable resources;
• analyse the issues that arise from conflicting demands on areas of great scenic attraction;
• analyse the effects of developments in technology on the exploitation of natural resources and the management of environments;
• explain the implications for international co-operation of resource and environmental management; and
• examine critically the concepts of sustainable development, stewardship and conservation.

17.39 National Curriculum history, also planned for 1991, will draw on the built environment, historic buildings and sites to bring the study of the past to life.

The National Curriculum will provide a sure basis for developing and improving environmental education

---

Some links between environmental education and other areas of the curriculum

English
1 Skills of communication, e.g. the ability to discuss
2 Research skills: the ability fo find and select information
3 Response to literature: in particular an appreciation of material about the environment

Geography
1 Mapping skills
2 Field study skills
3 Use of aerial and ground photographs and of satellite imaging
4 Investigation of physical and human conditions
5 A grasp of local, national and global scales of activity

History
1 A sense of time and chronology
2 A sense of continuity and change
3 Use and respect for evidence
4 Understanding the historical development of the environment

Religious Education
1 The attitudes of different religions to environmental issues
2 Moral considerations - e.g. on the use and sharing of resources

Mathematics
1 Statistical techniques: recording, displaying and interpreting data
2 Understanding patterns and shapes
3 Operational research

Foreign Languages
1 The exploration of other cultures and environments

Science
1 Skills of scientific investigation
2 An understanding of materials, energy, ecology, living things, scientific laws
3 Scientific aspects of the provision and use of energy, the water supply, waste disposal, biotechnology in food production and other industries
4 Conservation and pollution

Art and craft, design and technology
1 Awareness and appraisal of the environment, e.g. its aesthetic qualities
2 The concept of design as it affects the environment
3 Identification of the needs of individuals and groups
4 The choice and use of resources
5 Technological concepts, e.g. efficiency
6 The consequences of technology for the environment

Music and drama
1 The expression of ideas and responses to the environment

Physical education
1 First hand experience of the environment through outdoor activities in various settings

In addition to the links with the subjects outlined above, there is also much overlap with other cross-curricular themes such as political education, health education, education for economic understanding, consumer education and personal and social education.

Schools: other steps

17.40 The National Curriculum provides the essential legal framework, but leaves schools and teachers free to plan their teaching. Many local education authorities and schools have policies for environmental education. Her Majesty's Inspectorate has published the booklet "Environmental Education from 5 to 16". This underlines the distinctive contribution to pupils' learning that the environment can make, and outlines approaches to course planning and teaching. It gives guidance to the co-ordinators that schools appoint to work with colleagues to establish objectives and attainment targets for environmental education.

17.41 In its latest curriculum guidance - "Environmental Education" - the National Curriculum Council are issuing guidance on environmental education. This provides more detail about this cross-curricular theme, setting it in context in relation to the whole school curriculum and to other themes such as citizenship and economic and industrial understanding. It will be sent to all schools and should provide a new impetus for properly planned, objective environmental education.

17.42 As well as providing guidance, HM Inspectors assess the quality of work in environmental education, wherever it features in the school curriculum. Local authorities' own inspectors carry out similar appraisals, and some authorities have appointed advisers to promote environmental education and to provide in-service training for teachers. The Government welcomes these initiatives.

17.43 Teachers need training in environmental education, as part of their training both on the National Curriculum and on cross-curricular themes. New entrants to the teaching profession are a small part of the total workforce. In-service training is therefore crucial if children are to have an up-to-date appreciation of environmental concerns. The Government supports local authority expenditure on in-service training with specific grant focused particularly on the implementation of the National Curriculum.

The 1991/92 specific grant will increase this provision, and will explicitly cover training in the content, organisation and delivery of environmental education as a cross-curricular theme.

17.44 The Government has also introduced new requirements for student teachers in 1990. Pre-service training has now to focus on the National Curriculum, and all courses are required to cover the teaching of environmental matters. The Council for the Accreditation of Teacher Education, which advises the Government on the approval of pre-service training courses, has been asked to ensure that these requirements are met.

17.45 Many public bodies help children to understand their environment, through activities in and out of school. For example, the Nature Conservancy Council distributes special publications, hosts school visits to its nature reserves, and has provided over £½ million in grants to schools to establish areas for wildlife. Such projects often involve parents and the wider community in environmental initiatives. The Countryside Commission and others have similar programmes. English Heritage encourage free school visits to the historic sites in their care and prepare materials for teachers.

17.46 Non-Government organisations too provide educational material and facilities for teachers and promote practical projects. The Royal Society for Nature Conservation organises its WATCH club for children and

The National Curriculum Council has given guidance to all schools to help them to provide properly planned, objective environmental education

Many organisations inside and outside the Government help children to understand the environment by providing educational material and facilities, promoting clubs and projects and running award schemes

has a project to monitor ozone levels in air. The World Wide Fund for Nature publishes material on topics ranging from rainforests to mathematics. It also administers the Government's Environmental Enterprise Award for schools and colleges, which rewards environmental schemes invented and developed by young people. Many other bodies, including the Civic Trust, the Wildfowl and Wetlands Trust and the Field Studies Council, receive Government grants for practical projects. The Government welcomes the educational work of these and other bodies such as the Royal Society for the Protection of Birds and the National Trust, which runs a membership scheme for schools, with regular newsletters for teachers and free school admissions.

17.47 Government grant also supports the work of some organisations directly involved in environmental education. For example, the Council for Environmental Education (CEE) has recently co-ordinated comments from its 70 member organisations on the proposals of the subject working groups on the National Curriculum. The National Curriculum Council has also taken advice from CEE on the development of environmental education in the curriculum. The Government has asked the CEE to produce a guide to who does what in environmental education and a database of relevant courses on offer at higher and further education establishments.

Higher and further education

17.48 Protecting the environment is an increasingly sophisticated task. Demand for the skills of professional experts such as pollution control managers, waste management experts and environmental health officers is increasing in step. It is correspondingly important that environmental concerns are reflected in science, engineering and other courses in further and higher education.

17.49 The Government's approach to further and higher education is that course providers should be free of unnecessary central controls, and thus be able to react quickly to the demands of students and of employers. The main influences on curriculum development come not from the Government but from the examining and validating bodies, and from professional institutions, guided by new developments and needs in the disciplines concerned. The Government, however, is anxious to help the environmental education market to function better. It will be guided by a current Training Agency research study designed to relate environmental management activities and labour requirements to training availability. But it also proposes to establish a higher profile expert committee, similar to the Stuart Committee on Biotechnology, to survey the current supply of environmental courses, compare it with likely demand for courses and qualifications over the next decade and make recommendations.

17.50 The Government will also:
• sponsor a series of conferences with a 'market place' function, bringing industry, educationalists, trainers and course providers together with a body such as the Environment Council or CEE in the lead; and
• produce a new leaflet, to inform those at school about careers in the environment and the qualifications needed.

The Open University

17.51 The Open University already makes an important contribution to environmental education, both through the courses on its undergraduate programme and through the packs of learning materials which are more widely on sale. The Government welcomes the University's plans for further integration of its current activities to strengthen environmental studies in its study programmes, and to produce more courses aimed at people who deal directly with environmental issues, as well as at others with a general interest in the environment.

Postgraduate education

17.52 Highly qualified people are needed in growing numbers to work in environmental research in industry and in the public sector. Relevant postgraduate training is provided by higher education institutions, mainly through one year taught MSc and diploma courses, and three year research training leading to a PhD. All the Research Councils provide studentships in relevant subjects. The Government will continue to make funds available to secure an adequate supply of very highly qualified manpower for research in industry and the public sector. The Natural Environment Research Council is providing about 40 additional postgraduate studentships each year from 1990 onwards, targeted on areas of particular need. The Science and Engineering Research Council will provide 100 studentships a year for its clean technology initiative. The Agriculture and Food Research Council and the Economic and Social Research Council will also be giving greater priority to environmental topics.

Continuing education and training

17.53 Improving the environment calls for a better trained and more aware workforce and will provide new job opportunities. Training must remain primarily the responsibility of employers. They are best placed to decide what skills they need. The Government's job is not to direct their training efforts, but to provide a national framework within which employers can meet their needs effectively and efficiently. Individuals must also play an important part by investing in training to adapt their skills to new environmental demands.

17.54 The establishment of Training and Enterprise Councils (TECs) represents a significant change in the planning and

delivery of training provision in England and Wales. They have the flexibility to tailor training to local needs, and board members are well placed to reflect local environmental concerns. Training programmes which include environmental elements can provide interesting and useful disciplines for young people, the long term unemployed and those at a disadvantage in the labour market. They enable them to improve their skills and compete for other jobs. For example, TECs can provide training in forestry, waste management and in skills needed for urban and rural conservation.

17.55 Government training programmes will therefore continue to make an important contribution to a better environment by using environmental projects to develop skills and by responding to demands for training related to environmental issues. Encouraged by the Government's Professional, Industrial and Commercial Updating Programme (PICKUP), universities, polytechnics and colleges have the freedom to respond quickly and flexibly to the needs of business. Businesses locally or nationally can put the case for change to these institutions if they are not meeting their needs.

17.56 The Training Agency helps to make training responsive to the environment by:
• encouraging the inclusion of a significant environmental element in programmes such as Employment Training and Youth Training;
• helping to ensure that relevant standards and qualifications are in place;
• raising awareness of the effect of increased environmental concern on the range of skills employers need; and
• working with a wide range of environmental agencies to identify needs and develop training policy and guidance.

17.57 In addition the Government will promote a greater focus on environmental issues through Regional Technology Centres. These allow collaboration between education and business, providing training and other services related to the commercial exploitation of new technology. It will establish a new environmental unit within the further and higher education sector to

The Government will sponsor a series of conferences to bring industry, educationalists and course providers together, produce a leaflet to inform young people about careers in the environment, and establish a new unit to improve communications between business, trainers and educators

Training Agency publications provide information about careers in various environmental areas

Training programmes which include environmental elements provide interesting and useful disciplines for young people, the long-termed unemployed or those at a disadvantage in the labour market

improve communications between education and business country-wide, and to complement the existing units based on single institutions. This unit will support environmental training geared to the specific needs of employers and their employees.

17.58 The Agricultural Training Board, working with agricultural colleges and other agencies, will continue to foster environmental awareness in the countryside.

17.59 The Government has established five centres of excellence for environmental training – in Edinburgh, Sheffield, Cardiff, Rossendale and Colchester. Their tasks are:
• to provide assistance to other environmental training projects and to sub-contractors to enable them to deliver effective training and useful environmental work; and
• to redesign and restructure existing projects to ensure that they deliver effective training, based on competencies and leading to

vocational qualifications.
In addition the Training Agency promotes environmental work and training within the Employment Training initiative by the private, public and voluntary sectors. This reflects the fact that the environment is increasingly an industry in its own right, and shows how important environmental improvement can be to economic regeneration.

17.60 In both training and education professional bodies need to be more proactive in developing vocational requirements for environmental work. The Engineering Council's decision to hold an assembly to foster awareness of environmental issues among that profession is a welcome example.

17.61 Through the Training Agency Standards Programme, the Government will ensure that vocational standards are in place across the whole range of environmental jobs including countryside work, urban conservation and all aspects of pollution control and waste management. This initiative will develop further the work of COSQUEC (the Council for Occupational Standards and Qualifications in Environmental Conservation), which has recently reviewed the occupational structure of the sector and is developing standards for some environmental occupations. The Waste Management Industry Training Advisory Board was established last year, and will develop standards conforming with legal requirements during 1991. The Training Agency has also been assisting other lead bodies with an interest in the environmental sector.

CONCLUSION

17.62 The Government is acting to ensure that all decisions can be taken on the basis of the best scientific and economic evidence available. It will support a comprehensive programme of research and monitoring, and it will publish regularly a new statistical report including all important data on Britain's environment. It will help consumers take the environmental decisions that they want by setting in place labelling schemes, preferably across Europe.

17.63 The Government is also ensuring that the education system adapts fully to the new interest in the environment. This will be reflected in the National Curriculum for schools which is placing new emphasis in environmental topics; and in initiatives being taken to ensure that the supply of higher and further education, of post graduate courses and of training courses are all tailored to meet the increased environmental needs.

INSTITUTIONS AND CONSULTATION

The Government will co-ordinate all its policies affecting the environment; a Minister in each Department will be nominated to follow up the White Paper

The Government will publish an environmental action guide for Departments

INTRODUCTION

18.1 Establishing new bureaucracies or juggling powers and responsibilities between Government bodies is never by itself a sufficient solution to environmental problems. But we need the right institutional arrangements in place to deliver successful environmental policies; and we need the right consultative machinery so that Government is open to positive suggestions on ways to perform better. This Chapter considers the way in which Government Departments and other public sector bodies are organised to carry out their environmental functions effectively and their methods of consulting people outside Government.

Government Departments

18.2 Environment policy affects all Government Departments: most or all of their policies have an impact on the environment, as does the way in which they manage the buildings and land for which they are responsible. So, just as on other issues which cross Departmental boundaries, the Government already seeks to ensure that all the environmental implications of policy decisions under discussion are considered before conclusions are reached. But to reflect the growing importance of environmental issues and the Government's determination to tackle them effectively, the Government is proposing a number of changes to existing arrangements which will integrate environmental concerns more effectively into all policy areas

18.3 First, it will keep in place the co-ordinating machinery established to work up this White Paper. This includes a standing committee of Cabinet Ministers to consider environmental policies, and to follow up the policies described here. This will ensure that environmental issues are tackled in a co-ordinated and effective way.

18.4 Second, a nominated Minister in each Department is to be responsible for considering the environmental implications of all of that Department's policies and spending programmes, and for following up the relevant parts of this White Paper. People outside Government who want to discuss things in the White Paper which are the responsibility of particular Departments will then know which Minister to approach.

18.5 To complement that, Departments' annual Departmental Reports, which set out their spending plans, can also set out the action they have taken to follow up the White Paper and any other environmental initiatives which they are proposing.

Environmental analysis

18.6 During the preparation of this White Paper, each Government Department has reviewed the environmental implications of its existing policies and considered changes to them. Where this has resulted in proposals for change, these are included in the relevant chapters. To build on that exercise, and to ensure that the environmental implications of decisions are fully considered beforehand, the Government has carried out a review of the way in which the costs and benefits of environmental issues are assessed within Government. The review has looked at the range of analysis which is available on environmental costs and benefits, recognising the need for an integrated approach which takes account of all the consequences of a measure for the environment, favourable and unfavourable. It has concluded that there is scope for a more systematic approach within Government to the appraisal of the environmental costs and benefits before decisions are taken. The Government has therefore set work in hand to produce guidelines for policy appraisal where there are significant implications for the environment. These will be published in due course. The aim is to provide general guidance to departments, not to set out a rigid set of procedures to be followed in all cases.

Purchasing and building management

18.7 Decisions by individual Government departments on what materials to buy and how to manage their buildings and land can have a huge environmental impact. The Civil Estate totals some 8,000 properties, covering some 11 million square metres, and the Government spends about £7 billion each year on goods and services. Departments have taken major steps in recent years to adopt more environmentally-friendly policies and practices. The Department of the Environment's Property Holdings organisation has carried out a review to examine all aspects of purchasing, building management and land holding by Government departments, and to assess how the environmental impact of these activities can be improved by cost-effective measures. The outcome will be an environmental action guide which shows managers step by step, from photocopying to air conditioning, how to assess the environmental impact of their operations and what they can do to improve it. It will include technical notes on specific topics. This guidance will be adopted across Government and the Government is

encouraging other public bodies to follow it too. It should ensure that environmental issues are central to all purchasing, building and land decisions by Government. It will also be published by HMSO to allow others to draw on its advice. A striking feature of the guidance is the extent to which measures which are good for the environment also make good business sense. The Government will launch it shortly.

Pollution inspectorates

18.8 A number of separate pollution inspectorates exist at the moment, in addition to other pollution control functions carried out by Government Departments and local authorities. Effective pollution control requires strong and authoritative regulatory agencies or inspectorates. The following paragraphs briefly describe the functions of three key regulatory bodies.

18.9 In England and Wales Her Majesty's Inspectorate of Pollution (HMIP) is part of the Department of the Environment. The Government set it up in 1987, and is further strengthening its powers in the Environmental Protection Bill. HMIP is responsible for controlling all the major emissions to air, land and water from the most polluting industrial processes; for policing the storage and disposal of radioactive substances and wastes; and for overseeing local authorities' performance of their waste regulation functions under the Environmental Protection Bill.

18.10 The National Rivers Authority (NRA) was established in 1989 to protect and improve the water environment. It controls effluent discharges into, and abstraction from, Britain's rivers, lakes and coastal waters; it is also responsible for defence against flooding from rivers and the sea, and for fisheries and navigation.

18.11 The Health and Safety Commission (HSC) and the Health and Safety Executive (HSE) were established by the Health and Safety at Work etc Act 1974. The HSC's duties are to ensure that there is adequate legislation, research, training and information

Her Majesty's Inspectorate of Pollution is set to become a separate executive agency within Government, controlling pollution from industrial processes

The new inspectorates are making good progress in establishing their roles and earning credibility

to protect workers and the public from risks to their health and safety arising from work activities. The HSE has day to day responsibility for enforcing the legislation.

Options for change

18.12 The Government's first objective has been to establish effective inspectorates to help raise the quality of the environment. HMIP and NRA are making good progress in firming up their organisations and establishing their roles. The Government believes that the overriding need is to give them both time to settle down and establish credibility. Some, however, argue for further institutional change in the short term.

18.13 The commonest suggestion for change is for an amalgamation of some or all of the three regulatory bodies listed above. The main arguments in favour of some such change are that it might make it easier for industry and others to have only one inspectorate to approach; that with separate organisations there is always the risk of some overlap or duplication of effort; and that combining the bodies under one management might lead to greater consistency of approach across all pollution types and environmental media. Some people have suggested that HMIP cannot be sufficiently independent from Government, since it is part of the Department of the Environment.

The Government's proposals

18.14 The Government has concluded that the case for such an amalgamation is insufficient to outweigh the disadvantages of further administrative upheaval at just the time when the new organisations are getting into their stride. It does not therefore propose to alter the present functions of the existing regulatory bodies for the time being.

18.15 The Government does however propose to strengthen HMIP's position. First, it proposes that HMIP should be a candidate for becoming a 'Next Steps' agency, (ie a separate executive agency within Government), as soon as possible. Although still part of the Department of the Environment,

HMIP should thereby have an enhanced status and a clearly separate identity, which should strengthen its authority in controlling pollution. Second, to ensure that HMIP is able to draw on views and advice from a wide range of informed opinion, the Government will appoint an independent committee to advise HMIP on all its responsibilities.

Medium term options

18.16 The disbenefits of administrative change will diminish over time, and experience with the new systems may add to the case for some further rationalisation of these structures. One option which the Government will wish to consider in due course would be to create a new umbrella body responsible for overseeing the pollution control work of the NRA and HMIP. Under such an arrangement these bodies would keep their separate identity and independence, but the new umbrella body would oversee their implementation of pollution control and work for greater consistency of approach.

18.17 A second possibility would be to expand the role of HMIP in relation to the regulation of waste disposal, and perhaps to give it the leading responsibility for it. Under the Environmental Protection Bill HMIP will already have the duty of auditing the performance of local authorities in their task of regulating waste disposal operations. But many people have suggested that the regulation of waste disposal needs to be co-ordinated over a wider area than that of a single authority.

18.18 The regulation of waste disposal is an important and increasingly technical subject, and the Government accepts that it needs to be co-ordinated between local authority areas, at least on a regional basis. The Government has asked the local authorities concerned to establish appropriate arrangements for co-operation between them to secure this necessary co-ordination. HMIP will have the task of keeping these arrangements under review and reporting if problems arise. The Government will review the position further in the light of experience with these regional arrangements, and the evolution of HMIP.

Countryside and wildlife agencies

18.19 There are a number of public sector agencies which operate in the countryside. The Government greatly values their work, which is described in Chapter 7. The Environmental Protection Bill contains proposals for reorganising two of them. The following paragraphs briefly describe the arrangements once that Bill is implemented, and the Government's response to suggestions for further changes.

18.20 The Nature Conservancy Council (NCC) is at present responsible for nature conservation throughout Great Britain. It advises on policies affecting nature conservation; designates and protects sites of special scientific interest and nature reserves; and is responsible for nature conservation research.

18.21 The Countryside Commissions, one for England and Wales and one for Scotland, are responsible for the conservation of the countryside and its enjoyment by the public. They advise on the conservation and enhancement of the natural beauty of the countryside; promote public access to it; provide financial support towards conservation of and access to the countryside; take the lead in designating national parks and areas of outstanding natural beauty; and are responsible for heritage coasts and national trails.

18.22 The Rural Development Commission advises on all matters relating to the economic and social development of rural areas in England; provides industrial premises for sale or rent; advises and gives financial help to small businesses in rural areas; and gives financial help to other organisations, usually voluntary bodies, to carry out measures likely to further social development. In Wales the Development Board for Rural Wales and the Welsh Development Agency carry out these tasks. In Scotland a similar role is played by the Scottish Development Agency and the Highlands and Islands Development Board.

18.23 The Environmental Protection Bill divides the NCC into three separate agencies for England, Scotland and Wales; and provides for a single new Welsh agency to take over responsibility for all countryside matters in Wales. In Scotland the Government has announced its intention to legislate to amalgamate the new Scottish NCC with the Countryside Commission for Scotland. The Government has, however, announced that there is no present intention to merge the NCC and the Countryside Commission in England.

Options for change

18.24 As with the pollution inspectorates, the Government's main objective now is to allow the new organisations established by the Bill to find their feet, and that predisposes it against proposals for further change. The change most commonly suggested is an amalgamation of the NCC and Countryside Commission in England, which would mirror the arrangements being made in Scotland and Wales. The case for such a change was made recently in the House of Lords Science and Technology Committee's Report on the NCC, and the Government recognises the force of some of the arguments in that report. These included the closeness of the interrelationship between nature conservation and countryside conservation; their need for common data and expertise; and their tendency to concentrate their attention on the same landscapes.

The Government's proposals

18.25 But in addition to the need to avoid further institutional change on top of the proposals in the Bill, the Government sees other arguments against an immediate amalgamation in England. The greater size and complexity of the existing agencies in England when compared with those in Scotland and Wales would make an effective merger greatly more difficult to achieve; and although the Government accepts that there is a close relationship between countryside and nature interests, they nevertheless remain distinct, and amalgamation would risk subordinating

The Nature Conservancy Council and Countryside Commission will continue as separate bodies in England, and the Government will review the case for change in the longer term

some concerns to others. In the short term therefore the Government has decided not to proceed with a merger of the NCC and the Countryside Commission in England. For the longer term, however, the Government will review the options as it assesses the performance of the newly established NCC for England.

Local government

Local authorities play a crucial part in environmental policies; central and local government will work closely together

18.26 Local authorities have a key part to play in environmental policy. Not only do they have a range of specific powers and functions which have a direct impact on their local environment, but also, as with Government Departments, almost everything which local authorities do has some impact on the environment. The best local authorities have an enviable environmental record, and are pioneering ways of co-ordinating their environmental strategies and activities on a corporate basis.

18.27 The Government greatly welcomes the current initiative from the local authority associations in preparing a guide to environmental best practice by authorities, for publication later in 1990. It should be a particularly valuable reference source for authorities wishing to improve their environmental performance, as it draws together the best examples from all spheres of local government. It will complement the useful work by the Local Government Training Board, which published general

guidance on environmental issues earlier in 1990, and other similar publications.   The Government is very happy to endorse these valuable aids to the work of local authorities.

18.28 The Government will need to work closely with local government on the development of environmental policies and on their implementation. It will continue to consult the local authority associations as now on particular propositions. In addition the Secretary of State for the Environment, proposes to invite the leaders of the local authority associations to have regular meetings to discuss more general environmental concerns, perhaps also inviting Ministers from other Departments as appropriate.

Business

18.29 Many firms in all sectors of the business community are looking for ways to reduce the damage which their products and their processes do to the environment. Some businesses are exemplary in demonstrating how organisations can include environmental considerations in every aspect of their activities. These changes in approach make good commercial sense, since they are a direct response to pressures in the marketplace from consumers and investors. The Government fully supports this development, and is endorsing the very useful guidance to company chief executives issued by Business in the Environment. This stresses the need for all companies to establish clear environmental policies and procedures at the highest level. The CBI produces a range of information on environmental issues for companies of all sizes and is currently developing an environmental audit package for small businesses. The Environment Council, a charity which acts as an umbrella organisation for 45 environmental groups, runs a Business and Environment programme. Managers from over 450 companies support this programme which runs seminars and produces a handbook for those participating. The Government is a joint sponsor of the 'Better Environment Awards for Industry ' scheme administered by the Royal Society for the encouragement of Arts, Manufacturers and Commerce, and is considering with them ways of developing this scheme in the future.

18.30 In pursuing all its environmental policies, the Government is anxious to consult the business community at every stage, and to take full account of the implications for business. The Government already consults business interests about particular issues, such as the implementation of integrated pollution control and the phase-out of ozone depleting chemicals; and in some cases it has convened expert groups including representatives from industry at early stages of policy formulation, including groups on recycling and eco-labelling.

18.31 The Government wants to build on this experience and proposes to set in place the following arrangements for consulting business about environmental policies.
• It will continue to consult business on particular topics, at the earliest possible stage of policy formulation; in particular it will regularly discuss with business the implications of integrated pollution control in Britain and the implications for business of forthcoming environmental items on the EC agenda.
• Second, in order to help the business community to find its way around the Government Departments concerned with the various aspects of environmental policy, the Government will publish a guide setting out who does what within Government on environmental issues and on ways to advise and help business.
• Third, the Secretaries of State for the Environment and for Trade and Industry propose to establish a new discussion and advisory body with members drawn from a wide spectrum of business interests; this could advise on the implications for business of the strategic and practical environmental issues of the day, including measures to meet targets and the priorities and content of the action programmes of the two Departments relevant to environmental technology and other environmental issues.
• Fourth, the Departments of Trade and Industry and of the Environment will, with the help of HMIP and other Departments, make efforts at regional level to explain

Many businesses are responding to widespread public concern about the environment; the Government will consult business more

developments on environmental regulation and other environmental issues affecting business, and to encourage businesses to use the help which Government Departments can offer them; this will involve business, business advisers and local authorities.

Voluntary organisations

18.32 Voluntary organisations in Britain deserve much of the credit for the great increase in public interest in the environment in recent years. They have brought to the debate on the environment an invaluable commitment and expertise, which have rightly challenged the existing practices, home and abroad, of Governments, central and local, businesses and individuals. The success of the environmental voluntary organisations in exciting public interest is shown by the substantial increase in their membership: conservation and environmental groups in Britain now claim some 4 million members, compared with under 2 million in 1980.

18.33 The Government remains very keen to support voluntary activity in this area, and to build its environmental policies in partnership with the responsible environmental voluntary groups. There are numerous instances of successful co-operation, particularly in international conferences where the Government has worked closely with British voluntary organisations. The following paragraphs set out the Government's proposals to build on such examples.

Britain has excellent voluntary environmental organisations; the Government will work closely with them and give some financial support

18.34 First, the Government is anxious to continue to involve voluntary environmental bodies in the evolution of environmental policies, and will initiate discussion with them on how current practice might be improved. Discussion at national level is needed to address several issues common to all voluntary groups, including the need for effective arrangements at regional level to support and co-ordinate their activities, the need to achieve value for money, monitoring arrangements, general funding issues, and the opportunities for voluntary bodies to help each other to increase the contribution of their members to improving the environment. Individual voluntary organisations must of course continue to have regular access to Ministers and to Departments on their specific topics of interest; but in the Government's view, if the contribution of the voluntary sector is to be optimised, it is also important to discuss on a national basis the sort of general issues mentioned above. The Government will pursue this in the first instance with the National Council for Voluntary Organisations.

18.35 Second, the great strength of voluntary organisations lies in their local expertise and ability to pull together local voluntary effort. In the Government's view it is important for environmental organisations to improve communications at regional and local level with each other, with Government, central and local, and with local business interests. In a number of areas voluntary groups have established regional environmental networks to bring together voluntary organisations operating in the area, to address regional environmental concerns and to seek agreement on joint projects. The Government supports this approach, and the Department of the Environment will stand ready to respond to such initiatives at regional as well as national level.

18.36 Third, another strength of the voluntary sector is its reliance on volunteer effort and on financial contributions voluntarily offered. But the Government accepts that some projects need some Government money to help get them started.

It already gives substantial financial support to a range of voluntary organisations, directly through the Department of the Environment's Special Grants Programme and through agencies like the Countryside Commission and Nature Conservancy Council. In addition the Government proposes to set up a new ring-fenced fund to help finance specific initiatives proposed by voluntary organisations to further policies set out in this White Paper. The Department of the Environment will publish details and set aside funds for this purpose in 1991-92.

Royal Commission on Environmental Pollution

18.37 The Royal Commission was established in 1970 'to advise on matters, both national and international, concerning the pollution of the environment; on the adequacy of research in this field; and the future possibilities of danger to the environment'. It has produced 13 reports and successive Governments have greatly valued its work and its authoritative advice.

18.38 The Government has already taken steps to increase the resources available to the Royal Commission, both within its secretariat and for consultancy work. This is to enable the Royal Commission to improve its database, and to produce more rapid reports on matters of topical interest as well as the traditional style of fuller reports based on formally submitted evidence. The Government proposes to discuss with the Royal Commission whether further strengthening might be advantageous.

Conclusion

18.39 Just as the increase in public interest in the environment has permanently altered the behaviour of individuals and firms, this Chapter shows how increased emphasis on the environment is altering the institutions of Government and its arrangements for consulting others. The Government believes that the changes proposed here will make it better able to respond to the environmental challenges ahead.

19

THE ENVIRONMENT
IN WALES

Above: Snowdonia: part of the beautiful mountain landscape of Wales

Above right: The Brecon Beacons are one of three large National Parks which cover one fifth of the land area of Wales

INTRODUCTION

19.1 Wales and England share common systems of law, land tenure and local government. The Secretary of State for Wales is responsible for carrying out Government policy in the Principality in most areas described in other chapters. This broad range of responsibilities allows him to examine the relationship between his Department's individual functions in coming to decisions that take the interests of the environment fully into account. This Chapter illustrates this process and describes how some key policies referred to in other chapters are applied in Wales, dealing in turn with:
• the landscape and roads;
• agriculture;
• countryside;
• urban revival;
• built heritage;
• water;
• waste management;
• energy efficiency; and
• education and training.

19.2 The varied landscape of Wales ranges from mountains of over 3,000 feet in Snowdonia to lowland coastal plains. Much of the country is rural, and the large tracts of upland open country are very beautiful. Its countryside and the diverse flora and fauna it supports are major assets, with about one fifth of the land falling within the three National Parks of Brecon Beacons, Pembrokeshire Coast and Snowdonia. Wales has five Areas of Outstanding Natural Beauty, and 40% of the coastline is designated as Heritage Coast. Conservation and the sensitive use of these varied and important natural environments are a high priority.

19.3 The modernisation of industry in Wales brings with it social and environmental improvements to areas left derelict by past generations of heavy industry. The many areas of natural beauty in Wales and its distinctive cultural heritage have encouraged the development of leisure facilities and an increase in tourism.

THE ENVIRONMENT IN WALES

The landscape and roads

19.4 Since almost one quarter of Wales is recognised as of exceptional landscape quality and designated as either a National Park or an Area of Outstanding Natural Beauty, particular care is required in designing road improvement schemes. The main issues are relating the line of the road to the landscape and landscaping the finished road to blend in with its surroundings. The A55 Conwy crossing scheme provides a prime example of the weight given to environmental factors. The original proposals were for a bridge, but the Government decided that the road should be carried in a tunnel in order to preserve the setting of Conwy Castle and the estuary.

19.5 An innovative approach was also taken in considering improvements to the A470 through the Lledr Valley in Snowdonia. The route between Blaenau Ffestiniog and Betws-y-Coed has been studied as a whole; the characteristics of individual sections of the road have been highlighted; and improvement solutions drawn up based jointly on engineering and landscape considerations. These will now be used as a guide in developing improvement schemes.

19.6 Care is taken in finishing schemes to achieve a proper blend with the immediate surroundings. Between 1979 and 1988, 158 landscape schemes were undertaken. In 1988-89 about a quarter of a million trees and shrubs were planted around 17 new road schemes.

Agriculture

19.7 Over 80% of Welsh land is in agricultural use, but nearly 80% of that is within Less Favoured Areas. The combination of poor soils and climatic and other physical constraints over a large area of Wales means that a high proportion of the land is devoted to grassland farming systems. Welsh agriculture is therefore dominated by livestock production, and the countryside has suffered less than some other areas from insensitive farming practices. Indeed, much of the attractiveness of the countryside is due to the positive environmental benefits flowing from good practice of livestock farmers.

Overgrazing is not a serious problem except on some areas of common land. Nevertheless the Government has accepted that some local protection is needed and two Environmentally Sensitive Areas (ESAs) have been designated in Wales. The Cambrian Mountains ESA was first designated in 1987 and extended in 1988 so that the total area included is now 155,000 hectares. The Lleyn Peninsula ESA covering about 40,000 hectares was designated in 1988.

19.8 Welsh farmers generally have become much more aware and concerned about the need to conserve the environment. Their attitude is motivated by both ecological considerations and the obvious amenity value of an attractive countryside, which itself generates income from tourism. The conservation of the countryside can be an inherent part of good practice in livestock farming, and agricultural policy aims to ensure that basic support for agriculture will also provide environmental benefits in large parts of Wales.

Countryside

19.9 To conserve flora, fauna and geological formations, 45 National Nature Reserves and some 730 Sites of Special Scientific Interest have been designated in Wales. Britain's second Marine Nature Reserve – the waters around the island of Skomer – was designated earlier in 1990. The Nature Conservancy Council is planning for another Reserve, in the Menai Strait.

19.10 The countryside is also a valuable recreational asset. The Government seeks to encourage a proper balance between leisure and other interests that sometimes conflict. The Wales Tourist Board is very conscious of the impact that tourism can have on the countryside and works with the various conservation organisations to minimise it. The Board and the three National Parks in Wales have signed an accord recognising the important role that tourism plays in sustaining the economy of rural areas, but accepting that the environment must take precedence over tourism when the two are in irreconcilable conflict.

The Government encourages Welsh farmers to make conservation an inherent part of farming practice

239

two basic industries such as coal, steel or slate. The decline in the employment they provided led to serious urban deprivation, a huge legacy of derelict, contaminated land and other problems normally associated with inner cities. In Wales this occurred in isolated urban communities and in the coastal towns. Improving the environment of these communities is an essential element in the Government's strategy for their revival.

19.13 Land reclamation has been a key first step in urban revival in Wales. The Welsh Development Agency's (WDA) Derelict Land Grant is supporting one of the largest and most sustained reclamation programmes in Europe. Some 750 hectares a year are being cleared, a threefold increase over the past 10 years. This has already transformed many of the ugliest scars on the landscapes of North and South Wales, and there is now a real prospect that dereliction in Wales will be substantially cleared by the end of the century.

The Government will establish the new Countryside Council for Wales to improve countryside protection and nature conservation

19.11 As part of a wider reorganisation of countryside and conservation bodies throughout mainland Britain, the functions of the Countryside Commission and the Nature Conservancy Council for Wales are to be carried out by a single new body, the Countryside Council for Wales. This new Council is expected to assume its responsibilities from April 1991. The new arrangements should result in more efficient delivery of conservation and countryside policies with greater sensitivity to the needs of Wales.

19.14   The WDA is also engaged in a programme of environmental and town improvements. The last five years have seen £9 million committed to over 500 schemes. This work is complemented by grants to projects which contribute to the improvement of the environment as part of the Government's Urban Programme.

Urban revival

19.12   Urban revival policy in Wales aims to contribute to solving the interrelated economic, environmental and social problems that result from long term changes in the economic structure of Welsh cities and older industrial urban areas. Many communities in Wales were traditionally dependent on one or

19.15 Housing improvements are essential to improve the Welsh urban environment. A third of the urban housing stock in Wales was built before 1919. Housing policy is therefore directed at making sustained improvements through Home Renovation

The Government is transforming derelict urban land in Wales through the Derelict Land Grant programme

The Government is reclaiming once derelict land through the Programme for the Valleys, providing for new industrial and commercial development, leisure and housing.

Grants and area renewal, local authorities' own improvement programmes and the involvement of housing associations in rehabilitation schemes.

19.16   Unused and unsightly land and buildings are being brought back to life through the Urban Investment Grant (UIG) scheme and its predecessor the Urban Development Grant. These encourage private sector investment and expertise to enable development projects, such as the Swansea Marina, to go ahead in areas of high depriva tion and derelic-tion. So far, some £44.5 million in both grants has secured nearly £200 million of private sector investment and created over 11,000 jobs.

19.17   The Cardiff Bay Development Corporation was established in 1987 to secure the physical, social and economic regeneration of the South Cardiff area including the former docklands.   The aim is to introduce new housing, employment and a better environment to the area, and the strategy includes a proposal to construct a

barrage across the estuary of the Taff and Ely as a key feature. Over 160 hectares of land have already been brought forward for redevelopment.

19.18 The Programme for the Valleys is a special drive by the Government, other agencies and local authorities to improve economic, environmental and social conditions in the deprived urban communities of the South Wales Valleys. The Programme started in June 1988 and will run until March 1993. It has already resulted in significant economic, social and environmental improvements. Town centres have been enhanced, over 5,500 houses have benefited from area renewal schemes and 500 hectares of derelict land have been reclaimed for industrial and commercial development, leisure and housing.

The built heritage

19.19 The built heritage of Wales is a major asset which contributes both to the quality of life and to economic activity through tourism. The Government's policy is to promote its conservation and public appreciation and enjoyment of it.

19.20 There are over 2,600 scheduled monuments in Wales and an assessment programme is under way to ensure that the protection provided is both relevant and adequate. There are 13,000 listed buildings (compared with 8,000 in 1979), and a current resurvey is expected to add 20,000 to the list.

The Government is encouraging development projects, such as the Swansea Marina, in once-derelict areas

The Government will improve protection of the built heritage

Water

19.23 Water resources and quality are important in Wales, and Welsh water is supplied not only to customers in Wales but to many in England. Welsh rivers are generally of high quality. Many are important fishing rivers and 94 % of Welsh river length was identified in the 1985 River Quality Survey as of good or fair quality. In 1989 over 80% of identified Welsh bathing waters complied with the requirements of the EC Bathing Water Directive. Welsh Water will invest about £1.75 billion up to the year 2000 in order to improve water quality still further.

19.24 All water companies have conservation and recreation duties. Welsh Water owns over 36,000 hectares in Wales, much of which is in National Parks or designated as Sites of Special Scientific Interest. In 1989 it donated over 17,000 hectares of the Elan Valley to a charitable trust to safeguard the area for the benefit of the public. It has also entered management agreements to ensure that other important land in its ownership is properly managed and conserved.

Waste management

19.25 District councils in Wales undertake both waste collection and disposal functions and also regulate waste disposal operations. But following a Government review of the responsibility for waste disposal in Wales the district councils' operations are watched over by regional and national steering groups. The provisions of the Environmental Protection Bill require the Government to keep the regulation of waste under review, and any improvements needed will build on the regional arrangements already in place.

Energy efficiency

19.26 Energy production has been an important feature of the Welsh economy since the industrial revolution. Over the years the Principality's coal reserves have powered many industries. Now Wales is at the forefront in the development of equipment to harness renewable sources of

19.21 The Government gives financial support for repairs to the built heritage, and spending in Wales increased to £2.8 million in 1989/90. Churches and chapels in Wales already enjoy substantial support for conservation (more than £2.3 million in 1985-1990), and this will continue to be a priority. The need to extend assistance to cathedrals in Wales under these arrangements will be examined further.

19.22 The Government manages 127 historic properties in Wales. These include the castles built by Edward I at Conwy, Caernarfon, Harlech and Beaumaris which are classified as World Heritage sites. They also include smaller monuments such as the prehistoric burial chamber at Pentre Ifan and industrial remains at Blaenavon. It is a major task requiring considerable expertise to ensure that all these monuments are conserved for the future and well presented to the public. In 1984 the Government therefore established 'Cadw: Welsh Historic Monuments.' Cadw, which takes its name from a Welsh word meaning "keep, preserve", has improved guide books and publications and provided imaginative displays and more educational activities at sites. Cadw is an announced candidate for executive agency status under the Government's 'next steps' programme. As such, Cadw would be expected to build on these initiatives and deliver further improvements.

energy. The Centre for Alternative Technology at Machynlleth and the Centre for Solar Energy at University College Cardiff are involved in this field.

19.27 Energy efficiency policy in Wales is broadly similar to that in the rest of Britain. But the Government has a specific strategy for the efficient use of energy in Wales. The Welsh Office has set up four Energy Managers Groups which provide a forum for the exchange of information and experience and thus encourage and assist public and private sector organisations to make the most of energy.

Education and training

19.28 All Welsh Local Education Authorities have a policy statement for the curriculum, covering the 5-16 age range and containing references to the role of the environment. The National Curriculum applies to schools in Wales just as in England (see Chapter 17).

19.29 Initial teacher training courses in Wales now give a growing place to environmental work. All colleges and institutes of higher education have for some time provided primary curriculum courses which contain a compulsory environmental

and humanities component, in addition to science. They also have longstanding experience in offering main subject courses, such as geography and biology, which contain significant environmental emphasis. Some colleges offer outdoor education as a main study within the BEd degree, while some offer a BA degree which involves either a prominent environmental component or, in the case of one college, a multi-disciplinary BA degree directly related to the environment. Two colleges offer environmental courses in both English and Welsh.

19.30 Much of the thematic work in primary schools derives from topics with an environmental and often local emphasis. One specific development since 1988 in selected primary schools in Wales is the second phase of the Paris-based 'Environment and School Initiatives Project' sponsored by the Organisation for Economic Co-operation and Development (OECD). This is a research study of how schools are using the environment in teaching. The environmental dimension also figures strongly in current work undertaken in science and geography in secondary schools. This emphasis is reinforced and extended to pupils aged 5 to 16 within the programmes of study and attainment targets of the National Curriculum in science and in the Secretary of State's proposals for geography, all of which are common to England and Wales. The study of environmental topics and issues looms large in public examination courses in science, biology and geography at age 16+ and 18+.

19.31 The importance of the environment is also recognised in post-school education, including teacher training. Main subject courses such as geography and biology have significant environmental emphasis while a range of courses at the levels of both further and higher education include environmental aspects. Two colleges offer environmental courses through the medium of both English and Welsh and the Polytechnic of Wales is co-operating with the local authorities in Mid Glamorgan on a joint environmental study of its surrounding area.

19.32 Two prominent committees promote environmental education in Wales - the Prince of Wales Committee and the Environmental Education Group. Both have secured financial support from various agencies to sponsor a wide variety of business, commercial and educational projects and have conducted research into environmental matters. Each year, they make awards to schools for achievements in promoting environmental work. In 1988 the Prince of Wales Committee accepted an offer from the Gwent College of Higher Education to provide facilities for a Welsh Centre for Environmental Education.

CONCLUSION

19.33 The environmental policies set out in this White Paper are of particular importance to Wales which has on one hand problems of urban decay and on the other a priceless heritage of historic buildings and monuments and countryside of outstanding beauty. The White Paper sets out the Government's general principles and policies for the environment; in Wales the Secretary of State with his wide range of functions and his territorial responsibilities is well placed to carry them out and ensure that this inheritance is handed on to our children in good shape.

Research – Wales

The Welsh Office funds research into environmental matters which are of particular relevance to the Principality.
Examples of such research, valued at £0.2m in 1989/90, are projects on
• the effects of ozone and acidic pollutants on vegetation in Wales
• body burdens in Wales following exposure to heavy metals
• a radon survey of homes in Wales
• the effect of upland management on water resources and water quality in Wales
• movement of sediments in Swansea Bay
• effects of storm water overflows on Welsh river water quality
In addition much work in Wales is funded by the Department of Environment, the Ministry of Agriculture, Fisheries and Food, the Nature Conservancy Council, the Research Councils and other bodies.

THE ENVIRONMENT
IN SCOTLAND

INTRODUCTION

20.1 Scotland shares many of the environmental challenges of Britain generally, and policy is based on a similar approach. But Scotland's climate, geography and history give rise to distinctive challenges and opportunities, and this Chapter concentrates on aspects where there are significant differences of emphasis.

20.2 Many areas are of outstanding natural beauty with a rich diversity of species and habitats, and tourism has become one of Scotland's most important industries. But environmental problems remain in some towns and cities, especially in the Central Lowlands. Rural conservation and urban renewal both require measures attuned to Scotland's special circumstances.

Scotland has the world's largest colony of gannets as well as habitats and species which are unique in Britain

INSTITUTIONS

20.3 Responsibility for all aspects of environmental policy and land use in Scotland rests with the Secretary of State for Scotland. Within the Scottish Office these functions are administered by Departments responsible for Agriculture and Fisheries and for the Environment. The Secretary of State is jointly responsible, with the Secretary of State for Wales and the Minister of Agriculture, for the Forestry Commission. One of the Scottish Ministers is appointed by the Secretary of State to take responsibility for coordinating all policies in Scotland which affect rural areas.

20.4 The Scottish Office handles all planning matters which are not dealt with by local authorities and has its own professional staff

to advise on planning issues. It also has its own pollution inspectorate (HM Industrial Pollution Inspectorate) and Hazardous Waste Inspectorate. Outside the areas of the three Islands Councils, which exercise the functions themselves, the quality of water in rivers, estuaries, lochs and off the coast is the responsibility of the seven River Purification Boards. The provision of water supplies to consumers is the responsibility of the nine Regional and the three Islands Councils. The Scottish Office controls dumping at sea and monitors the marine environment and fish stocks in Scottish waters.

20.5 There is a separate Countryside Commission for Scotland (CCS) with functions similar to those of the Countryside

Commission in England. The Government has decided to bring forward early legislation to amalgamate the CCS with the new Scottish Nature Conservancy Council to create a powerful body responsible for all aspects of nature and landscape conservation, access and enjoyment.

20.6 The powers of the Scottish Development Agency have played a particularly important part in urban and environmental renewal in conjunction with the local authorities. Similar powers are now available to Scottish Homes in areas of run down housing, whether in urban or rural areas.

TOWN AND COUNTRY

Land use and planning

20.7 The existence of large areas which are poorly endowed for agriculture and the effect of past industrial history largely account for the size and distribution of the Scottish population. Around 80 % is located in the Central Lowlands. Some of the rural areas have a weak economic base and are among the most sparsely populated to be found anywhere in Europe. The overall density is only 66 persons per square kilometre, which compares with 235 persons for Britain as a whole.

20.8 The physical planning system is the centrepiece of policy to ensure that development and land use are compatible with proper care for the environment. The system in Scotland is very similar to that in the rest of Britain. But the high quality of so much of the natural environment, the densely populated Central Lowlands with its need for economic restructuring, especially in areas of unemployment, and the fragile economic base of sparsely populated rural parts all offer special challenges.

20.9 In the past decade the most important of these challenges were: the growth of oil activities in the North Sea and on land, the provision of new infrastructure, especially roads, airports, pipelines and housing and the task of regenerating the older conurbations and industrial areas. Local authority structure plans and policies played a major part in meeting these challenges with an outstanding degree of success which is not always publicly recognised.

20.10 A key element in this approach has been the development by the Scottish Office

of National Planning Guidelines aimed at facilitating development while protecting the environment. These cover a wide range of subjects and the Government will review them to ensure that they take full account of environmental considerations. Those which apply to ski-ing will require particular attention following the Secretary of State's proposed deletion of the proposal for expansion of ski-ing into Lurcher's Gully, Cairngorms, in the Highland Region structure plan.

20.11 In recognition of the importance to Scotland of the development of forestry, the Government has encouraged Regional Councils to prepare indicative forestry strategies and to include them in their structure plans. The Secretary of State has already approved the strategy for Strathclyde Region and the preparation of others is well advanced. A similar initiative for Caithness and Sutherland including the Flow Country has already been approved by all interested parties.

20.12 The Nature Conservancy Council has identified a series of Marine Consultation Areas to safeguard the conservation interest around the Scottish coast. The Government will consider the role of these areas in all

A framework has been agreed to protect the peatlands of Caithness and Sutherland, including the Flow Country, while allowing the development of a viable forestry industry

decisions affecting marine development, but the major development which has taken place in fish farming, to which Scotland's unpolluted waters are well suited, is of particular relevance. Salmon farms, mainly in the north west mainland and the islands, have brought much needed employment to sparsely populated and economically fragile areas. Hatcheries for salmon and trout farms have also developed in freshwater locations.

20.13 The Government has already taken a number of important steps to ensure that this industry develops in harmony with the local environment and scenery. For marine sites, the Crown Estate follows consultation procedures agreed with the Secretary of State before granting seabed leases. The procedures include reference to an Advisory Committee of cases where there is sustained objection by one of the major consultees. In addition the Government intends to prepare strategic guidance on environmental aspects of the location of marine fish farming. Discharges of effluents from fish farms are subject to control by River Purification Authorities. For freshwater areas an amendment has been made to the General Development Order which confirms that fish farms are subject to control by planning authorities.

20.14 The development of policy for the countryside and coastal areas requires detailed monitoring and survey information. The Government has therefore commissioned a major aerial photographic survey covering the entire land area of Scotland to secure a comprehensive classification of land cover. This will be used with other data to develop a geographical information system which will enable change in land use to be monitored and will test the potential effect of alternative policy options.

Conservation and countryside

20.15 The northerly location, the climate and the landform give parts of Scotland, notably the Highlands and Islands, more physical affinity with Scandinavia than with the rest of Britain. They provide an exceptionally rich range of habitats for plants and wildlife, some of which are not found elsewhere in Britain or in the European Community as a whole.

20.16 Scottish Natural Heritage (SNH), the new body which will come into existence through the merger of the Countryside Commission for Scotland and the Scottish Nature Conservancy Council, will have an important part to play in the conservation of both wildlife and landscape. Scotland has 47% of the total area of Sites of Special Scientific Interest (SSSI) in mainland Britain and 67% of the National Nature Reserves. Fully 10% of Scotland's area is SSSIs and 13% is classified as National Scenic Areas. But the role of SNH will go well beyond these specially designated areas; it will give advice to Government, land owners, developers and other public bodies on all countryside conservation issues, taking an approach related to the particular circumstances of Scotland. SNH will be more powerful than either of its two predecessors; it will have direct access to the Secretary of State and be an effective voice for conservation.

20.17 As well as speaking for conservation when issues are in dispute, the new body will aim to foster a greater understanding and appreciation of conservation issues and to promote access to and enjoyment of the countryside. Its management will be decentralised to ensure local involvement, and it will be available to discuss proposals for development to ensure that they avoid damage to the environment and provide for sustainable growth. There will be continuing dialogue through, for example, the Highlands and Islands Environment Group and with the voluntary sector through the Forum on the

The Government is tackling the planning and pollution control challenges presented by the growth of fish farming in Scotland

Rural Environment.

20.18 Agriculture is by far the most important rural activity in Scotland, almost 80 % of Scotland's land area being used for agricultural production. With over 90 % of the land classified under EC legislation as Less Favoured Area, extensive livestock production is the predominant agricultural activity. Cultivation is restricted to one-seventh of the land area. The measures to integrate environmental protection into agricultural policies as described in Chapter 7 are operated on broadly the same lines both north and south of the border. Measures for the future described in that Chapter will also extend to Scotland with appropriate adjustments where necessary to reflect particular Scottish circumstances. Specifically Scottish measures already in place help farmers to continue to play their part in the preservation of the countryside. For instance, the five Environmentally Sensitive Area schemes in Scotland provide for specific funding of

positive measures to enhance the environment. Grant-aided measures for the protection of the environment feature in the partly EC funded Agricultural Development Programme for the Scottish Islands. Over 50 % of Programme participants have adopted environmental management procedures on parts of their holdings. A similar concept is being developed for the Rural Enterprise

The Central Scotland Woodlands Initiative will bring major environmental improvements to many former industrial areas

Programme which will be brought into operation in the Highlands and Islands later in 1990.

20.19 The Government will continue the work of environmental renewal in areas suffering from the scars of past industry. Greater attention will be given to central Scotland, building on the work of the Central Scotland Countryside Trust and the Countryside Around Towns Projects. Organised through companies established especially for the purpose, work will focus on landscape improvement, habitat creation, amenity and community woodland planting, improved access and the extension of informal recreation facilities. But the most important and largest initiative is being undertaken by Central Scotland Woodlands Ltd in the area between Edinburgh and Glasgow. This was set up at the instigation of the Secretary of State for Scotland in1989 and will provide, through the planting of multi-purpose woodlands, for major environmental improvement to the land area between Glasgow and Edinburgh, much of which still shows the ravages of past oil shale and coal mining. This will provide a wide range of habitats for wildlife and an economic resource, while improving opportunities for recreation. It is the most ambitious project of its kind ever attempted in Scotland.

20.20 Scotland is fortunate in the skill and commitment of its voluntary environmental

The Government is exploring distinctive Scottish ways of further integrating environmental protection with agricultural policies

sector on which the success of these important initiatives will depend. Groups range in size from the small and local to those of national significance with membership into thousands. The Government would like to see the further development of this effort. It will continue to provide special funding for projects and for core administrative support and will look to Scottish Natural Heritage to work in partnership with local groups.

20.21 With increasing leisure time, prosperity and mobility, recreation in the countryside offers many opportunities for economic development. A major challenge for the future will be to ensure that development, including tourism, now a major industry, is able to provide increasing prosperity for Scotland's rural communities while preserving the benefits of a healthy and attractive environment. The Government is encouraging opportunities for environmentally sensitive tourism and will pursue on a wider basis the investigations currently being carried out in the Highlands.

20.22 Access to the Scottish countryside is a major issue. The long-standing tradition of freedom of access is coming under pressure as more and more people seek recreation in the uplands and in the urban fringe. Sensible management allows free access with a minimum of conflict in the local authority

Regional Parks in Scotland provide access and recreational opportunities while respecting land owners' rights and livelihoods

country parks and in the three regional parks, and the Government will consider sympathetically proposals for the expansion of this network. But in other areas visitors' wishes are often at odds with the needs of landowners and farmers, and their numbers

exceed the physical capacity of the land, and especially the paths, to carry them. The Government therefore supports the work of repairing Scotland's mountain footpaths and welcomes the establishment of Pathcraft Ltd to undertake this work on a commercial basis. It looks forward to the examination by the Countryside Commission for Scotland of access both in the wider countryside and in countryside around towns.

20.23 Scotland's most important landscapes are protected as National Scenic Areas. While this form of protection will remain for

In many parts of the Highlands the challenge is to conserve outstanding natural beauty and provide for viable economic activity

the present, the Government intends to review the position in the light of the Countryside Commission for Scotland's report 'The Mountain Areas of Scotland'. This recommends the establishment of National Parks in the Cairngorms, Loch Lomond, Ben Nevis/Glencoe/Blackmount, and Wester Ross. The Government will consider carefully views from the public and from all interested parties on these proposals and on the question of land designation generally with a view to developing a broadly based system of wildlife and landscape protection which could be administered by Scottish Natural Heritage. Agreements with landowners and farmers provide an important element in Environmentally Sensitive Areas, National Scenic Areas and SSSIs at present and have great potential for extending environmentally sensitive practices throughout Scotland. The Government intends to encourage the greater use of management agreements with associated financial support.

Urban environment

20.24 Urban decay stemming from the decline of Scotland's older traditional industries has led to some of the country's worst environmental problems. In their heyday some of these industries had a grossly polluting effect on the surrounding areas. The rapid growth of population in the cities, which was associated with their development, led to problems of overcrowding and squalor which left Scotland with a legacy of exceptionally poor housing conditions. Slum clearance in the 1950s and 1960s increased the proportion of public sector housing, which accounted for more than 54% of the total housing stock as recently as 1979. The drab uniformity of some of these estates, the absence of social facilities and problems of structural maintenance have themselves contributed to a depressing environment on the edge of many Scottish cities and larger towns.

20.25 Over the last 15 years a determined effort has been made by the Government, the Scottish Development Agency and local authorities to tackle these problems. The Glasgow Eastern Area Renewal project,

Glasgow has been outstandingly successful in regenerating its inner city areas

which was initiated by Government, started this process and successfully brought about the physical regeneration and transformation of a large area within Glasgow's inner city in the 1970s and 1980s. The subsequent development of schemes for the Merchant City and the Broomielaw has brought the process into the city centre itself. Glasgow is now regarded as an outstanding example of a large industrial city which is successfully transforming itself through urban renewal. Similar schemes, though more modest in scale, have been mounted in Leith, Dundee, Clydebank and a number of other Scottish industrial towns.

20.26 These efforts have been mainly directed at inner city and town centre problems. The Government decided to build on this success by tackling the problems of some of the worst peripheral housing estates. These range in population from 10,000 to about 35,000, and Glasgow alone has a population of approximately 100,000 in four such estates. The Government announced its policies for urban renewal in Scotland in the 1988 White Paper 'New Life for Urban Scotland'. Under the strategy put forward in that document, four major new Government-led Partnership initiatives have been set up in large peripheral housing estates: Castlemilk (Glasgow), Ferguslie Park (Paisley), Wester Hailes (Edinburgh) and Whitfield (Dundee).

20.27 'New Life' emphasised the importance of local residents taking responsibility for helping themselves and their communities, the potential contribution of the private sector and the need for partnership to achieve

comprehensive and self-sustaining regeneration. The Partnerships are putting these principles into action, each developing its own local strategy after a period of analysis and discussion. This involves tackling simultaneously problems of unemployment, training, housing, crime and health.

20.28 In May 1990 a further document 'Urban Scotland into the 1990s – New Life Two Years On' was published, reviewing progress made in the Partnership areas. That progress is striking. Over 2,100 unemployed adults (34% of the total) of working age in the areas were helped to find jobs in the period from January 1989 to May 1990, and about 800 entered training. Strengthening the economic base of the community will help to secure the success of direct measures to improve the environment. More than 3,000 houses have been or are being modernised in the areas, a substantial number of those with the worst structural problems have been demolished and over 400 have been built or are being rebuilt.

20.29 Many of Scotland's other peripheral housing estates are being tackled under the leadership of the local authorities, the Scottish Development Agency, Scottish Homes or the private sector. Similar work is being undertaken in Perth and Motherwell with further initiatives, recently announced by Scottish Homes, in Alloa and Kilmarnock. The Government also contributes to urban regeneration through the Urban Programme, which supports social development and improvements in the quality of life in the most disadvantaged areas. Urban programme projects have increased considerably in recent years with a budget allocation for 1990/91 of £69 million – an increase of almost 60% on the allocation two years earlier.

20.30 The Scottish Development Agency also undertakes environmental improvements away from the worst areas of urban dereliction. Between 1975 and 1991 the Agency will have spent well over £500 million on its environmental programmes and it will spend £72 million in 1990/91. Scottish Enterprise and Highlands and Islands Enterprise will inherit the Agency's environmental powers on their creation in 1991.

Built heritage

20.31 The Secretary of State for Scotland has powers to schedule monuments which he considers to be of national importance and to list buildings of special architectural or historic interest. There are at present over 4,500 scheduled monuments in Scotland. Some 330 monuments are in the direct care of Historic Buildings and Monuments, the Directorate responsible for the built heritage in the Scottish Office. In age these range from the internationally famous 3000 BC village at Skara Brae to the 19th century Biggar Gas Works; in type they range from Scotland's biggest tourist attraction, Edinburgh Castle with one million visitors a year, to the ruined medieval church on the almost inaccessible Orkney island of Eyn-hallow. Protecting these monuments from decay caused by weather and pollution, and in a few cases from the pressure of visitors, is a major task requiring expenditure of £9.2 million in 1990/91.

20.32 Scotland has over 36,000 listed buildings. A resurvey is underway to review the list completely by 1997. This is likely to give greater prominence to themes, such as industrial archaeology, which have not to date been fully represented on the list. Repairs to outstanding listed buildings, including churches and cathedrals, are eligible for consideration for historic buildings repair grant. Over five years the resources devoted to this grant have doubled to a total of £8.6 million in 1990/91.

20.33 The better people understand Scotland's built heritage, the more readily will they enjoy it and appreciate the need to maintain it. Some 2.5 million visits a year are made to monuments in the Secretary of State's care. The Government will continue to seek improvements in interpreting monuments in a way which is both historically and architecturally accurate and conducive to public understanding and enjoyment. It has introduced a free educational service to schools as a way of fostering this wider understanding.

Modern building

20.34 The standards of modern building are of great importance to the quality of the living environment. Like the rest of Britain, Scotland has its share of both good and bad modern buildings. In the former category the Burrell Gallery and the Princes Square shopping development in Glasgow are noteworthy examples. At the other extreme some of the soulless, system built, public sector housing of the 1960s shows standards at their worst. But modern housebuilding in Scotland, whether by housing associations, the private sector or the local authorities, shows welcome improvement in the quality of finish and setting. New guidance is being prepared on the location and design of rural housing to ensure it is in keeping with the high quality of Scotland's landscape.

The 3000BC village of Skara Brae, Orkney, is one of over 300 monuments in the Government's direct care

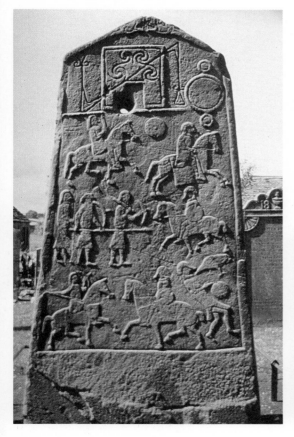

Left: The Government is encouraging a wider appreciation of Scotland's heritage

Right: The Burrell Gallery Glasgow is an internationally acclaimed example of modern architecture

POLLUTION CONTROL

Air quality

20.35 Local authorities' extensive smoke control programmes have proved very effective in reducing levels of smoke and sulphur dioxide in Scotland's atmosphere.

Nowhere is this more apparent than in Glasgow and the Clyde Valley, where there has been a transformation since the early 1960s. The success of smoke control can be gauged by the fact that when the EC Smoke and Sulphur Directive came into effect in

1983 only four districts in Scotland required temporary derogation from its requirements, and of these only two remain. These are taking steps to ensure early compliance with the Directive. The Government has played its part in providing local authorities with both grant-aid and testing and monitoring equipment.

20.36 Industry has seen significant changes over the last 10 years and the impact of land-based oil and gas terminals has been carefully controlled by HM Industrial Pollution Inspectorate. The construction of new plants has gone hand in hand with reductions in emissions to the atmosphere, and improvements have been made at existing works as new control technology has been commissioned. In the petrochemical industry the use of ground level flare systems has proved to be environmentally acceptable. For the future permitted emission levels will continue to decrease.

20.37 Acidification caused by sulphur and nitrogen oxide emissions from power stations, motor vehicles and industrial plant is a problem which is of particular concern to Scotland because of the high natural acidity of much of the soil in upland areas. Scotland's own electricity industry causes relatively little damage to the environment. Some 60% of the electricity supplied to Scottish consumers can be provided from non-fossil fuels, including nuclear and hydro-electric, which give rise to neither sulphur nor nitrogen oxide pollution. From 1992, when the supply of gas from the Miller Field to Peterhead is due to commence, a further amount of electricity will be available from gas-fired generation, where these emissions are very low. This will be as much as 20% in the early peak years of gas supply. Finally, the coal available from Scottish sources to generate the remainder of electricity needs has a low sulphur content and releases much lower amounts of sulphur dioxide into the atmosphere than most other coal burnt in power stations.

20.38 Despite this, many upland areas in Scotland, especially in the south west, do suffer from acidification, much of which is air borne from industrial plants and power stations elsewhere. A few inland lochs in Galloway can no longer sustain fish life. Because the effects of acidification are so marked in Scotland, Scottish universities and research organisations have focused considerable effort and resources on understanding the chemical processes involved and exploring how best to combat their effects.

Water

20.39 Scotland is particularly proud of the quality of its waters. Ninety-nine per cent of its rivers are of good or fairly good quality and support abundant fish life. In part this reflects the predominance of short, fast-flowing rivers and the lower pressure of population and industry on the environment north of the border.

20.40 Great credit is also due, however, to the work of the Scottish River Purification Boards and of the Regional and Islands Councils. The efforts of these bodies, together with those of industry, have improved the quality of discharges and transformed the conditions of some previously polluted rivers. A notable example is the lower River Clyde where salmon have become re-established after an absence of more than 130 years.

20.41 Over 97% of the population is served by public sewerage systems. Given the concentration of population around the coast, sea disposal of sewage has been widely used and marine treatment from long sea outfalls accepted as the Best Practicable Environmental Option. However, the Government's recent decision that all substantial discharges of sewage should be treated at sewage treatment works will further improve the quality of both coastal and inland waters. This initiative will also contribute to an overall improvement in the general quality of bathing waters around the Scottish coast. Although good progress has already been made (70% of waters monitored in 1989 complied with the requirements of the EC Bathing Waters Directive compared with 52% in 1988), more work still needs to be done. New treatment facilities being planned will produce significant improvements. Although monitoring has revealed no significant environmental effects, the parallel decision that dumping of sewage sludge at sea – involving some 60% of sludge – should cease by the end of 1998 will provide another safeguard for coastal water quality. The two local authorities involved, Lothian and Strathclyde, are now planning alternative means of disposal.

20.42 These new policies on sewage treatment will have significant implications for Scotland where the cost of compliance is likely to exceed £400 million in addition to other planned improvements. Accordingly, the Government intends to make available a grant of £130 million over three years to Regional and Islands Councils for work on sewerage systems, sewage treatment and disposal.

20.43 Most public water supplies are drawn directly from upland lochs and rivers (only some 3-4% comes from underground sources) and are of excellent quality. However, owing to the very soft water in much of Scotland and the prevalence of lead piping, mainly in buildings, the lead content of water at consumers' taps has been a serious problem in the past. Great progress has been made in tackling this problem by treatment to reduce plumbosolvency and removal of lead piping; and it is expected that the few remaining public supplies where some consumers may experience lead levels above the EC standard will conform by the end of 1992. Measures to ensure compliance with other EC standards are being implemented as fast as practicable.

20.44 The continuing improvements to water quality and sewage treatment will require high investment over the next decade or so. Capital expenditure provision for the Scottish water and sewerage programme has increased substantially in recent years, rising from £95 million in 1985/86 to £142 million in 1990/91. It is set to rise further to £170 million in 1991/92 and £190 million in 1992/93.

Integrated Pollution Control

20.45 A number of legislative changes have been and are being introduced to strengthen the control of pollution. The most recent are in the Environmental Protection Bill, which establishes a new pollution control regime – Integrated Pollution Control. In Scotland this will be operated by Her Majesty's Industrial Pollution Inspectorate and the River Purification Authorities. The new legislation will require HMIPI and the RPAs to work closely together before an authorisation is issued for a prescribed process. As in England and Wales local authorities will have improved powers to control air emissions from less polluting processes.

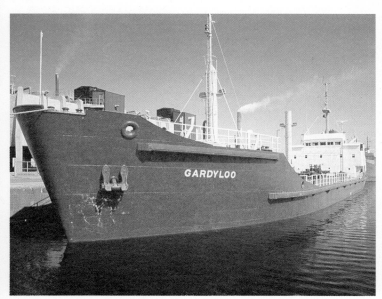

Dumping sewage sludge at sea will stop by the end of 1998

RESEARCH

20.46 Many of the issues outlined in this Chapter require high quality research if they are to be properly understood. Without it policies cannot be soundly based. The eight Scottish universities have developed considerable strengths in the life sciences, in agriculture, forestry and other subjects of relevance to environmental policy. For the most part, however, the research undertaken in the universities is funded by the Research Councils, which have a role covering the whole of mainland Britain and are referred to in Chapter 17.

20.47 Important research of relevance to environmental policy is carried out in Scotland by the Department of Agriculture and Fisheries Marine Laboratory in Aberdeen and Freshwater Fisheries Laboratory in Pitlochry. There has been recent concern about breeding failure in certain seabird populations around Shetland, and the Government has initiated research projects to look at the interaction between seabirds and sand-eel stocks. A new three year study of the ecology of seals and their interaction with prey species and fisheries in the Moray Firth has been commissioned. This will be a major contribution to the international programme of studies of marine life agreed at the Third North Sea Conference in March 1990.

20.48 The Macaulay Land Use Research Institute in Aberdeen has been commissioned to compile a map of Scotland, identifying places where the natural soil conditions are less able to neutralise acid deposition. This contract followed a major Government-sponsored symposium in Edinburgh in 1988. The Scottish Agricultural College, the Institute of Terrestrial Ecology and the Natural Environmental Research Council Dunstaffnage Marine Laboratory also undertake valuable research.

20.49 For the future the Government intends that Scottish Natural Heritage must be properly supported by research to ensure that its policies for nature conservation and the countryside are properly informed and directed. While SNH will have its own high quality scientific resource, it is expected to commission work from those universities and institutes both in Scotland and outside which are able to undertake high quality work in the appropriate subjects.

20.50 The Government is concerned that there should be specialist advice on environmental health matters including possible risks to health from the environment. In 1989 the Environmental Health (Scotland) Unit was established as a centre of expertise and reference point on epidemiological and medical aspects of environmental hazards.

The research community in Scotland has devoted significant resources to understanding acid rain and improving nature conservation

Environmental studies in Scottish primary schools have benefited from a Government development project which began in 1984

EDUCATION AND AWARENESS

20.51 It is essential, if environmental policies are to achieve their objective, that there is wide public awareness of the issues at stake and their importance to the future of the planet and to subsequent generations. Education has an essential part to play, and the Government has given environmental issues priority at all levels of the Scottish educational system.

20.52 The national Primary Education Development Project was set up in 1984 to improve the quality of environmental studies. The Government is reviewing the whole curriculum to ensure a coherent and progressive experience for all pupils in the age range 5-14. Environmental education continues to be an important theme in secondary schools, and the Scottish

Consultative Council on the Curriculum make it plain in their guidelines to secondary headteachers that care of the environment is one of the key skills and elements which are essential to every pupil's development. Awareness of the environment also figures prominently in teacher training. A new course leading to the award of the Primary Environmental Studies Certificate has been developed, and in-service training pays significant attention to environmental matters.

20.53 Environmental education is not confined to the classroom. Education authorities and schools in Scotland maintain good links with the statutory and voluntary bodies engaged in environmental work. Illustrated talks, visits and field trips are a normal part of school activity and help to develop in young people the right values at the formative stage of their lives. Links are maintained with developments in other countries, for example through Scotland's current participation in an Organisation for Economic Co-operation and Development (OECD) project to identify and share good practice in teaching about the environment. The Government is keen to see environmental education develop in a more coordinated way, and as a first step a working party has been set up to advise the Secretary of State.

The Clean Forth Campaign shows what can be achieved by community effort

CONCLUSION

20.54 The Government is well aware of Scotland's distinctive environment. The beauty of its countryside and the richness of its wildlife are unquestioned and must be kept secure for future generations. The Scottish environment also has a darker side – a formidable legacy of urban decay and dereliction. However, substantial progress has already been made to regenerate and transform the older conurbations and improve the quality of life.

20.55 In the 1990s the Government will seek to achieve healthy and sustainable economic development which is compatible with the high quality of Scotland's natural environment.

The challenge is to strike the right balance.

20.56 The Government will lead through policies and decisions which give weight to the importance of environmental issues. It will set up a major new and authoritative environmental body – Scottish Natural Heritage – to bring together the work of nature conservation and the presentation and enjoyment of the countryside. It will secure a better physical environment by tangible improvements in water quality, sewage treatment and pollution control; by a further vigorous regeneration of urban areas; and by major improvements such as the Central Scotland Woodlands Initiative.

Research – Scotland

Some examples of additional public sector research relevant to Scotland are projects
• to develop monitoring methodologies to assess the impact in Scotland of Environmentally Sensitive Areas and of farming diversification, extensification and set-aside – Department of Agriculture and Fisheries for Scotland (£1.4m in 1989/90)
• to study the role of farm livestock in the management of hill and upland vegetation – Department of Agriculture and Fisheries for Scotland (£1.0m in 1989/90)
• to determine the effects of agricultural practices on water quality and help to understand the processes involved in soil and water acidification – Department of Agriculture and Fisheries for Scotland (£0.35m in 1989/90)
• to investigate the management, treatment and disposal of farm waste and the effect of pollutants on agricultural land in Scotland – Department of Agriculture and Fisheries for Scotland (£0.6m in 1989/90)
• to protect and manage the Scottish countryside through landscape conservation and public access – Countryside Commission for Scotland (£0.3m in 1989/90)

• to support work on water quality including chemical and biological research to improve pollution control of rivers and surface waters in Scotland – River Purification Boards (£0.25m in 1989/90)
• to study and monitor pollutants and their impact on marine life to help to develop and apply pollution control policies – Department of Agriculture and Fisheries for Scotland (£1.8m in 1989/90)
• to study the impact of oil and gas exploration and exploitation on fisheries and other marine life – Department of Agriculture and Fisheries for Scotland (£0.7m in 1989/90)
• to conduct a land cover inventory of Scotland by interpreting an aerial photographic survey in order to evaluate and model change in the countryside – Scottish Development Department (£0.3m in 1989/90)

In addition much work in Scotland is funded and undertaken by bodies such as the Department of the Environment, the Natural Environment Research Council, the Nature Conservancy Council and the Commission of the European Communities.

THE ENVIRONMENT IN NORTHERN IRELAND

Northern Ireland is rich in natural beauty

INTRODUCTION

21.1 Northern Ireland is one of the most unspoilt areas in Britain and indeed in Europe. It is rich in mountains, moorlands, lakes and wetlands, plant and animal life. It has suffered much less than most of Europe from intensive industrial development and agriculture or from over-population. The Government's aim is to ensure that the benefits of this are not lost. This Chapter describes the broad objectives which flow from that aim – the preservation and enhancement of the countryside, the control of pollution, the protection and enhancement of the man-made environment, the efficient use of energy and the promotion of an increased awareness of the needs of the environment.

PRESERVING AND ENHANCING THE COUNTRYSIDE

Agriculture

21.2 Some 80% of the land area of Northern Ireland is in agricultural use. A further 4% is forest, owned by the Department of Agriculture for Northern Ireland (DANI), and 1% is privately owned forest. The proportion of Northern Ireland's GDP provided by agriculture is three times that for Britain as a whole.

21.3 The Secretary of State for Northern Ireland gave a commitment to Parliament in 1986 to balance the promotion and maintenance of a stable and efficient agricultural industry with the economic and social interests of rural areas, the conservation and enhancement of the countryside and enjoyment of it by the public. Practical examples of what this means are described in a new publication from DANI, 'Countryside Management – the DANI Strategy'.

21.4 In keeping with this integrated approach the Government has designated two internationally famous areas (the Mourne Mountains and the Glens of Antrim) as Environmentally Sensitive Areas. The Government has also introduced expert advice to farmers on conservation and incorporated conservation and environmental elements into the courses provided at agricultural colleges.

21.5 The Government has various research programmes directed towards the environmental aspects of agriculture in Northern Ireland. A major proportion of the assistance given under national capital grant schemes and the Northern Ireland Agricultural Development Programme is for the prevention of pollution from farms.

21.6 In applying the national measures set out in Chapter 7, the Government will take account of Northern Ireland's special conditions and needs and seek both to conserve and to enhance the rural environment in line with the main objectives laid down in its countryside management strategy:

• to pursue vigorously a reduction in pollution from farms through advice, research and grant aid to farmers;
• to take action against people who cause fish to be killed by deliberate or careless pollution of rivers;
• to promote and encourage environmentally sensitive farming; and
• to adopt good conservation practices in the management of its own estate particularly in relation to direct activities in drainage, forestry and fisheries.

Conservation of the countryside and wildlife

21.7 Maintaining a healthy and prosperous rural economy in Northern Ireland must be combined with special protection for the most valuable areas. This will be done wherever possible in partnership with the owners of the land (principally farmers). These areas will be protected by voluntary effort or, where they are especially vulnerable to damage, by law.

21.8 The Government is responsible in partnership with landowners for the conservation of wildlife and plants through the protection of habitats. It has declared 26 Areas of Special Scientific Interest (ASSIs), the Northern Ireland equivalent of SSSIs. Protection for ASSIs against damaging land use or management changes is achieved mainly by voluntary cooperation between landowners. The survey and declaration of

The Government encourages environmentally sensitive farming in Northern Ireland

ASSIs will be completed. Over 40 National Nature Reserves have been declared. These are selected as examples of important habitats and because of their potential for education or research. Most have open access but some are restricted because of the need to protect fragile features.

21.9 These arrangements are especially valuable in areas which are internationally important such as Lough Neagh and Strangford Lough. Lough Neagh with nearby Lough Beg has been designated as a Wetland of International Importance under

The Government ensures protection of the internationally important habitats for wildfowl and plant life at Strangford Lough and Lough Neagh

the Ramsar Convention. It is an outstanding habitat for wintering wildfowl, breeding birds and plant and animal life. Strangford Lough is famous for wintering wildfowl and for marine life. It enjoys ASSI and in part National Nature Reserve protection and will be designated as a Marine Nature Reserve.

21.10 The Government gives protection to Areas of Outstanding Natural Beauty, and a review is taking place. The emphasis is now on combining conservation with public enjoyment of the countryside. A notable example is the Causeway Coast (which includes the Giant's Causeway): this is a National Nature Reserve and part of an Area of Outstanding Natural Beauty, besides being a World Heritage site.

21.11 The integration of public and private effort extends beyond the designation of an area. The critical element in its protection is its subsequent management. Wide consultation with all interests - the key to sound management - will remain a fundamental principle of the Government's approach.

THE CONTROL OF POLLUTION

The Government monitors and controls industrial air pollution. It supports the creation of smoke control areas in towns

21.12 The high quality of the countryside in Northern Ireland and the needs of its people demand vigorous action to prevent pollution of water, air and the land itself. This is not just a matter of strict regulation: it requires the cooperation of industry (including agriculture), voluntary bodies and the Government. It must be based on an awareness of the threat which pollution poses. This alliance of interests is already achieving notable results.

Air

21.13 The absence of intensive industrialisation has prevented widespread man-made damage to the air in Northern Ireland. Moreover, naturally occurring radioactivity occurs at levels either similar to the national average (as in the case of radon) or below the average.

21.14 There are residual threats caused by such factors as emissions from inefficient industrial plant and the heavy dependence of Northern Ireland upon solid fuel, especially for domestic heating. Here the key elements are effective monitoring, increased public awareness and cooperation between Government and the private sector.

21.15 The control of industrial emissions lies with the Northern Ireland Alkali and Radiochemical Inspectorate. Its intensive programme of monitoring is ensuring that the use of Best Practicable Means prevents the emission of pollutants and renders any emissions harmless.

21.16 A comprehensive smoke control programme is under way in areas where problems of smoke and sulphur dioxide occur. In Belfast especially the programme has had significant results. The levels of sulphur dioxide in the city have declined markedly since 1957. The Government will continue to support the creation of smoke control areas so that levels of smoke and sulphur dioxide fall still further.

21.17 Vehicle fuels continue to pose a problem though traffic is much less intense than in Britain as a whole. Vigorous promotion of lead-free petrol has led to an increase from 60 to over 700 in the number of stations supplying it since January 1989. The response of the public has exceeded expectations. The Government will promote a further increase in the use of unleaded petrol in Northern Ireland.

Water

21.18 The quality of the waters in Northern Ireland is high. The Government aims to protect them by setting proper standards, measuring water quality and regulating pollution. The key to this, as with air quality, is effective scientific monitoring to

identify problems, measure progress in tackling them and anticipate threats to stretches of water whose quality is already high. Monitoring of river waters in 1989 indicated that over 95% were of good or fair quality. The Government aims to bring the remaining 5% up to this standard.

21.19 The improvement of the River Lagan (whose catchment area contains well over one-third of the population of Northern Ireland) follows substantial capital expenditure on refurbishing sewage treatment. The upper reaches are already of good quality. The Lagan will be a key element in the regeneration of the river front and dock area of Belfast over the next decade.

21.20 The quality of lough and estuarine water is also improving. Lough Neagh is a prime example. The largest lake in the country, it produces 40% of the daily water needs of Northern Ireland. Significant progress has been made in the reduction of phosphorus in the Lough, which had led to a serious algae problem.

21.21 The quality of Northern Ireland water is particularly good in its bathing areas. In 1989 all of its 16 beaches designated under the EC Bathing Water Directive complied with the mandatory standards. The one at Magilligan has won a Blue Flag Award from the Foundation for Environmental Education in Europe.

21.22 The Government will maintain and build on these successes. Monitoring of water quality is being extended to rivers not yet covered, to all the main estuaries and to Strangford Lough. Capital expenditure will lead to improved sewage treatment. The sea disposal of sewage sludge will be ended. Pollution from private sources (the cause of over 80% of known pollution incidents) will continue to be tackled by monitoring discharges, advice to industry and to farmers, the control of harmful commercial or recreation practices and the prosecution of persistent offenders. The response of industry and especially the farming community has been both encouraging and highly effective in preventing irreparable damage to Northern Ireland's water.

Above left: Over £30 million has been spent on improving water quality in the River Lagan

Above: All designated bathing beaches in Northern Ireland meet the EC water quality standards

MAN-MADE ENVIRONMENT

The urban environment

21.23 The conservation of the best of the man-made heritage can add to the quality of urban life. Post-industrial decay in the larger cities and the decline of local market economies in smaller towns and villages have

created run-down areas which are unattractive to live, work, shop or invest in. The Government regards as vital the encouragement of local (especially community-based) investment in improvements both to the economy and appearance of urban areas.

21.24 Increased investment in Belfast and Londonderry city centres is one of the most encouraging features of life in the Province. The most deprived inner city areas will receive specific assistance. Investment in the smaller towns and villages will help the recovery of the rural economy. The response to the Action Team initiative in Belfast indicates the success of this policy.

The Government protects Northern Ireland's rich heritage of historic buildings and monuments, like the 5,000 year-old tomb (above right)

Heritage

21.25 The cultural heritage of Northern Ireland is no less valuable than the natural environment. The protection of its historic buildings and monuments for present and future generations to enjoy is an important priority. The emphasis must be on encouraging active public involvement.

21.26 Substantial progress is being made in listing buildings of architectural or historic interest, the designation of Conservation Areas and the payment of grant aid. Between 1980 and 1990, the Government listed 2,626 buildings, bringing the total to 7,646, and it grant-aided 3,260 schemes. During the same period it declared 15 Conservation Areas. The Government will complete by 1994 the survey and listing of all pre-1960 buildings of architectural or historic interest.

21.27 The Government maintains an integrated archaeological service combining protection, survey, record, excavation, conservation and presentation. Between 1980 and 1990 the number of sites in state care has grown from 140 to 168 and scheduled monuments from 437 to almost 1,000. Two examples illustrate the progress made. First, to protect Navan Fort, the ancient capital of the Kings of Ulster in County Armagh, limestone quarrying nearby has stopped. An independent group is now raising funds to implement ambitious plans for protecting and presenting the Navan landscape. Second, the Government is committing resources for a major scheme to improve the presentation of the Anglo-Norman Carrickfergus Castle. Such schemes will generate employment, contribute to tourism and provide valuable educational and recreational resources. The Government will complete by 1995 the survey of all historic monuments and provide by 1992 a publicly accessible Monuments and Buildings Record.

USE OF ENERGY

21.28 Energy efficiency can contribute both to the reduction of global threats and to a healthier economy. It is being vigorously promoted in the Province.

21.29 Northern Ireland has currently no access to natural gas, nuclear power or hydro-electricity. It is highly dependent on oil to meet primary energy needs - oil accounts for two-thirds of needs and coal the remainder. Some 70% of electricity generation is oil-fired compared to 20% in England and Wales. Northern Ireland's energy bill is estimated at £1 billion annually. The transport and domestic sectors are the largest consumers at £480 million and £333 million respectively.

21.30 The Department of Economic Development promotes energy efficiency across all sectors through seminars, practical advice and schemes of financial assistance. In the industrial and commercial sectors, Northern Ireland is participating in the National Best Practice Programme. Large energy users are also encouraged to engage consultants to obtain expert advice on the scope for savings within their organisations through the Energy Efficiency Survey Scheme which offers grants for this purpose. The Government will take enabling powers which will, if appropriate, allow the replication of the Home Energy Efficiency Scheme.

21.31 In the public sector, energy savings of 10% have been achieved most notably in the

The Government provides practical advice on how to save energy for example by cavity wall insulation

Health and Prison Estates which account for almost half of the public sector's total energy bill of £44 million. As with the rest of the British public sector, a further target saving of a 15% reduction in energy usage by 1995 has been set.

21.32 Many of the national and EC initiatives for reducing carbon dioxide emissions through the promotion of good energy practice across all sectors of the economy apply directly to Northern Ireland. The Government is preparing an energy conservation and efficiency strategy and action plan for the Province.

ENVIRONMENTAL EDUCATION

21.33 An underlying theme of this Chapter is the significance of the partnership of private, voluntary and public sectors in the protection of Northern Ireland's environment. Increased public awareness is vital to that partnership, and the importance of environmental education in achieving this cannot be overstated.

21.34 The current programme of reform of curriculum and assessment in Northern

Ireland has goals similar to those of the reforms being implemented in England and Wales. Under the statutory common curriculum, two of the areas of study in particular - 'Environment and Society' and 'Science and Technology' - will ensure that all children experience environmental education throughout their period of compulsory education. Two themes - health education and cultural heritage -will focus on a range of environmental matters.

21.35 Substantial financial support is given to work related to a third compulsory theme - education for mutual understanding. Environmental issues have in practice formed a focus for much of this work, through shared involvement of pupils from both sides of the community. Joint groups have undertaken beach studies, river studies, land use studies, the study of woodland trails and investigations of local history.

21.36 The Government is determined to take the opportunity afforded by the implementation of the new common curriculum in Northern Ireland to build on and extend existing good practice so that the development of environmental awareness is an integral part of everyone's education.

Environmental projects are an increasingly important feature of school activity in Northern Ireland

CONCLUSION

21.37 The Government is safeguarding the environment in Northern Ireland by integrating conservation and economic policies for the countryside, protecting the most valuable habitats for wildlife and plants, improving air and water quality, protecting and enhancing the man-made environment, encouraging the more efficient use of energy and promoting environmental education. An essential part of this strategy is to encourage an increased public awareness that the protection of its rich heritage is the responsibility of everyone in Northern Ireland.

Research – Northern Ireland

Some examples of additional public sector research relevant to Northern Ireland are projects
• on ecosystems and conservation to support policies on air and water pollution control- Department of the Environment for Northern Ireland (0.9m in 1989/90)
• to survey landscape features, wildlife habitats and the use of the countryside by the public in support of policy on countryside and nature conservation - Department of the Environment for Northern Ireland (£0.2m in 1989/90)
• to investigate the interface between agricultural practices and water quality Department of Agriculture for Northern Ireland (£0.63m in 1989/90)
• to investigate alternatives to peat as a horticultural potting compost - Department of Environment for Northern Ireland (£0.9m in 1989/90)
• to provide a sound scientific basis for the management of Environmentally Sensitive Areas, hedgerows and associated flora and fauna - Department of Agriculture for Northern Ireland (£0.11m in 1989/90)
• to assess hill land management regimes and alternative farm enterprises and their impact on the environment - Department of Agriculture for Northern Ireland (£0.2m in 1989/90)
• to study farmers' knowledge, attitudes and practices with respect to conservation - Department of Agriculture for Northern Ireland (£0.6m in 1989/90)
• to study ways to protect, conserve and develop recreational and commercial fisheries in fresh and marine waters - Department of Agriculture for Northern Ireland (£0.31m in 1989/90)
• to understand freshwater and marine ecosystems supporting commercially exploitable fish populations - Department of Agriculture for Northern Ireland (£0.17m in 1989/90)

22

ACTION FOR ALL

TAKING STOCK

The action which the Government is taking is summarised at the close of Chapter 1. But responsibility for a good environment does not rest with government alone. This final Chapter offers a short checklist of the areas where individuals, businesseses and local authorities can help.

ACTION FOR INDIVIDUALS

As **householders** we can reduce energy consumption (Chapter 5) in a number of ways, for example, by:
• doing more to insulate and draughtproof homes;
• choosing the most energy efficient model when replacing heating boilers and electrical appliances such as fridges, freezers, washing machines and dishwashers;
• switching off unused lights and appliances, using low energy light bulbs and fitting timeswitches and thermostats on immersion heaters; and
• setting temperature controls at reasonable levels.
All these actions not only save us money, but also reduce the emission of greenhouse gases which cause global warming. The Energy Efficiency Office can provide more details. Householders can also take care to ensure that their homes and fires are properly ventilated to avoid pollution indoors. Using smokeless fuels reduces pollution outdoors.

As **travellers** our decisions influence greenhouse gas emissions (Chapter 5), as well as air pollution (Chapter 11) and the quality of urban life (Chapter 8). Ways to help include:
• adopting less aggressive driving habits to save fuel;
• keeping cars well-tuned;
• choosing cars fitted with a catalyst;
• buying more fuel-efficient cars;
• sharing car journeys to work with colleagues;
• using train or bus when we can;
• walking, or cycling where it is safe; and
• using unleaded petrol.
All this could save us money, as well as improving our environment and health.

As **shoppers** we can influence retailers and manufacturers, and take account of how the goods we choose will affect the environment as we use or dispose of them (Chapter 1). We can help the environment by:
• reading labels carefully when choosing products (Chapter 17);
• not buying environmentally damaging products, such as those which contain CFCs, or use CFCs in their manufacture (Chapter 5);
• buying recycled products where available;
• not buying overpackaged goods, or goods in packaging that cannot be recycled (Chapter 14);
• making our views known to retailers and manufacturers, especially those who do not provide sufficient environmental information to help us choose (Chapter 17); and
• not purchasing goods made of scarce materials – such as hardwoods unless they come from a managed source.

As **consumers** we can reduce the need for waste tips or for new domestic waste incinerators, by reducing our waste (Chapter 14). We can help by:
• recycling where possible all our paper, rags, cans and glass, pressing our local authority or supermarket chain to provide better recycling facilities, where necessary;
• making the most of the products we use – for example by reusing plastic carriers;
• composting waste vegetable matter for use in gardens;
• disposing of fridges containing CFCs in accordance with local authority guidance; and
• disposing of batteries, waste motor oil or household chemicals properly.
Children can make a special input to recycling of wastes such as aluminium drinks cans.

As **gardeners** we can:
• encourage urban wildlife with trees and ponds;
•use garden chemicals only when absolutely necessary;
• choose alternatives to peat, such as bark chips for mulching and compost for planting; and
• dispose of unwanted chemicals responsibly (Chapter 13).
Planting trees can also help reduce global warming as they absorb carbon dioxide from the atmosphere (Chapter 5).

As **good neighbours** we can help by:
• keeping noise to levels that do not disturb (Chapter 16);
• putting litter in bins or taking it home (Chapter 14) and keeping our dogs from fouling public places;
• improving the appearance of our home and garden (Chapter 8);
• protecting any historic features of our homes and streets (Chapter 9); and
• avoiding bonfires or smoking where it affects others.

As **investors** we can:
• seek information about the environmental practices of the companies we invest in, and make our views known (Chapter 17).

As **responsible citizens** we can:
• take steps to inform ourselves of the facts relating to our environment through adult education and the Open University (Chapter 17);
• join voluntary bodies active in the environment (Chapter 18);
• involve ourselves in local planning;
• alert the relevant bodies to possible breaches of planning or pollution controls;
• encourage local authorities to provide facilities for recycling; and
• make our views on the environment clear, not only by what we do, but also by telling local councillors, Members of Parliament, and Members of the European Parliament what we think.

As **parents** we can teach our children all these things, and be ready to learn from them as they gain new environmental knowledge at school (Chapter 17).

As **young people** we can join the groups run by and for young people, carrying out projects to improve the environment, including the Royal Society for Nature Conservation's youth branch 'Watch', and the 'Young National Trust'. Local schools or youth groups can also get involved in environmental projects, such as recycling schemes and local environmental studies, and the National Curriculum will encourage more action of this kind.

The Department of the Environment will publish a more detailed guide on the action individuals can take later this year.

ACTION FOR BUSINESSES

Many businesses have realised that environmental issues have increasing influence on the competitive success of firms in the market, and are responding accordingly. So, apart from helping to achieve a better environment, good environmental management increasingly makes good business sense in its own right.

Business organisations such as the International Chamber of Commerce and the Confederation of British Industry have published guidelines on the integration of environmental considerations into business strategy, both generally and in specific areas such as waste minimisation. The Government welcomes this guidance.

Many companies have developed a corporate environmental strategy to help ensure they achieve and sustain improved environmental management and maintain their competitive edge. Steps they can take include:
• reviewing all aspects of the business that may affect the environment, including products (design, development and production and the impact of their use and disposal), production processes (emissions,

waste management and opportunities for recycling), energy use, building construction and management, transport and distribution, services and public relations (including the possibility of corporate sponsorship of environmental groups);
• identifying ways to improve the firm's environmental performance, including improvements in products, processes and support services (the options include minimising the use of raw materials and guarding against accidents which may give rise to costs and pollution; for smaller firms expert advice may be available under the Department of Trade and Industry's Consultancy Initiatives);
• assessing the costs of all the possible actions identified and the benefits to be gained;

• setting out in a policy statement the business's broad environmental objectives (such statements should say how the objectives are to be achieved, and how they affect organisational structure and responsibilities in the firm);
• involving staff at all levels in the environmental planning;
• reviewing progress to ensure that the environmental policies and objectives chosen are delivered effectively;
• consider publishing the firm's environmental performance in the annual report or elsewhere; and
• keeping up to date with environmental issues relevant to the business, updating and improving the action plan regularly.

ACTION FOR LOCAL AUTHORITIES

Local authorities have always been in the front line in the protection and improvement of the environment, and in dealing with problems of pollution. Almost all local authority services affect the environment and environmental concerns need to be built into the way in which they are organised and administered.

Many local authorities have already reviewed their policies and programmes to ensure that all environmental concerns are properly taken into account in all aspects of their work. The local authority associations are developing advice for their members, based on actual examples, on ways in which authorities can develop their environmental role.

Issues which authorities should consider are:
• corporate management of environment issues within local authorities (how best to ensure that environmental concerns are properly taken into account by members and officers);
• reviewing and monitoring the state of the local environment (facts are the essential basis for action at local as at national level);
• reviewing policies and practices that affect the environment (authorities should examine how all their activities can influence the local environment);
• the preparation of environmental strategies or programmes, covering such areas as energy conservation, recycling, monitoring and minimising pollution, environmental education, transport and planning policies, waste management, environmental protection and enhancement, environmental health, consumer protection, purchasing and own use of resources; and
• involvement of the local community (local authorities are particularly well placed to work in partnership with voluntary groups, the public and the private sector on environmental issues).

ANNEX A

ECONOMIC INSTRUMENTS FOR ENVIRONMENTAL PROTECTION

INTRODUCTION

A.1 People, whether as consumers or producers, respond to differences in prices. If price signals reflect the full costs of each activity, the market place ensures that economic needs and aspirations are met in the most efficient way. This is the experience of this Government - indeed it is the experience throughout the world, as current developments in Eastern Europe illustrate. But markets often fail to take into account all the environmental costs and benefits. We need better analysis of these costs and benefits. We also need new ways of getting them reflected in prices. The need to adjust market forces so that price signals better reflect environmental gains and losses was one of the main themes of the report which the Department of the Environment commissioned last year from Professor David Pearce of University College, London *(Blueprint for a Green Economy).*

A.2 The aim of a market-based approach to the environment is, therefore, to give consumers and industries clear signals about the costs of using environmental resources. A market-based approach would not, as some people have put it, 'sell pollution rights': nor does the use of markets imply that the Government would relax its environmental objectives. The approach is simply one way for achieving the goals specified by government. It is, however, an effective way, since it allows producers and consumers rather than regulators to decide how best to alter their demands in order to meet environmental needs. This has a number of

beneficial consequences: freedom of choice is not constrained; those who find it cheapest to reduce emissions will make the biggest reductions; there will be an incentive to develop more efficient technology; there is a continuing incentive not to misuse the environment.

A.3 Governments throughout the world have been considering possibilities for introducing 'market-based' instruments of environmental control to achieve the correct price signals. In some cases markets can be improved by removing existing distortions; in others there are possibilities for using economic instruments to create new markets or directly to set new prices. The terms 'economic instrument' and 'market-based instrument' tend to be used interchangeably both in the international debate and in this Annex. A wide variety of measures is covered, and it is difficult to find a precise definition (the OECD distinguishes five types of economic instrument: charges; subsidies; deposit/refund schemes; market creation; and enforcement incentives). For purposes of policy, the key attribute of full market-based measures is that they provide incentives by establishing prices for environmental services. Modest use has already been made of economic instruments to protect the environment, both here and elsewhere. In most cases these are charges which finance environmental expenditures. It is as yet rare to find a full market-based approach, in which prices reflect all environmental costs and benefits.

A.4 The alternative to economic instruments is some form of direct regulation by means of administrative controls. Direct regulation enforces standards or ensures that firms use the right equipment to control pollution. Any form of regulation imposes costs either on industry, most of which are passed on to consumers in the form of higher prices, or directly on consumers. While the effect on prices in the former case may not be immediately apparent, it is real. Indeed, the total economic burden of achieving a given environmental target by direct regulation is generally likely to be higher than if a successful market-based instrument can be devised. In the USA, savings from using market-based instruments (notably tradeable permits) rather than traditional regulatory approaches seem, according to some estimates, to have been substantial. But regulation can in some circumstances be very efficient. The most effective approach must be sought for each situation.

A.5 This Annex looks at the ways in which governments can deliver environmental policies. The main point of reference is pollution control, though the use of economic instruments as a means of conserving valuable environmental resources is also considered. Administrative approaches and market-based instruments are examined as means of control. In each section details are given either of instruments which are currently in use in Britain or of the Government's approach – these details are contained in the italicised paragraphs.

THE RANGE OF INSTRUMENTS

Administrative controls

A.6 Where the release of certain pollutants is extremely damaging, governments will always rely on administrative controls, backed up as necessary by criminal sanctions. But administrative controls have been applied more widely. Regulation by way of prescriptive standards tends to be rigid and inflexible. At its best, regulation is more flexible than this: regulators can respond quickly to new events and technologies, and rules can be made to fit the circumstances of particular plants and localities.

A.7 Even if economic instruments become more widely used, there will remain an important role for administrative regulation as the basis for delivering environmental policy goals and defining property rights, and for monitoring and enforcement activity. Regulation also has a role in improving the workings of markets by requiring that better information be made available to consumers, notably by schemes of environmental labelling. Another means by which independent checks on polluters' behaviour can be obtained is, as is planned, to make more information available in public records about firms' performance (see paragraph 17.26).

Administrative controls will for the foreseeable future remain at the heart of Britain's system of environmental control - just as they are in many other countries in the world. But the Government is committed to investigating and testing these new approaches, particularly as the means of handling new problems. The Government will also seek to improve the availability of information about environmental controls and to improve education in environmental matters - as means of improving market choices.

Correcting market distortions

A.8 The object of market-based instruments for environmental protection is to improve price signals – yet the most direct means of doing this may be to make existing markets work better. In the market for water, the privatisation of the industry has brought into the open the scale of the investment needed to provide consumers with good quality water and to dispose of their waste in an environmentally acceptable manner. Over the next 10 years the water companies will spend £28 billion (in 1989 prices). This cost will be borne by the customer. As a result the true costs of using water will become more apparent to consumers, though the efficient use of water also depends on the structure of prices. The Office of Water Services (OFWAT), the regulatory body for the water industry, is encouraging a public debate about charging for water with the aim of moving the water industry towards charges which correctly signal to consumers the environmental and other costs which their demands impose. OFWAT will issue a consultation paper in the autumn of 1990.

A.9 In a different way, the introduction of competition into the electricity supply industry and its privatisation will lead to better decisions based on the costs of the different fuels, including the cost of energy from renewable sources. The fossil fuel levy makes the cost of nuclear power clear, and the costs of renewable energy sources will be made explicit when each tranche of the Non-Fossil Fuel Obligation is agreed (see Annex C, paragraph 6).

Privatisation is an important force serving to promote market transparency.

A.10 Waste disposal is another area where action is being taken to establish the conditions in which prices will better reflect costs. This is consistent with the 'polluter pays' principle whereby those responsible for waste discharges should pay for the social cost of disposing of that waste. It also provides the incentive to find alternatives to waste disposal, like waste minimisation or recycling.

The Environmental Protection Bill sets new environmental standards for the disposal of waste. In addition it separates the waste disposal companies from the local authorities. This means that the costs of waste disposal should then be fully assessed and attributed. As a result prices will tend to rise to levels consistent with the full cost of finding and running new and scarcer sites. In the case of industrial waste disposal these costs will be passed back directly to the generators of waste in disposal charges.

A.11 Charging systems are sometimes difficult to devise. In the case of household waste, the ideal would be to charge for each bag collected. That would give a clear incentive to the householder to reduce waste and to recycle it instead. However, it would

also provide an incentive to dump waste illegally. An alternative approach is to give a similar incentive to the waste collection authorities by giving them a financial credit for reducing the amount of waste they send for disposal.

The Environmental Protection Bill introduces a system of 'recycling credits' or rebates through which savings in landfill costs will be passed back to those removing materials for recycling from the waste stream, thereby providing an incentive for more recycling.

Charges to recover the costs of administration

A.12 If the costs of administering the system by which pollution is regulated can readily be established, it is fair that the polluters should pay these costs.

In Britain examples of charges which recover administrative costs are the new charges for Her Majesty's Inspectorate of Pollution (HMIP) and National Rivers Authority (NRA) discharge consents. Other examples are charges for licensing waste disposal sites and for holding and disposing of radioactive materials.

A.13 Generally charges which cover administrative costs are related to such things as the number of visits made or the number of sites covered, but they may, in some circumstances, be based on measures of the nature and volume of releases into the environment. This is a more complex method of regulation which offers a direct economic signal – since there is then a cost to producing more pollution. Charges for discharges set to recover administrative costs only are likely to be low in relation to the wider costs imposed on society by that pollution which remains. Similarly NRA's charges for consents to abstract water are currently low in relation to the wider costs which abstraction can impose on the environment and on other water users. Higher charges related to the amount of pollution or of abstraction might therefore be worth considering for the longer term (see paragraph A.19).

The Water Act empowers the NRA to recover the costs of administering discharge consents and monitoring compliance with them. When the NRA's full cost-recovery charging scheme is introduced it is likely that the levels of charges will reflect different levels of discharge.

Industry levies, product levies and deposit/refund schemes

A.14 Charges are used in some countries to recover not just administrative costs but also to finance specified pollution control measures. In this case, a homogeneous group of polluters should be defined: charges are then imposed on the output of these polluters, and the proceeds devoted to the cost of clean-up or to expenditure to reduce the level of emissions within the group. In France, Germany and the Netherlands charges of this kind are made on a variety of discharges, but notably on discharges to water.

A.15 Where a material or product would prove costly or dangerous to handle as waste, the consumer should ideally meet this cost on the 'polluter pays' principle. One possibility is, therefore, to charge a levy when that product is sold, and to make this levy available to firms, or even voluntary bodies, who arrange to deal with the product as waste.

The Government is discussing possibilities for introducing a levy on tyres to help subsequent problems of disposal (see paragraph 14.31). Its preferred scheme would be a voluntary one, introduced by the industry.

A.16 Another possibility is to use a system of deposits and refunds to give users the incentive to return a material or product. The Government's interest in such schemes stems from their potential either to avoid disposal problems and litter or to save resources. In the past, industry has itself organised voluntary deposit/refund schemes (eg for bottles), but these are less frequent than they were: this is a result partly of changes in the products available to consumers, and partly of changes in the ways in which products are distributed. Some

countries have imposed schemes on industry, but this is a drastic solution, tending to forestall the development of more appropriate schemes. There are cases where intervention has produced unintended consequences, with examples of over-supply of recycled materials and the supply of contaminated materials to recycling points.

In the case both of levies and deposit/refund schemes the Government would prefer industry itself to come up with workable schemes, but it will take the lead where the environmental benefits are clear and a cost-effective scheme can be devised.

Charges on producers for damage to the environment

A.17 There is a good case for charges which show polluters and others the costs which their use of the environment imposes on the community as a whole. In these circumstances, the authorities could set charges related either to the scale of the release (to land, air or water) or to the use of the environmental resources. Such charges may often be seen as the local equivalent of taxes. Firms would be able to choose to use the environment at a given level and pay the charge, or to invest in new, less environmentally damaging, methods of production and, in part at least, avoid the charge. All firms are likely to make some investments in equipment to control pollution, and the introduction of a charge on the remaining pollution may be unpopular with industry. However, a pollution charge is no more than a price for using scarce resources.

The Government will be examining the potential for using charges to control the amount of noise. Some airports already have some differentiation in landing charges according to the level of noise made by each aircraft (see paragraph 16.21). The Government will also consider the scope for introducing an economic incentive to encourage those who currently hold land derelict and vacant for a considerable time to bring it back to beneficial use (see paragraph 6.66).

A.18 Charges would still require administrative support because the level of emissions, or whatever it is that provides the basis for the charge, would have to be measured and monitored. This may sometimes be more difficult and expensive than regulatory options (which is one reason why regulatory solutions, like the specification of equipment standards, have so often been preferred in the past).

A.19 A problem with the use of charges is to determine their level. A charge could be altered if its effects were not as originally anticipated, but there are advantages in giving industry a relatively stable and certain regime. Another approach is to accompany regulations establishing a basic requirement for pollution abatement with a charge on emissions. This would give a more certain outcome, while still providing firms with an incentive to do better.

The Government is considering, with HMIP and NRA, whether a greater degree of incentive charging could in the longer term be incorporated in their charging schemes and will be commissioning studies into the possibilities. Incentive charging would require legislation.

Environmental charges on products or materials

A.20 An alternative to putting a charge on releases would be to add an environmental charge or tax directly to the price of materials used or products and services sold. In many cases environmental damage is associated with production rather than consumption, and a charge on sales would tend to distort choices because producers would lack an incentive to find the least damaging processes or materials. Nevertheless, where it is the consumption or disposal of a good or service rather than its production which has adverse effects, an environmental charge might, in principle, be put on each purchase. A charge or tax related to the quantity consumed would generally be more closely matched to the environmental effects than one based on the value of the product or service.

The case for all kinds of environmental charges and taxes is being considered in both the EC and the OECD. Each country will want to decide for itself whether particular ones are justified. In particular any impact on international competitiveness needs to be considered.

A.21 There has been discussion of the possible use of taxes to reduce the emission of environmentally harmful gases, notably CO_2, from various sources of energy. From an environmental point of view there would be advantages in relating any taxation to the quantity of CO_2 emitted, so as to encourage producers to move to less environmentally harmful patterns of production and consumers to move to less environmentally harmful choices of goods and services.

Taxes can be the most effective means of tackling environmental problems, and so merit serious examination. However, their use raises wider economic, social, and industrial consequences which need to be weighed in the balance (see paragraphs 5.25-26).

A.22 Environmental taxes can be used to encourage as well as discourage. Taxes can be levied at differential rates to reflect the fact that one course of action is less environmentally damaging than another.

The differential between the tax charged on leaded and unleaded petrol, which the Government introduced in 1987, is a good example of a market-based instrument of this kind: sales of unleaded petrol have risen to about 35% of the total in three years.

Tradeable quotas

A.23 Where a ceiling on total emissions has been set, either locally or nationally, there is a case for allowing industry to have a say in the allocation of this total between plants or processes. The basis for this is that industry may have better information about the full range of technical opportunities than administrators.

HMIP will regulate individual processes to ensure that Best Available Techniques Not Entailing Excessive Costs (BATNEEC) are being employed to limit pollution, utilising the Best Practicable Environmental (Discharge) Option. Subject to BATNEEC being satisfied, HMIP may permit offsets between different processes to ensure that overall standards are satisfied.

A.24   A different approach would be to allow permissions to emit specified quantities of pollutants to be bought and sold within a given industry or, if appropriate, between different industries - a system of 'tradeable permits'.   A system based on a market for pollution rights holds the prospect of increases in efficiency since, by trading, producers would find the cheapest way of meeting a given pollution target. Alternatively, bigger cuts in pollution could be obtained at the same cost. If a well functioning market could be established, the range of alternative possibilities for pollution abatement which could be taken into account would be likely to be wider than is possible within an administrative system. A tradeable permit system does not do away with the need for accompanying regulatory activity. In particular, somebody would have to oversee the trades and make sure that emissions were being kept within specified limits.

A.25   There are important issues concerning the initial allocation of permits. The practice in the USA, where such schemes have been used, has generally been to give 'grandfathered' rights, allowing existing firms to continue to emit their previous levels of discharges, at least for a specified period. Other systems could be envisaged: for example, permits might be leased for a specified period of time or periodically re-auctioned. One problem is that if the markets in which permits were sold were not sufficiently competitive it might be difficult to accommodate new entrants. There would also be problems if markets were limited because pollution controls were applied at the local level, and the permits were, as a result, applicable only to a small number of producers.

The Department of the Environment has commissioned an external research project to examine possibilities for using market mechanisms, including tradeable permits, as a means of delivering longer term acid deposition control strategies, based on critical loads, which will be developed when the existing UNECE Protocol is revised (see paragraph 11.39).

Legal liability and schemes of private compensation

A.26   The extent to which a polluter is financially liable for the effects of his activities under both criminal and civil law will influence his behaviour. In this sense aspects of legal liability have some of the characteristics of economic instruments. Under a system of strict civil liability, a characteristic of a number of continental legal codes and of many international environmental agreements, it is not necessary to show that a polluter is negligent or at fault in establishing his liability for damage done to other parties. In Britain it is not uncommon for strict liability to be imposed for criminal offences, including those committed under anti-pollution legislation, but so far as civil action is concerned, negligence generally has to be established.

The Environmental Protection Bill strengthens the incentive effects of criminal law with regard to several offences which will now carry exceptional maximum penalties of £20,000 in magistrates' courts, and unlimited fines in the High Court (there is an example in paragraph 12.24).

A.27   Some people have suggested that a system of strict civil liability for environmental damages would increase the incentives on polluters to carry out their activities with a greater degree of care. It might be difficult to obtain insurance for some environmental risks which could limit the potential for this approach. These ideas are under active discussion within the Council of Europe and the European Community. They raise a number of complex issues.

A.28   Whatever the structure of legal liability, the operators of polluting activities may themselves decide to offer compensation directly to those affected by pollution. Compensation schemes are generally likely to be inadequate substitutes for more comprehensive and direct incentives, since the polluter is not likely to cover all the costs of pollution. Even so, voluntary compensation may sometimes be worthwhile as a means of reducing the costs of providing compensation and of increasing the certainty that payments will be made. The way in which it fits into the structure of civil liability needs careful consideration.

Subsidies and schemes of public compensation

A.29 In Europe as a whole, decreasing use is being made of subsidies as means to secure reductions in pollution. European Community rules on state aids limit the scope for such use, and given the 'polluter pays' principle, which the Government supports, subsidies are generally recognised as both inequitable and inefficient. There are dangers that subsidies will be distributed wastefully to projects which would have gone ahead in any case and that firms would become dependent on subsidies rather than accepting responsibility for the pollution they cause.

A.30 Outside the field of industrial pollution control, different considerations apply, particularly in cases where the ability to finance environmental improvements is in doubt or where the extent of an individual's contribution to pollution is uncertain.

In pilot Nitrate Sensitive Areas, farmers can be compensated for the loss of income arising from voluntary restrictions on nitrate applications, going beyond good agricultural practice (see paragraph 12.20).

A.31 Government policy towards the countryside is to encourage farmers and landowners to seek markets for those environmental goods which offer considerable amenity value. It recognises,

however, that there is need to provide incentives where the market fails to produce the right outcome. It therefore has in place various schemes to encourage owners of private resources to manage them in ways which conserve the countryside and benefit the general public.

A range of government payments is available to help farmers and landowners to maintain, protect and enhance landscape features and wildlife habitats (see paragraphs 7.55-57).

A.32 Existing agricultural subsidies can be modulated to achieve environmental as well as social and economic objectives.

MAFF intends, where possible and worthwhile, to introduce environmental conditions into agricultural support schemes (paragraph 7.19-20).

A.33 A further type of support is Government grant-aid to assist industrial research and development carrying a high technological or commercial risk but which has the potential to yield higher environmental standards, or wider access to innovation, and broader social and commercial benefits. Such assistance can embrace a range of environmental issues including clean technology, waste minimisation, and recycling.

There are a number of schemes of this kind: for example the proposed Environmental Technology Innovation Scheme to be run by the Department of Trade and Industry and the Department of the Environment (see paragraph 14.7); and the Department of Energy's renewables programme.

CONCLUSION

A.34 The particular contribution of market-based instruments to environmental policy will continue to be examined in Britain and abroad. Britain will continue to take a full part in studies of the scope for using market-based instruments in both the European

Community and the Organisation for Economic Co-operation and Development (OECD).

A.35 The different environmental instruments, both administrative and economic, will need to be assessed against a range of criteria - environmental effectiveness; economic burden; compliance costs; the effect on international competitiveness; administrative costs; encouragement to innovation; effects on different groups; and the effect on competition in product markets. There are circumstances in which each has its place. The precise choice will be influenced by such factors as: the ease with which releases can be measured; the scale and nature of the problem; the number of polluters; market structures; and prospective changes in technology.

A.36 There is no doubt that a mix of measures - both administrative and economic - will be needed to deal with the full range of environmental problems. Major economic changes are implied, and we shall need to guard against the danger of unforseen consequences if action is taken in advance of a proper analysis of the likely effects. But the potential for achieving environmental protection more efficiently than by direct regulation is clear and the new possibilities will be pursued with vigour.

Research - economic instruments

Many Government departments are undertaking research projects in the economics of the environment at international, national and regional levels. In all cases the objective is to achieve a more sustainable use of the environmental resources. Examples include projects
• to support the development of economically efficient policies to control pollution and protect the environment - Department of the Environment (£0.3m in 1990/91)
• to study the economics and technologies of recycling - Warren Spring Laboratory for Department of Trade and Industry (£0.1m in 1990/91)
• to study the ways in which environmental effects should be quantified and valued in

transport appraisals - Department of Transport (£0.5m in 1990-91)
• to study ways of valuating environmental change - Scottish Office and Scottish Development Agency (£0.1m in 1990/91)
• to understand the dynamics of the rural economy - Department of the Environment (£0.1m in 1990/91)
• on policies in developing countries to combat localised and global environment problems - Overseas Development Administration (up to £0.5m a year)

In addition the Economic and Social Research Council has a new programme to study the economic and social implications of global environmental change.

ANNEX B

STATISTICAL REPORT ON THE ENVIRONMENT

INTRODUCTION

This Annex lists the statistical series that the Government proposes to include in statistical reports on the environment, which will also include charts, explanatory notes and commentary.

The reports are intended mainly to bring together available and reliable data relating to the UK environment. Where UK activity is relevant to the description of international issues, as for example with the UK contribution to global carbon dioxide emissions, the reports will refer to internationally agreed statistics. The reports will not however focus primarily on comparisons between UK figures and those for other countries; documents produced by the OECD, the UN or the EC will carry out that function.

The Government will consult widely on the topics to be covered in the reports and the statistical series to be used, on the basis of the list of topics below.

PART 1:
BACKGROUND

- Climate - rainfall, temperatures (very long time series for climate change comparison), hours of sunshine.
- Physical relief, land drainage and soils. Maps showing population centres, major industrial regions, power stations, extractive industries, agricultural use, etc.

PART 2:
STATE OF THE ENVIRONMENT

AIR

Global issues

Global climate change
- Relative contribution of different gases (carbon dioxide, methane, nitrous oxide, ozone, CFCs) to greenhouse effect.
- UK emissions of greenhouse gases - trends in emissions and sources for carbon dioxide, methane, nitrous oxide.
- Concentrations in atmosphere of greenhouse gases (global).
- Effect of climate change - trends in sea level, trends in wave heights.

Stratospheric ozone depletion
- Annual appearance/sizes of polar ozone holes.
- Ultraviolet-B measurements for Europe.
- CFC (chlorofluorocarbon) production and consumption in EC.

European issues

Acid deposition and acid rain
- Maps showing acidity of rain and acid deposition.
- Effects of acid rain - eg trends in quality of selected upland waters.

Tropospheric ozone
- Ozone episodes in UK and elsewhere (location, concentrations, duration).
- PAN measurements (peroxylacetyl nitrate is an indicator of photochemical activity).

UK issues

Emissions of local significance
- Smoke - sources, trends in emissions, breaches of EC limit values, urban concentrations, smoke control orders and maps of areas covered.
- Sulphur dioxide - sources, trends in emissions, emissions from large combustion plants and EC targets, breaches of EC limit values, urban concentrations.
- Nitrogen dioxide - sources, trends in emissions, emissions from large combustion plants and EC targets, concentrations.
- Volatile organic compounds - sources, trends in emissions.
- Carbon monoxide - sources, trends in emissions, concentrations.
- Lead - trends in emissions, uptake of unleaded petrol, trends in concentrations of lead in air.
- Trace elements - concentrations of zinc, arsenic, selenium.
- Number of contraventions of air pollution acts, central government expenditure on clean air grants.

WATER

International issues

Marine water quality issues
- North Sea - source and amount of metal inputs, oil discharges, quality indicators, phytoplankton blooms (type, area, duration, time), biological monitoring for birds, seal counts, cetaceans and marine species.
- Dumping of sewage sludge, industrial waste and dredgings - total amounts and metal content.

UK issues

Sources of Pollution
- Water pollution incidents and prosecutions
- Trends in numbers, causes (industry, farms, sewage).
- Sewage - compliance of treatment works with discharge consents, sludge disposal routes, sewage works by size of population served, expenditure.

Inland water quality
- River and canal water quality - trends in lengths in quality classes, annual average concentrations of selected determinands. Indicators of water quality for selected lakes.
- Groundwater quality - concentrations of nitrates and pesticides.

Drinking water quality
- Compliance with standards for lead, nitrates and pesticides by supply zone.
- Ground and surface water withdrawal.
- Fluoridated water (map).

Marine water quality
- Oil pollution - trends in spills and clean-up costs, mortality and oiling of sea birds.
- Bathing water quality - compliance with EC Directives.
- Effects of toxic substances on marine life - TBT (tributyl tin) concentrations.
- Contaminant levels in fish, water, sediments and shellfish.

Natural effects
- Floods and droughts - number of drought orders, hydrological data for floods.
- Coastal erosion - map, expenditure on flood defence, sea defence and coastal protection.

WASTE

- Main sources of waste - estimated waste arisings from agriculture, mines and quarries, power stations, industry, sewage sludge, commercial, household.
- Trends in waste collected and disposed of by local authorities - amounts and costs.
- Transport of household waste.
- Recycling - reclamation by local authorities, trends in weight and of recycled scrap (glass, paper, metals) and proportion of total consumption in manufacture.
- Waste incineration/heat recovery.
- Landfill - numbers of sites with potential gas problem.
- Litter - public attitudes.
- Hazardous and special waste - amounts imported, countries of origin.

RADIOACTIVITY

- Sources of radiation.
- Natural radiation - radon concentrations in dwellings, gamma-ray dose rates in dwellings, Gamma-ray dose rate measurements from the RIMNET system used to monitor for nuclear accidents.
- Radiation from nuclear establishments - trends in atmospheric and liquid emissions, solid waste disposal.
- Concentrations in air, rain water, drinking water, milk, fish, shellfish.
- Trends in public radiation exposure to radioactive liquid waste, collective doses from fish and milk.

NOISE

- Noise levels
- Complaints and prosecutions - trends by source (roads, aircraft, domestic, etc), sources of complaints about domestic noise.
- Motor vehicle noise - trends in noise offences.
- Aircraft noise - trends in areas and population affected around Heathrow, Gatwick and Luton, complaints received, sound insulation grants.
- Exposure - effects on hearing impairment of exposure to varying levels of noise, numbers claiming and awarded Industrial Disablement Benefit for occupational deafness, estimates of numbers exposed to differing levels of noise at work.

TOXIC SUBSTANCES

- Concentrations of heavy metals - blood lead concentrations, concentrations of cadmium in kidneys, cadmium and lead intake by adults.
- Dioxins - emissions to the atmosphere, concentrations in soil.
- Chemical notification systems - results.
- Pesticides - approvals, numbers of reported incidents, concentrations in birds, fish and wildlife.

WILDLIFE

- Species - number of fully and partially protected species, numbers of species at risk.
- Ecological indicators - trends for selected species.
- Trade in endangered species - from CITES.

LAND USE

General

- Land cover and use - distribution of main land uses (agriculture, forestry, other) by country, current land use change.
- Agriculture - details of land use and information on special categories when available (Environmentally Sensitive Areas, Farm Woodland Scheme, Set-Aside and Nitrate Sensitive Areas).
- Forestry - forestry area broken down between broadleaved and coniferous and by age class, trends in forests planted.
- Mineral workings - area of permissions, area covered by satisfactory reclamation conditions.
- Soil - types in UK, suitability for agriculture or forestry, important threats (erosion, contaminated land, acidification).

Rural

- Changes in land cover and linear features (hedgerows etc) - information on stock and change during the 1980s for land cover, vegetation, species, etc.
- Designated and protected areas - numbers and areas of national parks, areas of outstanding natural beauty, heritage coasts, national nature reserves, sites of special scientific interest (SSSIs), special protection areas (SPAs), biosphere reserves, Ramsar wetland sites, environmentally sensitive areas (ESAs), marine nature reserves, national trails, etc.
- Damage to SSSIs.
- Forest health surveys; tree preservation orders.

Urban

- Area of green belt land.
- Derelict land - area, type of dereliction, area justifying reclamation, minerals involved in reclamation, end use of reclaimed land, changes 1974-82-88, expenditure on reclamation.
- Vacant land - results of recent survey.

- Area reclaimed for garden festivals.
- Dwelling stock and completions, slum clearance, home improvement grants (number of dwellings and total grant paid).

Heritage
- Number of buildings 'listed' and 'scheduled' in last 10 years.

PART 3:
SOURCES OF PRESSURE, AND RESPONSES

Agriculture, Forestry and Fishing

Agriculture
- Crop areas and livestock population numbers.
- Yields of major arable crops, milk and eggs.
- Production of major agricultural commodities.
- Value and quantity of fertilizers and pesticides purchased and used.

Forestry
- Standing volumes and production.
- Environmental assessment.

Fishing
- Stocks of freshwater, migrating and marine fish and shellfish.
- Landings of fish.

Energy
- Trends in energy consumption by user.
- Trends in energy production by source.
- Trends in fuels used to generate electricity.
- Energy efficiency.
- Renewable sources.

Industry and business
- Trends in industrial output.
- Mineral production and use.
- Production and consumption of environmentally important materials.
- Expenditure on environmental protection, pollution charges.
- Number of visits, licenses issued and notices and prosecutions served etc by HMIP.
- Notices and prosecutions served by HSE

under the Food and Environmental Protection Act and the Control of Pesticides Regulations.
- Hazards and accidents - number of sites covered by the Control of Major Hazards and Notification of Hazardous Installations Regulations, industrial accidents of environmental significance, planning applications and fire certificates issued in relation to major hazard industrial installations.
- Notification of planned releases of genetically manipulated organisms.
- Attitudes of managers to the environment.

Transport
- Trends in use - passenger transport by mode, freight transport by mode, road traffic by type of vehicle, traffic at UK airports and ports, number of road vehicles (by fuel type and capacity), public road lengths.
- Energy consumption, changes in fuel consumption of new cars, petrol and diesel prices and duties.

Population
- Population trends (urban/rural), density, birth and death rates.
- Public attitudes to the environment.
- Membership of environmental organisations.
- Recreational activities - visits by overseas residents to the UK and by domestic UK tourists by region and season, recreational and sporting use of forestry land, visitor numbers to national parks.
- Education and training - enrolments in courses on environmental studies.

Government
- Expenditure on environmental protection, government grants made to environmental bodies.
- Research - Expenditure on environmental research and development.

(NB. Consideration would be given to including some of the series in Part 3 in relevant sections in Part 2 and to cross-referencing).

ANNEX C

ACTION ON GLOBAL WARMING : ENERGY EFFICIENCY AND RENEWABLE SOURCES OF ENERGY

INTRODUCTION

C.1 This Annex sets out the action that the Government is taking towards achieving the target that it is prepared to set, if other countries take similar action, of reducing presently projected emissions of carbon dioxide to 1990 levels by 2005.

C.2 In the transport sector, the Government is taking action to make people more aware of the environmental effects of their transport decisions, to improve vehicle fuel consumption and to continue policies for public transport which increase choice and reduce congestion. This action is set out in paragraphs 5.41 to 5.64. This Annex describes more fully the action on energy efficiency and renewable sources of energy summarised in paragraphs 5.27 to 5.40.

A. ENERGY EFFICIENCY

C.3 The Government is taking major init-iatives on energy efficiency in four areas:
• electricity generation and supply;
• industry and commerce;
• buildings; and
• the European Community.

I ELECTRICITY GENERATION AND SUPPLY

C.4 The Electricity Act 1989 will lead to very substantial reductions in CO_2 emissions.

Competition

C.5 The Act paved the way to the privatisation of the electricity supply industry. Privatisation introduces competition among electricity generators, giving them a strong incentive to generate electricity more efficiently. One consequence of this is that gas, in combined cycle gas turbines (CCGTs), is emerging as the first choice of fuel for power generation. CCGTs are both more efficient and significantly less costly to build than most other power stations. CCGTs have environmental advantages over existing plant, since their high efficiency means up to 40 per cent less CO_2 produced per unit of power generated compared with coal-fired stations, and their use of natural gas (which is low in sulphur) reduces acid emissions too.

Non fossil fuels

C.6 The Act also encourages electricity generation from non-fossil fuels, such as nuclear power and renewable sources of energy, which emit little or no CO_2. The extra cost being borne by public electricity suppliers for the sake of environmental and other benefits of non-fossil fuels will be shared out by means of a fossil fuel levy. This will be paid by all licensed electricity suppliers on the energy they have sold to final customers which was generated using fossil fuels (See section B on renewables).

Promoting energy efficiency

C.7 The Electricity Act 1989 created the

new post of Director General of Electricity Supply. He has a duty to take account of the effect on the physical environment of activities connected with generation, supply, or distribution of electricity. Public electricity suppliers' licences specify that they must give information and advice to their customers on the efficient use of electricity. The DGES is responsible for monitoring the performance of the suppliers in meeting their licence obligations, and has powers to instruct suppliers to issue such information as he believes necessary.

II INDUSTRY AND COMMERCE

C.8 Industry and commerce are responsible for about 30% of national CO_2 emissions. The Energy Efficiency Office (EEO) targets its work on this key sector of the economy.

Best practice programme

C.9 In April 1989, the EEO launched the Best Practice programme, building on the success of its previous demonstration and research and development programmes. The new programme provides authoritative independent information and advice on energy use and efficiency in industry and commerce, and also in the public sector and in housing.

C.10 Under the Best Practice programme, the EEO provides a full range of guidance on energy efficiency technologies and management techniques. The EEO also encourage the development and marketing of goods and services which lead to improved energy efficiency, helping the energy efficiency industry to get in touch with potential customers and to spot market opportunities for both equipment and consultancy services. Guidance and help from the EEO is available at a national level and through a network of regional offices.

C.11 The Government intends to develop further EEO services during 1991 to help energy users to get expert advice, specific to their circumstances, on the purchase, design, operation and improvement of energy-using equipment and of buildings. This could include assistance with project management for smaller companies who want to put consultants' recommendations or EEO advice into practice but lack the management resources to do so.

Combined Heat and Power

C.12 Combined Heat and Power (CHP) is a highly fuel-efficient technology which generates electricity and puts to good use heat which would otherwise be wasted. CHP plant can be of any size and be operated on any fuel. It is already widely used in British industry and buildings and in the right circumstances is a very cost effective means of meeting a given energy demand. Because of its high fuel efficiency, CO_2 emissions are reduced. CHP, therefore, has the potential to improve the environment and reduce energy costs for users in all sectors of British industry and commerce. The Energy Efficiency Office will continue to promote the technology under its Best Practice programme and will aim to ensure that an identified potential of a further 2,000 megawatts of capacity by the year 2000 will if possible be achieved, doubling present capacity.

III BUILDINGS

C.13 Heating, lighting and electrical appliances in houses and other buildings account for nearly half of Britain's total energy use. The Government is therefore putting special effort into improving the energy efficiency of both new and existing buildings.

C.14 A major part of the EEO's Best Practice programme (see para 9) covers buildings. It assesses the effectiveness of techniques and technologies, helps to develop and spread new methods of improving energy efficiency and provides independent and authoritative advice to owners, occupiers and building professionals.

Building Regulations

C.15 Amendments to the Building

Regulations 1985, which came into force on 1 April 1990, include higher thermal insulation standards for new houses and other buildings in England and Wales. The equivalent standards in Scotland and Northern Ireland are also under review. The new requirements should achieve a saving of about 20% in energy requirements for space and water heating compared with a building constructed to the former standards. Detailed practical guidance has been issued on ways in which the new requirements can be met, and on how the technical risks which are sometimes associated with thermal insulation measures can be avoided. The way in which the new requirements operate in practice is being monitored by the Building Research Establishment, and, once the construction industry has had time to adjust to them, the Government will be looking carefully at the scope for further improvements. At the same time, the Government will examine how far it would be practical to strengthen energy conservation requirements where an alteration is being made to an existing dwelling.

Energy labelling of buildings

C.16 The Government wishes to give every encouragement to the adoption of even higher standards of thermal insulation on a voluntary basis wherever this is reasonably possible. In relation to housing, energy labelling helps to make both house-builders and house-owners more aware of how different factors affect energy consumption, and to identify ways in which this can be reduced or minimised. It also helps a purchaser to compare the likely space and water heating costs of different houses. The Building Research Establishment has developed the BREDEM computer model for assessing energy requirements in dwellings, and the Government warmly welcomes the use that is now being made of this model as the basis of energy labelling schemes. It is considering how best the application of such schemes should be developed and encouraged. The Government's intention is that energy labelling should be sufficiently developed to enable it to be incorporated into the Building Regulations when these are next amended.

Lighting

C.17 High efficiency lamps are proving slow to penetrate the housing sector, although the initial outlay is quickly repaid in energy savings. The EEO is considering with the industry how barriers to greater uptake might be overcome.

Attitudes to energy conservation

C.18 The Government has for some years conducted extensive marketing analyses of the barriers to take-up of energy efficiency measures by home owners. It will continue this work with the aim of targeting its marketing campaigns to encourage home owners as effectively as possible to save energy.

Local authority housing

C.19 Some £3.5 billion is spent annually in England on repairing and maintaining the local authority housing stock. About one quarter goes on work which improves energy efficiency, since many council houses and flats have poor standards of insulation and inefficient heating systems. A similar proportion of the resources distributed through the Department of the Environment's Estate Action programme goes on energy efficiency measures. This programme was established in 1985 to tackle the serious social and economic problems of run-down council estates. Where energy efficiency measures can contribute to a project, Estate Action will continue to encourage them. In addition, consideration is being given to launching a separate pilot programme of energy-saving measures in the local authority stock.

Housing associations

C.20 New houses built for housing associations will, of course, comply with the new Building Regulations. The Government will discuss with the Housing Corporation and the National Federation of Housing Associations the scope for further measures to encourage the promotion of energy efficiency in their housing stock, including the introduction of an energy auditing scheme involving some of the larger associations.

Private sector housing

C.21 The new system of renovation grants which came into force on 1 July 1990 in England and Wales enables local authorities to continue to help people less well off in housing which is not energy efficient. Where a property does not meet a new fitness standard (which includes adequate provision for heating), an applicant is entitled to assistance, subject to a test of his financial resources. Even if the standard is met authorities can also give grants both for home insulation and for heating.

The Home Energy Efficiency Scheme

C.22 The Energy Efficiency Office is introducing a new scheme of advice and grants for lower-income households in both public and private sector housing. The scheme will encourage improvements in energy efficiency through draught-proofing and the insulation of lofts, tanks and pipes. By improving the energy efficiency of housing, the scheme will improve the quality of life for many people on lower incomes, as well as cutting energy consumption. The Home Energy Efficiency Scheme will complement the work already being done by local authorities to improve standards of insulation for both home-owners and tenants.

Energy-related environmental research

C.23 The Government sponsors a major research programme at the Building Research Establishment (BRE) which is aimed at improving the energy efficiency of buildings. This includes work on the development and monitoring of Building Regulations requirements, including the assessment of any associated technical risks such as condensation and rain penetration and of how these risks can be avoided. The continuing development of the BREDEM energy requirements model is also part of this research programme. In addition, BRE maintains a continuing review of energy conservation and practice in both this and other countries. In the area of construction in general, BRE is developing

design criteria for low energy buildings. Research is also proceeding on the use of natural lighting, energy efficiency methods for electric lighting, thermal modelling and the development of more effective controls for environmental services in buildings. In addition, BRE helps to stimulate energy efficiency improvements in buildings by managing the EEO's Best Practice programme, which provides guidance and information based on case studies and is targeted at a wide range of building professionals.

Government buildings

C.24 The Government is alive to its responsibility for saving energy in its own buildings as well as encouraging others to save energy in theirs. The EEO promotes, co-ordinates and monitors initiatives to increase the efficiency with which energy is used in the public sector. The present campaign by all major Departments aims to achieve further savings in the Government estate rising to £45 million a year (15% of the total energy bill prior to the start of the campaign in 1989) over a 5-year period.

C.25 The need to promote energy efficiency as a major environmental objective is a central theme of the 'environmental action guide' which the Department of the Environment's Property Holdings organisation will soon issue to Government departments.

Local authority buildings

C.26 All new school buildings have to comply with design energy targets recommended in a Department of Education and Science Design Note, which gives guidelines on environmental conditions and conservation of fuel in educational buildings. These guidelines ensure that new school buildings are energy-efficient.

C.27 The DES has been actively encouraging local education authorities and other building owners to save energy. Good progress has already been made in reducing consumption of energy in educational buildings. In 1987-88, local education authorities in England were spending £41 million a year less on energy for heating than they did in 1985-86. This is equivalent to about 200,000 tonnes of carbon dioxide emissions. DES will be funding further research on energy efficiency, carrying out development projects and disseminating information, which should achieve further savings.

C.28 There is scope for still greater savings in local authority buildings as a whole. Earlier this year, a report by the Audit Commission suggested that there was potential in this area for energy efficiency savings of £100 million a year. The Government is considering how to encourage local government to make these savings.

IV THE EUROPEAN COMMUNITY

C.29 The Government proposes to pursue two initiatives in the European Community. First, it will press for agreement on a common scheme for energy efficiency labelling of electrical appliances. Second, it will argue for minimum standards for a wide range of appliances - for example central heating boilers, fridges, washing machines and industrial heating equipment. It makes sense to align our approach with that of our European partners because, as the internal market nears completion, goods manufactured in one member state are increasingly sold throughout the Community.

Labelling

C.30 Energy-efficient freezers, fridges, cookers, washing machines, boilers, lamps and so on are often more expensive to buy, but are cheaper to run and more environmentally friendly. It is important that customers are in a position to make an informed choice. The energy efficiency standard of goods on sale in high street stores varies enormously. Some freezers use 50% less electricity than others. Condensing boilers use up to 20% less gas than other central heating systems. The price of energy-efficient light bulbs is higher than that of normal bulbs, but they last longer, use much less

electricity and will more than repay the initial cost.

C.31 In many cases, manufacturers of appliances have already given information about energy efficiency in promotional literature, but there is evidence that it fails to make an impact on purchasers. One problem is that the information is not always clearly displayed. Customers are therefore unlikely to choose on energy saving grounds. Indeed, customers often choose cheaper models, unaware that these use more energy and are thus more expensive in the long run. The Government believes that customers should have ready access to this kind of information and that energy labelling schemes would be the best way of achieving it.

C.32 The Government favours a voluntary approach in the first instance. Since manufacturers already provide data in their brochures, measured to international standards, it is clear that there are no major technical problems. The European Commission has put forward some initial proposals on electrical appliances but these have made little headway. The Government will encourage and help the Commission with the more detailed development that is needed to devise a workable scheme of the kind that manufacturers would be willing and able to comply with. For the voluntary approach to succeed, it will also be important for consumers to keep up the pressure for clear and informative energy labelling by manufacturers.

Minimum standards

C.33 The Government will also urge the European Community to negotiate effective voluntary agreements on minimum standards of energy efficiency for domestic and industrial appliances, and if necessary to bring forward regulations prescribing those standards. Such agreements, or regulations if necessary, could strengthen the effectiveness of the labelling schemes, removing grossly inefficient appliances from the market and encouraging industry to manufacture products which are more environmentally friendly.

B. RENEWABLE SOURCES OF ENERGY

C.34 Chapter 5 discusses the Government's intentions for speeding up the development of renewable sources of energy through means including:
• research and development;
• demonstration; and
• promotion.
The first part of this section explains what technologies exist for producing renewable energy. The second part describes the future action on renewable energy that the Government proposes to help achieve the aims referred to in paragraph 5.40.

I RENEWABLE ENERGY TECHNOLOGIES

Small-scale hydropower

C.35 Small-scale water-power (less than 5 megawatts per site), has been exploited for centuries, at first with water wheels and later using a variety of turbines. Today we can take energy from rivers and reservoirs more efficiently, using modern turbines with low hydraulic heads. Most of the potential for larger schemes has already been realised. However, there is some further scope for small-scale projects. The 1989 Water Act encourages small-scale hydro schemes which are connected to the electricity grid for England and Wales by exempting them from water abstraction charges. The Government will encourage water authorities to take up the available small-scale technology, and research will continue into improved plant control and new systems which can work with lower water pressures.

Wind energy

C.36 Wind turbine generators produce electricity when their blades are spun around by the wind. There are two basic designs, with either a horizontal or vertical axis. These can be sited on land or offshore, though the costs would be higher offshore. As a result of the strong prevailing winds in Britain, wind energy on land has the potential to supply up to 10% of current electricity needs. However, there are planning constraints because technically favourable sites are often in areas of natural beauty or of importance to wildlife. Government spending on wind energy was £4.8 million in 1989/90. It has already led to the building and operation of a range of experimental wind turbines (from 0.1 to 3 megawatts) and an extensive programme of research which will continue into the next decade. Plans are in hand for the first commercial wind farms, using machines of around 0.3 megawatts, in areas such as Cornwall, Wales, Yorkshire and the North West.

Tidal power

C.37 Tidal energy can be extracted from an estuary by building across it a barrage equipped with sluices and turbines. If necessary, locks can be incorporated to allow ships through. The UK has unusually favourable tides for energy generation. The Severn Estuary, for example has the second largest tidal range in the world. There are a great number of estuaries and inlets along the western shores of England and Wales which could be exploited. Tidal power has the technical potential to produce the equivalent in power to burning as much as 26 million tonnes of coal a year. It could play a significant part in reducing national emissions of CO_2 and sulphur dioxide.

C.38 Scientists are studying in detail the effects of barrages on the surrounding environment. These are complex and would vary according to local conditions. Patterns of sedimentation in the estuary would change, affecting populations of small creatures on which birds feed. The migration of fish may also be affected, and the relationship with local water quality and water tables needs careful scientific assessment. There have already been preliminary feasibility studies on the Severn, Mersey, Loughor and Conwy estuaries. Work will continue to confirm the costs, performance and regional and environmental impact of the projects so that industry is well placed to construct the barrages if the outcome of the studies is favourable. Barrages are very expensive to build but they last much longer than conventional power stations, perhaps for over 100 years.

Passive solar design

C.39 Passive solar design uses building design to capture sunlight so as to help heat buildings and cut down the need for electrical lighting. For example, double-glazed windows fitted with blinds may be concentrated on the south side of buildings, with smaller windows to the north.

C.40 Simple measures like these can lead to major reductions in the energy needed for heating, cooling and lighting houses, offices, schools and hospitals. Field studies, design studies, and information gathering by the Building Research Establishment and others are all in train to gain a better understanding of how buildings can capture energy from the sun. We also need to increase awareness of the benefits among developers, designers and clients.

Biofuels

C.41 'Biofuels' are fuels derived from biological materials. It has been estimated that they could provide up to 15 million tonnes of coal equivalent, equivalent to about 13% of Britain's current coal use, by 2025. They can be used in their original state (solid, liquid or gas) or converted to fuels such as methane. The Government believes that three areas are the most promising.

Gas from wastes

C.42 Methane gas is produced as wastes break down naturally in landfill waste disposal sites. Methane from landfill sites can cause explosions and is also a potent greenhouse gas. We can use landfill gas as a fuel to generate electricity. Tapping the methane that would otherwise leak into the atmosphere will both improve safety and reduce emissions of greenhouse gases. Work will continue on a detailed programme to

develop landfill gas technology.

C.43 Sewage sludge emits a mixture of gases, of which about 65% is methane. This can be used by sewerage undertakers to generate electricity. Its use in Combined Heat and Power Systems is well established at many large sewage works. Any surplus electricity can be returned to the grid by arrangement with the local electricity supply company. The gas could provide up to 30% of the annual energy needs of the water industry.

C.44 A programme of research and development is in hand to look at the potential for the controlled anaerobic digestion of municipal waste as an alternative to landfilling. Residues from this process could be used as soil conditioners, which would help to reduce the use of peat.

Burning dry wastes

C.45 Dry refuse, industrial wastes, straw and forestry waste can also be processed and used directly as solid fuels. These wastes have a more variable energy content than fossil fuels because they often contain materials which do not burn. Burning them produces CO_2, but they allow waste to be disposed of in a useful way and can be cost-effective. In fact some biofuels such as wood waste (ie. offcuts and sawdust), used as fuel in the timber industry, are already commercially established. Research and development will now concentrate on developing cheaper ways of processing and using dry wastes.

Biofuel crop planting

C.46 Crops can be grown specifically with energy production in mind, either on marginal land or on land in set-aside. The energy potential of forestry, either conventional or using modern short-rotation coppicing techniques, is significant and the Government is funding work, worth £0.5 million in 1990/91, to develop low cost technologies for both producing and using wood as fuel.

II FUTURE ACTION

Research and Development

C.47 Governments have already spent over £160 million on programmes of research and development, and this Government has increased its support on renewables in the programme to £20 million in 1990/91. The programme will focus on technologies with prospects for the later 1990s. A key objective will be to encourage industry to take up the technologies: the Government will encourage industry to increase its funding from 25% to 50% of the cost of the programme by the mid-1990s.

Demonstration

C.48 As technologies achieve greater commercial viability the task for the Government will be to persuade industry that the technologies can perform satisfactorily. One way of doing this is the successful demonstration of full-scale plant. The Government will reinforce its existing programme for demonstrating renewable technologies.

Promotion

C.49 Renewable technologies will not achieve their full potential unless industry and people at large are aware of their potential. The Government will expand its promotional efforts to raise public awareness of renewables and stimulate the commercial application of the technologies.

Creating a market

C.50 Some renewable technologies are at the point where commercial exploitation is possible. But, for a number of reasons, electricity from some of them is not yet competitive with that from existing fossil fuel power stations. The Government's new arrangements for the privatised electricity industry will offer renewables special opportunities which were not available before. These start from the fact that electricity suppliers, because they have to buy and sell electricity in a competitive market, would be unlikely on commercial grounds to take power from renewables except in nominal amounts. To allow the technologies to prove themselves, and to secure their environmental benefits, the Government is using its powers under the Electricity Act 1989 to provide a level of financial support.

C.51 The Electricity Act 1989 provides for a Non-Fossil Fuel Obligation (NFFO) to be placed on public electricity suppliers in England and Wales. These suppliers are successors to the Electricity Area Boards and are to be privatised in November. This arrangement permits the Secretary of State to require the suppliers to contract for a specified minimum amount of non-fossil electricity capacity. Because at present electricity from renewables tends to be more expensive to produce than electricity from other sources, the Act provides for the suppliers to be compensated for the extra cost that the Obligation involves. Paragraph 6 describes how this compensation is financed in turn by a levy on sales of electricity produced from fossil fuels.

C.52 An Order relating specifically to renewables came into effect in September 1990. It requires the suppliers to contract in total for some 102 megawatts (MW) of renewable capacity by 1998. The suppliers have entered into contracts to meet this requirement. The contracted capacity is made up of landfill gas, waste incineration, wind power, hydro electricity and sewage gas.

C.53 The Government is aware of a number of further potential renewables projects that were not yet ready for contracting when the Order was laid. Further projects are also likely to be planned over the next few years. The Government announced when the Electricity Act was going through Parliament that further Orders would be laid for up to a further 600 megawatts of renewable capacity. The next Order will be made next year, with a specific provision for wind power.

Mersey barrage

C.54 Among those projects not yet ready for contracting was a proposal by a local consortium for a tidal barrage in the Mersey estuary. This is an exciting project which would provide very substantial quantities of energy and could open the way for more extensive exploitation of tidal energy. The Government proposes to contribute further to the studies needed to complete the technical definition of the proposal and to assess the wider benefits that such a barrage could bring. The results of this assessment will be made available next year.

Policy review

C.55 In 1988 the Department of Energy published a policy document setting out its strategy for the development of renewables. In view of the developments since then, including greater concern about the environment, the Department intends to carry out a fundamental review of its strategy next year to assess whether the targets and resource needs identified in it need revision.

The European Community

C.56 An extensive research and development programme covering all major aspects of renewable energy is under way, funded by the European Commission. The Government will take action to ensure that this programme is as effective, and cost-effective, as possible.

C.57 The Government will call on the European Commission:
• to pursue its efforts to bring forward renewable energy through its support for research and demonstration projects, and to ensure that the technologies selected for support include those relevant to Britain;
• to ensure that the contribution of renewable energy to the Community's energy supplies is properly taken into account in any Community response to environmental issues; and
• to ensure that the Community's own policies do not hinder the development of renewable and other energy sources which can help in meeting environmental concern: particular attention may need to be paid to the completion of the internal market for energy and to any constraints on the take-up of renewable energy created by competition measures.

C.58 The Government will continue its efforts to publicise the availability of finance for renewable energy from the Community and to encourage British companies to take advantage of these opportunities.

DIAGRAMS IN THIS WHITE PAPER HAVE BEEN PRODUCED ON THE BASIS OF INFORMATION FROM THE FOLLOWING SOURCES:-

★Digest of Environmental Protection and Water Statistics No.12 – Government Statistical Service

WE ARE GRATEFUL TO THE FOLLOWING FOR PERMISSION TO REPRODUCE THE PHOTOGRAPHS

ADAS; p.99
Aerofilms; pp.71 left, 87
Ardea, London; pp.38 top left (Robert T. Smith), 53 top right (Stegan Meyers)
Automobile Association; p.90
Douglas W. Barnett; p.252
Belfast Development Office, Dept. of the Environment, Northern Ireland; p.264 top
Berwick-upon-Tweed Borough Council; p.133 right
R. J. C. Blewitt; p.179
Philip Bier/Sunday Times Magazine; p.120 top right
Blue Circle Industries PLC, p.139 top
Janet & Colin Bord; p.134
Brintons Ltd; p.139 bottom
British Antarctic Survey; pp.216 centre left, 216 right (J. Paren)
British Gas plc; p.157 right
British Nuclear Fuels plc; p202
British Steel plc; pp.92 left (Aerofilms), 92 right
Brüel & Kjaer; p.214
BTA/ETB/SI; pp.32 top right, 95, 104 top right, 105, 106, 164
The Builder Group; p.212 bottom
Building Research Establishment; p.220 right
CADW; p.242
Laurie Campbell; p.245
R. W. Carter; p.263 right
The J. Allan Cash Photolibrary; cover (countryside) and pp.40 bottom, 141, 197 left.
Central Office of Information; p.62
Central Scotland Countryside Trust; p.249 top (Mark Hamilton)
Chemical Industries Association; p.175
Clyde River Purification Board; p.248
Bruce Coleman Ltd; p.52 (O Langrand)
Coleraine Girls Secondary School; p.266
Cologne Cathedral; p.149 top
Colorific!; p.151 (Ted Spiegel/Black Star)
Cory Environment Ltd; pp.38 top right, 195
Countryside and Wildlife Branch, Dept. of the Environment, Northern Ireland; pp.259, 261 bottom
Countryside Commission; cover (foxgloves–F. B. Pearce), pp.98 bottom, 101 top, 104 bottom right, 109 top left
Mike Davis DOE/DTp Photographic Club; p.207
Dept. of Agriculture, Northern Ireland; p.261 top
Dept. of Employment; p.227
Dept. of Environment, pp.41 top, 46 top right and bottom left (R. Shaw), 47 (R. Shaw), 85 bottom, 94, 97 left, 98 top, 100 right, 115 left, 124, 155 bottom, 184, 213
Dept. of Transport; pp.117 top, 212 top
English Heritage Education Service; p.128 bottom
English Heritage Library; p.130 right
Environment Council; p.227 top
Environmental Picture Library; p.136 top right
Environmental Protection Division, Dept. of the Environment, Northern Ireland; pp.262, 263 left
Farmers Publishing Group Picture Library; p.83 bottom
Finishing Services Ltd; p.186 left (J. Stewart McLaucklan)
Forestry Commission; pp.77, 96 right, 100, 103
Friends of the Earth Trust; p.190
Greenpeace Communications; pp.60, 171 (Gieizes), 196 (Greig)
Nicholas Grimshaw & Partners/Jo Reid & John Peck; p.118 left
V. K. Guy Ltd; p.96 left
Peter Hall; p.88
Harwell Laboratory; p.71 right
David Hay; p.253 top right
Historic Buildings & Monuments, Scotland; pp.251 (Michael Brooks), 253 left (David Henrie)
Historic Monuments & Buildings Branch, Dept. of the Environment, Northern Ireland; p.264 bottom
HMIP; p.136 top left (Dr. Feates) p.220 left, p.221 right (R. G. Wakeford)
Terry Hope/Imagination Design and Communication; p.120 bottom right
Hulton-Deutsch; p.146
ICI; p.11, p.219 left, p.219
Keep Scotland Beautiful; p.257 bottom
A. F. Kersting; p.32 bottom
Kirklees Metropolitan Borough Council; p.234
Landwise; p.228 right
Frank Lane Picture Agency; pp.51 (Leo Batten), 54 left (Marc Webber), 54 right (S. McCutcheon), 147 (D A Robinson), 215 (W.Wisniewski)
Ian D Leith; p.256
Eli Lilly International Corporation; p.183 top
Loch Fleet Management Committee; p.254 top
London Borough of Richmond upon Thames; p.85 top
London Transport Museum; p.75
London Waste Regulatory Authority; p.186 centre left

Printed in the United Kingdom for HMSO on Envirocote from James McNaughton Paper Group Ltd..
Design by Banks & Miles, London
Dd 0506582 9/90 C120 51-6701 39462 O/N 119592